STATE RESPONSES TO MINORITY RI...

Increasing religious diversity in nations a[...] minority religions in many countries. This [...] together seventeen respected experts who [...] ...ost nation responses to the appearance of minority religions in their midst.
David G. Bromley, Virginia Commonwealth University, USA

The response of states to demands for free exercise of religion or belief varies greatly across the world. In some places, religions come as close as imaginable to autonomous existences with little interference from government. In other cases religion finds itself grinding out a meagre living, if at all, under the jealously watchful eye of the state.

This book provides a legal and normative overview of the variety of responses to minority religions available to states. Exploring case studies ranging from Islamic regions such as Indonesia, Pakistan, and the wider Middle East, to Western Europe, Eastern Europe, China, Russia, Canada, and the Baltics, contributors include international scholars and experts in law, sociology, religious studies, and political science. This book offers invaluable perspectives on how minority religions are currently being received, reviewed, challenged, or ignored in different parts of the world.

Ashgate Inform Series on Minority Religions and Spiritual Movements

Series Editor: Eileen Barker,
London School of Economics, Chair and Honorary Director of Inform

Advisory Board:
Afe Adogame, University of Edinburgh, UK,
Madawi Al-Rasheed, King's College, London, UK,
François Bellanger, Université de Genève, Switzerland,
Irena Borowik, Jagiellonian University, Krakow, Poland,
Douglas E. Cowan, University of Waterloo, Ontario, Canada,
Adam Possamai, University of Western Sydney, Australia,
James T. Richardson, University of Nevada, Reno, USA,
Fenggang Yang, Purdue University, USA

Inform is an independent charity that collects and disseminates accurate, balanced and up-to-date information about minority religious and spiritual movements. The Ashgate Inform book series addresses themes related to new religions, many of which have been the topics of Inform seminars. Books in the series will attract both an academic and interested general readership, particularly in the areas of Religious Studies, and the Sociology of Religion and Theology.

Other titles in this series:

Revisionism and Diversification in New Religious Movements
Edited by Eileen Barker

Prophecy in the New Millennium
When Prophecies Persist
Edited by Sarah Harvey and Suzanne Newcombe

Spiritual and Visionary Communities
Out to Save the World
Edited by Timothy Miller

State Responses to Minority Religions

Edited by

DAVID M. KIRKHAM
Brigham Young University, USA

ASHGATE

© David M. Kirkham and the contributors 2013

All rights reserved. No part of this publication may be reproduced, stored in a retrieval system or transmitted in any form or by any means, electronic, mechanical, photocopying, recording or otherwise without the prior permission of the publisher.

David M. Kirkham has asserted his right under the Copyright, Designs and Patents Act, 1988, to be identified as the editor of this work.

Published by
Ashgate Publishing Limited
Wey Court East
Union Road
Farnham
Surrey, GU9 7PT
England

Ashgate Publishing Company
110 Cherry Street
Suite 3-1
Burlington, VT 05401-3818
USA

www.ashgate.com

British Library Cataloguing in Publication Data
A catalogue record for this book is available from the British Library

The Library of Congress has cataloged the printed edition as follows:
Kirkham, David M.
  State responses to minority religions / by David Kirkham.
    pages cm —(Ashgate inform series on minority religions and spiritual movements)
  Includes bibliographical references and index.
    ISBN 978-1-4724-1646-9 (hardcover)—ISBN 978-1-4094-6579-9 (pbk)—
  ISBN 978-1-4724-1647-6 (ebook)—ISBN 978-1-4724-1648-3 (epub) 1. Religion and state. I. Title.

  BL65.S8K57 2013
  322'.1—dc23

2013019344

ISBN 9781472416469 (hbk)
ISBN 9781409465799 (pbk)
ISBN 9781472416476 (ebk – PDF)
ISBN 9781472416483 (ebk – ePUB)

Printed in the United Kingdom by Henry Ling Limited, at the Dorset Press, Dorchester, DT1 1HD

Contents

List of Contributors ix
Preface xiii
Foreword by Heiner Bielefeldt xvii
List of Abbreviations xxi

PART I: MINORITY RELIGIONS AND INTERNATIONAL LEGAL AND ETHICAL NORMS – AN OVERVIEW

1 State Reactions to Minority Religions: A Legal Overview 3
  W. Cole Durham, Jr

2 The UN Human Rights Committee and Religious Minorities 15
  Nazila Ghanea

PART II: MINORITY RELIGIONS AND ISLAM

3 Religious Minorities and Conversion as National Security Threats in Turkey and Iran 31
  Ziya Meral

4 Springtime for Freedom of Religion or Belief: Will Newly Democratic Arab States Guarantee International Human Rights Norms or Perpetuate Their Violation? 45
  Robert C. Blitt

5 Indonesia: Between Religious Harmony and Religious Freedom 65
  Renata Arianingtyas

6 A Legal Analysis of Ahmadi Persecution in Pakistan 81
  Asma T. Uddin

PART III: ATLANTIC MODELS – RELIGIOUS MINORITIES, DIVERSITY AND THE 'EUROPEAN WEST'

7 Public Policies in European Case Law: Between Security, Non-discrimination, and Public Information   101
   Louis-Léon Christians

8 The French System against Sectarian Deviations   115
   Hervé Machi

9 The French 'War on Cults' Revisited: Three Remarks on an On-going Controversy   121
   Etienne Ollion

10 Switzerland and Religious Minorities: Legal, Political and Educational Responses   137
   Brigitte Knobel

PART IV: MOVING EASTWARD – EMERGING DEMOCRACIES AND THE COMMUNIST LEGACY

11 Recognition, Registration, and Autonomy of Religious Groups: European Approaches and their Human Rights Implications   151
   Jeroen Temperman

12 The State, New Religious Movements, and Legislation on Religion: A Case Study of Three Baltic States   167
   Ringo Ringvee

13 With Fear and Favour: Minority Religions and the Post-Soviet Russian State   183
   Marat Shterin

14 China's Responses to Minority Religions   199
   Ping Xiong

PART V: MINORITY RELIGIONS IN NON-EUROPEAN DEMOCRACIES: CANADIAN AND SOUTH AFRICAN MODELS

15 Expanding the Scope of Regulation: Some Reflections on Religious Minorities in Canada   217
   Lori G. Beaman

| 16 | The Constitutional Protection of Religious Practices in Canada
Richard Moon | 231 |
| 17 | Religious Minorities' Right to Self-Determination
Johan D. van der Vyver | 243 |

Bibliography 257
Index 269

List of Contributors

Series Editor:

Eileen Barker is Professor Emeritus of Sociology with Reference to the Study of Religion. Her research interests explore the social reactions that come from 'cults', 'sects' and new religious movements, and investigate changes in the religious situation in Eastern Europe. In 1988, with the support of the British Home Office and the mainstream Churches, she founded the Non-Governmental Organization, The Information Network on Religious Movements.

Editor:

David M. Kirkham, PhD, JD, is Senior Fellow for Comparative Law and International Policy at the Brigham Young University (BYU) Law School's International Center for Law and Religion Studies and a professor in the BYU Department of Political Science. He is also former associate dean and professor at the George C. Marshall European Center in Germany, and former Senior Humanitarian Affairs Officer for the United Nations in Switzerland.

Foreword:

Heiner Bielefeldt is the present United Nations Special Rapporteur for Freedom of Religion and Belief, and a professor of human rights and human rights policy at the Friedrich-Alexander University of Erlangen-Nuremberg.

Authors:

Renata Arianingtyas has been engaged actively in freedom of religion and minority rights movements in Indonesia for several years. She is currently a programme manager for Human Rights and Justice at Tifa Foundation; founder of the Indonesia Legal Resource Center; and a lecturer in the Graduate School for Diplomacy of Paramadina University and in the Political Science Department of the University of Indonesia.

Lori G. Beaman, PhD, is Canada Research Chair in the Contextualization of Religion in a Diverse Canada, professor in the Department of Classics and Religious Studies at the University of Ottawa, and director of the *Religion and Diversity Project* (religionanddiversity.ca).

Robert C. Blitt is an associate professor of law at the University of Tennessee. He served in Washington, DC as an International Law Specialist for the US Commission on International Religious Freedom and spent time in the Middle East where, among other things, he clerked for the Chief Justice of the Supreme Court of Israel.

Louis-Léon Christians is professor and chair at the Catholic University of Leuven of Religious Law, Belgian, European and International Canon Law and Comparative Religious Rights, and Law and Religious Studies. He is also director of the Interfaculty Master of Religious Studies programme. Since 1999, he has served on the board of the Belgian Federal Agency on Harmful Cults, (http://www.uclouvain.be/en-chaire-droit-religions.html).

W. Cole Durham, Jr is the director of the International Center for Law and Religion Studies and the Susa Young Gates University Professor of Law at Brigham Young University. He is co-editor-in-chief of the *Oxford Journal of Law and Religion,* a member of the Organization for Security and Cooperation in Europe/Office for Democratic Institutions and Human Rights (ODIHR) Advisory Council on Freedom of Religion or Belief, and current president of the International Consortium for Law and Religion Studies.

Nazila Ghanea teaches International Human Rights Law at the University of Oxford. She serves as a member of the ODHIR Advisory Panel of Experts on Freedom of Religion or Belief. Her publications include nine books, four UN publications and a number of journal articles and reports. She has obtained research funding from a range of institutions, lectured widely and carried out first-hand human rights field research in a number of countries including Malaysia, Qatar and the United Kingdom.

Brigitte Knobel was trained as a sociologist at the University of Lausanne and is the director of the *Centre intercantonal d'information sur les croyances* in Geneva, a non-profit specializing in new religious movements.

Hervé Machi, a judge, graduated from Sciences-Po Paris and from the French National School for the Judiciary. He has been a deputy to the Prosecutor in the Paris Appeal, and from 2010 to 2012 was the General Secretary of Inter-ministerial Mission for Monitoring and Struggling Against Sectarian Deviations (MIVILUDES, the French national agency in charge of monitoring cults).

List of Contributors

Ziya Meral is a London-based Turkish researcher, writer and a PhD candidate in politics at the University of Cambridge. He publishes widely on Middle East, religion and human rights issues, and comments in the international media on Middle East affairs.

Richard Moon is a professor in the Faculty of Law, University of Windsor. He is also the author of *The Constitutional Protection of Freedom of Expression*, editor of *Law and Religious Pluralism in Canada* and a contributing editor to *Canadian Constitutional Law* (4th edn).

Etienne Ollion holds a PhD in sociology from the School of Higher Studies in Social Sciences (Paris). Currently a post-doctoral researcher at Sciences-Po Paris, he has taught at the University of Chicago, at the Université Paris–1 La Sorbonne and at the Ecole Normale Supérieure.

Ringo Ringvee is advisor in the Religious Affairs Department at the Estonian Ministry of the Interior, and a historian of religion.

Marat Shterin is senior lecturer in the Sociology of Religion at King's College London. He has researched and published widely on religion and society in Russia, including minority groups, state and law.

Jeroen Temperman is assistant professor of public international law at Erasmus University in Rotterdam, and editor-in-chief of *Religion and Human Rights: An International Journal*.

Asma T. Uddin is the founder and editor-in-chief of *altmuslimah.com*. She is a Legal Fellow with the Institute for Social Policy and Understanding and an international law attorney with The Becket Fund for Religious Liberty in Washington, DC.

Johan D. van der Vyver is the I.T. Cohen Professor of International Law and Human Rights at Emory University. He is a former professor of law at the University of the Witwatersrand in Johannesburg, South Africa, and is an expert on human rights law.

Ping Xiong is a senior lecturer at the Law School of University of South Australia, and a member of the International Law Association and the Australia and New Zealand Society of International Law.

Preface

State responses to demands for free exercise of religion or belief wear a wide array of apparel. In some places, religions of all sorts live near-autonomous, peaceful existences with little interference from government. In others religion grinds out a meagre living, if at all, under the jealously watchful eye of the state. New and minority religious movements are of course bound to be more affected by religious freedom policies and practices than large, established religions and movements. Societal interests, ranging from cultural identity to security concerns, evoke a variety of governmental responses to new and unfamiliar religious societies, running the spectrum of cooperation, accommodation, separation, unintentional insensitivity, hostility and overt persecution. Some states give the widest berth to new and minority religions; others give no berth at all.

This variety of state reactions suggests the need for serious study of these phenomena and to this end this book was accepted as a part of the Ashgate/Inform Series on Minority Religions and Spiritual Movements under the direction of Professor Eileen Barker. The actions of some nominally religious groups in recent years – most dramatically the collective suicide of the Order of the Solar Temple in Switzerland, France and Canada – revived the debate regarding the possibly dangerous nature of some New Religious Movements (NRMs), leading both the Council of Europe and many European states to call for objective information on NRMs. Several European states set up parliamentary committees or ordered official reports to analyse the 'sectarian' phenomenon and its possible attendant risks, resulting in some cases in legislative and administrative measures to prevent criminal acts related to NRMs. Other countries have preferred to promote information rather than repression. Still others have not reacted at all or have chosen totally to ignore NRMs.[1]

This book brings together 17 leading international scholars and experts in law, sociology, religious studies, political science and other disciplines who have taken on the challenge to provide unique but compatible perspectives on how minority religions are currently being received, reviewed, ignored, challenged or (rarely) cherished in key countries across the world. Nearly 18 years after the dramatic events of the Solar Temple, some countries are witnessing increasing secularism, while others see increasing religious influence, and still others are growing more concerned about religious extremism. In this context, it is vital to examine the effectiveness – or not – of state efforts to respond to challenges posed by NRMs

---

[1] Thanks to François Bellanger for his contribution to conceptualizing this view of the situation in Europe.

and religious minorities while still maintaining fundamental human rights of believers and belief communities.

These state reactions are examined in four parts. **Part I** provides a legal and normative overview of responses available to states, illustrating that these responses do not necessarily fall onto a convenient continuum of suppression on one hand or absolute license on the other. **Cole Durham** shows that as secularization increases, policies on religious minorities are affecting ever-increasing numbers of the global community, for good or for ill. **Nazila Ghanea** argues that although religious minorities triggered the creation of the international minority rights framework, they have been largely sidelined from its protections.

Part II presents case studies from Islamic-majority countries. **Ziya Meral** compares Iran and Turkey, showing how a nominally theocratic state and a nominally secular state can paradoxically pose similar challenges to religious minorities in their midst. **Robert Blitt** examines whether new, 'democratic' movements are moving towards compliance with international freedom of religion, thought and belief norms following the 'Arab Spring'. **Renata Arianingtyas** writes that Indonesia's government recognizes as religions only six of thousands of its belief systems and, despite having ratified the International Covenant on Civil and Political Rights (ICCPR), has implicated itself in serious challenges to religious freedom. **Asma Uddin** focuses on the Ahmadiyyas of Pakistan, exploring the historical, social and religious undercurrents behind state hostility toward this group and tracing the case law, statutes and legal arguments made against their recognition.

Part III highlights the situation in Western Europe, paying particular attention to the rise in the twentieth century of the 'sect' or cult phenomenon. **Louis-Léon Christians** examines how three kinds of public policies in Europe – state recognition and registration, criminal prosecution of abusive proselytism and psychological destabilization, and public informational campaigns – aim to prevent abuse of religious freedom by minority groups. Christians asserts that the European Court of Human Rights has created some ambiguity regarding religion's status in secular Europe by limiting but not prohibiting these policies. **Hervé Machi** illustrates, as a case in point, the French government's efforts to protect its citizens from the behaviour of 'sects', adding that what constitutes a sect, or a religion for that matter, is not legally defined by law. Machi suggests that many public and private actors protect victims of sectarian aberrations while ensuring both freedom of belief and other individual freedoms, particularly for those deemed vulnerable or weak. **Etienne Ollion** builds upon this, illustrating how shifts in the definition of 'cult' have brought many more groups, including some non-religious actors, under the French anti-cult policy umbrella in recent decades, to their direct detriment. **Brigitte Knobel** explicates similar challenges for neighbouring Switzerland, although its policy, both locally and nationally, is intended to guarantee freedom of belief while anticipating and managing conflicts, preventing abuses, and addressing citizen concerns via political, legal and educational measures.

In **Part IV**, **Jeroen Temperman** bridges East and West, in examining Central and Eastern European approaches to religious registration, Western European approaches to autonomy and their respective human rights implications. **Ringo Ringvee** discusses the legal frameworks regarding religious minorities in the Baltic States – Estonia, Latvia and Lithuania – focusing primarily on their differences, despite a shared history. **Marat Shterin** looks at minority religions in post-Soviet Russia, where some minority groups have become targets of unfair treatment and even persecution, despite relatively liberal religious freedom laws and mechanisms. Finally, **Ping Xiong** analyses in its cultural and historic context the situation for religious minorities in China, including a case study of Falun Gong.

Part V opens with **Lori G. Beaman's** consideration of the dynamic and layered contexts in which religious minorities and NRMs exist, using Canada's recent jurisprudence as a frame of reference. **Richard Moon** adds that, while the line drawn by the Canadian Supreme Court between the private and political spheres has insulated certain religious practices from state action, the Court has made it easy to justify the restriction of religious practice over public or civic concerns. Finally, **Johan D. van der Vyver** examines how South Africa's 'rainbow nation' offers both hope and challenges in its effort to balance zero tolerance for discrimination while at the same time allowing minority groups to follow their conscientious dictates.

A word about vocabulary: given cultural and language differences, this discussion risks brewing confusion in its varied uses of 'cult', 'sect', or NRM. In several European languages, the term 'sect' and its cognates approaches in meaning the pejorative term 'cult' in English (whereas, for example, 'culte' in French comes closer to the meaning of 'worship'). To avoid the confusion and non-objective, even negative connotations of these terms, social scientists have adopted the term 'New Religious Movements' (though some are not very new at all) to describe in an encompassing way most of the minority faith communities discussed in this book. As this simple explanation, we hope, eliminates what we believe to be most ambiguities, we have chosen to let the individual authors make their own terminology choices, as most of them define within the context of their analysis how the different uses of these terms should be understood.

In conclusion, let me express deep thanks to all who have contributed to the creation of this volume. It is no exaggeration to say the book would not exist without the editing and organization efforts of my assistant, Chad McFadyen. This is our third collaboration and I believe our efforts have become the proverbial 'well-oiled machine', anticipating one another's moves and needs at a high level of serendipitous harmony. To this, Eileen Barker, as long-suffering series editor, has been the perfect overseer: quick to respond with counsel when requested, otherwise allowing full and patient autonomy. I also thank Professor Melvin J. Thorne, director of the BYU Humanities Publication Center, who rallied his student editing assistants to the tedious task of note checking, as well as Kellie Daniels of the BYU Department of Political Science, and law students Samuel

Packard, Rebecca Skabelund, Aaron Worthen, Cherise Bacalski, Joshua Bishop and Joey Leavitt for their painstaking editing contributions. Thanks goes also to the faculty and staff of BYU Law School's International Center for Law and Religion Studies, especially Deborah Wright, but also Cole Durham, Donlu Thayer, Bob Smith, Gary Doxey, Elizabeth Clark, Marshall Morrise and Brett Scharffs. Also in our third collaboration, I thank Sarah Lloyd and many behind the scenes at Ashgate, talented professionals all – and did I mention, patient? Finally, I thank my loving family: Judy and the children. Many evenings and weekends have seen time that should have been theirs go to this book. I cherish their cheerful support.

David M. Kirkham

Foreword

Heiner Bielefeldt

Whoever works on behalf of the implementation of freedom of religion or belief will inevitably be confronted with the vulnerable situation of persons belonging to religious or belief minorities. In my reports to the Human Rights Council or to the General Assembly's Third Committee, including the country-related reports, this topic has always been present. It also constitutes an important part of the communication that I have with government on individual cases. In this light, I welcome the present volume, *State Responses to Religious Minorities*, with its varied but engaged treatment of key religious minority issues.

Persons belonging to religious or belief minorities often suffer from violations of their human rights, including their freedom of religion or belief. Abuses are perpetrated by states and/or non-state actors, sometimes in a climate of impunity. They may originate from different political, religious, ideological or personal motives. Practical examples of violations include arbitrary bureaucratic restrictions and burdensome administrative stipulations imposed on minorities; compulsory indication of religious affiliations in passports; denial of legal personality status for certain communities; lack of an infrastructure needed for upholding religious community life; intimidating effects of criminal law sanctions (for example, for possessing and distributing religious literature); indoctrination of children from religious minorities in public schools; violations of parents' rights to educate their children in conformity with their own convictions; discriminatory structures in family law; threatened loss of custody rights for children in divorce cases; and arbitrary confiscation of property and partial exclusion of members of minorities from certain public services, such as education, health care and social security. Furthermore, people belonging to religious minorities suffer from stereotypes and public demonizing, acts of vandalism on their houses of worship, desecration of cemeteries, mob violence and even incidents of torture, ill-treatment and extra-judicial killings. While people from virtually all religious or belief backgrounds, when living in a minority situation, may be exposed to anti-minority victimization, certain religious communities have a particularly impressive and long-lasting history of discrimination, harassment and even persecution.

Initiatives to secure the rights of persons belonging to religious or belief minorities should consistently be based on a human rights perspective. This clarification is necessary, since minority issues are often associated with protection concepts that historically emerged outside of the human rights framework. However, amalgamating different concepts of 'minority protection' harbours the danger that the specific profile of the human rights approach becomes blurred. It is all the more important to reiterate that the rights of persons belonging to religious minorities as established in the context of international human rights law naturally share all the characteristics of the human rights approach in general, which is based on the principles of (1) normative universality, (2) freedom and (3) equality/non-discrimination.

(1) Based on the assumption that all human beings are rights holders in international human rights law, they all deserve respect for their self-understanding in the area of religion or belief. Given the experience that self-understandings of human beings in questions of religion or belief can be very diverse, freedom of religion or belief accordingly must have a broad scope of application and should be implemented in an open, inclusive manner. A broad and inclusive understanding must also guide the interpretation of the rights of persons belonging to religious minorities. Accordingly, the term 'religious minority' should be conceptualized in such a way as to cover all respective groups of persons, including traditional as well as non-traditional communities or large and small communities. One should also take into account the situation of internal minorities, that is, minority groups within larger minorities. Against a widespread misunderstanding, it seems important to emphasize that the rights of persons belonging to religious minorities are not anti-universalistic privileges reserved to the members of certain predefined groups. Rather, all persons factually living in the situation of a religious or belief minority should be able to fully enjoy their human rights on the basis of non-discrimination and benefit from measures which they may need to develop their individual and communitarian identities. The question which individuals or groups of individuals fall under the specific guarantees of Article 27 of the ICCPR and similar minority rights provisions should be established on the basis of the self-understanding of the concerned persons in conjunction with an empirical assessment of their actual need of promotional measures in order to keep and develop their identity.

(2) Measures used to promote the identity of a specific religious minority always presuppose respect for the freedom of religion or belief of all of its members. Thus, the question how they wish to exercise their human rights finally remains left to the personal decisions of each individual. This in turn means that the state cannot, strictly speaking, 'guarantee' the long-term development or identity of a particular religious minority. Instead, what the state can and ought to do is create favourable conditions for persons belonging to religious minorities to ensure that they can take their faith-related affairs in their own hands in order to preserve and further develop their religious community life and identity. Positive measures are often urgently needed to facilitate the long-term development of a religious minority and its members. This requires a broad range of activities, such as subsidies for schools and training institutions, the facilitation of community media, provisions for an appropriate legal status of religious minorities, accommodation of religious festivals and ceremonies, inter-religious dialogue initiatives and awareness-raising programmes in the larger society. Without such additional support measures the prospects of long-term survival of some religious communities may be in serious

peril which, at the same time, would also amount to grave infringements of the freedom of religion or belief of their individual members.

(3) Combating discrimination on the grounds of religion or belief obviously is a complex task that implies state obligations at different levels. First, it requires a consistent policy of non-discrimination within state institutions, like for instance, accessibility of public positions in administration, public services, police force, military, public health, and so on, to everyone regardless of their religious or belief orientations. Moreover, states should also combat discriminatory practices within society at large, such as the labour market, the housing market, the media and other societal systems. This may require promotional activities that go beyond policies of formal non-discrimination, such as positive outreach and promotional measures on behalf of minorities. Finally, states should critically address the root causes of societal discrimination, that is, existing stereotypes and prejudices against members of religious minorities, and they should foster a general climate of societal openness and tolerance, for instance, by providing fair information about different religious or belief traditions as part of the school curriculum, facilitating encounters of people from different denominations and encouraging inter-religious communication. Members of religious minorities also typically suffer from hidden forms of discrimination, such as structural or indirect discrimination. For instance, seemingly neutral rules relating to dress codes in schools or other public institutions, although not openly targeting a specific community, can amount to discrimination against persons belonging to a religious minority if they feel religiously obliged to adhere to an alternative dress code. Similar problems can occur with regard to dietary rules, public holidays, labour regulations, public health norms and many other issues. To prevent or rectify discriminatory consequences, states should generally consult with representatives of religious minorities when issuing legislation that may seriously infringe on their religious or belief-related convictions and practices. Moreover, systematic attention should be given to forms of multiple and intersectional discrimination; for instance, discriminatory patterns in the intersection of religious and gender discrimination.

In my daily work I receive many reports of grave violations of freedom of religion or belief of persons belonging to religious minorities in different parts of the world. Given the number and gravity of human rights violations, the need for concerted action to better safeguard the human rights of persons belonging to religious minorities is more than obvious. In this light we should look for practical recommendations addressed to different stakeholders, including states, civil society actors, media professionals, religious or belief communities and international human rights bodies.

With the publication of this book, David Kirkham, Eileen Barker and Ashgate Publishing have brought together in one setting leading thinkers on freedom of religion or belief from around the world. Here, with nuanced analysis and sensitivity, these scholars and professionals lend timely thought and counsel to the on-going challenges facing minority religion or belief communities. The varied case-studies and analyses in this book, from China and Indonesia to Turkey and Tunisia to Canada, Switzerland and more, present themselves as well-researched, well-thought-out, well-balanced, readable approaches to the concerns confronting the freedom of religion or belief norm and ideal today. To the end of furthering our understanding of and commitment to this freedom, I commend this work to the reader.

List of Abbreviations

AI	Amnesty International
AKP	Adalet ve Kalkınma Partisi (Justice and Development Party)
ASALA	Armenia Secret Army for the Liberation of Armenia
BKKI	*Badan Kongres Kebatinan Indonesia*
BYU	Brigham Young University
CAIMADES	Cellule d'assistance et d' intervention en matière de dérives sectaires (a special French police force dedicated to aberrant sectarian movements)
CCMM	Centre contra les manipulations mentales (Centre Against Mind Control)
CDU	Christlich Demokratische Union (Christian Democratic Union, Germany)
CEDAW	Committee on the Elimination of Discrimination Against Women
CFR	Federal Commission against Racism
CIA	Central Intelligence Agency
CIC	Centre d'information sur les croyances (Information Centre on Beliefs)
CPC	Country of Particular Concern
CPPCC	Chinese People's Political Consultative Conference
CRCS	Centre for Religious and Cross-cultural Studies
ECHR	European Convention on Human Rights or European Commission on Human Rights
ECtHR	European Court of Human Rights
EU	European Union
FGM	Female Genital Mutilation
FKUB	Forum Kerukunan Umat Beragama (Inter-religious Harmony Forum)
HRC	Human Rights Commission
ICERD	International Convention on the Elimination of All Forms of Racial Discrimination
IJABI	Ikatan Jamaah Ahlul Bait Indonesia (a Shiite sect in Indonesia)
INFORM	Information Network Focus on Religious Movements
IRFA	International Religious Freedom Act
IRNA	Islamic Republic News Agency
JCP	Justice and Construction Party
JW	Jehovah's Witness
MBC	Muslim-background Christian

MENA	Middle East/North Africa
MIVILUDES	Mission interministérielle de vigilance et de lutte contre les dérives sectaires (Inter-ministerial Mission for Monitoring and Struggling Against Sectarian Deviations)
MP	Moscow Patriarchate
MRIG	Minority Rights Group International
NATO	North Atlantic Treaty Organization
NFA	National Forces Alliance
NGO	Non Governmental Organization
NRM	New Religious Movement
NPC	National People's Congress
NTC	National Transitional Council
ODHIR	Office for Democratic Institutions and Human Rights
OIC	Organization of Islamic Cooperation
OSCE	Organization for Security and Cooperation in Europe
OTS	Ordre du Temple Solaire (Order of the Solar Temple)
PRC	People's Republic of China
SARA	State Administration for Religious Affairs
SCAF	Supreme Command of the Armed Forces
SGP	Reformed Protestant Party (*Staatkundig Gereformeerde Partij, Netherlands*)
SILICC	Saint Ireneus of Lyons Information and Consultation Centre
SPC	Supreme People's Court of the People's Republic of China
SPP	Supreme People's Procuratorate
UDHR	Universal Declaration of Human Rights
UN	United Nations
UNADFI	Union Nationale des Associations de Défense des Familles et de L'individu (a French anti-cult association founded in 1974)
UNDM	United Nations Declaration on the Rights of Persons Belonging to National or Ethnic, Religious and Linguistic Minorities
US	United States
USCIRF	United States Commission on International Religious Freedom

PART I
Minority Religions and International Legal and Ethical Norms – an Overview

Chapter 1
State Reactions to Minority Religions: A Legal Overview

W. Cole Durham, Jr[1]

Introduction

According to the Pew Forum on Religion and Public Life, there are 2.2 billion Christians on earth (32 per cent of the global population), 1.6 billion Muslims (23 per cent), 1 billion Hindus (15 per cent), nearly 500 million Buddhists (7 per cent) and 14 million Jews (0.2 per cent), with 400 million (6 per cent) practising various folk or traditional religions, and slightly less than 1 per cent belonging to other religions, including the Bahá'í faith, Jainism, Sikhism, Shintoism, Taoism, Zoroastrianism, and so on.[2] About 1.1 billion (16 per cent) have no religious affiliation,[3] which could mean that they do not adhere to any particular religion or that they question or disavow adherence to religion altogether. From a global perspective then, we are all members of religious or belief minorities.[4] In fact, there are no countries on earth without at least some religious minorities, whether as a result of distribution of the major world religions, or due to fissures within major religions such as Islam and Christianity.[5]

---

[1] The author wishes to thank Cherise Bacalski for research assistance in the preparation of this chapter.

[2] The Pew Forum on Religion and Public Life, 'The Global Religious Landscape: A Report on the Size and Distribution of the World's Major Religious Groups as of 2010' (18 December 2012) (Executive Summary), http://www.pewforum.org/global–religious–landscape–exec.aspx. The *World Christian Encyclopedia* reports similar number for the same period: Christianity constitutes 33.2 per cent of world population, Islam 22.4 per cent, Buddhism 6.8 per cent and Hinduism 13.7 per cent. David B. Barrett, George T. Kurian and Todd M. Johnson, *World Christian Encyclopedia: A Comparative Survey of Churches and Religions in the Modern World*, 2 volumes (Oxford: Oxford University Press, 2001).

[3] Ibid.

[4] In the United States, even the largest religion, Roman Catholicism, includes less than 30 per cent of the population. Thus, an essay I wrote several years ago about religious minorities in the United States covered all religions in the country. See W. Cole Durham, Jr, 'Treatment of Religious Minorities in the United States', in *The Legal Status of Religious Minorities in the Countries of the European Union*, ed. European Consortium of Church–State Research (Thessaloniki: Sakkoulas Publications, 1994), 323–79.

[5] See Wolfgang Lutz and Vegard Skirbekk, 'The Demography of Religions and their Changing Distribution in the World', in *Universal Rights in a World of Diversity: The Case*

Of course, it remains true that particular religions tend to preponderate in certain areas. In general, however, a significant percentage of every major religion's adherents lives in regions where the religion is not dominant.[6] About 27 per cent of the world's population lives as religious minorities.[7] Moreover, this figure does not include subgroups of the major religions (for example, Shia Muslims living in Sunni majority countries). Christianity in general and Protestantism in particular are highly fractionalized.[8] The result is that many Christians in Christian majority countries nonetheless find themselves in minority positions. Similarly, there are major divisions in Islam and Buddhism. Moreover, in every tradition there are significant ranges of interpretation and understanding of religious doctrines, teaching and practice, and different degrees of strictness in compliance with various teachings, which may lead to situations in which individuals find themselves in minority positions. This can make significant differences for various subgroups in the population, such as women[9] or ethnic minorities.

Types of state reactions to minority religions

The realities of pluralism require all states to deal with religious minorities, but the ways that different states handle this differ markedly. State reactions to minority religions can be divided broadly into restrictive and facilitative responses. With respect to restrictive approaches, it is important to distinguish between restrictions imposed by government and more general constraints flowing from social hostilities.[10] Of course, there is a high correlation between social hostilities and government restrictions,[11] since the former often create pressures for government response, either because dominant social groups affirmatively call for the restrictions, or because government is forced to intervene to avoid

---

of Religious Freedom, eds Mary Ann Glendon and Hans F. Zacher (Vatican City: Pontificia Academia Scientiarum Socialium, 2012), 91, 102–7, citing *World Religion Database,* eds Todd M. Johnson and Brian J. Grim (Brill, Online at: www.worldreligiondatabase.org/wrd_home.asp).

[6] See Pew Forum, 'Global Religious Landscape', Chart showing Geographic Distribution of Religious Groups.

[7] Ibid., Section on Living as Majorities and Minorities.

[8] See Pew Forum, 'Global Christianity', 21.

[9] See Bahia G. Tahzib-Lie, 'Dissenting Women, Religion or Belief, and the State: Contemporary Challenges that Require Attention', in *Facilitating Freedom of Religion or Belief: A Deskbook*, eds Tore Lindholm, W. Cole Durham, Jr, and Bahia G. Tahzib-Lie (Leiden: Koninklijke Brill N.V., 2004), 455–95.

[10] See Pew Forum on Religion and Public Life, Global Restrictions on Religion (December 2009): 27–31 (differentiating government restrictions and social hostilities).

[11] Brian J. Grim and Roger Finke, *The Price of Freedom Denied: Religious Persecution and Conflict in the Twenty-First Century* (Cambridge: Cambridge University Press, 2011), 215–22.

violence, discrimination, or other problems. But it is important to remember that governmental and social reactions to religious minorities can be different. For example, China has very high government restrictions on religion in a society with low to moderate social hostilities toward religion, whereas India has very high social hostilities, with only moderate to high government restrictions.[12]

In compiling its annual International Religious Freedom Report, the United States government's Bureau of Democracy, Human Rights and Labor has identified five types of restrictive responses as it has surveyed global practice.[13] In this typology, the most severe abuses are perpetrated by authoritarian governments. All too often, such regimes 'seek to control all religious thought and expression as part of a more comprehensive determination to control all aspects of political and civic life'.[14] Religious groups are treated as enemies or at least threats to the state because of their potential to challenge loyalty to the state's authoritarian leaders. Other factors such as national security may be cited to justify restrictions, but the result is the same.

The second type of reaction is hostility toward non-traditional and minority religions. State control over religious life is less extensive in such regimes, but intimidation and harassment is typical, and social abuses against minorities are tolerated. In severe cases, government authorities may coerce renunciation of faith or force minority groups to relocate or leave the country. These patterns are often exacerbated where ethnic tensions exist.[15]

A third type of reaction involves failure to address societal intolerance. The state itself may have passed laws aimed at discouraging discrimination and religious intolerance, but enforcement remains passive, and governments fail to prevent socially-based abuses.[16] Those engaged in persecution or harassment have de facto immunity.

A fourth type of reaction consists of institutionalized bias, either in the form of formal adoption of discriminatory legislation or, more typically, of concrete actions by state officials that have discriminatory purposes or effects. As the State Department report notes, 'These circumstances often result from historical dominance by a particular religious group, and can result in institutionalized bias against new or historically repressed religious communities'.[17] Sometimes such patterns simply reflect unthinking assumptions about the status quo and about

---

[12] Pew Forum on Religion and Public Life, Global Restrictions on Religion, 3.

[13] US State Department Bureau of Democracy, Human Rights and Labor, 'Executive Summary', *International Religious Freedom Report, 2010*, http://www.state.gov/j/drl/rls/irf/2010/148659.htm. Subsequent reports have not expressly mentioned this typology, but it clearly remains relevant.

[14] Ibid.
[15] Ibid.
[16] Ibid.
[17] Ibid.

long-standing 'normal' practice; in other settings, the discrimination can be more intentional.

The fifth type of reaction treats particular groups as illegitimate, and improperly denies them religious freedom protections. This approach is evident in states that hold that certain groups are 'illegitimate and dangerous to individuals or societal order'; such groups are described as '"cults" or "sects", thereby perpetuating the stigmatization of the groups and encouraging or implicitly condoning acts of violence against them'.[18] This approach can be seen in countries such as China, which do not extend constitutional protection to 'evil cults' that are not 'normal',[19] or in a number of Islamic countries that refuse to recognize followers of Bahá'í or Ahmadi religions. But such practices are 'relatively common even in countries where religious freedom is otherwise respected'.[20]

On the positive side, states may react to religious minorities by effectively maintaining a regime of benevolent neutrality among all religious groups. They may also go further, in a variety of ways. For example, states can adopt affirmative action measures designed to remedy past discrimination, or more straightforwardly, they may accommodate religious differences out of respect for conscientious objection of various types (for example, objection to military service, to activities that conflict with religious days of rest, or to participation in various types of medical procedures). Legislative majorities often display strong sympathy for religious minorities. In the United States, legislatures in recent years have often been much more solicitous of minority concerns than supposedly counter-majoritarian courts.[21] Many states allow more affirmative forms of state cooperation, including facilitation of religious instruction and subsidies of various types of religious activities.

---

[18] Ibid.

[19] Chinese Constitution, Article 36.

[20] 2010 International Religious Freedom Report Executive Summary.

[21] Thus, it was the judicial branch that lowered the standard for constitutional protection of religious freedom in *Employment Division v. Smith*, 494 US 872 (1990), and *City of Boerne v. Flores*, 521 US 507 (1997), and Congress that sought to reverse this pattern by adopting the Religious Freedom Restoration Act of 1993 ('RFRA'), 42 U.S.C. § 2000bb to 2000bb-4, and subsequently, after *Flores* held RFRA unconstitutional as applied to the states, by adopting the Religious Land Use and Institutionalized Persons Act ('RLUIPA'). 42 U.S.C. §§ 2000cc 5. Many state legislatures have also adopted legislation insisting on heightened protection of religious freedom. See William W. Bassett, W. Cole Durham, Jr, and Robert T. Smith, *Religious Organizations and the Law* 1 (Thomson Reuters West, 2012), § 2.63. A similar pattern is evident in individual cases. For example, when the US Supreme Court rejected a claim of a Jewish Air Force officer seeking an exemption from a dress code that banned wearing a yarmulke, *Goldman v. Weinberger*, 475 US 503 (1986), Congress promptly passed corrective legislation. 10 U.S.C. § 774.

Implications of religion–state structures for minority religions

In the end, state reactions to religious minorities depend heavily on the general religion–state structures that a particular nation adopts and implements. Elsewhere, drawing on work with students and other colleagues, I have developed a robust scheme for analysing the full range of possible religion–state relationships,[22] which can be represented by the following diagram:

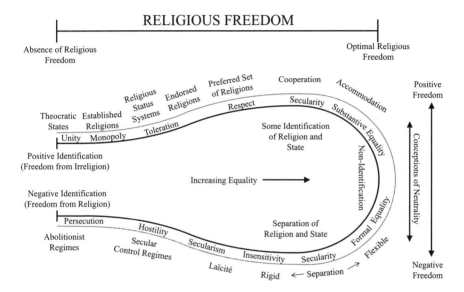

Figure 1.1   Diagram Representing Comparative Religion–State Relationships

---

[22]   W. Cole Durham, Jr, 'Patterns of Religion–state Relations', in *Religion and Human Rights: An Introduction*, eds John Witte and M. Christian Green (Oxford: Oxford University Press, 2011), chapter 22; W. Cole Durham, Jr and Brett G. Scharffs, *Law and Religion: National, International and Comparative Perspectives* (Austin: Aspen Publishers, Wolters Kluwer Law & Business, 2010) 113–22; W. Cole Durham, Jr, 'Perspectives on Religious Liberty: A Comparative Framework', in *Religious Human Rights in Global Perspective*, eds J.D. van der Vyver and J. Witte, Jr (The Hague: Martinus Nijhof Publishers, 1996), 1–44; George R. Ryskamp, 'The Spanish Experience in Church-State Relations: A Comparative Study of the Interrelationship Between Church–State Identification and Religious Liberty', *Brigham Young University Law Review* (1980): 616–53.

Without repeating in detail here what has been described in prior work, the main aim of the schema is to lay out the broad array of the world's religion–state systems on a continuum stretching from regimes with positive (absolute) identification of state with (a particular) religion to those with negative identification (for example, positive identification with an anti-religious ideology). The continuum is curved in a horseshoe loop to reflect the fact that the two ends of the continuum correlate with absence of religious freedom, while the middle zone of the loop corresponds to a variety of systems that optimize religious freedom. Arrayed along the inner and outer bands of the identification continuum are two sets of types of religion–state relations. The outer band focuses on structural features of the various types of religion–state relationships: theocratic states, established religions, religious status systems, and so forth. The inner band focuses on the posture or attitude of the state toward religion. While there is a rough correlation between institutional structure and general state attitude toward religion, there is considerable flexibility. The established religions of the United Kingdom and Scandinavia (now disestablished in Sweden and Norway), for example, have long exhibited high degrees of toleration, respect, equal treatment, and secularity in their interactions with minority religions. In that sense, the position of institutional structures in the outer loop has considerable elasticity and can 'slip around' the loop.

The schema as it has been described in earlier work focuses on the relationship of the state to religion in general and on the implications of that relationship for the neutrality of the state and for the conceptions of freedom and equality embodied in different religion–state models. Other authors have used this schema to analyse how a country's religion–state identification affects a state's compliance with human rights law more generally,[23] and to show how a religion might understand its relationships with a variety of states (as opposed to how various states might understand their relations with religions).[24] Here my focus is on implications of the schema for minority religions. This focus brings out the degree of variation in treatment within particular systems that the abstract character of the schema necessarily obscures. That is, description of a particular regime as theocratic, established, cooperationist, separationist or laicist says something in broad terms about relations of the state with prevailing religions or religion in general, but gives no detail about how particular regimes deal with the range of smaller religions in each country. Nonetheless, the schema has significant implications for understanding state reactions to minority religions and for suggesting preferred approaches.

---

[23] Jeroen Temperman, *State-Religion Relationships and Human Rights Law: Towards a Right to Religiously Neutral Governance* (Leiden: Martinus Nijhoff Publishers, 2010).

[24] F. Russell Hittenger, 'Political Pluralism and Religious Liberty: The Teaching of *Dignitatis Humanae*', in *Universal Rights in a World of Diversity: The Case of Religious Freedom*, eds Mary Ann Glendon and Hans F. Zacher (Vatican City: Pontificia Academia Scientiarum Socialium, 2012), 39–55.

First, and most obviously, a high degree of *either* positive *or* negative identification with religion bodes ill for religious minorities, because it commits the regime to opposing belief systems other than that favoured by the state. Strong identification tends to be totalistic and exclusive, and minority religions in this context constitute threats to the legitimacy and loyalty structures that support the regime. High degrees of identification also tend to be polarizing, inducing defensive reaction by non-preferred groups, thereby heightening divisive tensions among religions in society.

Second, focus on religious minorities highlights a major social dynamic that in fact lies behind the schema. That is, the reality of growing pluralization in societies around the globe underlies the trend signalled by the arrow pointing toward increased equality and suggesting movement over time toward the institutional arrangements at the middle of the loop. As societies become more religiously diverse, and as religious minorities become more visible, state identification with any one group becomes less politically sustainable. Distinctions between religion, state and society become more evident, making it conceptually easier to imagine a society with multiple religions. As experience with greater diversity increases, religious differences seem less threatening. Religious homogeneity no longer represents the vital 'social glue' holding society together. The Lockean insight that respecting difference can strengthen social stability rather than fragmenting it[25] is increasingly validated by practical experience, and can take hold in the form of increased commitment to religious freedom norms that protect minority rights.

Third, reflection on the challenges faced by minorities underscores problematic state responses at various positions along the loop. Here two recurrent examples may suffice. A frequent feature of cooperationist regimes is specific agreements or concordats with major religions designed to spell out specific features of state cooperation with religion. Historically, concordats with the Roman Catholic Church were a standard way of structuring church-state relations. In recent decades, efforts to equalize cooperation with other groups have resulted in parallel agreements with other religious communities.[26] Too often, however, there is insufficient political will to extend the benefits of such agreements to other religious groups, leading to violations of fundamental equality principles.[27] Another example flows from wooden application of rule-of-law principles. In separationist regimes, commitment to the rule of law can

---

[25] For discussion of the Lockean insight, see Durham, 'Perspectives', 7–12.

[26] See Silvio Ferrari, 'Religious Communities as Legal Persons: An Introduction to the National Reports', in *Churches and Other Organisations as legal Persons: Proceedings of the17th Meeting of the European Consortium for Church and State Research 3–8*, ed. Lars Friedner (Brussels: Uitgeverij Peeters 2007).

[27] Cf., *Savez crkava 'Riječ života' and Others v. Croatia* (ECtHR, App. No. 7798/08, 9 December 2010) (holding that legislation that deprived minority religions of access to certain benefits granted to major churches resulted in unequal protection of religious freedom rights of minority groups).

lead to inflexible and excessively formalistic interpretations of legal rules that fail to accommodate religious practices. In the United States, the well-known case of *Employment Division v. Smith*[28] took this approach by holding that any neutral or general law would trump religious freedom claims. The result of this approach is to deny protection to minority religious practices inconsistent with general and neutral rules, even where reasonable alternative accommodations are available and no compelling reason to deny them exists. The extent of minority protections is often the real test of the level of religious freedom in a particular legal system.

Fourth, focus on minority rights leads to recognition of the nature of inter-religious competition that lies behind the religion–state structures of a given country. When one first surveys the array of religion–state systems in the world, there is a tendency to see them as fixed institutional models. In fact, however, the systems in place in any particular country reflect social equilibrium points in on-going historical processes that involve constant debate, tension, adjustment, and revision of relationships between various actors in the domain of state, religion and society. With that in mind, it becomes clear that the arrangements in place at any particular time reflect interactions between the state and the full spectrum of religious groups in society. Unsurprisingly, the conduct of dominant religious groups, whether in public or behind-the-scenes, can parallel the anti-competitive practices of monopolies and oligopolies trying to preserve their share in economic markets. For example, they advance arguments that privileged status is necessary for social stability; national security; nation identity, prestige and culture; to avoid foreign dependence; and to prevent fraud.[29] Reacting to these pressures, states all too often adopt structures that raise barriers to entry against new religions, leading as in economic markets to reduction in service, reduced options for religious 'consumers', and in the end, reduced liberty. Religious registration laws, which persist in many countries, are a practical example of this.[30]

Fifth, restrictive practices are based all too often on stereotypical images of new religious movements. For example, the provisions of the 1997 Russian Law on Freedom of Conscience and Religious Associations setting the eligibility conditions for acquiring legal entity status read like a laundry list of stereotypical cult behaviours. Under these provisions, grounds for dissolution of a religious organization include *inter alia*:

---

[28] 494 US 872 (1990).

[29] See Shima Baradaran-Robison, Brett G. Scharffs, and Elizabeth A. Sewell, 'Religious Monopolies and the Commodification of Religion', *Pepperdine Law Review* 32 (2005): 885.

[30] For a review of the relevant law, see W. Cole Durham, Jr, 'Legal Status of Religious Organizations: A Comparative Overview', *The Review of Faith & International Affairs* 8 (2010): 2, 3–14; see also, for example, *Manoussakis v. Greece* (ECtHR, App. No. 18748/91 29 August 1996).

creation of [an] armed formation; propaganda of war and incitement of social, racial, national, or religious enmity and misanthropy; compulsory dissolution of the family; religious use of drugs and psychotropic substances and hypnosis; encouragement of suicide or refusal of medical care for religious motives for persons whose life or health are threatened; prevention of acquiring obligatory education; compulsion of members and adherents ... to alienate property ... for the use of the organization; [and] prevention of a citizen's leaving the religious association under threat of harm to life, health, or property ... .[31]

So-called 'mental manipulation' laws or other legislation seeking to impose special constraints on 'brainwashing' and other forms of religious 'undue influence' often have stereotypical images of cult behaviour as their basis.[32] While these provisions do identify some legitimate problems, they are overbroad and in effect authorize and encourage state officials to prosecute religious individuals and groups merely because they fit a stereotypical profile. Moreover, the law reinforces in the public mind the unjustified notion that religious minorities tend to have many of these problematic characteristics, when that is often not the case. Legislation of this type, unfortunately, can spring up in regimes located at virtually any point around the loops, though it is less likely in regimes that provide optimal protection of religious freedom.

Sixth, stereotypical thinking is not the only source of legislation that can arise without regard for particular religion–state structures and can be particularly problematic for minority religions. In this regard, one thinks of the spate of anti-extremism laws adopted in the aftermath of 9/11, and of the defamation of religion legislation that has been encouraged by the Organization of Islamic Cooperation in recent years.[33] Anti-extremism legislation tends to be overbroad,

---

[31] Federal Law No. 125-FZ on the Freedom of Conscience and Religious Associations (Russia 1997), art. 14(2).

[32] See, for example, James T. Richardson, 'Regulating Religion: Sociological and Historical Introduction', in *Regulating Religion: Case Studies from Around the Globe*, ed. James T. Richardson (New York: Kluwer Academic/Plenum Publishers, 2004), 1; James T. Richardson, "Brainwashing' Claims and Minority Religions Outside the United States: Cultural Diffusion of a Questionable Concept in the Legal Arena', *BYU Law Review* (1996): 873; Willy Fautré, Alain Garay, and Yves Nidegger, 'The Sect Issue in the European Francophone Sphere', in *Facilitating Freedom of Religion or Belief: A Deskbook*, eds Tore Lindholm, W. Cole Durham, Jr and Bahia G. Tahzib-Lie (Oslo: Oslo Coalition on freedom of Religion or Belief, 2004).

[33] Frank La Rue et al., Joint Declaration on Defamation of Religions and Anti-Terrorism and Anti-Extremism Legislation (December 10, 2008), http://www.article19.org/pdfs/other/joint-declaration-on-defamation-of-religions-and-anti-terrorism-and-anti-ext.pdf; Leonard A. Leo, Felice D. Gaer and Elizabeth K.I. Cassidy, 'Protecting Religions from "Defamation": A Threat to Universal Human Rights Standards', *Harvard Journal of Law and Public Policy* 34 (2011): 769; L. Bennett Graham, 'Defamation of Religions: The End of Pluralism?', *Emory International Law Review* 23 (2009): 71. The Organization of

and empowers regimes to harass religious minorities.[34] Defamation of religion legislation, often ostensibly passed to defend religious minorities, paradoxically often has the opposite effect. This is because religious minorities are often too intimidated to invoke such legislation because doing so may simply attract additional social hostility, whereas in contrast religious majorities may feel quite safe invoking the legislation against speakers from minority backgrounds. Anti-conversion legislation also poses serious problems for minority religious communities, particularly those that engage in missionary outreach activities.[35] Like some of the other forms of problematic legislation, this often trades on perceptions that religious minorities use inappropriate inducements to procure conversions, but is structured in ways that inhibit legitimate religious persuasion.

Conclusion

In conclusion, state reactions to religious minorities are as diverse as the states and the religions involved, and variations are compounded by the personalities of the government officials that implement those reactions. A brief essay such as this cannot hope to describe the infinite variations involved in any detail. But it is helpful to survey the types of reactions and see how they relate to broader patterns of interaction between states and religions. Three broad generalizations do seem to emerge from the foregoing discussion. First, the presence of religious minorities is a pervasive feature of contemporary societies, and in our highly mobile world, pluralization is only likely to increase with time. Second, optimal protections for religious minorities are most likely to be found in regimes that seek to maximize equal religious freedom for all. Third, while historical evolution over the past several centuries has followed a path of increasing secularization of society (that is, the movement from established religions to cooperationist, accommodationist, and separationist regimes), it is possible for secularization to go too far. Insofar as secularization results in the creation of religion–state systems that provide a neutral framework capable of accommodating a broad range of religions, minority religions will clearly benefit. To the extent that secularism as an ideology becomes an end in itself, religious minorities are likely to suffer along with religion generally. Indeed, since they are smaller, have weaker defences, and may become

---

Islamic Cooperation recently changed its name; during much of the period it was pushing the 'defamation of religion' agenda, it was known as the Organization of Islamic Conference.

[34] Alexander Verkhovsky, *Inappropriate Enforcement of Anti-extremist Legislation in Russia in 2011*, 27 April 2012, http://www.sova–center.ru/en/misuse/reports–analyses/2012/04/d24302/.

[35] See, for example, James Andrew Huff, 'Religious Freedom in India and Analysis of the Constitutionality of Anti-Conversion Laws', *Rutgers Journal of Law and Religion* 10 (2009): 12.

targets or scapegoats, they are likely to suffer even more. We owe much that we have learned about the ideal of religious freedom to the experience and thought of religious minorities,[36] and we should take care to extend that heritage for the future, remembering that in our shrinking world, we are all minorities.

---

[36] Nicholas P. Miller, *The Religious Roots of the First Amendment: Dissenting Protestants and the Separation of Church and State* (Oxford: Oxford University Press, 2012).

Chapter 2
The UN Human Rights Committee and Religious Minorities[1]

Nazila Ghanea

Originally it was religious minorities that spearheaded minority rights concerns onto the regional and later international level. Through the experience of protection for religious minorities, minority rights first attempted to be established at the League of Nations and later slowly percolated the United Nations (UN) human rights norms and mechanisms. Nevertheless, though minority rights eventually – after some decades of uncertainty – gained currency in the UN, persons belonging to religious minorities never came to be re-integrated into the concept of minorities in anything other than passing mention. Religious minorities are formally covered in human rights protections offered by minority rights – these being in addition to human rights standards that apply to all. However, they are largely excluded from their mechanisms and procedures.

Historical antecedents

Migration has had religious overtones throughout history, with the very emergence and spread of religion – and the subsequent linkages related to that religious civilization – leading to minority demands and concerns in many lands. One such example is the history of the spread of Islam across the Middle East, Asia, North and East Africa and across Europe. Some of these patterns led to relatively progressive norms coming into being. However, others, such as when Christianity was imposed through colonialist ambition, led to devastating human rights violations, for example against indigenous populations. These patterns of religious migration were later built upon to establish trade between the horn of Africa and East Africa, Oman, and India; and subsequently led to an increase in the presence of religious minorities on these soils. Though they were ethnic minorities too, they were primarily conceived of and catered to as religious minorities. Religious minorities have also been a serious Islamic concern from the outset of its revelation, since

---

[1] An earlier version of this chapter appeared as Nazila Ghanea, 'Are Religious Minorities Really Minorities?', *Oxford Journal of Law and Religion* 1 (2012): 57–79, reprinted in part here with the permission of the copyright holder.

the Quran gave explicit textual recognition to 'People of the Book',[2] for example as indicated by the later Millet system. Religious minorities, meanwhile, had long established themselves as a matter of enduring European concern, not least due to the religious underpinnings of the devastating Thirty Years War, 'wars which pitted subordination to a universalizing religion (the Catholic church) against national independence, which also appeared to require religious independence'.[3]

From this European experience, the protection for religious minorities could hardly be of a higher pedigree. It has a record dating back to the mid- to late 1500s,[4] when successive treaties sought to provide protection for religious minorities. The post-First World War period and the Treaty of Versailles re-focused concern on religious minorities and a new generation of religious minority protection clauses were enshrined as non-negotiable elements of emerging peace treaties. In sum, it is no exaggeration to suggest that the roots of minority rights can be found in the protection of religious minorities, not only in Europe where related protections were enshrined explicitly in bilateral and multilateral treaties over three centuries,[5] but with traces over other continents and eras too. Such concern with religious minorities pre-dated by centuries not only the emergence of modern human rights but also international concern with racial minorities. This precedence is all the more remarkable considering that the proposed League of Nations Article 21 had failed on grounds that protection for racial minorities was deemed unpalatable by the great powers. Protection for religious minorities was not an issue. Now, some 90 years on, however, racial minorities enjoy protections[6] that religious minorities have largely lost.

The scope of these historical legal protections, however, should not be overstated or romanticized. The underlying concern was security, and the scope of protection was tightly drawn in terms both of geography and beneficiaries. The

---

[2] For a discussion of both the limitations and opportunities offered by the 'People of the Book' status, see Nazila Ghanea, 'Phantom Minorities and Religions Denied', *Shi'a Affairs Journal* 2 (2009).

[3] Asbjorn Eide, 'Minority Situations: In Search of Peaceful and Constructive Solutions', *Notre Dame Law Review* 66 (1990–1991): 1316.

[4] For a discussion, see Malcolm Evans, *Religious Liberty and International Law in Europe* (Cambridge: Cambridge University Press, 1997), 42–82.

[5] As Eide observes, the issue of religious minorities 'first emerged between Catholics and Protestants in the seventeenth century, and later between Christians and the Islamic world of the Ottoman Empire in the eighteenth and early nineteenth century'. This was followed later in the peace settlement after World War I with five special treaties, five peace treaties, five declarations, and two conventions. See Eide, 'Minority Situations: In Search', 1316–17.

[6] For example as upheld in the UN Convention on the Elimination of all Forms of Racial Discrimination. For a discussion see Nazila Ghanea, 'Religious or Minority?', *Religion, State and Society* 36 (2008): 303–25; and David Keane, 'Addressing the Aggravated Meeting Points of Race and Religion', *Maryland Law Journal of Race, Religion, Gender and Class* 6 (2007): 353–91.

protections were discrete rather than generally applicable and the objective was the maintenance of the status quo rather than motivated by broader humanitarian concerns. In essence, the aim was the containment of religious minorities and tit-for-tat guarantees of protections between empires and later states. It was not underpinned with a concern with freedom of religion or belief as enshrined in international human rights standards since 1948, nor indeed with our principled rationales for minority rights today.

The separation of religious minorities from minorities

Religious minorities are formally covered under both freedom of religion or belief and minority human rights protections – these being in addition to human rights standards that apply to all. The UN recognizes minority rights as 'special rights' that accrue to persons belonging to minorities on the understanding that equality alone would not provide sufficient protection against discrimination. One could, in fact, consider minority rights as a means of ensuring substantive equality for a specific category of rights holders. Henrard declares non-discrimination as the '*condition sine qua non* for adequate minority protection'.[7] She also distils the essential element of minority rights to the right to identity, which requires 'effective protection of their general human rights in combination with the right not to be discriminated against'; and one which is informed by and limited to a quest for the goal of real, substantive equality.[8]

International legal provisions regularly preface any reference to minorities with the designations 'ethnic', 'religious' or 'linguistic'. Religious minorities have always been assumed to be part and parcel of the minorities regime normatively, but have in fact rarely been protected through it. Though there has long been concern about the narrowness of these designations, this chapter seeks only to establish that, though religious minorities have been one of the three most explicitly recognized categories in the minority rights regime, they have largely been excluded from consideration under the umbrella of minority rights.

For historic reasons the UN era started out with 30 years of downplaying, if not outright rejecting, of minority rights. The UN had no appetite for minority provisions. In fact, the ideology of the time held that universal rights would be the panacea for all ills; equality presumably removed the premise for singling out rights holders by categories.[9]

---

[7] Kristin Henrard, 'Ever-Increasing Synergy towards a Stronger Level of Minority Protection between Minority-Specific and Non-Minority-Specific Instruments', *Eur. Y.B. Minority Issues* 3 (2003–2004): 29.

[8] Ibid., 16.

[9] For a broader and richer discussion, see Patrick Thornberry, *International Law and the Rights of Minorities* (Oxford: Oxford University Press, 1991).

It took several decades to realise that equal treatment could result in discrimination against those who started lower down the pecking order. If, for example, Brahmins and Dalits are treated 'equally' in India, the discrimination against Dalits only becomes further entrenched. The gloss of equal treatment could too easily merely conceal inequality. In 1976, the ICCPR came into force, Article 27 holding that, 'In those States in which ethnic, religious or linguistic minorities exist, persons belonging to such minorities shall not be denied the right, in community with the other members of their group, to enjoy their own culture, to profess and practise their own religion, or to use their own language'.[10]

The UN Human Rights Committee, however, took some years to feel comfortable with this provision and to utilize it. It eventually started reflecting on it in its jurisprudence, eventually interpreting it in its 1994 General Comment 23 on Article 27 of the ICCPR regarding the rights of minorities. Capotorti's 1977 UN Sub-Commission[11] study also contributed to a gradual return to a reinvigorated notion of minorities, this time under the UN's umbrella. A UN Sub-Commission expert, Capotorti held that a minority is 'a group, numerically inferior to the rest of the population of a State, in a non-dominant position, whose members – being nationals of the State – possess ethnic, religious or linguistic characteristics differing from those of the rest of the population and show, if only implicitly, a sense of solidarity, directed towards preserving their culture, traditions, religion or language'.[12] Capotorti emphasizes the shared desire to preserve different characteristics. However, others have widened their reading of the beneficiaries and the rationale for the enjoyment of minority rights. Van Dyke has stated

> The groups that enjoy [minority] rights seem to fall into two broad categories that sometimes overlap. One category includes groups characterized by weakness that calls for protection or disadvantage that calls for compensatory action. Special measures for such groups seem to be approved if their purpose and effect is to promote equality and not to establish or preserve inequality. The characteristic that distinguishes groups in the second category is a shared sense of a community of interest that is relatively fundamental, important, and enduring ... .[13]

---

[10] International Covenant on Civil and Political Rights, G.A res. 2200A (XXI), 21 U.N. GAOR Supp. (No. 16) at 52, U.N. Doc. A/6316 (1966), 999 U.N.T.S. 171, entered into force 23 March 1976, Article 27.

[11] Though the name of the UN Sub Commission on Prevention of Discrimination and Protection of Minorities (1947–1998) suggested a focus on minorities; in fact the scope of its work was much broader. In 1999 it changed its name to Sub-Commission on the Promotion and Protection of Human Rights and it held its final session in 2006.

[12] Francesco Capotorti, Study on the Rights of Persons Belonging to Ethnic, Religious and Linguistic Minorities, E/CN.4/Sub.2/384/Rev.1, published by the UN in 1991, Sales No. E.78.XIV.1.

[13] Vernon Van Dyke, 'Human Rights and the Rights of Groups', *American Journal of Political Science* 18 (1974): 741.

In 1978, the UN began drafting what would become the 1992 UN Declaration on the Rights of Persons Belonging to National or Ethnic, Religious and Linguistic Minorities. Later still, from 1995 to 2006, the UN sponsored the annual weeklong meeting of the UN Sub-Commission Working Group on Minorities. Since the change from the UN Commission on Human Rights to the UN Human Rights Council,[14] this group has been meeting for just two days per annum since 2008 as the Forum on Minority Issues.

Some 30 years had passed from the formation of the UN, therefore, before its concern for minorities came into full effect. This 30-year question mark over minority rights meant that 'minority protection ceased to be the primary vehicle through which religious freedoms were addressed on the international plane'.[15] When religious minorities face discrimination and persecution as a group, then, their case is addressed under the 'freedom of religion or belief' umbrella in international human rights and not under minority rights.

This observation can be deduced primarily from the examination of the jurisprudence of UN treaty bodies such as the Human Rights Committee, though it is also evident in how such violations have been handled by UN Charter-based bodies, as seen in 1235 and 1503 procedures and the lack of serious consideration to date to religious minorities by the Independent Expert on Minority Issues. The assessment below will focus on the jurisprudence regarding Article 27 of the ICCPR, since this is the most significant binding norm addressing minorities at the UN level. As a backdrop to this assessment, it should be kept in mind that some elements in minority rights complement and enhance protections offered through freedom of religion or belief, including religious culture, group rights in general, objective determination of the existence of religious minorities, positive measures of protection, effective participation by religious minorities in decisions affecting them, and the fact that in the protection of the 'survival and continued development' of religious minorities, the bar for protection is high.[16]

The void

The objective of this section is not to consider more broadly the limitations of UN Human Rights Committee jurisprudence. However, a few preliminary points need to be considered. First, we should note the criticism that has also been expressed with

---

[14] For a discussion of the implications of this change see Nazila Ghanea, 'From UN Commission on Human Rights to UN Human Rights Council: One Step Forwards or Two Steps Sideways?', *International and Comparative Law Quarterly* 55 (2006): 695–705.

[15] Evans, *Religious Liberty*, 183.

[16] See full discussion at Nazila Ghanea, 'Are Religious Minorities Really Minorities?', *Oxford Journal of Law and Religion* 1 (2012): 57–79.

regard to its jurisprudence regarding freedom of religion or belief: 'So far, the HRC [Human Rights Committee] has not concluded in many individual Communications to a violation of the prohibition of discrimination on the basis of religion'.[17] Second, the very language of Article 27 refers to 'persons belonging to' minorities rather than minorities as such and, furthermore, the individual communication procedure of the ICCPR does not allow for *actio popularis*.[18] A third point is that the Human Rights Committee has often reiterated that it understands 'minorities' to refer to minority status within the whole nation and not within a particular province or geographic area, as determined in the *Ballentyne et. al. v. Canada19* case and as has been reiterated since.[20] In *Ballentyne,* the Committee observed

> that this provision [art. 27] refers to minorities in States; this refers, as do all references to the 'State' or to 'States' in the provisions of the Covenant, to ratifying States. Further, article 50 of the Covenant provides that its provisions extend to all parts of Federal States without any limitations or exceptions. Accordingly, the minorities referred to in article 27 are minorities within such a State, and not minorities within any province. A group may constitute a majority in a province but still be a minority in a State and thus be entitled to the benefits of article 27. English speaking citizens of Canada cannot be considered a linguistic minority. The authors therefore have no claim under article 27 of the Covenant.[21]

This means that religious minorities fulfil the numerical aspect of their relevance to Article 27 by being numerically inferior in the State and not in a particular province or geographic area of that State.

These observations illustrate the narrowness of the scope of Article 27 jurisprudence in significant ways. Nevertheless, Article 27 still remains highly important for (religious) minorities. As Jabareen asserts

---

[17] Kristin Henrard, 'The Protection of Minorities', *International Journal of Minority and Group Rights* 14 (2007): 168.

[18] This has been reiterated in the 2009 case *Anderson v. Denmark*: 'The Committee observes that no person may, in theoretical terms and by actio popularis, object to a law or practice which he holds to be at variance with the Covenant. Any person claiming to be a victim of a violation of a right protected by the Covenant must demonstrate either that a state party has by an act or omission already impaired the exercise of his right or that such impairment is imminent, basing his argument for example on legislation in force or on a judicial or administrative decision or practice.' See *Fatima Andersen v. Denmark*, (1868/2009), CCPR/C/99/D/1868/2009 (7 September 2010), para. 6.4.

[19] *Ballantyne, Davidson, McIntyre v. Canada*, (359/1989 and 385/1989/Rev. 1), CCPR/C/47/D/359/1989 and 385/1989/Rev.1 (5 May 1993).

[20] See Peter Michael *Queenan v. Canada*, (1379/2005), CCPR/C/84/D/1379/2005 (26 July 2005).

[21] *Ballantyne, Davidson, McIntyre v. Canada*, para. 11.2.

if Article 27 is to have any noticeable effect on the position of minorities in a given society, and if the ICCPR is to achieve its goal of securing true equality, then Article 27 must be invested with more than a passive interpretation. If no such positive, forceful content is given to it, Article 27 adds nothing to the Covenant. This discussion is all the more important given that the ICCPR legally binds the largest number of states parties of any treaty containing minority rights and arguably has gained the status of customary international law[.][22]

The purpose of addressing Article 27 jurisprudence in this chapter is to observe the dearth of consideration of religious minorities as minorities. A brief review of UN Human Rights Committee jurisprudence regretfully reveals the overall exclusion of religious minorities from Article 27 consideration.

Article 27 jurisprudence on freedom of religion or belief runs the gamut of 'Faith' or ideological/anti-religion schools, the exclusion of minorities from particular spheres, the wearing of the Islamic headscarf, and registration of religious communities. Space limitations permit full discussion here of only the last two of these, but I have addressed them all elsewhere and the assessment supports the conclusions here concerning the absence of religious minority analysis.[23]

Headscarf or other headdress

The headscarf cases follow the pattern of excluding consideration of the headscarf as part of a minority – whether ethnic and/or religious – culture. If Article 27's implications received scrutiny, one would expect consideration of whether the headscarf can be deemed part of culture, whether positive measures may be necessary for minority members to enjoy this cultural and/or religious practice, participation of the religious minority in decisions concerning it, and whether the ban on the headscarf may jeopardize the survival and continuity of cultural, religious and social identity.

In *Hudoyberganova v. Uzbekistan*,[24] however, one finds no consideration of Article 27 at all. Though the claimant herself had not claimed violation of Article 27, the Committee could have brought this article within its purview and invoked its consideration. The Committee's consideration focuses on Article 18 and the limitations possible to manifestation of religion or belief and coercion in this regard. Since a violation of Article 18.2 is found, consideration of Article 27 would not necessarily have changed the finding. However, in relation to the State's claim that Ms Hudoyberganova's hijab constituted a 'cult dress'[25] and

---

[22] Yousef Jabareen, 'Toward Participatory Equality: Protecting Minority Rights Under International Law', *Israel Law Review* 41 (2008): 647.
[23] See Ghanea, 'Are Religious Minorities Really Minorities?', 57–79.
[24] *Hudoyberganova v. Uzbekistan* (931/2000), ICCPR, A/60/40 vol. II (5 November 2004).
[25] Ibid., para. 2.7.

assertion that 'Islam does not prescribe a specific cult dress',[26] consideration of the possible relevance of expression of minority religion as culture could have added this interesting consideration to Article 27 jurisprudence.

An older related case is that of *Bhinder v. Canada*,[27] where a Sikh worker claimed violation of Article 18 due to the refusal of the Canadian Railway Company to exempt him from wearing a hard hat, in effect disallowing him from wearing his turban. The State party, at that time, made a claim that should have served as a red flag to the Committee and compelled consideration of Article 27. Canada stated

> The State party further considers that article 18 does not impose a duty of 'reasonable accommodation', that the concept of freedom of religion only comprises freedom from State interference but no positive obligation for States parties to provide special assistance to grant waivers to members of religious groups which would enable them to practice their religion.[28]

Contemplation of Article 27 clearly would have made the positive duty towards a religious and ethnic minority pertinent to the Committee's considerations. However, the Committee did not flag up Article 27 but did consider Article 26, deciding that

> If the requirement that a hard hat be worn is regarded as raising issues under article 18, then it is a limitation that is justified by reference to the grounds laid down in article 18, paragraph 3. If the requirement that a hard hat be worn is seen as a discrimination de facto against persons of the Sikh religion under article 26, then, applying criteria now well established in the jurisprudence of the Committee, the legislation requiring that workers in federal employment be protected from injury and electric shock by the wearing of hard hats is to be regarded as reasonable and directed towards objective purposes that are compatible with the Covenant.[29]

The Committee decided that 'the facts which have been placed before it do not disclose a violation of any provision of the International Covenant on Civil and Political Rights'.[30]

However, another case has begun to unravel a faint connection between the Committee's views on the scope of cultural rights and their relevance for religious minorities. It concerns a Latvian national, a member of the Jewish, and Russian-speaking minorities, seeking to have his name corrected to its Russian Jewish

---

[26] Ibid., para. 2.8.
[27] *Karnel Singh Binder v. Canada*, (208/186), CCPR/C/37/D/208/1986, 9 November 1989.
[28] Ibid., para. 4.5.
[29] Ibid., para. 6.2.
[30] Ibid., para. 7.

form on his passport. In *Raihman v. Latvia*, the Committee found a violation of Article 17, noting 'with respect to the unilateral change of the author's name by the State party, the Committee does not consider it necessary to address whether the same facts amount to a violation of article 26, article 27, or article 2, paragraph 1, read in conjunction with article 17'.[31] Although the Committee does not consider Article 27, Mr Rafael Rivas Posada and Mr Krister Thelin, do so in their dissenting opinions in which no violation is found. They state that the reasoning and conclusions on the merits should instead have: (1) noted the claimant to be a member of the Jewish and Russian-speaking minorities in Latvia; (2) recalled that 'States parties to the Covenant may regulate activities that constitute an essential element in the culture of a minority, provided that the regulation does not amount to a de facto denial of this right';[32] and (3) considered that 'the imposition of a declinable termination on his name and surname did not adversely affect his right, in community with the other members of the Jewish and Russian speaking minorities of Latvia, to enjoy his own culture, to profess and practice the Jewish religion, or to use the Russian language', and hence no violation of Article 27 occurred.[33] Misters Posada and Thelin's reference back to the jurisprudence of the Human Rights Committee regarding the culture of indigenous peoples in relation to religious minority culture is promising, as it suggests that religious minorities are equal beneficiaries of the right to (religious) culture. One of the cases they reference in this connection is *Länsmann v. Finland*. They refer to this paragraph in particular:

> A State may understandably wish to encourage development or allow economic activity by enterprises. The scope of its freedom to do so is not to be assessed by reference to a margin of appreciation, but by reference to the obligations it has undertaken in article 27. Article 27 requires that a member of a minority shall not be denied his right to enjoy his culture. Thus, measures whose impact amount to a denial of the right will not be compatible with the obligations under article 27. However, measures that have a certain limited impact on the way of life of persons belonging to a minority will not necessarily amount to a denial of the right under article 27.[34]

---

[31] *Leonid Raihman v. Latvia*, (1621/2007), CCPR/C/100/C/100/D/1621/2007, 30 November 2010, para. 8.4.

[32] Ibid., dissenting opinion of Mr Rafael Rivas Posada and Mr Krister Thelin, para. 8.6. In making this point, they reference *George Howard v. Canada*, (879/1999), July 26, 2005, para. 12.7; *Kitok v. Sweden*, (197/1985), 27 July 1988; and *Länsmann v. Finland*, (511/1992 and 671/1995), 30 October 1996, para. 9.4.

[33] *Leonid Raihman v. Latvia*, dissenting opinion of Mr Rafael Rivas Posada and Mr Krister Thelin, para. 8.6.

[34] *Länsmann v. Finland*, para. 9.4.

In relation to persons belonging to religious minorities – albeit both ethnic and religious in this present case – they are therefore suggesting a similar judgment call regarding 'certain limited impact on the way of life' of the religious culture.

Registration of religious communities

In the context of cases addressing the registration of religious communities we find scant reference to Article 27, despite their implications in the protection of culture, the enjoyment of rights in community with other members of their group, the objective determination of the existence of the minority, and the 'survival and continued development' objective. The case *Malakhovsky et. al. v. Belarus*,[35] for example, concerned the registration of a religious community but gave no consideration to Article 27. Again, as in the *Hudoyberganova v. Uzbekistan*[36] case, the claimant does not claim violation of Article 27. Indeed this chapter suggests that both claimants and international mechanisms are serving to sideline religious minorities from the minority rights regime. Since persons belonging to religious minorities are largely focusing their claims solely on Article 18 without conjoining it, for example, with Article 27, we have to turn to the Human Rights Committee itself to invoke the relevance of Article 27 in pertinent cases before it.

The Committee observes in *Malakhovsky* the following:

> The State party's law distinguishes between religious communities and religious associations, and ... the possibility of conducting certain activities is restricted to the latter. Not having been granted the status of a religious association, the authors and their fellow believers cannot invite foreign clerics to visit the country, or establish monasteries or educational institutions. Consistent with its General Comment, the Committee considers that these activities form part of the authors' right to manifest their beliefs.[37]

They proceed to find a violation of Article 18.1. Article 27's implications for this case are, nonetheless, numerous and profound.

In the case of *Sister Immaculate Joseph et. al. v. Sri Lanka*,[38] the sisters did claim violation of *inter alia* Article 27 regarding the Sri Lankan Supreme Court's decision to deny incorporation of their Order, which was established in 1900 and was engaged in teaching, charity and community work.[39] They argued that

---

[35] *Sergei Malakhovsky and Alexander Pikul v. Belarus* (1207/2003), ICCPR, A/60/40 vol. II (26 July 2005).
[36] *Hudoyberganova v. Uzbekistan.*
[37] *Sergei Malakhovsky and Alexander Pikul v. Belarus*, para. 7.2.
[38] *Sister Immaculate Joseph and 80 Teaching Sisters of the Holy Cross of the Third Order of Saint Francis in Menzingen of Sri Lanka v. Sri Lanka*, (1249/2004), CCPR/C/85/D/1249/2004 (21 October 2005).
[39] Ibid., paras. 2.1, 2.2, 2.4 and 3.1.

to reject the Order's incorporation while many non-Christian religious bodies with similar object clauses have been incorporated violates article 26. In support, the author provides a (non-exhaustive) list of 28 religious bodies that have been incorporated and their statutory objects, of which most have Buddhist orientation, certain Islamic, and none Christian.[40]

The Human Rights Committee found violation of Article 18.1 and Article 26 and considered that Article 27 would not add anything and did not need separate consideration.[41]

In light of headscarf and registration jurisprudence, therefore, not to mention the faith schools and exclusion of minorities from political parties or similar spheres, we can say that by not considering religious minorities as minorities we are at risk of perpetuating discriminatory patterns against them and denying them equal rights. We are also impoverishing the jurisprudence of minority rights through the refusal to consider religious minorities within its ambit.

Obstacles

Having argued that religious minorities triggered the very concern for minorities as a whole in international law, and that religious minorities were intended for inclusion in the minority rights regime and should not be sidelined from its provisions and mechanisms, one must not naively assume reintegration of religious minorities into minorities protections regimes would be without challenges. Space again does not allow the full consideration here that I have given these challenges elsewhere,[42] but four areas particularly ripe for further study and consideration demand at least mention. They are state-religion or state-ideology relationships, categorization of who fits minority definition, religious leadership issues, and the implication of religion or belief laws.

The first of these, state-religion/ideology relationships, raises the concern that 'religious characteristic' may itself overlap with or subsume 'culture', 'traditions' and 'language'. The particularities in relation to recognition of the characteristics of religious minorities may therefore be multiple. In recognizing religious minorities we also need to make a clear distinction between numerical minorities and minorities as recognized in international human rights law. This in turn raises the complex question of state support. The state-religion or ideological

---

[40] Ibid., para. 3.1.
[41] Ibid., para. 7.6. As a contrast, see discussion of the variety of forms the legal status of religion in the state can take. Also see Anat Scolnicov, *The Right to Religious Freedom in International Law: Between Group Rights and Individual Rights* (London: Routledge, 2011), 67–125.
[42] See full discussion at Ghanea, 'Are Religious Minorities Really Minorities?', 57–79.

relationship may give rise to concerns in relation to state funding for religious schools or religious organizations, muscular state promotion of the religion or ideology, enforcement of religious law as state law, state penalties for 'non-believers' and so on. The complexities stemming from this largely distinguish themselves, or are often of a higher level of magnitude, compared to the state ethnic or linguistic relationship.

Since so-called nation building and the preservation of national unity can become highly dependent on reliance on an intolerant state–religion or state–ideology relationship, vigilance is required to ensure that states don't discriminate between religion–belief minorities in order to entrench their own political support base. The state and minority leaders should also not presume the membership of persons belonging to particular (religious or other) minorities, but allow for both change of religion or belief and voluntary ascription by individuals as to such belonging.

The second question, that of who fits the category of 'religious minority' poses further challenges, including whether 'religious' minorities include 'belief' minorities. As has been discussed elsewhere,[43] within freedom of religion or belief protections and mechanisms, belief enjoys equal protection as religion. It is not clear within minority rights instruments that the same holds, though the same rationale is relevant. Historically, the reason for the inclusion of belief with religion in the freedom of religion or belief instruments was the Cold War and the insistence of the Soviet Block for inclusion for atheism and non-religion. Over time a further explicit advantage of this broad scope has become evident, that being its relevance for states who tightly demarcate controls and rights for 'recognized' religions versus 'others'. However, noting the framework of minority rights as special and additional rights, it is not intended to broaden its scope to such an extent that its raison d'être is trivialized. If we considered extreme cases and concerns, without wanting to play into the 'securitization' of minorities discourse, we would be vigilant to groups that would want to claim 'religious minority' rights in order to advance political and even terrorist objectives. Hence, there would need to be some interrogation of 'religion' and 'belief' in order to ensure it is more than a façade. Realities make this demarcation difficult to draw and more debate and indicators may be helpful.

The third challenge, that of religious leadership, differs from leadership concerns of racial or linguistic minorities whose leadership structures are usually less rigid than that of religious leadership. They often use political, economic and electoral means to gain a following, in much the same way as others seeking leadership positions in their societies. Freedom of religion or belief human rights standards have soft norms acknowledging the freedom to choose their religious leaders, priests and teachers and to maintain their religious leadership structures;[44]

---

[43] Ghanea, 'Religious or Minority?', 303–25.
[44] Human Rights Committee, General Comment 22, Article 18, para. 4.

however this has not been effectively theorized within the minority rights regime and demands further consideration where religious minorities are concerned.[45]

The fourth challenge deserving at least mention here is the question of how religion or belief laws fit within the human rights landscape. Compared with racial and linguistic minorities we can generally observe that legal structures are one area where religious or belief minorities differentiate themselves from other minorities and therefore the impact of this needs to be unravelled. The question of the position of human rights norms and mechanisms on religious laws relates not only to their voluntary application to individuals who wish to apply them in their daily lives, but also to those within the community who may be compelled to apply them or may be sanctioned for not doing so. It also overlaps with the first point raised above regarding the state–religion or ideology relationship.

Again the full implications of such questions cannot be ignored and the above discussion is merely traced in outline, suggesting they must be raised in a more pronounced way if religious minorities are to be brought in from their de facto sidelining from the minority rights regime.

The chances of reconciliation?

This chapter has provided reasons to show that religious minorities have largely come to be sidelined from the minority rights regime. It has critiqued this fact, and outlined reasons why this proves detrimental to religious minorities. It also acknowledges, however, that religious minorities are not an easy 'fit' within the minority rights regime and at least suggests four reasons for pause and caution. Regardless, open debate towards overcoming obstacles is necessary in order to re-integrate religious minorities within their rightful place in the minority rights regime.

---

[45] See Ghanea, 'Are Religious Minorities Really Minorities?', 77–8.

PART II
Minority Religions and Islam

Chapter 3
Religious Minorities and Conversion as National Security Threats in Turkey and Iran

Ziya Meral

There is nothing unclear about the provisions of Article 18 of the Universal Declaration of Human Rights (UDHR), which states:

> Everyone has the right to freedom of thought, conscience and religion; this right includes freedom to change his religion or belief, and freedom, either alone or in community with others and in public or private, to manifest his religion or belief in teaching, practice, worship and observance.[1]

This article enshrines what we know to be a fundamental human right: freedom to be who we are, to form our own thoughts and values, to decide what we want to believe (or not believe) and to live accordingly. Human rights covenants that built on Article 18 have sought to protect this right and have obliged states that have ratified those covenants not only to ensure that individuals not be persecuted for the exercise of this fundamental right, but also that they are affirmatively enabled to fully enjoy this freedom.[2]

However, the extensive diplomatic debate surrounding each and every word of Article 18 during its drafting, and subtle changes in subsequent covenants show how states perceive and react to freedom of religion and belief.[3]

---

[1] The Universal Declaration of Human Rights, 1948.

[2] For an introductory book on religious freedom in international law see Paul Taylor, *Freedom of Religion: UN and European Human Rights Law and Practice* (Cambridge: Cambridge University Press, 2005).

[3] Due to diplomatic pressure, subsequent human rights covenants abandoned the wording of Article 18 in the UDHR: Article 18 of the International Covenant on Civil and Political Rights (1966): 'Everyone shall have the right to freedom of thought, conscience and religion. This right shall include *freedom to have or to adopt a religion or belief of his choice*, and freedom, either individually or in community with others and in public or private, to manifest his religion or belief in worship, observance, practice and teaching' (emphasis added). Article 18 of the Declaration on the Elimination of All Forms of Intolerance and of Discrimination Based on Religion or Belief (1981): 'Everyone shall have the right to freedom of thought, conscience and religion. This right shall include *freedom to have a religion or whatever belief of his choice*, and freedom, either individually or in

For those who perceive religious belief to be merely a matter of personal faith and private practice, it may come as a surprise to find that states have fought immense battles to ensure that the freedom to believe is protected or, conversely, controlled. Yet, as globalization increases exposure to previously unheard ideas, and modernization and rising levels of literacy enable individuals to take more and more control of their own lifestyles, high-level diplomatic fights over the wording of human rights texts have given rise to real life consequences.

In a worrisome trend, a growing number of countries around the world have passed legislation to criminalize conversion from officially sanctioned religions, punishing those who follow atheistic beliefs or join newly emerging faith communities. In Hindu-majority India, several states ban and punish those leaving the Hindu faith. In Buddhist-majority Sri Lanka, there have been attempts to copy Indian legislation to stop citizens from changing religions. In Muslim-majority Indonesia, Iran, Saudi Arabia, Egypt, Malaysia and Pakistan, those who have criticized or expressed disbelief in majority religions have found themselves facing life-threatening opposition from both society and the state.[4] Around the world, individuals who leave Islam for another religion face immense persecution.[5]

The question this chapter seeks to answer is: Why? Why do countries react so harshly to the exercise of a fundamental human right? While each country has its own domestic context that needs to be incorporated into the answer to this question, a comparison of Iran and Turkey in particular offers us key insights that might help us better understand the general principles behind this increasingly global human rights concern.

Both Iran and Turkey have a troubling track record of actively persecuting individuals on the basis of religious affiliation or belief, structurally blocking religious freedom, and denying religious minorities access to equal social, political and economic opportunities. While Turkey is a secular nation-state that based its state structures and laws on European models, Iran has been a theocracy since the 1979 revolution, enforcing religious adherence with a blend of traditional religious jurisprudence and secular structures. Yet despite their differences, when placed under the magnifying glass they appear almost identical in some important respects.

---

community with others and in public or private, to manifest his religion or belief in worship, observance, practice and teaching' (emphasis added).

[4] See Paul Marshall and Nina Shea, *Silenced: How Apostasy and Blasphemy Codes are Choking Freedom Worldwide* (New York: Oxford University Press, 2011).

[5] For a detailed survey of how conversion from Islam is handled by Muslim-majority states today, see Ziya Meral, *No Place to Call Home* (London: CSW, 2008).

The Islamic Republic of Iran

It is commonly said that one can scrutinize the political vision behind contemporary Iran starting at the very name of the country: the Islamic Republic of Iran. To what extent can Iran really be called Islamic? Or a Republic? Or in fact even truly Iranian? The answers to these questions highlight the idiosyncrasies of the country's ruling regime.

Contrary to popular belief, the 1979 revolution in Iran, which overthrew the regime of the Shah, was not an Islamic uprising, but a mass rebellion against a corrupt rule that involved large swaths of the Iranian public, including nationalists, leftists and communists, and the non-political middle class. It was only in the revolution's final stages that Ayatollah Khomeini returned to Iran from exile, utilizing the uprising's momentum to fill the post-revolutionary power vacuum and seize control of the country.[6]

Khomeini presented himself as the true, moral and independent Iranian who would put a stop to the Western powers' involvement in Iranian affairs, restore justice and equality, and most importantly provide authenticity for alienated Iranians. In the months and years that followed the fall of the Shah regime, however, Khomeini proved in fact to be a brutal ruler who would seemingly stop at nothing to maintain power and enforce his own vision for Iran upon its people. He did not take Iran back to an imagined era when Islam was said to be perfectly applied, but instead developed a unique blend of theological ideas which he appropriated to modern state structures to secure the jealously guarded power of a close-knit clerical elite.

Many clerics and Shiite scholars criticized Khomeini's theology as well as his decision to bring clerics into executive offices of the regime. Historically, many Shiite theologians and clerics had rejected participation in politics and the halls of power as mundane and impure distractions. Only on a few previous occasions had clerics and seminary students joined in protests against the state. Yet, clerics too faced harsh consequences if they publicly clashed with the Khomeini regime.

As Iran faced a prolonged war with neighbouring Iraq and growing isolation from the rest of the world due to its involvement in a wide range of militant networks across the world, the regime strengthened its powerful grip on the country. It continued to portray itself in a 'revolutionary' language, making the protection of the 'Islamic' 'Republic' of 'Iran' against external enemies and their internal collaborators a nationalistic duty for ethnically Farsi Iranians as well as a religious call that demanded personal dedication. Despite some signs of reform under President Khatami, the narratives and structures of the regime have not changed to this day, even after Ayatollah Khamanei replaced Ayatollah Khomeini as Supreme Leader.

---

[6] For a good review of the 1979 revolution and the birth of contemporary Iran, see Nikki R. Keddie, *Modern Iran: Roots and Results of Revolution* (New Haven: Yale University Press, 2006).

Religious freedom in Iran

It is difficult to obtain definite statistics for religious minorities in Iran, but multiple credible sources claim there are 13,000 Chaldean, Latin and Armenian Catholics; 122,000 Armenian, Assyrian and Greek Orthodox Christians; and 8,500 Protestants. There are also at least 30,000 Christians with Muslim backgrounds that meet in underground churches. In addition, there are around 300,000 Bahá'ís, making the Bahá'í community the biggest non-Muslim community in the country. The exact number of Jews residing in the country is difficult to establish, but the number is often said to be in the thousands. Estimates on the number of Zoroastrians in Iran range from 35,000 to 60,000.[7]

While it is beyond the scope of this chapter to discuss in detail the fortunes of all of these groups, we can classify the roots of the problems faced by religious minorities under two categories: legal status and actual treatment by the State.

The Iranian Constitution provides equality to every citizen to a limited degree. Article 19 of the Constitution guarantees that 'all people of Iran enjoy equal rights, whatever their ethnic group or tribe'. Article 13 recognizes Christianity, Judaism and Zoroastrianism as minority religions, and Article 64 guarantees two seats in parliament for Armenians and one each for Assyrian, Jewish and Zoroastrian communities. These recognized communities are allowed to establish charitable associations, cultural centres, and schools for children, and to use their own language in religious practices and in the instruction of their congregations. They can continue to enjoy such privileges as long as they follow strict regulations.[8]

However, these positive provisions are undermined by the constitution itself. First, by providing a list of protected religious minorities, the constitution *ipso facto* leads to persecution of groups that are not on this list, such as the Bahá'í community. Secondly, Article 12 of the Constitution declares Islam to be the state's official religion. Although the declaration of a state religion is not an inherent contradiction to international human rights law, the obscure provisions of Article 168 – which state, among other things, that the judiciary functions 'in accordance with the criteria of Islam' – open the door to clear contradictions with human rights covenants to which Iran is a signatory.

This problem is manifest even more obviously in Article 167, which allows judges to deliver verdicts 'on the basis of authoritative Islamic sources and authentic *fatwa*' (rulings on Islamic law) in the absence of any relevant codified law.

For example, though there are currently no codified laws that criminalize conversion from Islam to another religion, converts are regularly threatened with

---

[7] See US State Department's 2011 International Religious Freedom Report, Iran country section, for alternative estimates.

[8] For example, an Assyrian church in Tehran was shut down recently for allowing Christians with Muslim backgrounds to attend church services. Allowing Muslims to attend churches – to say nothing of helping them to convert – is a clear red line not to be crossed.

apostasy charges and the death penalty under Article 167 as traditional Islamic jurisprudence is unanimous on the punishment for apostasy.

Many other grounds for discrimination against non-Muslims are subtly enabled by Articles 12, 167 and 168 of the constitution due to Shari'a laws, such as the validity or credibility of the testimonies of non-Muslims compared with Muslims in court; the differing remuneration convicted criminals are required to pay as 'blood money' to non-Muslim victims' families compared to Muslim victims' families; and the illegality of Muslim women marrying non-Muslim men.

As precarious as the legal status of religious minorities is, their actual treatment is even worse. True, the government has shown great care in granting certain privileges to some minorities, such as Armenians – largely thanks to geo-political calculations and relations with Armenia. However, two groups in particular remain extremely vulnerable: Christians with Muslim backgrounds and Bahá'ís.

While at the time of the 1979 revolution there were no sizable communities formed by first generation converts from Islam to Christianity, today Iran is home to the largest number of Muslim-background Christians (MBCs) in the Middle East. Estimated to be at least 30,000 strong in the country, despite some unrealistic claims reaching hundreds of thousands, MBCs are increasingly attracting persecution. In 2008, the Iranian parliament voted on the Islamic Penal Code bill, which, inter alia, sought to codify the death penalty for male apostates and life-long or hard-labour imprisonment for female apostates. Following the initial vote, the bill was passed on to the Legal and Judicial Committee of the Parliament.

In June 2009, Ali Shahrokhi of the Committee told the Iranian state news agency (Islamic Republic News Agency, IRNA) that the Committee had decided to remove the death penalty from the bill, as this was not 'in the interest of the regime'.[9] In 2012, it was passed into the law without the provisions. However, persecution of MBCs continued. Between 2011 and 2012 alone, there have been at least 200 instances across the country of MBCs being arrested and detained. In most cases, they are detained for prolonged periods of time before being dragged into court and threatened with the death penalty unless they renounce their Christian faith. They are nevertheless usually released, but only after turning over the deeds to their properties and making hefty additional bail payments, all without ever being officially charged.

Even harsher treatment has been shown to Bahá'ís. Since 1979, around 200 Bahá'ís have been killed and 10,000 dismissed from government and university posts.[10] Their holy places have been destroyed, scores of followers have been arrested, and thousands of Bahá'í students have been denied access to university

---

[9] 'Press Release: Iran – Parliamentary Committee Scraps Death Penalty for Apostasy and Stoning', *Christian Solidarity Worldwide*, 26 June 2009, http://dynamic.csw.org.uk/article.asp?t=press&id=880&search=iran.

[10] For a detailed discussion on persecution of Bahá'ís in Iran, see 'The Bahá'í Question: Cultural Cleansing in Iran', *Bahá'í International Community*, September 2008, http://news.bahai.org/documentlibrary/TheBahaiQuestion.pdf.

education. Since the revolution, Bahá'ís have been portrayed by the regime as a threat to the homeland. They have been accused of being 'Zionists' since the Bahá'í World Centre is located in Israel. The Bahá'í faith is often declared by clerics to be a heretical apostate group, as it teaches of a prophet and a holy book after Prophet Muhammad and the Qur'an. All seven members of the Bahá'í national coordination group have been in prison since 2008, awaiting a verdict on charges of espionage for Israel, insulting religious sanctities and propaganda against the Islamic republic.

Reasons behind Iran's policies

During research visits to Iran, I have asked many people, both within minority communities as well as without, about the reasons behind the disparate treatment of religious minorities by the Iranian government. Most drew attention to the fact that the regime does not allow anyone to differ and denies freedoms for all, not simply minorities. Some pointed out that the powerful clerics' conservative religious views shape official attitudes towards non-Muslims. Some suggested that mistreatment of Muslims in other countries has caused reactionary discrimination in Iran. Finally, a smaller number indicated that some religious minorities secretly work with foreign powers to undermine the regime. Each of these four factors – state control, state ideology, negative reciprocity, and suspicion of allegiance – contributes to the problem to varying degrees.

The fact that Iran is a theocracy might tempt us to attribute the persecution of non-Muslims to Shiite Islam itself. But no matter how alluring it may be, this is an untenable position. First, if the reason were merely the religious beliefs of the Shiite Farsi majority, we would see widespread persecution of non-Muslims at the grassroots level across society, as in other parts of the Middle East and South Asia. But although Iran ranks highly in state restriction of religious freedom, it ranks low in social reactions shown. In other words, the vast majority of Iranians, a significant portion of whom are believing and practicing Muslims, do not participate in or condone the discriminatory acts of their state or demand more restrictions on non-Muslims. Over the last two decades, there are virtually no recorded cases of ordinary people in Iran carrying out attacks on non-Muslims, their properties or their businesses.

Secondly, there is a long tradition of tolerance toward non-Muslims – especially Christians and Jews – in traditional Islamic jurisprudence, which explains why Iran officially recognizes certain minorities. Thirdly, Iran shows tolerance toward Zoroastrians, who according to traditional Islamic views should be seen as pagans and thus banned. But since Zoroastrian beliefs are part of the officially sanctioned narrative of Persian civilization, they are protected in Iran. This theologically inconsistent stance demonstrates that when it is not aligned with its political vision, the Iranian regime is willing to live inconsistently with its self-professed commitment to traditional Islamic jurisprudence. Indeed, the regime has a long track record of changing its official declarations of Islamic convictions when they conflict with its interests. Such 'breakaways' are grounded in the doctrine of *maslahat*, which grants the Supreme Leader the right to override the provisions of Shari'a – even those relating to prayers and pilgrimage – if they contradict the good of society.[11] This utilitarian argument has been used continually in Iran, as we see in the examples of birth control initially being banned as anti-Shari'a then being actively promoted, and in the abandonment of the 2008 apostasy bill due to 'national interests'.

Yet one would also be wrong to completely overlook the role religious beliefs play in cementing negative attitudes. Take the example of the strong teachings of Ayatollah Khomeini on the idea of *najess*, which means impure. According to Khomeini, non-Muslims and apostates are *najess*, and any physical contact with them or products produced by them can therefore defile a Muslim's purity.[12] Khomeini argued that although a handshake with a non-Muslim was not *najess*, contact with the bodily liquids of a non-Muslim was. Thus, washing the clothes of non-Muslims and Muslims together; eating food touched by non-Muslims; or using utensils touched by non-Muslims could potentially be *najess*.

While there is undoubtedly a correlation between beliefs and negative attitudes, the story of Iran since 1979, its actual treatment of minorities, and the gap between state and public attitudes signal a much more fundamental causality. The most crucial factor which translates theological positions and ethnic attitudes into state policy is the reification of a particular reading of Islam and the enforcement of a rigid vision of what it means to be Iranian.

Maintenance of this vision has proven to be easier said than done. Economic and political problems have posed a serious challenge to the regime's legitimacy, which continually seeks to maintain its rule and shift public attention away from its failures through imagined and actual conflicts with internal and external enemies. The current political unrest in the country has served only to escalate the need for scapegoats and to increase the number of arbitrary acts of the heavy-handed rulers of the land, whose only remaining political legitimacy is the myth of being the guardians of the nation against its enemies.

These two very temporal aims – socially engineering a complex society into a homogenized ideal, and creating mythic domestic enemies, who pose no actual threat and can therefore be harassed without fear of repercussions, in order to maintain state power – are the main reasons why Iran has come to perceive and respond to religious freedom as a national threat. In the rigid story of what the 'Islamic' 'Republic' of 'Iran' ought to be and the supposed dangers against which Iranians have to fight, converts from Islam to another religion, Bahá'ís, and any Muslim who breaks away from an officially sanctioned version of Islam will

---

[11] See Ervand Abrahamian, *A History of Modern Iran* (Cambridge: Cambridge University Press, 2008), 165.
[12] See Eliz Sanasarian, *Religious Minorities in Iran* (Cambridge: Cambridge University Press, 2006), 23.

always find themselves portrayed as 'enemies' and 'moral deviants', no matter how faithful to the country they may actually be.

Republic of Turkey

Ever since the Justice and Development Party (Adalet ve Kalkınma Partisi, or AKP) came to power in 2002, the vast majority of nervous foreign commentary on the country has focused on a single question: Is Turkey becoming an Islamist nation and turning its face away from the West? The underlying anxiety is understandable; Turkey has been a major ally of the United States (US) and, as the North Atlantic Treaty Organization (NATO)'s only member with a majority Muslim population, has been a key supporter and protector of both European and American security concerns in its region. An 'Islamist' takeover would have major implications for international terrorism, on-going military campaigns in Afghanistan and Iraq, and precarious power balances in the region.

Somewhere in the cacophony of such radical doomsday scenarios, a more fundamental change in Turkey went unnoticed: the AKP represented a new era and a new trajectory somewhere between the anti-Western Islamist and secular modern nation extremes.[13]

When the Republic of Turkey was founded in 1923, its underlying vision was the creation of a robust nation-state from the ruins of a collapsed multi-ethnic and religious empire.[14] While the Ottoman Empire had ruled a vast stretch of land with pragmatic policies that granted autonomy and privileges to its diverse subjects on the condition that they pay taxes and accept the rule of the Ottoman Turks, the founders of Turkey saw those conditions as among the main reasons why, following the First World War, the Turks had both lost their empire and had their homelands invaded by Western forces in cooperation with domestic ethnic groups. The Empire was seen as regressive – held back by a corrupt monarchy and religious zealots who refused the modernization process that enabled European countries to assume so much power. The response to this problem was a harsh, top-to-bottom social and political reform project to bring the country together under a uniting narrative. A Turkish nation was born, with the vision of one race, one language, and one religion. 'Backward' religious and cultural attitudes were combatted and efforts made to assimilate ethnic differences. The state changed the Turkish alphabet from Ottoman–Arabic script to Latin, banned certain clothing, decommissioned the Islamic seat of authority and pursued industrial reform.

---

[13] For a detailed discussion on changes in Turkey, see Ziya Meral, *Prospects for Turkey* (London: Legatum Institute, 2009).

[14] For a discussion on the link between the legacy of the Ottoman Empire and the making of Turkish Republic and its implications for contemporary politics, see Kerem Oktem, *Angry Nation: Turkey Since 1989* (London: Zed Books, 2011).

Retrospectively, it is clear that the vast majority of these reforms were indeed necessary and have made Turkey what it is today. However, the initial foresight of the founding fathers of the nation eventually turned into a static state monopoly that increasingly struggled to cope with the complexities of the late twentieth century.

By 2000, the Turkish public was widely disillusioned with the ruling political and bureaucratic elite of the country. The economy, which was facing near bankruptcy, was disproportionately dependent on firms and investments in three major cities, which also symbolically represented 'modern' Turkey. The Turkish public was demanding a new politic beyond the 'left' and 'right' wings that dominated the party spectrum. They wanted economic reform, human rights, entry into the European Union and the freedom to cherish ethnic and religious differences.

The AKP's young leadership, coupled with its appeal to religious conservatism and emphasis on integrating Turkey into global markets and the European Union (EU), prompted a sizable ratio of voters to give it the benefit of the doubt in the absence of any other viable alternative. The party's surprising victory in its first ever election in 2002 unleashed a turbulent period of change in the country at a speed that was at once dazzling and worrisome. In the 10 years since then, the Turkish economy has gone from near bankruptcy to becoming one of the fastest growing in the world. From 2004 to 2011 the AKP's pursuit of EU membership became the most aggressive of any Turkish government to date. The AKP has galvanized Turkish foreign policy to almost hyperactive levels and drastically extended Turkey's global reach.

Yet this process has also involved immense power clashes between the AKP and its opponents in the traditional political establishment: the armed forces and the bureaucracy. Various shady networks from within the state sought to curb the AKP's rise to power through various political, judicial and social means. In the process, however, the old guard has lost much of its popular appeal and Turkey has entered a new and uncharted phase in its history with a new ruling political and economic elite.

Religious freedom in Turkey

It could perhaps be said that the shift from the old Turkey to the new shows itself nowhere more clearly than in the area of religious freedom. Though the old Turkish state called itself 'secular', it was not so in the fullest sense of the word. The Turkish doctrine of secularism meant state control of religion, not a separation of church and state affairs, and certainly not equal treatment of all religions.[15]

---

[15] For a study on how Turkish secularism differs from that of others, see Ahmet Kuru, *Secularism and State Policies toward Religion: The United States, France and Turkey* (Cambridge: Cambridge University Press, 2009).

Drawing from nineteenth century European secularism, the founders saw religion as a hindrance to modernization, but recognized that it was too powerful to escape. As the state enforced ethnic assimilation across the country, it sought also to enforce a similar religious assimilation. Through the creation of a Directorate of Religious Affairs, the state monopolized the interpretation of Islam and the activities of mosques, religious schools and religious education. All Islamic clerics became civil servants, sermons were written from a central authority, and independent Islamic networks were suppressed. The state's attempt to carve out its secular version of Islam also meant banning the public promotion of religion generally. In practice, this meant that any devout Muslim who did not conform to the officially endorsed version of Islam was driven from the public sphere; for example, Muslim women wearing the headscarf were banned from working for the civil service, studying at universities and even entering official state buildings. Any political movement with a religious outlook was treated as a national threat, prompting harsh measures, including impeachment of governments and even military intervention.

As for non-Muslims, the state perceived them as clear security threats – potential agents of foreign powers who might be used to weaken and infiltrate the country. This was helped neither by the treatment of Muslim Turks in the Balkans, nor by the memories of population exchanges between Greece and Turkey which led to the uprooting of Greeks and Turks in each country.

While the founding document of the Republic, the 1923 Lausanne Treaty, provided strong protection for non-Muslims, in practice the state read the provisions as only applying to Greeks, Jews and Armenians.[16] Legally, Turkey guarantees religious freedom both through Turkish law and international covenants it has ratified; yet in practice the state enforces a strict policy of exclusion and marginalization of non-Muslims.[17] Under the Ottoman Empire, non-Muslim ambassadors, state officials, and politicians were a common sight, but since the

---

[16] See Articles 37 to 45 of the Treaty of Lausanne, especially Article 38 that ensures that all residents of Turkey have the right to religious freedom.

[17] Both the Turkish constitution and criminal code have strong provisions on religious freedom. Article 10 of the constitution states that all individuals are equal regardless of religion or belief. Article 24 explicitly states that 'everyone has the right to freedom of conscience, religious belief and conviction'. Article 115 of the criminal code penalizes any attempt to prevent exercise of religious freedom and Article 119/I-e doubles the punishment of denial of religious freedom if state officials commit the crime. In addition to these, Article 90 of the constitution grants supremacy to international law over domestic law. This is a key provision as Turkey is not only a signatory to key UN human rights covenants that protect religious freedom, such as the International Covenant on Civil and Political Rights, but also to the European Convention on Human Rights (ECHR). What separates the ECHR from other UN covenants is that it has a court (European Court of Human Rights, ECtHR) that individuals can appeal to after domestic legal options have been exhausted. Turkey has been regularly challenged and found guilty of religious freedom denials at the ECtHR.

creation of the Republic the numbers of non-Muslims working for the state or playing political or diplomatic roles has dwindled to nothing.

A combination of tensions with Greece, the murders of Turkish diplomats abroad by the Armenian terror organization, the Armenia Secret Army for the Liberation of Armenia (ASALA), on-going tensions over whether or not the deaths of hundreds of thousands of Armenians in 1915 should be called a 'genocide', and public sensitivity over the Israel–Palestine conflict have triggered physical attacks, discriminatory media coverage, and incitement against non-Muslims by opportunistic political parties.

The slow but certain numerical decline of historic ethno-religious minorities in the country was inevitable. By the late 1990s, the number of non-Muslims in the country had fallen from millions in the early 1900s to just 100,000.[18] It became almost impossible for any Turk to engage with non-Muslims on a day-to-day basis, and non-Muslims practically retreated into well-guarded social enclaves with a deeply internalized sense of vulnerability. This made non-Muslims, as well as their lives and beliefs, into urban legends, the subjects of widely promoted paranoia about their position as tools of foreign powers.

These urban myths took a dangerous turn in 1999 when the Turkish media increasingly began reporting the phenomenon of Turks converting to Christianity and other religions. Sensational media accounts included wild stories of Bibles being given out with hundreds of dollars tucked into their pages, as well as Muslim youth being offered alcohol, sex and visas to Europe on the condition that they convert. When politicians and authorities began to appropriate these and similar stories, many took the accusations to be factually true.

Shortly thereafter, Christian activities – especially the promotion of the faith – were listed as a national security threat in the official security document of the Turkish National Security Secretariat.[19] The following years saw immense campaigns by state security officials, as well as clerics, the media and civil groups, to 'inform' the public that Christian missionaries had covered their land like a spider web. Police and gendarme forces regularly launched operations against suspected missionaries, though none were ever found to be committing a crime. Nevertheless, these myths were deeply engraved in the public psyche.

---

[18] The US State Department's 2011 International Religious Freedom Report states: 'While exact membership figures are not available, these religious groups include approximately 500,000 Shiite Caferi Muslims; 60,000 Armenian Orthodox Christians; 22,000 Jews; 20,000 Syrian Orthodox (Syriac) Christians; 10,000 Bahá'ís; 5,000 Yezidis; 5,000 Jehovah's Witnesses; 5,000 members of various other Protestant sects; approximately 3,000 Iraqi Chaldean Christians; and up to 2,500 Greek Orthodox Christians. There also are small, undetermined numbers of Bulgarian Orthodox, Nestorian, Georgian Orthodox, Roman Catholic, Syriac Catholic, and Maronite Christians.'

[19] Tarik Isik, 'Sagci da Solcu da Misyonerlik Alarmi Veriyor', *Radikal Gazetesi*, April 20, 2007.

When the AKP assumed power, religious freedom in the country entered a completely new phase. After suffering so long from a state religious monopoly which banned anything but its conservative brand of Islam, and determined to establish its democratic credentials in the face of growing international worry that it would Islamize Turkey, the AKP unleashed slow but substantial reforms on religious freedom.

While the EU and the international community welcomed these reforms, the old guardians of Turkey, who still held firmly to powerful positions in the military and bureaucracy, denounced them as attempts to weaken the secular state. The perceived destruction of the secular legacy left by the founders of the Republic became the main rallying cry for protests and campaigns against the AKP.

Interestingly, while thousands of Turks marched in the streets with Turkish flags, vowing to defend the secular Republic against Islamists, in almost all of the marches they also chanted and carried banners against Christian missionaries who were said to be destroying the country from within. From 2005 to 2008, this hysteria gave rise to fatal attacks on Christians across the country, taking the lives of clergymen and other Christian public figures and damaging church property.

Ironically, secularist Turkish press outlets reported these as yet more evidence of Islamists taking over the country, and the international media served only to amplify the ripples. In reality, the facts suggest otherwise. The profiles of the perpetrators and the mode of the attacks seem to indicate that secular nationalist networks were behind each of them. All of the attacks, as well as immense public demonstrations, stopped virtually overnight in 2008, when the AKP government survived a legal closure threat and emerged much stronger from the new elections, thus finding the power to clamp down on these nationalist networks.

Today, the reforms continue to achieve historic developments, such as the return of property that the Turkish state had seized from non-Muslims in the 1950s. Turkish security services no longer regularly detain or intimidate non-Muslims. However, there is still a long way to go, and deeply held mistrust towards non-Muslims continues to be widespread.

Reasons behind Turkey's policies

In this brief account of the dynamic story of the fall of the Ottoman Empire and the emergence of the Republic of Turkey, we see an interesting pattern. At the start of the twentieth century, we see a crumbling empire that accommodated religious diversity both for Muslims and non-Muslims. We then see painful episodes of killings, forced migrations, and population exchanges as the empire collapsed, followed by the decades-long creation of a new nation.

From the 1960s onwards, we see a well-defined secular nation with European laws and an iron hand that aggressively enforced the ideal vision of one language, one race and one religion. Ironically, this strong tide was only broken by the AKP, a government perceived to be pursuing a secret agenda of Islamizing Turkey.

With this wide historical progression in mind, it becomes clear that restrictions on religious freedom in 99.9 per cent Muslim Turkey since 1923 have been due not to Islam nor to some theological view held by its rulers but, on the contrary, to a strong nineteenth century European vision that promotes a strong state ushering a homogenized nation into a 'bright' future by any means necessary, no matter the human cost.

This strong structural cause behind the denial of religious freedom also prepares the ground for widely held public views of non-Muslims. Whether through amplified stories of how non-Muslims 'betrayed' Turks under the Ottoman Empire, or of how the Central Intelligence Agency (CIA) is now using Christian activities to destroy the 'soul' of the nation, the Turkish public is regularly bombarded with calls for 'vigilance'. Since such outlandish accusations against non-Muslims have gone unchallenged for so long, it might well be impossible to fully undo 90 years of engineered and promoted social paranoia about religious minorities.

Both of these factors – brutal enforcement of a homogenized nation state and officially sanctioned marginalization of non-Muslims – have made Christians, Jews and other smaller faith communities easy targets for sinister political agendas and mob violence. Religious conversion has come to be seen as treason against the Turkish nation, as leaving the country's officially enforced religious beliefs seems to equate with breaking from the entire vision behind the creation of the modern Turkish state. Thus, while an Armenian or a Greek can be shown 'tolerance' if they accept their place, an ethnic Turk converting to another religion cannot be accepted.

Conclusion

A comparison of Iran and Turkey reveals some startling insights as to why states see religious freedom and ethno-religious minorities as a security threat. In both countries, a host of theological and secular beliefs and assumptions serve to develop racial constructs as well as narratives of unity and differentiation of the society from the 'other'. These in turn provide a language and a seemingly cosmic and solid basis for the ruling elite to assert the privileges and entitlements of the preferred members of the public over those of the marginalized other.

While Iranian clerics use poetic and 'eternal' discourses that locate an extremely contextual theo-political vision in a cosmic story involving the beginning of time and its end with the return of the Hidden Imam, Turkish politicos use a similarly enduring narrative of Turkish superiority and history, blurring hundreds of different communities in different eras across Central Asia and Anatolia into a single meta-narrative. The beliefs, languages, and historical and theological assertions of both regimes support an identical political cause in both countries: the creation and enforcement of a rigid vision for their societies with no space allowed for the accommodation of any differences in culture, religion, or belief. Within that socially engineered vision, religious conversion undermines the foundations of the narratives promoted.

Ironically, this political cause is not an organic one that grew from within Iran or Turkey per se, but rather involved importing extremely modern nation-state visions and enforcing them from top to bottom. Both countries were home to flourishing communities and multicultural societies in the early 20th century. Yet, in the process of creating a nation-state, all had to be melted down and controlled. Sadly, this is not limited to Iran and Turkey. The entire 20th century is full of examples of the dangerous outcomes of such modernist macro nation-making projects.

Chapter 4
Springtime for Freedom of Religion or Belief: Will Newly Democratic Arab States Guarantee International Human Rights Norms or Perpetuate Their Violation?

Robert C. Blitt

Introduction

The Arab Spring has generated unprecedented and seismic political and social upheaval across the Arab world. The reasons for the outbreak of widespread and vociferous public protest are myriad, but are generally understood to include long-simmering resentment of government corruption and repression, underwhelming economic development, chronic unemployment and poor respect for human rights, including the treatment of individuals and groups affiliated with political manifestations of Islam.

The purpose of this chapter is to consider one narrow aspect of the Arab Spring, namely, what does this historic moment augur for securing the right to freedom of thought, conscience and religion or belief? Further, how – if at all – have the emerging post-Arab Spring governments differentiated themselves from their predecessors on issues including non-discrimination, equality, freedom of expression and the rights of religious minorities – including Muslims dissenting from state-sanctioned Islam, non-Muslims, NRMs and nonbelievers? In the end, this chapter argues that the revolutions hold the promise of correcting years of discriminatory and unequal treatment. However, such an outcome remains contingent upon overcoming a dangerous historical paradox that often finds formerly persecuted groups morphing into the role of persecutor. The direction emerging regimes tip will be determined by a combination of internal and external factors.

To better grasp the scope of the problem, the next section provides a brief survey of religious freedom conditions in Tunisia, Egypt and Libya in the period leading up to the Arab Spring revolutions.[1] This historical context defines the

---

[1] Due to space constraints, this chapter limits itself to a consideration of developments in Tunisia, Egypt and Libya. These states afford a clearer glimpse into emerging political realities because free and fair elections have already transpired there.

challenges new governments will face reversing years of entrenched and systemic discrimination impacting religious freedom. It will also serve as the springboard for exploring the extent to which the Arab Spring's promise of democracy is on track to implement relevant international human rights safeguards. Following this analysis, the chapter considers the function of the international community in facilitating a break away from the threat of a renewed cycle of religious persecution that historically has been responsible for denying countless thousands their freedom and in many cases their very lives.

Mubarak, Ben Ali, and Gadhafi: an abysmal legacy of religious repression, discrimination and inequality

Recognized as the birthplace of three monotheistic faiths, the Middle East/North Africa (MENA) region more recently has come in the eyes of many to represent a principal geographic hub for one side in the purported 'clash of civilizations', and a venue for religious oppression, sectarian conflicts, and revolution. States in the region are predominantly Muslim, with the vast majority having constitutions that declare Islam as a central source for law and/or establish Islam as the official state religion.[2] To what extent the role of Islam may be responsible for colouring conditions relating to respect for freedom of religion or belief[3] is a question that has occupied researchers across various fields including law, history and sociology.[4]

---

[2] See Tad Stahnke and Robert Blitt, 'The Religion–state Relationship and the Right to Freedom of Religion or Belief: A Comparative Textual Analysis of the Constitutions of Predominantly Muslim Countries', *Georgetown Journal of International Law* 36 (2005): 947–1077. See also Brian J. Grim and Roger Finke, 'Religious Persecution in Cross-National Context: Clashing Civilizations or Regulated Religious Economies?', *American Sociological Review* 72 (2007): 633–58; and International Religious Freedom Data, collected by Brian J. Grim and Roger Finke, Association of Religion Data Archives, 2008, http://www.thearda.com/Archive/Files/Downloads/IRF2008_DL2.asp.

[3] Here I specifically refer to the right to freedom of thought, conscience and religion or belief as defined and explicated under the Universal Declaration of Human Rights and the International Covenant on Civil and Political Rights. The UN Human Rights Committee's General Comment No. 22 is also instructive.

[4] See for example, Khaled Abou el Fadl, ed., *Islam and the Challenge of Democracy* (Princeton: Princeton University Press, 2004); Charles K. Rowley and Nathanael Smith, 'Islam's Democracy Paradox: Muslims Claim to Like Democracy, So Why Do they Have so Little?', *Public Choice* 139 (2009): 273–99; Eugene Cotran and Adel Omar Sherif, eds., *Democracy, the Rule of Law and Islam* (London-The Hague-Boston: Kluwer Law International, 1999); Nisrine Abiad, *Sharia, Muslim States and International Human Rights Treaty Obligations: A Comparative Study* (London: British Institute of International and Comparative Law, 2008); and John L. Esposito and John Obert Voll, *Islam and Democracy* (Oxford University Press, 1996).

One useful study of state practice that helps shed light on this complex issue asks a related question; namely, to what extent do variations in religious regulation – composed of *social* and *government* regulation – help explain levels of religious persecution?[5] The data points generated by this survey reveal that a significant majority of predominantly Muslim MENA states consistently place restrictions on foreign missionaries, the dissemination of religious literature and broadcasts, religious conversions, preaching and proselytizing. With respect to new religions, 70 per cent of predominantly Muslim MENA states had established or existing religions that sought to shut out new religions, and all but two states imposed restrictions on certain religious brands. Furthermore, the majority of these states displayed societal attitudes regarding other religious brands ranging from discrimination to open warfare, and the majority of citizens demonstrated intolerance towards 'non-traditional' faiths or groups perceived as new religions.[6]

Tunisia, Egypt and Libya specifically shared a dictatorial history where now-deposed rulers had identified their primary political opposition as emanating from Islamist circles and dealt with this opposition in similar, often brutal fashions. In Egypt, the Muslim Brotherhood, almost from the time of its establishment in 1928, oscillated in and out of severe government-sanctioned repression.[7] Essentially outlawed from the political arena since the Nasser era, the movement had only recently begun making 'authorized' inroads into Egypt's tightly controlled political space. Former President Hosni Mubarak viewed the Muslim Brotherhood – 'generally considered the most moderate and innocuous of Islamist groups'[8] – as 'inextricably linked with the more violent terrorist organizations in Egypt'.[9] In the 2000 elections, Egypt's Muslim Brotherhood fielded candidates as independents and secured 17 seats in parliament, despite a government-initiated harassment campaign involving detentions and trials of the organization's leaders.[10] By 2005, the Brotherhood was able to boost its political representation significantly, coming to represent 20 per cent of the legislature despite 'widespread government fraud and voter intimidation'.[11]

---

[5] Grim and Finke, 'Religious Persecution', 654. Note that the authors define the term 'persecution' very narrowly, limiting it to instances of killing or forced resettlement. Thus, acts of persecution exclude more 'routine' forms of discrimination and inequality that fall short of death or migration, such as denial of legal status, limits on personal freedom, arbitrary arrest and detention, etc.

[6] Data downloaded from the Association of Religion Data Archives.

[7] Mariz Tadros, *The Muslim Brotherhood in Contemporary Egypt: Democracy Redefined or Confined?* (Routledge 2012), 5–6.

[8] Charles Robert Davidson, 'Reform and Repression in Mubarak's Egypt', *The Fletcher Forum of World Affairs Journal* 24 (2000): 75, 85.

[9] Ibid., 85.

[10] David S. Sorenson, 'Global Pressure Point: The Dynamics of Political Dissent in Egypt', *The Fletcher Forum of World Affairs Journal* 27 (2003): 207, 216.

[11] Robert S. Leiken and Steven Brooke, 'The Moderate Muslim Brotherhood', *The Fletcher Forum of World Affairs Journal* 86 (2007): 113–114. Tadros, *The Muslim Brotherhood*.

In Tunisia, the Islamic movement, led primarily by the organization *en-Nahda* (Ennahda), also found itself on the receiving end of government repression. After seizing power in 1987, President Zine Abidine Ben Ali sought to liberalize and foster economic development in the country. But he soon 'became increasingly repressive', espousing a zero tolerance policy towards Islamic groups.[12] Like President Mubarak, Ben Ali also invoked the spectre of Islamic religious parties serving as 'vehicles for extremism', intolerance, hatred and terrorism.[13] And like Egypt, Tunisia's crackdown on Islamic groups was met with relative silence in the West. While appearing in certain respects to be progressive on women's rights, the Tunisian government restricted the right to manifest religion for the overwhelmingly Muslim population by, among other things, prohibiting the wearing of the hijab as a 'sectarian garment of foreign origin'.[14]

In Colonel Muhammar Gadhafi's revolutionary Libya, Islam was 'closely monitored and regulated ... to ensure that religious life lacked a political dimension'.[15] The government imposed its official interpretation of Islam on the country by overseeing mosque sermons and the publication of religious literature, and the Sufi Sanusi order remained outlawed due to its close association with Libya's pre-revolution monarchy.[16] Initially, Libya's orthodox Muslims backed Gadhafi's overthrow of King Idris. The Colonel rewarded this support by reinstating religious criminal codes, appointing orthodox Muslim leaders to prominent administrative positions, banning the sale and consumption of alcohol, and shuttering churches and cathedrals.[17] Yet by the late 1970s, Gadhafi – ever more confident in his grasp on power – turned on this community, 'abandon[ing] orthodox Islam [as] a source of legitimacy' by, among other things, urging the masses to 'seize the mosques', branding the religious leadership as a superfluous add-on to true Islam,[18] and calling his Green Book the 'gospel of the new era'.[19]

---

[12] David Mednicoff, 'The Importance of Being Quasi-Democratic – The Domestication of International Human Rights in American and Arab Politics', *Victoria University of Wellington Law Review* 38 (2007): 317, 330–31.

[13] US Department of State, 2009 Annual Report on International Religious Freedom: Tunisia.

[14] Ibid.

[15] US Department of State, 2009 Annual Report on International Religious Freedom: Libya.

[16] Ibid.

[17] Lisa Anderson, 'Religion and State in Libya: The Politics of Identity', *Annals of the American Academy of Political and Social Science* 483 (1986): 69–70. Gadhafi's renewed attachment to Islam heralded for many 'the beginning of an Islamic revolution; and until the Iranian revolution, [Gadhafi] held pride of place as the principal ruling spokesman of Islam as a political force' (70).

[18] Ibid., 70.

[19] Ibid., 71.

Ultimately, Libya's Islamists, alongside other regime opponents, came to be 'harshly suppressed'.[20]

In addition to restricting manifestations of political Islam and limiting certain Muslim religious and cultural practices, the triumvirate of Mubarak, Ben Ali and Gadhafi also actively restricted freedom of religion for other minorities, including 'traditional' denominations and NRMs. In Egypt, 'the government harassed [non-Sunni] Muslims who held heterodox views including Quranists, Shi'a and Ahmadiya Muslims',[21] failed to prosecute individuals responsible for acts of violence and incitement of religious hatred toward Coptic Christians and others, and discriminated against Christians and members of the Bahá'í Faith, 'especially in government employment and their ability to build, renovate, and repair places of worship'.[22] The government also maintained tiers of recognition for various religious groups, distinguishing among Muslims, *Ahl al-kitab* or 'people of the book', and others. For example, national identity cards recognized only Islam, Judaism or Christianity as classifications for religious affiliation. Consequently, Bahá'ís' and other unrecognized religious groups were 'compelled either to misrepresent themselves or to live without valid identity documents'.[23] Egypt's Law 263 of 1960 stripped Bahá'ís' of legal recognition and outlawed the religion's institutions and community structures.[24] Other NRMs fared equally poorly. For example, the government instituted a ban against the Jehovah's Witnesses in 1960 and subjected members to harassment and surveillance despite its 30-year presence in Egypt and prior status as an officially registered group.[25]

In Tunisia, the Ben Ali regime prohibited proselytizing to Muslims, including distribution of religious material in Arabic, and barred domestic inter-marriage between Muslim women and non-Muslim men. The government considered the Bahá'í faith 'a heretical sect of Islam' and permitted its adherents to practice their faith only in private.[26] In Libya, although no religious minority was singled out for harassment provided it avoided political activity, the government restricted places of worship to one per city for each Christian denomination, prohibited proselytism of Muslims, and actively prosecuted alleged offenders.[27] Members of

---

[20] 'Libya Drops Ban on Religion-based Parties', *Al Jazeera*, 2 May 2012, http://www.aljazeera.com/news/africa/2012/05/2012522304234970.html.

[21] US Department of State, 2009 Annual Report on International Religious Freedom: Egypt. Quranists are a small group of Muslims branded unorthodox because they consider the Koran to be the sole authority for Islam and reject other sources of Islamic law. US Department of State, 2010 Annual Report on International Religious Freedom: Egypt, 16.

[22] 2009 Annual Report on International Religious Freedom: Egypt.

[23] 2010 Annual Report on International Religious Freedom: Egypt, 9. Without valid identity cards, individuals 'encounter difficulty registering their children in school, opening bank accounts, and establishing businesses'.

[24] Ibid., 8.

[25] Ibid., 9.

[26] 2010 Annual Report on International Religious Freedom: Tunisia, 2.

[27] 2009 Annual Report on International Religious Freedom: Libya.

other non-Muslim religious groups, including Hindus, Bahá'ís', and Buddhists, were relegated to private observance in their homes.[28] Likewise, Libya's non-Arab ethnic groups, including Berbers (Amazigh), Tuareg and Toubou, which practice a version of Islam that differs from the majority Arab population, were the targets of longstanding governmental and societal discrimination.[29]

From this brief historical snapshot, the stark reality of persecution and discrimination across a wide swath of religious viewpoints becomes evident. Now-deposed autocrats consistently repressed political manifestations of Islam – including those views advocating peaceful regime change – and branded such expressions as being at odds with the state-sanctioned interpretation of Islam. Government and society also subjected to varying forms of intolerance and persecution those Muslims who espoused disfavoured or alternate views on Islam, maintained membership in a minority denomination, or dissented from or did not believe in the majority faith. Other longstanding, ostensibly 'traditional' religions such as Christianity likewise faced fundamental hardships, including the denial of societal acceptance as well as unequal and discriminatory treatment at the hands of government. Finally, so-called NRMs were also subject to discriminatory treatment and obstruction in their religious life.

The deficits outlined above cannot be explained away even when controlling 'empirically for levels of democracy, political rights and civil liberties'.[30] This reality has led some to conclude that strict enforcement of religious homogeneity 'is likely to be prejudicial to the development of free debate in … democratic politics'.[31] When coupled with indications that public opinion in Muslim-majority countries 'is more pro-democratic than elsewhere, but … less favourable to freedom, and especially to religious freedom',[32] the nature of the challenge becomes plain: securing the right to freedom of thought, conscience, religion and belief in the post-Arab Spring context is not a simple matter of substituting a tyrant regime for a democratically elected government. Rather, because these challenges may be rooted not in regimes per se, but in entrenched societal opinions about the nature of religion, focus on education and awareness-raising regarding, among other things, the nature of international human rights norms and treaty obligations at the public and governmental levels will prove essential in breaking the cycle of persecution.

---

[28] 2010 Annual Report on International Religious Freedom: Libya, 4.

[29] Louis Dupree, 'The Non-Arab Ethnic Groups of Libya', *Middle East Journal* 12 (1958): 33–44. See also Human Rights Council, Summary prepared by the Office of the High Commissioner for Human Rights in accordance with paragraph 15(c) of the annex to Human Rights Council Resolution 5/1, Libyan Arab Jamahiriya, 15 July 2010.

[30] Charles K. Rowley and Nathanael Smith, 'Islam's Democracy Paradox: Muslims Claim to Like Democracy, So Why Do They Have So Little?', *Public Choice* 139 (2009): 274.

[31] Ibid., 296.

[32] Ibid., 298.

The Arab Spring: curing or perpetuating the religious freedom deficit?

The removal of Presidents Gadhafi, Ben Ali and Mubarak from power prompted one Islamist legislator to declare, 'Now the Islamic tide is rising in the Arab world'.[33] Yet, the political landscapes in Egypt, Tunisia and Libya remain fluid, even volatile. Islamic parties must confront the complexity of compromise necessitated by coalition politics and overcome the lingering suspicion and concern held by minority communities and other elements of society. On the issue of religious freedom specifically, these emerging political parties are also faced with an historic choice: perpetuate the classic 'religious persecution paradox' cycle whereby the persecuted become the persecutor,[34] or break from this destructive pattern and embrace a new era of respect for human rights norms enshrined under international law. While a definitive conclusion at this stage may be premature, examining the 'tea leaves' of recent events, including the statements and actions of relevant political leadership relating to religious freedom, can provide an interim picture of the direction in which regimes may be pointing.

Tunisia

On the whole, ascendant Islamist political parties have thus far worked diligently to communicate a message of tolerance and moderation to the electorate and international community at large. In this regard, Tunisia, the epicentre of the Arab Spring, is no exception. Ennahda (the Renaissance Party), a long-suppressed Islamist opposition movement, emerged with the largest share of seats in Tunisia's new constituent assembly.[35] Hamadi Jebali, the country's new prime minister and Ennahda's secretary general, has insisted that his party will not convert the country into a theocracy and that the state will remain neutral towards religion: 'All Tunisian citizens – Muslims, Jews, or Christians – are citizens with equal rights and duties. ... Our understanding is [that] the state shall remain neutral towards religion. ... [It should] neither encourage nor interdict [manifestations of religion]'.[36] When asked specifically whether Ennahda would recognize all

---

[33] Remarks by Sahbi Atig, Ennahda Party Member, *Islamists in Power: Views from Within – Building New Regimes after the Uprising*, National Constituent Assembly of Tunisia, Carnegie Endowment for International Peace, 5 April 2012, Washington, D.C., 5, http://carnegieendowment.org/2012/04/05/building-new-regimes-after-uprisings/a6sm.
[34] W. Cole Durham and Brett G. Scharffs, *Law and Religion: National, International, and Comparative Perspectives* (New York: Aspen Publishers, 2010), 3–4.
[35] 'Final Tunisian Election Results Announced', *Al Jazeera*, 14 November 2011, http://www.aljazeera.com/news/africa/2011/11/20111114171420907168.html.
[36] 'Hamadi Jebali: 'L'essentiel est de respecter les libertés'', *Le Monde*, 20 October 2011, http://www.lemonde.fr/tunisie/article/2011/10/18/hamadi-jebali-l-essentiel-est-de-respecter-les-libertes_1589959_1466522.html.

religions, Jebali asserted, 'Absolutely. ... Islam obliges its adherents to respect all religions and this respect is a foundation of the faith'.[37]

Ennahda also appears poised to reject demands to enshrine Islamic law or sharia as a source of legislation in the country's new constitution. According to one Ennahda legislator, Tunisia's constituent assembly has settled that 'Islam and Arabism will be the main foundations' of the new constitution,[38] retaining a formula endorsed by the previous constitution. Ennahda's long-time leader Rachid Ghannouchi has reiterated this position, stating that the party will forgo seeking entrenchment of sharia as a binding source of law to which all civil legislation must conform.[39]

More generally, the closing statement to Ennahda's recent Congress pledged to maintain the political party as centrist and moderate.[40] Along these lines, Ennahda officials have expressed the view 'that there is no contradiction between Islam and democracy. ... Minority religious groups enjoy their rights as everybody else. We ... respect the individual freedoms and public freedoms ... and the ... rights of minorities'.[41]

Although statements such as these indicate Tunisia's new government will take measures to break with previous state practices restricting freedom of religion or belief, their authoritativeness is undercut in the face of conflicting declarations. For example, at the close of Ennahda's Congress, the party also pledged to 'criminalize any attempt to undermine sacred values',[42] a statement that bodes poorly for freedom of expression generally, but also may have severe implications for manifestations of religious belief deemed at odds with Islam. Prime Minister Jebali reinforced this position when, in response to a question whether publication of images of God or Islam's prophets would be protected under freedom of expression, he stated – without seeking further clarification or elaboration – that this would be 'more a provocation than a matter of freedom of expression'.[43]

Troublingly, these latter statements are more indicative of the reality unfolding in the country today, where a meaningful reduction in subjective and discriminatory prosecutions of expression premised on protecting religious beliefs remains difficult to discern. For example, consider the Tunisian government's decision to prosecute Nabil Karoui, the director of satellite broadcaster Nessma TV, for airing *Persepolis*,

---

[37] Ibid.
[38] Remarks by Sahbi Atig, 6–7.
[39] Tarek Amara, 'Tunisia's Ennahda to Oppose Sharia in Constitution', *Reuters*, 26 March 2012, http://www.reuters.com/article/2012/03/26/us-tunisia-constitution-idUSBRE82P0E820120326.
[40] Antoine Lambroschini, 'Ennahda Party Vows Moderate Islam in Tunisia', *AFP*, 17 July 2012, http://news.yahoo.com/ennahda-party-vows-moderate-islam-tunisia-200211510.html.
[41] Remarks by Sahbi Atig, 6–7.
[42] Lambroschini, 'Ennahda Party'.
[43] Jebali, 'L'essentiel est de respecter'.

an animated film that includes a brief representation of God as imagined from a child's point of view.[44] After suspected 'Salafist activists', firebombed his house,[45] a court found Karoui guilty and fined him $1,500 for 'disturbing public order and threatening proper morals'.[46] In a related incident, another Tunisian court upheld a seven-year conviction for Jabeur Mejri, a young Tunisian convicted for posting cartoons of the Prophet Mohammad to his Facebook account.[47] The government justified its prosecution on the basis of defending public decency.[48] The gravity of these incidents is only magnified by Ennahda's decision to introduce a bill in the National Assembly seeking to criminalize blasphemy against Abrahamic faiths with prison sentences ranging from two to four years.[49] Disturbingly, this approach is at odds with a UN-supported consensus that opposes criminalizing forms of expression that fall short of incitement to imminent violence[50] and signals a clear rejection of the promised principles of neutrality, freedom and non-coercion as cornerstones for the new Tunisian state.

Egypt

In Egypt, continued interference by the Supreme Command of the Armed Forces (SCAF) and a constitutional court ruling dissolving the elected parliament (where the Brotherhood's Freedom and Justice Party [FJP] maintained 47 per cent of the seats, followed by an alliance of ultraconservative Islamists with about 25 per cent)[51] overshadowed presidential run-off elections between the FJP's Mohammed

---

[44] The Franco-Iranian production directed by graphic novelist Marjane Satrapi contemplates the 1979 Islamic revolution and rule of Ayatollah Khomeini through the eyes of a young girl.

[45] 'Tunisia Must Drop Charges against TV Boss over 'Persepolis' Screening', *Amnesty International*, 20 January 2012, http://www.amnesty.org/fr/node/29264.

[46] Marc Fisher, 'Tunisian who showed 'Persepolis' on TV fined in free speech case', *Washington Post*, 3 May2012, http://www.washingtonpost.com/world/africa/tunisian-who-showed-persepolis-on-tv-fined-in-free-speech-case/2012/05/03/gIQA0GpzyT_story.html. The trial had been postponed several times between November 2011 and April 2012.

[47] Ghazi Beji, Mejri's friend who faced similar charges, fled the country but was similarly convicted and sentenced in absentia. See 'Tunisia Court Upholds Cartoon Blasphemy Conviction', *Associated Press*, 25 June 2012, http://news.findlaw.com/apnews/b6934e497ef647518bf3fb4029a1790a.

[48] Zoubeir Souissi and Lin Noueihed, 'Tunisian Loses Appeal over Cartoons of Prophet', *Reuters*, 25 June 2012, http://af.reuters.com/article/worldNews/idAFBRE85O0QO20120625?sp=true.

[49] 'Tunisia's Ruling Islamists File Blasphemy Bill', *AFP*, 2 August 2012, http://news.yahoo.com/tunisias-ruling-islamists-file-blasphemy-bill-234254228.html.

[50] For more on this issue, see Robert C. Blitt, 'Defamation of Religion: Rumors of Its Death Are Greatly Exaggerated', *Case Western Reserve Law Review* 62 (2011): 347–97.

[51] David D. Kirkpatrick, 'Islamists Win 70% of Seats in the Egyptian Parliament', *New York Times*, 21 January 2012, http://www.nytimes.com/2012/01/22/world/middleeast/

Morsi and Ahmed Shafiq, Mubarak's last prime minister. The country's Election Commission ultimately declared Morsi the winner with a narrow 51 per cent of the vote, but left him to confront an entrenched military poised to dominate the security apparatus, retain control over the state's purse strings, and oversee the expected constitutional drafting process.[52]

President Morsi has promised 'no imposition on women to wear the veil' and has assured Coptic Christians they will be 'national partners and have full rights like Muslims. ... They will be represented as advisers in the presidential institution, and maybe a vice president if possible'.[53] These assurances coincide with statements made by various FJP representatives. For example, Abdul Mawgoud Dardery, an FJP parliamentarian from Luxor, affirmed the party's support for lifting restrictions on building churches and other houses of worship.[54] When asked about an individual's right to criticize or doubt Islam, Dardery responded that religion is a human choice, and that Islam does not allow one to impose that choice upon another individual.[55]

On the role of Islam in the future Egyptian constitution, Dardery stressed a distinction between invoking Islamic principles and invoking Islamic rulings. According to him, FJP was opposed to enshrining the latter as a constitutional requirement because such a move would 'make it very difficult for Egyptian people, [would] make their life really difficult. And we're not interested in this'.[56] The FJP, according to Dardery, views the process of drafting a new constitution as belonging to all Egyptians, and not merely to the majority: 'It's un-Islamic to have just the majority write the constitution'.[57] The FJP's Foreign Relations Coordinator, Khaled Al-Qazzaz, has gone so far as to affirm that 'we actually want [the international community] to support us on [the values of democracy, freedom and rule of law]. We want you to help us. We want you to give ideas and actually believe in these values and believe in the right of nations to achieve these values.'[58]

---

muslim-brotherhood-wins-47-of-egypt-assembly-seats.html.

[52] 'Egypt Delays Runoff Result as Protests Loom', *Al Jazeera*, 21 June 2012, http://www.aljazeera.com/news/middleeast/2012/06/201262023501862710.html.

[53] Ivana Kvesic, 'Egypt's Muslim Brotherhood Candidate Wants Christians to 'Convert, Pay Tribute, or Leave' the Country?', *Christian Post*, 31 May 2012, http://www.christianpost.com/news/egypts-muslim-brotherhood-candidate-wants-christians-to-convert-pay-tribute-or-leave-the-country-75821/.

[54] 'Muslim Brotherhood and Egyptian Politics', *Georgetown University*, 4 April 2012, http://www.c-spanvideo.org/program/MuslimBr.

[55] Ibid.

[56] Dr Abdul Mawgoud Rageh Dardery, 'Islamists In Power: Views From Within – Building New Regimes After the Uprising', (lecture, Carnegie Endowment for International Peace, Member Freedom and Justice Party, People's Assembly of Egypt, Washington, D.C., 5 April 2012), Washington, D.C., 13, http://carnegieendowment.org/2012/04/05/building-new-regimes-after-uprisings/a6sm.

[57] Ibid., 11.

[58] Dardery, 'Islamists in Power'.

While statements like these may have assuaged some Washington policymakers, others maintain that the Brotherhood's 'liberal' discourse remains superficial. This shortcoming stems from the fact that the organization's founding ideology remains intact and continues to espouse a worldview whereby 'the governing authority [of the civil state is] an agent of Islam [and] the Quran remains the supreme constitution'.[59] Moreover, even the Brotherhood's liberal rhetoric is plagued by inconsistency. At a campaign rally before Cairo University students, candidate Morsi proclaimed:

> The Koran is our constitution, the Prophet is our leader, jihad is our path and death in the name of Allah is our goal. ... Today, Egypt is close as never before to the triumph of Islam at all the state levels. ... Today we can establish Sharia law because our nation will acquire well-being only with Islam and Sharia. The Muslim Brothers and the Freedom and Justice Party will be the conductors of these goals.[60]

Lingering suspicion and concern over the Muslim Brotherhood's political agenda remains strong among Egypt's minority and secular communities because of these inconsistencies. For example, despite assurances that minority religious rights would be protected,[61] Morsi early on courted the ultraorthodox Salafist movement[62] while the dominant Islamist parties in parliament moved to install their delegates in nearly two-thirds of the constitutional committee's available seats. This move prompted liberal and Coptic Christian members of the committee to walk out of meetings in protest, claiming the body was 'unbalanced' and stacked with an 'overwhelming number of representatives from Islamist groups'.[63] While the

---

[59] Hassan Hassan, 'Muslim Brotherhood Still Fails to Offer a 'Civil State' Solution', *The National (UAE)*, 18 June 2012, http://www.thenational.ae/thenationalconversation/comment/muslim-brotherhood-still-fails-to-offer-a-civil-state-solution. See also Hamza Hendawi, 'Egypt's Brotherhood Scrambling to Broaden Support', *Associated Press*, 28 May 2012, http://www.google.com/hostednews/ap/article/ALeqM5gzNYA47e-xN5zVteHShPkFOEE1_A?docId=4968227083af4a25854c7b47a13226c2; and William Wan, 'Muslim Brotherhood Officials Aim to Promote Moderate Image in Washington Visit', *Washington Post*, 3 April 2012, http://www.washingtonpost.com/world/national-security/muslim-brotherhood-officials-aim-to-promote-moderate-image-in-washington-visit/2012/04/03/gIQApqs1tS_story.html.

[60] 'Egypt Presidential Candidate Seeks Constitution Based on Sharia Law', *RIA Novosti*, 13 May 2012, http://english.ruvr.ru/2012_05_13/74584752/.

[61] Elena Suponina, 'Mursi Gave us Guarantees that Egypt Would not Become a Theocratic State', interview by Ayman Nur, *The Voice of Russia*, 2 July 2012, http://english.ruvr.ru/2012_07_02/80020988/.

[62] Tom Perry, 'Egypt's Morsy Goes from Prisoner to President', *Chicago Tribute*, 24 June 2012, http://articles.chicagotribune.com/2012-06-24/news/sns-rt-us-egypt-election-morsybre85n0dj-20120624_1_ahmed-shafik-fear-of-judgment-day-brotherhood-leaders.

[63] Wan, 'Muslim Brotherhood Officials Aim'.

ultimate fate of the constitutional committee remains in limbo,[64] Salafist members have forced human rights supporters out of the committee[65] and have threatened to abandon the process altogether if the constitutional provision establishing sharia as a source of legislation is not strengthened.[66] For their part, Coptic groups have called for protests against the proposed constitutional changes.[67] Related to this, in a series of surprise moves in August 2012, Morsi reversed the SCAF's executive and legislative power grab from several months prior. The net effect of this action has laid the groundwork for a strengthened executive office controlled by the Muslim Brotherhood that, among other things, notably retains exclusive power to appoint a new constitution-drafting committee if the existing body 'is prevented from doing its duties'.[68]

On balance, the transitional period has been decidedly unkind to Egypt, and particularly its religious minorities. In a damning 2012 report, the US Commission on International Religious Freedom (USCIRF) renewed its 2011 recommendation

---

[64] Following the committee's suspension by court order in April for failing to adequately represent Egyptian society, parliament struck a reconstituted committee in June. This second committee remains the subject of judicial challenge. See 'Egypt to Have Second Go at Constitution Assembly', *Reuters*, 9 June 2012, http://www.reuters.com/article/2012/06/09/us-egypt-parliament-constitution-idUSBRE85806320120609; and Bradley Hope, 'Salafists Threaten Walkout over Sharia Law Clause in Egypt's Constitution', *The National*, 27 July 2012, http://www.thenational.ae/news/world/africa/salafists-threaten-walkout-over-sharia-law-clause-in-egypts-constitution.

[65] Upon resigning, Manal Al-Taibi asserted that 'liberal members of the assembly are being harassed by Islamists to approve drafting several religious articles in a way that goes against liberties and human rights and the democratic ideals of the January 25 Revolution'. See Gamal Essam El-Din, 'Fierce Debates Plague Final Drafts of Egypt's Constitution', *Ahram Online*, 20 August 2012, http://english.ahram.org.eg/NewsContent/1/64/50821/Egypt/Politics-/Fierce-debates-plague-final-drafts-of-Egypts-const.aspx.

[66] Bradley Hope, 'Salafists Threaten Walkout Over Sharia Law Clause in Egypt's Constitution', *The National (UAE)*, 27 July 2012, http://www.thenational.ae/news/world/africa/salafists-threaten-walkout-over-sharia-law-clause-in-egypts-constitution; and Gamal Essam El-Din, 'Fierce Debates Plague Final Drafts of Egypt's Constitution', *Ahram Online*, 20 August 2012, http://english.ahram.org.eg/NewsContent/1/64/50821/Egypt/Politics-/Fierce-debates-plague-final-drafts-of-Egypts-const.aspx.

[67] Ekram Ibrahim, 'Coptic Group Calls for Protest Against Proposed Constitutional Changes', *Al Ahram*, 25 July 2012, http://english.ahram.org.eg/NewsContent/1/64/48699/Egypt/Politics-/Coptic-group-calls-for-protest-against-proposed-co.aspx.

[68] 'English Text of President Morsi's New Egypt Constitutional Declaration', *Ahram Online*, 12 August 2012, http://english.ahram.org.eg/News/50248.aspx. See also Matt Bradley, 'Egypt's New Leaders Target Judges' Power', *Wall Street Journal*, 17 August 2012, http://online.wsj.com/article/SB10000872396390444233104577595262292055968.html; and David Hearst, 'Mohamed Morsi is Changing the Balance of Power in Egypt', *The Guardian*, 13 August 2012, http://www.guardian.co.uk/commentisfree/2012/aug/13/mohamed-morsi-benefit-of-doubt.

that Egypt be listed as a 'country of particular concern',[69] characterizing conditions as having turned from hope to dismay:

> Human rights conditions, particularly religious freedom abuses, worsened dramatically under military rule. Authorities continued to prosecute and sentence citizens charged with blasphemy and allowed official media to incite violence against religious minority members, while failing to protect them or to convict responsible parties. Law enforcement and the courts fostered a climate of impunity in the face of repeated attacks against Coptic Christians and their churches. Rather than defending these minorities, military and security forces turned their guns on them … .[70]

With respect to enforcing blasphemy laws, there have been several high-profile cases underscoring a tendency towards perpetuating Mubarak's constraints on free expression. In one incident, billionaire Egyptian Coptic Naguib Sawiris tweeted a caricature of Mickey Mouse with a beard and Minnie Mouse in what was interpreted to be conservative Islamic garb.[71] This tweet landed Sawiris in court on two separate charges of defaming Islam.[72] While the court ultimately rejected the indictments on technical grounds, it failed to dismiss the legitimacy of a criminal offense grounded in protecting select religious beliefs from perceived insult.[73] Other defendants have been less fortunate. For example, a juvenile court in Assiut sentenced a 17-year-old Christian student, Gamal Abdou Massoud, to a three-year jail term 'after he insulted Islam and published and distributed pictures that insulted Islam and its Prophet'.[74] An appeals court affirmed the decision in

---

[69] Under the International Religious Freedom Act (IRFA), a 'country of particular concern' (CPC) designation is triggered where a government is identified as having engaged in or tolerated systematic, ongoing, and egregious violations of religious freedom. When the state department designates a country a CPC, IRFA requires the president to take one or more specified actions or to invoke a waiver where circumstances warrant.

[70] USCIRF, Annual Report 2012, 1. Commissioner al-Hibri dissented from the decision to recommend Egypt for CPC status.

[71] Mr Morsi branded the tweet an insult to Islam and led a boycott of Sawiris' cellphone company in response, even after Sawiris retracted the message and apologized. See David D. Kirkpatrick, 'In Egypt Race, Battle Is Joined on Islam's Role', *New York Times*, 23 April 2012, https://www.nytimes.com/2012/04/24/world/middleeast/in-egypt-morsi-escalates-battle-over-islams-role.html?_r=1&pagewanted=all.

[72] 'Egypt Businessman Naguib Sawiris Faces Blasphemy Trial', *BBC News*, 9 January 2012, http://www.bbc.co.uk/news/world-africa-16473759.

[73] 'Egypt Court Dismisses Sawiris Insulting Islam Case', *BBC News*, 28 February 2012, http://www.bbc.co.uk/news/world-middle-east-17192283; and 'Court Dismisses Islam Insult Case Against Tycoon Sawiris', *Egypt Independent*, 3 March 2012, http://www.egyptindependent.com/news/court-dismisses-islam-insult-case-against-tycoon-sawiris.

[74] 'Egypt Sends Christian Student to Jail for Insulting Islam', *Reuters*, 4 April 2012, http://af.reuters.com/article/topNews/idAFJOE83309420120404.

May 2012.[75] Notably, during this period, the FJP-dominated parliament took no steps to amend, suspend, or abolish Mubarak-era legislation restricting freedom of religion and associated rights, including Article 98(f) of Egypt's notorious penal code, which operates as a de facto prohibition on blasphemy by criminalizing 'disparaging or showing contempt for any divinely-revealed religion'.[76]

Other developments that in isolation may seem trivial suddenly loom ominously for the future of religious freedom and women's rights when considered collectively. When asked by a TV interviewer to clarify what Islamist rule might mean for the presence of bikinis on Egypt's beaches, Morsi described the matter as only 'very marginal, very superficial and affecting a very limited number of places'.[77] Yet Morsi has previously 'argued for barring women and non-Muslims from Egypt's presidency on the basis of Islamic law'[78] and also has voiced support for overturning Egypt's ban on female genital mutilation, declaring the matter 'a private issue between mothers and daughters … that families, not the state, should decide'.[79] Related to this, reports also have emerged of self-appointed gangs policing their communities unimpeded for what they deem inappropriate religious behaviour.[80] Finally, other ostensibly authoritative post-revolution human rights statements, such as the one issued by the august Al-Azhar University, continue to express a hamstrung view of religious freedom, limited in application to so-called 'heavenly revealed' religions.[81]

Perhaps most telling of the FJP's intention regarding the future of human rights in Egypt is the party's failure to endorse a set of measures proposed by the human

---

[75] 'Teen's Sentence for Defaming Islam Upheld', *UPI*, 30 May 2012, http://www.upi.com/Top_News/World-News/2012/05/30/Teens-sentence-for-defaming-Islam-upheld/UPI-54911338388775/. Consider also the case of septuagenarian comic actor Adel Imam, who lost his appeal contesting a three-month jail term for 'defaming Islam' in several of his films. See also 'Adel Imam is Sentenced to Jail over Islam Insult', *BBC News*, 2 February 2012, http://www.bbc.co.uk/news/entertainment-arts-16858553.

[76] Egyptian Penal Code, 1937, Article 98(f).

[77] Shaimaa Fayed, 'Don't Destroy Beach Tourism, Egypt's New Leader Told', *Reuters*, 18 July 2012, http://www.reuters.com/article/2012/07/18/uk-egypt-tourism-idUSLNE86G01M20120718.

[78] Kirkpatrick, 'In Egypt Race'.

[79] Abeer Allam, 'Egypt: A Toxic Mix of Tradition and Religion', *Financial Times*, 7 July 2012. In May, the FJP was 'accused of launching a medical campaign for FGM in the southern governorate of Minya. The party denied the report, but human rights groups filed a complaint to the attorney-general and governor of Minya to stop the campaign'.

[80] Nick Meo, 'US Secretary of State Hillary Clinton Meets Egypt's Muslim Brotherhood President Mohammed Morsi in Historic First', *The Telegraph*, 14 July 2012, http://www.telegraph.co.uk/news/worldnews/africaandindianocean/egypt/9400749/US-Secretary-of-State-Hillary-Clinton-meets-Egypts-Muslim-Brotherhood-president-Mohammed-Morsi-in-historic-first.html. These groups reportedly harass unveiled women as well as individuals who purchase alcohol.

[81] USCIRF Annual Report 2012, 62.

rights NGO Amnesty International (AI). In advance of parliamentary elections, AI asked 54 Egyptian political parties to sign a 'human rights manifesto', signalling their support for genuine human rights reform.[82] The FJP was one of only three parties that failed to respond substantively – ignoring meeting requests and providing no feedback on the manifesto – despite 'considerable efforts by Amnesty International to seek its views'.[83] From this vantage point, what Egypt's FJP has refused to say appears more telling than what has been proffered in various Western media outlets as evidence of its moderation.

Libya

Even before the fall of Tripoli, the National Transitional Council's (NTC) support for a democratic Libya appeared mixed from a rights perspective. As part of its 'aspirations for a modern, free and united state', the NTC called for respecting 'international humanitarian law and human rights declarations'.[84] But it failed to expressly endorse religious freedom for Libya's citizens.[85] The NTC's Constitutional Declaration for the Transitional Stage also struck a discouraging precedent. Article 1 of this document provides that 'Islam is the Religion of the State and the principal source of legislation is Islamic Jurisprudence (Sharia)'.[86] Although the maintenance of an established state religion is not per se incompatible with international human rights law, the text fails to elaborate on key questions including whose interpretation of sharia shall govern during the transitional period, to whom sharia shall be applied, or what will occur in the event of potential conflicts between sharia and human rights guarantees. The constitutional declaration itself provides only that the state 'shall guarantee for non-Moslems the freedom of practicing religious rituals',[87] a formulation which

---

[82] '10 Steps For Human Rights: Amnesty International's Human Rights Manifesto for Egypt', *Amnesty International*, October 2011, http://www.amnesty.org/en/library/asset/MDE12/046/2011/en/78828d97-ab01-4a77-bd74-f3098647ded9/mde120462011en.pdf.

[83] 'Egypt: Parties Pledge to End State of Emergency, Many Stop Short of Committing to Women's Rights', *Amnesty International*, 24 January 2012, http://www.amnesty.org/en/news/egypt-parties-pledge-end-state-emergency-many-stop-short-committing-women-s-rights-2012-01-24.

[84] Preamble, 'A Vision of a Democratic Libya', The Libyan Interim National Council, www.ntclibya.org/english/libya/.

[85] Ibid., Article 7(d).

[86] Article 1, The Transitional National Council of Libya, 'Draft Constitutional Charter for the Transitional Stage', *Cline Center for Democracy*, 3 August 2011, http://portal.clinecenter.illinois.edu/REPOSITORYCACHE/114/w1R3bTIKElG95H3MH5nvrSxchm9QLb8T6EK87RZQ9pfnC4py47DaBn9jLA742IFN3d70VnOYueW7t67gWXEs3XiVJJxM8n18U9Wi8vAoO7_24166.pdf.

[87] Article 1, The Transitional Nat'l Council of Libya. The final version of the Constitutional Declaration omits a guarantee of 'respect for [non-Muslim] systems of personal status'. See Article 1, The Transitional Nat'l Council of Libya, http://pomed.

suggests a restrictive understanding of the international right to manifest freedom of religion or belief and, moreover, on its face denies protections for non-believers and Muslims who may dissent from the state's official interpretation of Islam.[88] In light of this approach, the formulation of Article 7, which provides that 'Human rights and ... basic freedoms shall be respected by the State' and 'commit[s the state] to join the international and regional declarations and charters which protect such rights and freedoms',[89] is, while promising, wholly inadequate.

In October 2011, during his first address to the Libyan people in celebration of 'liberation' day, former Gadhafi justice minister and NTC chairman Mustafa Abdul Jalil declared that sharia would serve as the basis of the country's new constitution and that any laws to the contrary would be rescinded: 'We as a Muslim nation have taken Islamic sharia as the source of legislation, therefore any law that contradicts the principles of Islam is legally nullified.'[90] The NTC maintained this position throughout the transitional period, including during the run up to parliamentary elections, recommending that Libya's incoming elected parliament 'make sharia the main source of legislation. ... And this should not be subject to a referendum'.[91] This emphatic position conflicted with the NTC's own Constitutional Declaration, which stipulates that Libya's new constitution 'shall be referred to the people for a plebiscite'.[92]

Not surprisingly, Libya's Muslim Brotherhood has affirmed the NTC's consistent endorsement of establishing sharia as the principal source of legislation. According to the Brotherhood's Mohamed Gaair, Libya is distinct from Egypt and Tunisia insofar as 'there is no large polarization between the Islamists and the liberals ... Shariah is now a demand for all Libyans. It's not restricted to a particular group of the Libyans'.[93] To translate this vision into reality, the

---

org/wordpress/wp-content/uploads/2011/08/Libya-Draft-Constitutional-Charter-for-the-Transitional-Stage.pdf.

[88] Human Rights Committee, General Comment No. 22. See especially paras. 2 and 4.

[89] Article 1, The Transitional Nat'l Council of Libya, 3 August 2011.

[90] 'Libyan Protesters Storm Government Headquarters in Benghazi', *Al Arabiya*, 21 January 2012, http://english.alarabiya.net/articles/2012/01/21/189534.html. See also Tasha Kheiriddin, 'Arab Spring Leads to Sharia Autumn', *National Post*, 26 October 2011, http://fullcomment.nationalpost.com/2011/10/26/tasha-kheiriddin-arab-spring-leads-to-shariah-autumn; and Elizabeth Tenety, 'Sharia law for Libya?', *Washington Post*, 24 October 2011, http://www.washingtonpost.com/blogs/under-god/post/sharia-law-for-libya/2011/10/24/gIQATDrhCM_blog.html.

[91] Imed Lamloum, 'Sharia Should be 'Main' Source of Libya Legislation: NTC', *AFP*, 5 July 2012, http://www.google.com/hostednews/afp/article/ALeqM5jX7Q1meMlZyHeccNoSuRZyq6Y3qw?docId=CNG.b918f47fa06e0e3e9fdee19bf4e2ae76.511. See also 'NTC: Libya Doesn't Need Referendum to Adopt Sharia Law', *Middle East Online*, 5 July 2012, http://www.middle-east-online.com/english/?id=53221.

[92] Article 30, The Transitional Nat'l Council of Libya, 'Draft Constitutional Charter for the Transitional Stage', 3 August 2011.

[93] 'Islamists in Power'.

organization established the Justice and Construction Party (JCP),[94] which, according to many observers, was expected to dominate elections for the General National Congress and thereby gain significant input into the task of drafting a new constitution.[95] But in a surprise upset, the JCP lost to the National Forces Alliance (NFA)[96] – a coalition of over 50 political parties headed by Mahmoud Jibril[97] – prompting widespread speculation that the country was tilting away from Islam in favour of liberalism.[98] Voters casting ballots against the JCP expressed the sentiment that the party offered little to distinguish itself in a crowded field: 'In Libya, we are Muslims. [The JCP] can't take away my identity and claim that it's only theirs.'[99] Indeed, on the topic of Islam's role in Libya's political future, most party platforms were of one mind, including the NFA. Despite being widely touted as a liberal alternative to the JCP,[100] the NFA has echoed many identical positions, including a pledge to establish Islamic law as a main source of legislation under the constitution.[101]

As parliament takes shape, actual implementation of human rights protections remains uncertain. One of the National Congress' first acts was to elect Mohammed

---

[94] Omar Ashour, 'Libya's Muslim Brotherhood Faces the Future', *Foreign Policy*, 9 March 2012, http://mideast.foreignpolicy.com/posts/2012/03/09/libya_s_muslim_brotherhood_faces_the_future. The party is sometimes referred to as the Justice and Development Party (JDP). Associated Press, 'Muslim Brotherhood Forms Political Party in Libya', *USA Today*, 3 March 2012, http://www.usatoday.com/news/world/story/2012-03-03/Muslim-Brotherhood-party-Libya/53348332/1.

[95] 'Libya Bans Religious Political Parties', *BBC News*, 25 April 2012, http://www.bbc.co.uk/news/world-africa-17844280.

[96] Voters in the July election cast ballots for 80 political party representatives and 120 independent candidates. The MB won only 17 of those 80 seats.

[97] Because of his position in the interim government, Mr Jibril himself was barred from running as a candidate.

[98] Associated Press, 'Libya Election Results Put Liberal Alliance First', *USA Today*, 17 July 2012, http://www.usatoday.com/news/world/story/2012-07-17/libya-election-results/56282270/1.

[99] Omar Ashour, 'Libyan Election Another Arab Spring Paradox', *Japan Times*, 23 July 2012, http://www.japantimes.co.jp/text/eo20120723a5.html.

[100] See for example, Margaret Coker, 'Libya's Liberals Seem to Have Edge Over Islamists in Vote', *Wall Street Journal*, 8 July 2012, http://online.wsj.com/article/SB10001424052702303292204577514842797430140.html, See also Esam Mohamed and Maggie Michael, 'Libya Liberal Alliance Cleans up Election, Leaving Islamists Far Behind', *Toronto Star*, 17 July 2012, http://www.thestar.com/news/world/article/1227936--libya-liberal-alliance-cleans-up-election-leaving-islamists-far-behind; and Jomana Karadsheh, 'Liberal Coalition Makes Strides in Historic Libyan Election', *CNN*, 18 July 2012, http://www.cnn.com/2012/07/17/world/africa/libya-election/index.html.

[101] According to one expert, 'What we will see is a lot of Islamist sensibility. But I think it will be much more of a nationalist movement here'. See Nancy A. Youssef, 'Muslim Brotherhood Runs out of Steam in Libya', *Miami Herald*, 11 July 2012, http://www.miamiherald.com/2012/07/11/2890698_p2/muslim-brotherhood-runs-out-of.html.

el-Megarif as president. Megarif, a long-time Gadhafi opponent, had lived in exile as a fugitive since the 1980s and is 'seen as close to Islamist parties'.[102] Moreover, developments on the ground signal that support for genuine religious freedom in Libya remains tenuous at best. In one act of vandalism apparently directed against non-Muslims, armed men smashed the graves of British and Italian soldiers killed during the Second World War.[103] Video of the desecration showed one man 'pulling from the ground a headstone bearing a Star of David' and a different man uprooting another headstone exclaiming, 'This is a grave of a Christian.' The NTC apologized for the episode, stating the 'action is not in keeping with Islam'.[104]

In another alarming incident, David Gerbi, a Libyan-born Jew who had travelled from Italy to join the rebellion against Gadhafi, generated intense hostility following his effort to re-consecrate the abandoned Dar al-Bishi synagogue in Tripoli's walled Old City.[105] Gerbi hastily cut short his stay in fear for his life when, shortly after entering the dilapidated synagogue, protests erupted in Tripoli and Benghazi. Protesters, bearing placards reading 'There is no place for the Jews in Libya', and 'We don't have a place for Zionism', demanded Gerbi be deported. Others reportedly attempted to storm Gerbi's hotel. Rather than applaud efforts to clean accumulated trash out of an historical religious site and restore a part of Libya's heritage, or plead for a new era of religious tolerance, the government issued a police summons against Gerbi, alleging unauthorized entry into an archaeological site.[106] An NTC spokesman denied that Gerbi had been granted permission by the transitional government to enter the synagogue: 'It's an illegal act because he has not [received] permission from anybody. ... I think it's a very sensitive issue at a very critical time. You are inciting something by not going through the proper channels.'[107] Following diplomatic interventions, Gerbi boarded a military plane bound for Rome 'to ease the tension'.[108] In Gerbi's words, the incident was a missed opportunity for the NTC and other Libyan leaders to 'demonstrate their

---

[102] Esam Mohamed, 'Mohammed el-Megarif, Former Gaddafi Foe, Elected Interim President of Libya', *Huffington Post*, 9 August 2012, http://www.huffingtonpost.com/2012/08/09/mohammed-el-megarif-interim-president-libya_n_1762796.html.

[103] Oren Kessler, 'Libyans Desecrate British, Italian, Jewish Graves', *Jerusalem Post*, 4 March 2011, http://www.jpost.com/International/Article.aspx?id=260393.

[104] Kessler, 'Libyans Desecrate British'.

[105] Gil Shefler, 'Talks to Return Jewish Assets in Libya Set for 2013', *Jerusalem Post*, 15 June 2012, http://www.jpost.com/JewishWorld/JewishNews/Article.aspx?id=273947.

[106] Lisa Palmieri-Billig, 'Following Calls for Deportation, Gerbi to Return to Rome', *Jerusalem Post*, 10 October 2011, http://www.jpost.com/MiddleEast/Article.aspx?id=241109.

[107] Lourdes Garcia-Navarro, 'Hostile Crowd Forces Libyan Jew Out of Synagogue', *NPR*, 3 October 2011, http://www.npr.org/2011/10/03/141014576/hostile-crowd-forces-libyan-jew-out-of-synagogue.

[108] Palmieri-Billig, 'Following Calls for Deportation'.

seriousness about democracy and human rights by breaking with Libya's past and welcoming back Jews and other minorities'.[109]

Such expressions of religious discrimination have not been limited to endorsement of anti-Semitism. Libya's Sufi communities across the country have suffered the desecration of graves belonging to their saints and sages and the destruction of mosques and religious schools, with little evidence the government is taking measures to condemn the violence or apprehend the attackers.[110] In a bizarre demonstration of its commitment to religious freedom, Libya's new government permitted Salafist extremists to proceed unimpeded with the demolition of a Sufi mosque in the centre of Tripoli in broad daylight. According to a government official, authorities attempted to stop the armed group from bulldozing the Al Sha'ab mosque, but retreated 'after a small clash' and opted instead 'to seal off the area while the demolition took place to prevent any violence from spreading'.[111]

Women's rights are similarly implicated in the emerging pattern of discrimination. At the historic handover ceremony transferring NTC authority to the new national assembly, audience members directed shouts of 'Cover your head! Cover your head!' at the event's host, Sarah Elmesallati, and one conservative legislator from Misrata walked out in protest because Elmesallati refused to wear a hijab. As his final act as leader of the NTC, Chairman Jalil insisted that Elmesallati exit the stage and be replaced by a male host for the rest of the ceremony.[112]

Conclusion

No one can predict the direction post-Arab Spring regimes will take on the road to delivering on the promise of democracy. What is clear, however, is the need for an outcome that respects human rights, including freedom of religion or belief. According to one human rights Non Governmental Organization (NGO): 'The huge changes taking place across the Middle East and North Africa, while increasing hopes for democratization, represent for both religious and ethnic minorities perhaps the most dangerous episode since the violent break-up of the

---

[109] David Gerbi, 'Next Year in Tripoli', *Foreign Policy*, 22 March 2012, http://www.foreignpolicy.com/articles/2012/03/22/the_last_jews_of_libya.

[110] Tom Heneghan, 'Freed from Gaddafi, Libyan Sufis Face Violent Islamists', *Reuters*, 1 February 2012, http://www.reuters.com/article/2012/02/01/us-libya-sufis-idUSTRE8101LA20120201; Hadi Fornaji, 'Massive Damage to Major Sufi Shrine Follows Fatal Zliten Clashes', *Libya Herald*, 24 August 2012, http://www.libyaherald.com/?p=13135; and Hadi Fornaji, 'Another Sufi Mosque Attacked', *Libya Herald*, 25 August 2012, http://www.libyaherald.com/?p=13209.

[111] Reuters, 'Libyan Islamists Raze Sufi Sites in Bold Attacks', *New York Times*, 25 August 2012, http://www.nytimes.com/2012/08/26/world/africa/islamists-in-libya-brazenly-attack-sufi-sites.html.

[112] George Grant, 'Jalil in Headscarf Controversy as First Row Erupts at National Congress', *Libya Herald*, 9 August 2012, http://www.libyaherald.com/?p=12444.

Soviet Union and the former Yugoslavia'.[113] Available evidence suggests that these emerging governments are aware of international scrutiny and accordingly are willing – at least verbally – to endorse international human rights standards. However, in practice, other indicators point to a potentially divergent and decidedly more troubling outcome.

To be certain, genuine and unqualified validation of international norms on the part of new governments – in the form of constitutional safeguards and appropriate legislative and judicial follow up – would signal a sweeping gesture capable of discarding the underwhelming track record of previous regimes and breaking the cycle of state-sanctioned religious persecution. However, the international community also has a critical role to play while remaining cognizant of the need to balance respect for state sovereignty and international human rights norms. Concerned states must move beyond previous 'soft' engagement and implement a more assertive policy designed to educate and advocate at all levels on behalf of domestic human rights safeguards in post-Arab Spring countries using all feasible and relevant options. Ironically, the extent to which domestic and international actors may be able to gauge success in this undertaking is encapsulated in a simple test derived, coincidentally, from a chapter in Egyptian president Morsi's life. As a student, Morsi moved to the United States to complete his PhD. Some time thereafter, his wife Naglaa Ali Mahmoud travelled from Cairo to join him in Los Angeles where she began volunteering at the University of Southern California's Muslim Student House. Her responsibilities included 'translating sermons for women interested in converting to Islam'.[114] Morsi and other post-Arab Spring leaders must be asked: Will a non-Muslim in the new Egypt, Libya, or Tunisia share the same freedom? If the answer is no, continued unqualified support of these governments will serve only to establish donor states as witting accomplices in the denial of human rights and the perpetuation of religious persecution, discrimination and inequality. In the name of the victims of past repression, casualties of the Arab Spring, and those aspiring to freedom, the international community must assert itself as a proactive force in ensuring successful delivery of the promise of democracy.

---

[113] 'Minorities Face Attack as Revolutions Sour in Middle East and North Africa', Assyrian International News Agency (AINA), 24 May 2012, http://www.aina.org/news/20120524131848.htm. Syria, Libya, Egypt and Yemen are among the most significant risers in Minority Rights Group International's (MRIG) global ranking of minority communities most at threat of mass killing.

[114] Mavy El Sheikh and David D. Kirkpatrick, 'Egypt's Everywoman Finds Her Place Is in the Presidential Palace', *New York Times*, 27 June 2012, http://www.nytimes.com/2012/06/28/world/middleeast/naglaa-ali-mahmoud-an-egyptian-everywoman-in-the-presidential-palace.html.

Chapter 5
Indonesia: Between Religious Harmony and Religious Freedom

Renata Arianingtyas

Introduction

Indonesia's population of 237,641,326 people[1] is well known as one of the most multicultural in the world, with 1,128 ethnic groups[2] (not including Papua province's 2,868 tribes[3]) boasting their own cultures, dialects (and, in many cases, entirely distinct languages) and belief systems. Despite its eclectic religious identity, however, Indonesia only recognizes six religions, as reflected by its 2010 Census: Islam (87.18 per cent of the population); Protestantism (6.96 per cent); Catholicism (2.92 per cent); Hinduism (1.69 per cent); Buddhism (0.72 per cent); and Confucianism (0.05 per cent). Every other religion is lumped into the category 'Other' (0.13 per cent).[4]

The meaning of 'religious minority' in Indonesia

The term 'minority' has many different definitions in many contexts. Francesco Capotorti, United Nations Special Rapporteur on Prevention of Discrimination and Protection of Minorities, proposed a definition in 1991 that tried to encompass all of them:

> A group numerically inferior to the rest of the population of a State, in a non-dominant position, whose members – being nationals of the State – possess

---

[1] Badan Pusat Statistik, *Kewarganegaraan, Suku Bangsa, Agama dan Bahasa Sehari-hari Penduduk Indonesia: Hasil Sensus Penduduk 2010*, http://sp2010.bps.go.id/files/ebook/kewarganegaraan%20penduduk%20indonesia/index.html.

[2] 'Indonesia Miliki 1.128 Suku Bangsa', *Jawa Pos Group Online*, 3 February 2010, http://www.jpnn.com/berita.detail-57455.

[3] Nurlina Umasugi, 'BPS Menemukan 2.868 Suku Terasing di Papua', *Okezone News*, 22 June 2010, http://news.okezone.com/read/2010/06/22/340/345588/bps-temukan-2-868-suku-terasing-di-papua.

[4] Badan Pusat Statistik, *Kewarganegaraan, Suku Bangsa*. Of those interviewed, 0.38 per cent did not answer or were not asked about their religion.

ethnic, religious or linguistic characteristics differing from those of the rest of the population and show, if only implicitly, a sense of solidarity, directed towards preserving their culture, traditions, religion or language.[5]

In order to ensure the fulfilment of minorities' rights, the UN accepts minority status under both objective and subjective criteria:

> Objective criteria focus on the shared characteristics of the group such as ethnicity, national origin, culture, language or religion. These categories derive from the only global standard on minorities, the UN Declaration on the Rights of Persons Belonging to National or Ethnic, Religious and Linguistic Minorities (UNDM) ... and Article 27 of the International Covenant on Civil and Political Rights (ICCPR) concerning the rights of persons belonging to ethnic, religious and linguistic minorities.
>
> [...]
>
> Subjective criteria[, on the other hand,] focus on two key points: the principle of self-identification and the desire to preserve the group identity. According to the principle of self-identification, individuals belonging to minority groups have the right to self-identify as a minority or to not self-identify as a minority (see UNDM Article 3.2). A minority community has the right to assert its status as a minority and thereby to claim minority rights. Individuals can claim their membership in a minority community on the basis of objective criteria, including shared ethnicity, culture, language and religion. The preservation of the minority group identity depends on the expressed will of the minority community.[6]

By these standards, a religious community can be identified as a minority when its members: (1) share a common religion; (2) share a desire to preserve their religion, traditions, or group identity; (3) are numerically inferior;[7] (4) are nationals of the state; and (5) are in a non-dominant position.

Of the above characteristics, the latter is most subject to debate. Like the term 'minority', 'non-dominant' can have various meanings. One could be lack of

---

[5] 'Minority Rights: International Standards and Guidance for Implementation', United Nations Human Rights Office of High Commissioner, 2010, HR/PUB/10/3, http://www.ohchr.org/Documents/Publications/MinorityRights_en.pdf.

[6] 'Marginalized Minorities in Development Programming', UNDP Resource Guide and Toolkit, May 2010, 7, http://www.ohchr.org/Documents/Issues/Minorities/UNDPMarginalisedMinorities.pdf.

[7] This by itself does not equate to minority status as defined here. As the demographics clearly show, any non-Muslim religion is technically in the minority in Indonesia. However, the five other state-recognized religions are what Amy Chua would call 'market dominant minorit[ies]': they wield significant economic power even though numerically they are relatively insignificant. See Amy Chua, *World on Fire: How Exporting Free Market Democracy Breeds Ethnic Hatred and Global Instability* (New York: Random House, 2004).

state recognition. In Indonesia, this meaning would imply that any belief group other than the six officially recognized religions (along with a few others such as Zoroastrianism and Judaism, which are also respected)[8] is a minority. In other situations, 'non-dominant' may simply encompass any group whose beliefs or practices are considered outside of the mainstream. When new religious movements began to emerge (or rather, re-emerge) in Indonesia in the 1960s, the government issued Law No. 1/Pnps/1965, intended to prevent these movements from gaining a solid cultural foothold in the new Indonesian regime. Under this law, a large number of minorities were considered to have broken the law, disturbed national unity, and defamed religion.[9] As recently as 2010, the Constitutional Court upheld the Law, whose Article 1 prohibits any person from

> intentionally conveying, endorsing or attempting to gain public support in the interpretation of a certain religion embraced by the people of Indonesia or undertaking religious-based activities that resemble the religious activities of the religion in question; where such interpretation and activities are in deviation of the basic teachings of the religion.

This means that any denomination that fails to conform to the beliefs or practices of any one of the mainstream religions may be considered a minority. Under this law, a large number of minorities have been considered to have broken the law, disturbed national unity, and defamed religion[10] – especially where these groups deviate from the most important mainstream civil-religious doctrine in Indonesia: Belief in the One and Only God.

Belief in the One and Only God: the first principle of Indonesia

The principle of Belief in the One and Only God was present in some of the Republic of Indonesia's foundational moments, including during the 'Birth of Pancasila' and the drafting of the Constitution in 1945. Indonesia's National Revolution came about at the end of the Second World War as the Dutch Empire, which the Japanese had expelled during its wartime occupation of Indonesia, attempted – unsuccessfully – to reassert colonial dominance as the Japanese Empire's influence began to wane. In his defining speech on Pancasila – now known as 'The Birth of Pancasila' – on 1 June 1945 in the midst of the Revolution, Soekarno, who would become the first president of the Republic of Indonesia and is considered the Father of the Nation, envisioned Indonesia as an independent state in which the people were devoted to Almighty God:

---

[8] Article 4, Explanation of Law No. 1/PnPs/1965 jo. Law No. 5/1969.
[9] Ibid.
[10] Ibid.

> [Pancasila] means that all Indonesians believe in God, in the sense that the Christians believe in God in harmony with the teachings of Jesus Christ; the Muslims in line with the teachings of Mohammed; the Buddhists practice their religion as prescribed in their holy scriptures. But we all together believe in God.[11]

Soekarno taught that a belief in God had been ingrained into Indonesian culture by its history, as an agrarian society deeply connected to the land. He believed that since the beginning of civilization, human beings had praised God as the giver of life. Anciently, religion was devoted to tangible Gods of nature. Over time, God became recognized as an invisible being or force in control of the physical universe. Soekarno believed that Indonesia's people had resisted the post-Industrial concept that man had created God, in part because they had retained their agrarian roots. Thus, a belief in God was part of Indonesia's identity, and Soekarno institutionalized this in the principle of Belief in the One and Only God.[12] He emphasized, 'Indonesian people believe in God.[13] ... In our country, all religions will have space to live, and our country also believes in God[; indeed, it] is based on the One and Only God'.[14] He further stated, 'Religion in Indonesia is a civic religion, which means that religion should inspire and guide the people to manage the public sphere including political and social life'.[15]

In an effort to incorporate Soekarno's narrative into the Indonesian Constitution, its drafters included Belief in the One and Only God, and, in Article 29, a guarantee that each citizen could embrace his or her religious beliefs.[16] This language remains the law today, though critics contend that it fosters intolerance toward non-dominant belief systems, including by contributing to a tradition of preoccupation with religious harmony at the expense of religious freedom.

---

[11] PSP UGM and Yayasan Tifa, *Pancasila Dasar Negara: Kursus Presiden Soekarno tentang Pancasila* (Yogyakarta: PSP UGM and Yayasan Tifa, 2008), 21; see also the translation in Abdurrahman Mas'ud, 'Arah dan Kebijakan,Pembangunan Bidang Kerukunan Hidup Beragama', in *Kerukunan Umat Beragama dalam Sorotan: Refelksi dan Evaluasi 10 (sepuluh) Tahun Kebijakan dan Program Pusat Kerukunan Umat Beragama*, eds. Abdurrahman Mas'ud et al. (Jakarta: Pusat Kerukunan Umat Beragama Sekretariat Jendral Kementrian Agama RI, 2011), 40.

[12] PSP UGM and Yayasan Tifa, *Pancasila Dasar Negara*, 55–80.

[13] Ibid., 78.

[14] Ibid., 22.

[15] Yudi Latif, *Negara Paripurna: Historitas, Rasionalitas dan Aktualitas Pancasila* (Jakarta: Gramedia, 2011), 119.

[16] Ali Machsan Moesa, *Nasionalisme Kiai: Konstruksi Sosial Berbasis Agama* (Yogya: LKIS, 2007), 120.

Religious harmony vs religious freedom

Many government publications on religious plurality in Indonesia emphasize the overarching importance of harmony and peace and see religious plurality as its eternal enemy. Thus, religious harmony has been an explicit paradigm of Indonesian government since 1967, when the Minister of Religious Affairs, Muhammad Dahlan, spoke in the first Inter-religion Conference on 30 November 1967 in response to increasing social tensions due to proselytism and other facets of religious rivalry.[17] Dahlan defined religious harmony as

> a situation in which the relation of religious followers (parishioners) is based on toleration, understanding, respect, equality in practicing religious teachings and cooperation in social and national life under the unitary state of Indonesia, Pancasila and the Constitution.[18]

However, this definition would change over time. During the period in which Minister Alamsyah Ratu Perwiranegara issued Ministerial Decree No. 3/1981, the Ministry of Religious Affairs developed what it called the 'Trilogy of Harmony', a formula for an ideal, conflict-free society *in spite of* pluralism:[19] (1) inter-religious harmony; (2) internal religious harmony; and (3) harmony between religious adherents and the government.[20]

This approach has been implemented in many different policies, such as the recent Bill of Religious Harmony, drafted in 2003 by the Ministry of Religious Affairs and revised in 2011 under a parliamentary initiative. Collectively, these policies illustrate three widespread assumptions about religious harmony:[21] (1) Religion is a source of conflict, and thus religious life is inherently fraught with potential discord; (2) Religious clerics and followers are subject to *pembinaan*,[22]

---

[17] Ahmad Syafii Mufid, 'Taman Bunga dan Buah Kerukunan: Pergumulan Lintas Agama selama Lima Tahun di Jakarta', in *Kerukunan Umat Beragama dalam Sorotan: Refleksi dan Evaluasi 10 (sepuluh) Tahun Kebijakan dan Program Pusat Kerukunan Umat Beragama,* eds. Abdurrahman Mas'ud et al. (Jakarta: Pusat Kerukunan Umat Beragama Sekretariat Jendral Kementrian Agama RI, 2011), 277.

[18] Mas'ud, 'Arah dan Kebijakan Pembangunan', 48.

[19] Laporan Tahunan Kehidupan Beragama di Indonesia 2011 (Yogyakarta: CRCS, 2011), 8, http://crcs.ugm.ac.id/annualreport.

[20] Instruksi Menteri Agama No. 3 Tahun 1981, http://www.kemenag.go.id/file/dokumen/INMENAG381.pdf; Mas'ud, 'Arah dan Kebijakan', 44.

[21] Laporan Tahunan Kehidupan, 22.

[22] *Pembinaan* is a series of effective and efficient efforts to get a better result (Kamus Besar Bahasa Indonesia); directing staff to keep working toward the organizational objective (Roland & Rowland); and attempting to ensure there are no clashes of interests (Urwick). Basically, this word involves power in relation from the stronger to the weaker. *Pembinaan* is a process of cultivating, making, and creating a 'better' condition led by the strongest for a person or group of persons.

or oversight, from the government; and (3) religious harmony is a permanently endangered construct that must be created, monitored, maintained, and controlled by the state.[23] Thus, religious harmony is a state tool meant to protect political and social stability (along with the existing regime)[24], not citizens' rights.

As such, inter-religious dialogue in Indonesia is initiated and engineered by the government. To that end, the Ministry of Public Affairs, under the direction of Muhammad Dahlan, founded the Inter-religion Contact/Communication Agency, later changed to the Inter-religious Council, and now known as the Inter-religious Harmony Forum (*Forum Kerukunan Umat Beragama*, or FKUB). The FKUB is a council of religious leaders that facilitates coordination between faith groups and the government to ensure religious harmony – including by nudging religious groups toward cooperation with the government's agenda, especially *Pancasila* and national unity and development.[25] Although the FKUB is ostensibly a democratic forum meant to empower the people to develop and maintain harmony on their own terms,[26] its ultimate goal is state security. Therefore, government appointees, rather than religious representatives, steer it toward its conclusions.

The religious representatives that comprise the FKUB are, as might be expected, predominately from majority religions, with minority religions usually occupying only one or two of the 21 (at a provincial level) or 17 (at a district level) seats. Because decision-making is based on majority rule, the influence of minorities is limited.[27] This is by design, and is typical of many Indonesian programmes that protect stability instead of promoting, respecting and protecting religious freedom.

Nevertheless, Indonesia has taken some steps to develop religious freedom through legal instruments both national and international. It has ratified and acknowledged as national law the ICCPR under Article 7 of the Human Rights Law of 1999. The Constitution of Indonesia also acknowledges freedom of religion

---

[23] Trisno Sutanto, 'Negara, Kekuasaan, dan 'Agama' – Membedah Politik Perukunan Rezim Orba' in Zainal Abidin Bagir, et.al., *Pluralisme Kewargaan – Arah Baru Politik Keragaman di Indonesia,* Mizan and CRCS, 2011, 116–48.

[24] Ibid.

[25] Atho Mudhzar, 'Memelihara Kerukunan Umat Beragama: Jalan Landai atau Mendaki?', in *Kerukunan Umat Beragama dalam Sorotan: Refelksi dan Evaluasi 10 (sepuluh) Tahun Kebijakan dan Program Pusat Kerukunan Umat Beragama,* eds. Abdurrahman Mas'ud et al. (Jakarta: Pusat Kerukunan Umat Beragama Sekretariat Jendral Kementrian Agama RI, 2011), 27.

[26] Joint Decree of Ministry of Religious Affairs and Ministry of Home Affairs No. 8-9/2006.

[27] See Salim Ruhana, 'FKUB sebagai Forum Kerjasama Antar Umat Beragama', http://isjd.pdii.lipi.go.id/admin/jurnal/830098091_1412-663X.pdf; see also Ihsan Ali Fauzi et al., 'Disputed Churches in Jakarta', *Center for Religious and Cross-cultural Studies*, 11 June 2012, http://crcs.ugm.ac.id/news/786/Serial-Monograph-Disputed-Churches-in-Jakarta.html.

in Articles 28e, 28i, and 29.[28] However, the Constitutional Court's Decision on the Constitutionality of the Blasphemy Law (PNPS No. 1/PnPs/1965 jo UU No. 5/1969) seems to take Indonesia's *Pancasila* principles for granted, including Belief in the One and Only God. The decision emphasizes that

> Indonesian State respect for various conventions and instruments of international law, including human rights, must be based on the philosophy and the Constitution of the Unitary State of the Republic of Indonesia. Hence the uniqueness of Indonesia's constitutional system need not be the same as *rechtsstaat*, the rule of law, individualism or even communalism.[29]

In other words, although Indonesia's Constitution adopts concepts from both *rechtsstaat* (the continental European system) and the Rule of Law (the Anglo-Saxon conception), it need not necessarily incorporate those systems' rationale. While the central concern of the Rule of Law and *rechtstaat* is the respect and protection of human rights, Indonesia's system is more concerned with having harmonious relations between the government and its people. Under this framework, conflict or tension should be resolved by majority rule so that there

---

[28] The Constitution of Indonesia recognizes the bill of rights in Articles 28a to 28j. Freedom of religion is protected under Article 28e: '(1) Every person shall be free to embrace and to practice the religion of his/her choice, to choose one's education, to choose one's employment, to choose one's citizenship, and to choose one's place of residence within the state territory, to leave it and to subsequently return to it. (2) Every person shall have the right to the freedom to hold beliefs (*kepercayaan*), and to express his/her views and thoughts, in accordance with his/her conscience. (3) Every person shall have the right to the freedom to associate, to assemble and to express opinions'; Article 28i: '(1) The rights to life, freedom from torture, freedom of thought and conscience, freedom of religion, freedom from enslavement, recognition as a person before the law, and the right not to be tried under a law with retrospective effect are all human rights that cannot be limited under any circumstances. (2) Every person shall have the right to be free from discriminative treatment based upon any grounds whatsoever and shall have the right to protection from such discriminative treatment. (3) The cultural identities and rights of traditional communities shall be respected in accordance with the development of times and civilizations. (4) The protection, advancement, upholding and fulfilment of human rights are the responsibility of the state, especially the government. (5) For the purpose of upholding and protecting human rights in accordance with the principle of a democratic and law-based state, the implementation of human rights shall be guaranteed, regulated and set forth in laws and regulations'; Article 29: '(1) The State shall be based upon the belief in the One and Only God. (2) The State guarantees all persons to have religion and the freedom of worship, each according to his/her own religion or belief'.

[29] Margiono, Muktiono, Rumadi, Sulistyowati Irianto, *No Middle Road: a Public Examination of the Decision of the Constitutional Court Concerning Review of Law No. 1/Pnps/1965 Regarding the Abuse and/or Defamation of Religion* (Jakarta: Indonesian Legal Resource Center, 2011), 30.

will be a balance of rights and communal obligations, the court being only the very last resort.[30] This structure invariably leads to minority persecution.

Persecution of religious minority groups

In its 2011 report on religious freedom and tolerance, the Wahid Institute indicated that there were 93 violations of religious freedom (an 18 per cent increase from the previous year) and 184 instances of religious intolerance (a 16 per cent increase) in Indonesia.[31] The same year, the Setara Institute Report on Freedom of Religion/ Beliefs observed 244 violations in the previous five years, with the highest number of violations occurring against Ahmadiyyas during 2008. Similar findings were reported by the Ministry of Religious Affairs, the Islamic University of Jakarta, and the Center for Strategy and International Studies.[32]

The government of Indonesia emphasizes that most religious intolerance cases deal with relatively innocuous conflicts, such as proselytism and the construction of places for worship.[33] However, the Wahid Institute Report on Religious Freedom and Tolerance in 2011 found that many cases dealt with more active restrictions

---

[30] Marwan Effendy, *Kejaksaan RI Posisi dan Fungsinya dari Perspektif Hukum* (Jakarta: Gramedia, 2005), 32, http://books.google.co.id/books?id=fnGtQk0JBBQC&p g=PA32&lpg=PA32&dq=rule+of+law,+rechtsstaat,+indonesia&source=bl&ots=pKB6 BdBJAR&sig=nOk7RzkRjMF7vY8xDyY0YSIwcQk&hl=id&sa=X&ei=pBcQUMajF IrKrAfn6oGwCQ&ved=0CFsQ6AEwBQ#v=onepage&q=rule%20of%20law%2C%20 rechtsstaat%2C%20indonesia&f=false.

[31] The Wahid Institute, *Lampu Merah Kebebasan Beragama: Laporan Kebebasan Beragama dan Toleransi di Indonesia* (Jakarta: The Wahid Institute, 2011), http:// wahidinstitute.org/files/_docs/LAPORAN%20KEBEBASAN%20BERAGAMA%20 DAN%20TOLERANSI%20TWI%202011.pdf. This report of the Wahid Institute analyzes the trend of violations and intolerance in several provinces such as Jakarta, West Java, Central Java, West Nusa Tenggara, Yogyakarta, Makasar and Riau.

[32] The CSIS's survey in June 2012 found that 68.2 per cent of people in Indonesia do not want to have other religious worship places near their houses. Similarly, LaKIP's (Institute for Peace and Islamic Studies) survey in 2011 found 40.9 per cent of teachers supported the destruction of problematic places of worship. Worse still, 51.3 per cent of their students expressed willingness to participate in the destruction. For more on this, see 'RI Becomes More Intolerant', *Jakarta Post*, 6 June 2012, http://www.thejakartapost. com/news/2012/06/06/ri-becomes-more-intolerant.html; and 'Radikalisme Remaja Meng khawatirkan', *ICRP Online*, 24 October 2011, http://icrp-online.org/102011/post-693. html.

[33] See Hadi Mustofa, '10 Tahun PKUB: on the Right Track Mewujudkan Kerukunan dan Citra Positif Indonesia', in *Kerukunan Umat Beragama dalam Sorotan*, (Jakarta: Pusat Kerukunan Umat Beragama, Sekretariat Jenderal, Kementrian Agama RI, 2011). See also M. Ridwan Lubis, 'Religious Harmony In The Biggest Moslem Country: The Experience From Indonesia', *Puslitbang Kehidupan Keagamaan*, 29 September 2006, http://puslitbang1.balitbangdiklat.kemenag.go.id/index.php?option=com_content&view

on worship, including heresy and blasphemy charges, hate speech, violent threats toward religious minorities and forced conversions. The victims were almost all religious minorities – both individuals and entire communities.

Although the Constitution officially protects religious freedom, the government's response to these issues rarely enforces the law, as under the harmony paradigm it analyzes the situation through the lens of security rather than rights. The only notable exception is where it sees the principle of Belief in the One and Only God threatened. Exemplary of this problematic situation are the struggles of the *aliran kepercayaan* community.

Aliran kepercayaan

Adherents of belief systems that are not recognized as official religions may be considered blasphemers or heretics. Although Law No. 1/Pnps/1965 states that all beliefs deserve respect, it was actually enacted specifically to prevent *aliran kepercayaan* – a blanket term for various indigenous spiritual systems[34] – from solidifying its place in Indonesia, allegedly because it violated the principle of religious freedom.

In 1953, the Ministry of Religious Affairs reported that *aliran kepercayaan* failed to conform to the Ministry of Religious Affairs' definition of a legitimate religion and thus did not deserve government protection. However, after Indonesia's first election in 1955, the *aliran kepercayaan* community mobilized against government suppression, forming a coalition of members called *Badan Kongres Kebatinan Indonesia*, or BKKI. In the face of strong opposition from Islamic groups, the *aliran kepercayaan* followers were virtually friendless until the increasingly influential Indonesian Communist Party, looking for political support during the 1950s, stepped in to defend them. However, when the Communists' influence subsequently disintegrated, it left the BKKI more vulnerable to its rivals than ever, as its relationship with the Communists had eroded its religious capital in the eyes of many.[35] President Soekarno considered this conflict a potential threat to national security and state unity, and pushed for a quick resolution. Under this imperative, the Ministry of Religious Affairs (and later the Ministry of Justice[36])

=article&id=31:religious-harmony-in-the-biggest-moslem-country-the-experience-from-indonesia&catid=12:ilmiah&Itemid=205.

[34] *Aliran kepercayaan* can cover indigenous religions as well as other forms of Eastern or mystical beliefs.

[35] See the Proceeding of Constitutional Court Session on the Case No. 140/PUU-VII/2009, Session VI, 24 February 2010, pages 76–7, http://www.mahkamahkonstitusi.go.id/index.php?page=web.RisalahSidang&id=1&kat=1&cari=140%2FPUU-VII%2F2009.

[36] Niels Mulder, *Kebatinan dan Hidup Sehari-Hari Orang Jawa: Kelangsungan dan Perubahan Kulturil* (Jakarta: Gramedia, 1983), 5, as cited in Uli Parulian Sihombing, *Menggugat Bakor Pakem: Kajian Hukum Terhadap Pengawasan Agama dan Kepercayaan di Indonesia* (Jakarta: ILRC & Hivos, 2008), 25–6.

was given the authority to monitor new religious movements, especially the *aliran kepercayaan*, to prevent them from stirring up discord. In 1965, President Soekarno further burdened the *aliran kepercayaan* by issuing the decree that would later become Law No. 1/Pnps/1965.

Discrimination became even more systematic after the People's Assembly Instruction TAP MPR No. IV/MPR/1978 on State Guidelines stated categorically that *aliran kepercayaan* was not a religion.[37] The Ministry of Religious Affairs followed this up with Instruction No. 14/1978, which stated that the Ministry of Religious Affairs should continue to monitor the *aliran kepercayaan* community to provide information to the Minister on how to deal with them. Declaring *aliran kepercayaan* a non-religion affected the citizenship status of its adherents, as well as their ability to obtain proper documentation for marriages, burials, and other civilly-recognized ceremonies. *Aliran kepercayaan* adherents were prohibited from 'register[ing for recognition as a citizen with] the Civil Registration Office unless they agree[d] to voluntarily adhere to one of the religions recognized in Law No. 1/Pnps/1965'.

After Indonesia's reformation of 1998, the state finally took some steps to guarantee adherents of *aliran kepercayaan* their religious rights. President Abdurrahman Wahid issued Presidential Decree No. 6/2000 to repeal Presidential Instruction No. 14/1967 on the Prohibition of Practicing Chinese Rituals and Beliefs, followed that same year by the Circular of Home Affairs Ministry to All Governors and Heads of Districts in Indonesia No. 477/805/SJ, which marked a departure from recognizing only the six dominant religions. However, officials have been slow to implement these changes, and many still fail to recognize the burdens their regulations place on the *aliran kepercayaan* community.

For example, Citizenship Administrative Procedural Law No. 23/2006, though well-intentioned, still marginalizes *aliran kepercayaan* by referring to it as an unrecognized religion. Article 81 of Government Regulation No. 37/2007 declares that for adherents of *aliran kepercayaan* to register a marriage, it must be endorsed by a religious official that has registered with the Ministry of Education and Culture.[38] This is often very difficult, as most indigenous communities in Indonesia depend upon religious structures that have existed for centuries without formal organization. This social incongruity must be overcome before *aliran kepercayaan* practitioners can enjoy full access to their rights. But these inconveniences pale in comparison to many other forms of state discrimination against minorities.

---

[37] TAP MPR No. IV/MPR/1978 Tentang Garis-Garis Besar Haluan Negara, 36, 12 July 2012, http://www.tatanusa.co.id/tapmpr/78TAPMPR-IV.pdf.

[38] Since *aliran kepercayaan* was not recognized as a religion but was considered an expression of culture, the Ministry of Religious Affairs removed them from their responsibility and it was moved to the Ministry of Education and Culture, and then moved again to the Ministry of Tourism and Culture. Recently, the responsibility again moved to the Ministry of Education and Culture.

Discrimination against religious minorities

Blasphemy law

In the last 11 years, 120 people have been taken to court under blasphemy laws.[39] Article 1 of Law No. 1/PnPs/1965 states:

> Every individual is prohibited in public from intentionally conveying, endorsing, or attempting to gain public support for the interpretation of any religion embraced by the people of Indonesia – or undertaking religious-based activities that resemble the religious activities of the religion in question – where such interpretation and activities deviate from the basic teachings of the religion.

Article 4 further states:

> Any person who intentionally and publicly expresses a feeling or commits an act: a) which is principally hostile in nature, or an abuse or defamation of a religion adhered to in Indonesia; [or] b) with the intent that people will not adhere to any religion whatsoever which centres on the Belief in the One and Only God [shall be penalized with imprisonment for a maximum of five years].

Most blasphemy cases follow a predictable pattern of provocation against a minority, conflict between the minority and its persecutors, and finally intervention by the state, which almost always results in prosecution against the minority.[40]

Pre-conflict: provocation

The pre-conflict stage of blasphemy cases usually starts with suspicion toward the minority, whether from religious figures, government officials or radicals. Usually the antagonists band together against the minority at this stage, as they seek to validate and legitimize their fears. This is frequently accomplished when Muslim clerics are brought on board to issue a *fatwa*, or religious decree, confirming that the minority's beliefs or practices are indeed heretical. Blasphemy charges usually ensue. In some cases, local governments make the discrimination official by issuing regulations meant to inhibit the minority's ability to function.

---

[39] Melissa Crouch, 'Law and Religion in Indonesia: The Constitutional Court and the Blasphemy Law', *Asian Journal of Comparative Law* 17 (2012): 1.

[40] Lembaga Bantuan Hukum, Komisi Untuk Organ, and Hilang dan Tindak Kekerasan, *Laporan Investigasi Kekerasan Terhadap Jama'ah Ahmadiyah di Manislor, Kuningan, Jawa Barat & Lombok, NTB, Kekerasaan Terhadap Jama'ah al Qiyadah al Islamiyah Siroj Jaziroh, Padang, Sumatera Barat, Kekerasaon Terhadap Jemaat Jemaat Gereja di Bandung, Jawa Barat* (Jakarta: LBH, 2008), 79–81; 'Yearly Report on Religious Freedom and Tolerance', The Wahid Institute, 2009–2011.

Conflict

Often, this leads to hate speech meant to marginalize or even incite violence toward the minority. Law enforcement agencies often fail to protect the minority from such violence, and thus the group is fully stigmatized as heretical outsiders who must fend for themselves. Over time, this tension builds up to a violent eruption. After its followers are galvanized into action, the minority group eventually attempts to enforce its rights, increasingly triggering public clashes with its oppressors. At this point, the government is usually compelled to become involved, as the majority presses for action against the minority, which is accused of disrupting the all-important public order.

Post-conflict: state prosecution of the minority

The minority is usually regarded as the aggressor after any confrontation, and the state responds with varying degrees of harshness. Some cases involving, for instance, the Ahmadiyya have resulted merely in mandates to build dialog between the parties involved, whereas others have resulted in the eviction and displacement of entire communities. In many instances, the group's status as heretics has prevented them from access to the most basic civil rights. In 2011 alone, the Wahid Institute recorded 34 religious freedom violations against Ahmadiyya, including children being banned from schools; forced residential segregation; failure to investigate or prosecute incidents of sexual violence against Ahmadiyya women; and other human rights failures that have left the community deeply traumatized.[41]

This unfair treatment finds support in various laws and regulations, most notably Law No. 1/Pnps/1965 and Law No. 16/2004,[42] which establish that:

---

[41] Laporan Pemantauan Ham Komnas, *Perempuan: Perempuan dan Anak Ahmadiyah: Korban Diskriminasi Berlapis*, 22 May 2008, http://www.komnasperempuan.or.id/wp-content/uploads/2010/08/Perempuan%C2%A0dan%C2%A0Anak%C2%A0AhmadiyahKorban%C2%A0Diskriminasi%C2%A0Berlapis-Copy.pdf.

[42] Musdah Mulia listed 13 implementing regulations of Law No. 1/Pnps/1965 (Chandra Setiawan, 2006). Those regulations are, among others, Home Affairs Ministerial Decree No 221a tahun 1975 with annex No. 477/74054 on Procedure to fill the Religion Column in the ID Card; Attorney General Decision No. KEP-108/J.A./5/1984 on the formation of Belief Monitoring Coordination Team (Bakorpakem) that functions to monitor the existence of belief groups; Religious Affairs Minister Instruction No. 8 year 1979 on Education, Assistance and Monitoring of the Islamic Organizations and Islamic Sects that may be against the Islamic teachings; Religious Affairs Minister Instruction No. 4/1978 and No. 14/1978 on Policy on *Aliran kepercayaan*; Religious Affairs Minister Letter to Ministry of Home Affairs No. B.VI/5996/1980 on marriage, ID Card and Deceased of Followers of *Aliran kepercayaan*; Letter of Ministry of Religious Affairs to all Governors No. B.VI/11215/1978 on titling 'Religion' on Marriage, Oath and Burial that is different from *Aliran kepercayaan*; etc.

a. Religion is inseparable from the State of Indonesia. 'As the first foundation, the Belief in the One and Only God not only places a moral basis on the State and Government, but also assures that there is a National unity with the axis of religiosity. The statement of the first principle of *Pancasila* (Belief in the One and Only God) cannot be separated from religion as it is one of the primary pillars of human living, and to the nation of Indonesia, it is the pivot of the life of the State and an absolute component in nation-building efforts'.[43]
b. In order to maintain public order and safety, the State may intervene to prevent any religious minority group from modifying the religious teachings of a religion recognized in Indonesia.
c. The government may monitor and investigate the activities of religious minority groups that are considered dangerous to social order.

Persecutors of minorities have depended upon Law No. 1/Pnps/1965, along with Article 156a of the Criminal Code, as justification for violating the religious liberty of many thousands of victims.[44] As of June 2012, there have been 50 Article 156a cases brought to court.[45] The punishments have varied, but at least 13 people have been sentenced to the maximum penalty of five years in prison.[46] Often, though not always, the impetus behind these cases has been the Coordinating Board for Monitoring Mystical Beliefs in Society (*Badan Koordinasi Pengawas Aliran kepercayaan Masyarakat*) or Bakor Pakem.

Bakor Pakem

Bakor Pakem is a branch of the Attorney General's Office that 'normally sits under the intelligence division of the public prosecution office, and works closely with the Ministry of Religious Affairs, the police, the military, local governments, and religious establishments'.[47] It is meant to monitor 'religious beliefs that could endanger society and the state',[48] and exists on both national and state levels to prevent religious minorities from evading negative attention for long.

---

[43] Elucidation on Law No. 1/Pnps/1965.

[44] Article 4 of Law No. 1/Pnps/1965 states, 'In the Penal Code a new article is produced, composed as follows: "Article 156a: Penalized with imprisonment of a maximum of five years any person who intentionally in public expresses a feeling or commits an act: a) which is principally hostile in nature, an abuse or defamation of a religion adhered to in Indonesia; b) with the intent so people will not adhere to any religion whatsoever, which centred on the Belief of the One and Only God."'

[45] The number of cases is tabulated by the author from the data tabulated by Melissa Crouch and the current data from the Wahid Institute, June 2012 (unpublished).

[46] Crouch, 'Law and Religion in Indonesia', 14.

[47] 'Indonesia: Shia Cleric Convicted of Blasphemy', *Human Rights Watch*, 12 July 2012, http://www.hrw.org/news/2012/07/12/indonesia-shia-cleric-convicted-blasphemy.

[48] Law No. 16 of 2004 on the Public Prosecution Service.

For example, on 16 April 2008, the national Bakor Pakem decided after investigating the Ahmadiyya community that its interpretation of Islam disturbed the public order, and recommended that the state put a stop to their religious practices. Consequently, the Ministry of Religious Affairs, the Ministry of Home Affairs and the Attorney General issued Joint-Ministerial Decree No. 3/2008; No. 199/2008; Kep–033/A/JA/6/2008 warning all followers and leaders of Ahmadiyya in Indonesia to passively refrain from practicing their religion in order to preserve harmony.[49]

The local branch of Bakor Pakem in West Sumatra proved itself no less zealous in its persecution of another Islamic minority, Al Qiyadah Al Islamiyah. In 2007, after a series of *fatwas* by the Islamic Ulama Council of West Sumatra on the heretical nature of Al Qiyadah Al Islamiyah, the Bakor Pakem issued its Decision No. 5 recommending action by the state. The West Sumatran governor, Attorney General's Office, police department and provincial office of the Ministry of Religious Affairs all responded by together issuing a joint decree on 10 October 2007 forbidding the teaching and other religious activity of Al Qiyadah Al Islamiyah in West Sumatra. Shortly thereafter, Dedi Priadi and Gery Lutfi Yudistira, two followers of Al Qiyadah Al Islamiyah, were arrested for violating Article 156a Criminal Code. Each was subsequently sentenced to three years in prison.[50] While not all Bakor Pakem branches are so uncompromisingly efficient, there is no shortage of other groups ready to make life harder for religious minorities in Indonesia.

Bakor Pakem was not even involved, for instance, in the case of Tajul Muluk, the head of Ikatan Jamaah Ahlul Bait Indonesia (IJABI), a Shiite sect in Sampang, East Java. On 1 January 2012, the Islamic Ulema Council of Sampang issued *fatwa* No. A–035/MUI/Spg/I/2012, declaring Tajul Muluk's teachings heretical deviations from mainstream Islam. The next day, Roisul Hukama, another religious leader in Sampang (who also happened to be Tajul Muluk's disaffected brother), reported Muluk to police for blasphemy. The Sampang Police Department referred the case to the Provincial Police Department of East Java, which prepared the case for prosecution by the East Java Attorney General's Office. On 13 July 2012, Tajul Muluk was found guilty of defaming Islam, and sentenced to two years in prison under Article 156a of the Criminal Code.[51]

These cases, while grievous and ubiquitous across Indonesia, represent just a fraction of religious minorities' problems there. Even those able to avoid similar difficulties are still likely to encounter the most common obstacle to their existence in Indonesia: building and maintaining a place of worship where they can practice their religion in peace.

---

[49] Uli Parulian Sihombing, *Menggugat Bakor Pakem*, (ILRC, 2009): 36–7.
[50] Ibid., 52–5.
[51] AKBB-Alliance for Freedom of Religion and Belief, 'Chronology of the Shi'ite Case in Sampang', (unpublished manuscript, 13 July 2012), brief court proceeding of Tajul Muluk.

Problems surrounding minority houses of worship

According to several religious freedom reports, the most prevalent forms of state abuse toward religious minorities implicate their houses of worship. According to Joint Decrees No. 8 and 9 of 2006, securing a construction permit consists of two phases: first, religious groups must obtain 90 signatures from group members and 60 signatures from neighbours of the proposed site; second, they must obtain written recommendations from local officials in both the Ministry of Religious Affairs and the FKUB. The first phase is usually relatively straightforward, as churches rarely fail to find sufficient support from neighbours. It is quite common, however, for minorities to encounter opposition from local officials.

Various factors might prompt officials to withhold approval for construction.[52] First and foremost, the stigma of being the 'Other' naturally breeds intolerance. Furthermore, as officials – most of whom belong to majority religions – see the expansion of other religions, the fear of lessening their religion's dominant position becomes a powerful deterrent.[53] For example, in majority Christian provinces, the presence of mosques is often considered a threat to Christianity,[54] and vice-versa in majority Muslim provinces. Socio-economic self-interest is also a factor: where the presence of a minority house of worship does not bring any obvious benefits to its majority neighbours, there may be little motivation to tolerate the hassle of its construction. In rare cases, the officials' constituents may demand action against proposed construction. However, much more often it is a vocal minority of religious radicals that pressures officials to block construction.[55] This was the case for GKI Yasmin, a Christian church that recently obtained a permit only to see it revoked by district officials under pressure from local Muslim radicals. Officials are allowed to revoke a permit on various grounds, including the claim that local residents oppose construction or that construction will cause a public disturbance. Although GKI Yasmin already had the permit in hand and the law was on their side, the district worked its way around it, and the church remains unbuilt.[56]

Many similar cases exist, but thankfully not all minorities face such problems. Those that avoid opposition often maintain good relationships with local governments and citizens, who can be their strongest advocates, especially against the opposition of non-local radical groups that mobilize to prevent construction. This is usually only possible, however, when a strong local government, including law enforcement agencies, can flex its muscles to prevent violence and fend off opposition. Where the local government is weak or indecisive in enforcing minority rights, even its best intentions usually fail to ensure the right of minorities

---

[52] There are several research reports and monitoring reports on the places of worship. This paragraph is meant to summarize the diverse causal factors those reports analyze.
[53] Fauzi et al., 'Disputed Churches in Jakarta'.
[54] Laporan Tahunan Kehidupan, 40–53.
[55] *Laporan Investigasi*, 78, 89, 92.
[56] Fauzi et al., 'Disputed Churches in Jakarta'.

to gather unharassed. Of course, all too often, local governments lack even the desire to protect minorities. Instead, they dedicate their resources to preserving harmony, ostensibly intervening in conflicts to serve justice, only to backhandedly force the minority to accept the quickest and least controversial resolution, which usually leaves them without a place to worship. This was the experience of Johanes Baptista Church, Sang Timur and Yohanes Maria Vianney Church.

According to data gathered by the Christian group Daikonia, there were still 56 religious construction disputes from 2007 to 2010,[57] and the CRCS reported 36 such incidents in 2011 – 26 involving churches and 10 involving mosques.[58] And there is, of course, no guarantee that successfully building a house of worship signals an end to opposition. During the Soeharto Regime, there were 450 churches destroyed or closed down under the authority of the Joint Decree of the Ministries of Home Affairs and Religious Affairs No. 1/1969. Since the Soeharto regime, there have been more than 580 churches destroyed, including more than 100 during the first term of President Yudhoyono.[59]

Conclusion

Both Indonesia's government and its dominant religious communities consider new religious movements potential threats to public order. They are often stigmatized as the 'Other' and regarded with suspicion. Religious and cultural differences lead to tension in the absence of preventive action by the government. However, the state does not view building dialog among religious communities as its role; it leaves it up to the communities themselves to initiate such efforts. However, because the state has almost always enforced the dominant groups' agendas when inter-group disputes have arisen, there is little motivation for dominant religions to compromise with minorities. If any progress is to be made, the state must take it upon itself to create a level playing field for all religious groups, regardless of size or influence. That will only happen when the state overcomes its preoccupation with preserving religious harmony at the expense of religious freedom. Fortunately, regulations are already in place that signal a willingness to change; Indonesia need now only get serious about enforcing them.

---

[57] Data Bidang Diakonia, PGI 2007–2010, http://khotbah-populer.reformata.com/search/label/Data%20Perusakan%20Gereja?max-results=100.

[58] Laporan Tahunan Kehidupan, 40–53.

[59] Melissa Crouch, 'Implementing the Regulation on Places of Worship in Indonesia: New Problems, Local Politics and Court Action', *Asian Studies Review* 34 (2010): 405–6.

Chapter 6
A Legal Analysis of Ahmadi Persecution in Pakistan

Asma T. Uddin

Introduction

In February 2012, Abdul Qudoos, schoolteacher and president of a chapter of the Ahmadiyya Muslim Community in Rabwah, was illegally detained for 46 days,[1] during which police brutally tortured him into confessing to a murder he did not commit. He was also forced to implicate the Ahmadiyya leadership in other made-up offenses.[2] There was no evidence connecting him or them to the crimes, and no charges were ever brought against him,[3] yet he was hung upside down and beaten and also pinned to the floor as police crushed him with a weighted wooden roller.[4] He died as a result of internal injuries shortly after police released him.[5]

Such suffering is unfortunately nothing new for Qudoos' community. In May 2010, gunmen entered two Ahmadi mosques during Friday prayer in Lahore, Pakistan, and attacked the assembled worshipers.[6] The gunmen threw grenades, shot AK-47s, and detonated suicide vests, claiming 94 lives and injuring more than 100 people.[7]

The Ahmadiyya is a minority religious group founded in 1889 by Mirza Ghulam Ahmad. Ahmadis consider themselves Muslims, although orthodox

---

[1] 'Pakistan: In a Hate Campaign against the Ahmadis the Police Tortured to Death an Innocent School Teacher', *Asian Human Rights Commission*, 3 April 2012, http://www.humanrights.asia/news/urgent-appeals/AHRC-UAC-057-2012.

[2] 'UK: Shaheed Master Abdul Qudoos Death by Torture Matter Raised during Parliamentary Q&A', *Ahmadiyya Times*, 30 April 2011, http://ahmadiyyatimes.blogspot.com/2012/04/uk-shaheed-master-abdul-qudoos-death-by.html.

[3] Usman Ahmad, 'A Murder Most Foul: How Master Abdul Qudoos Was Tortured and Killed', *Pak Tea House*, 2 April 2012, http://pakteahouse.net/2012/04/02/a-murder-most-most-foul-how-master-abdul-qudoos-was-tortured-and-killed/.

[4] 'UK: Shaheed Master Abdul Qudoos'.

[5] Ibid.

[6] Banyan, 'State Persecution and Pakistan's Ahmadi Sect: We Decide Whether You're Muslim or Not', *The Economist*, 10 June 2010, http://www.economist.com/blogs/banyan/2010/06/state_persecution_and_pakistans_ahmadi_sect.

[7] 'Pakistan: Massacre of Minority Ahmadis', *Human Rights Watch*, 1 June 2010, http://www.hrw.org/news/2010/06/01/pakistan-massacre-minority-ahmadis.

Muslims disagree with this portrayal because of the group's variant belief about the finality of the Prophet Muhammad.

There are approximately two million Ahmadis in Pakistan.[8] While anti-Ahmadiyya sentiment was relatively absent at Pakistan's founding, it has intensified in the years since and was codified into law in the 1980s by General Zia-ul-Haq, who gave new life to blasphemy laws previously on the books but rarely enforced.[9] Since then, more than 1,000 people have been arrested for blasphemy, 40 per cent of them Ahmadi.[10] Sections 298B and 298C of Pakistan's Penal Code, added in 1984 through Ordinance XX, are dedicated entirely to the persecution of Ahmadis.[11]

Legitimated by this draconian law, social hostility against Ahmadis is common. Other Pakistanis frequently ransack their homes and businesses. The government, afraid of retribution by extremist groups, refrains from punishing these anti-Ahmadi criminals, while Ahmadis continue to be arrested and jailed merely for practicing their faith.[12] Any criticism of these laws is met with violence: in 2011, Salman Taseer, the governor of Punjab, and Shahbaz Bhatti, Islamabad's Minister for Minorities, were both assassinated merely for speaking out against the blasphemy laws.[13]

This chapter will explore the historical, social and religious undercurrents of Pakistani state hostility toward the Ahmadiyya. It will first explore the conflict between Pakistan's constitutional religious liberty provisions and its history of anti-Ahmadi hostility. It will then lay out the case law, statutes and legal arguments made against recognition of the group, and conclude with proposed solutions.

Religious freedom in Pakistan

Founded in 1947, Pakistan was the result of decades of British oppression and religious violence between Hindus and Muslims in India, which together led to a movement by Muhammad Ali Jinnah to create a state that could serve as a safe haven for Muslims while also maintaining religious plurality. Jinnah's vision for Pakistan was to elevate the status of both South Asian Muslims and Islam

---

[8] Ibid.
[9] 'Pakistan: Massacre'.
[10] Amjad Mahmood Khan, 'Testimony of Amjad Mahmood Khan', presented at United States House of Representatives Tom Lantos Human Rights Commission: House Committee on Foreign Affairs, March 21, 2012, http://tlhrc.house.gov/docs/transcripts/2012_3_21_South%20Asia/Amjad%20Khan%20Testimony.pdf.
[11] 'Pakistan: Massacre'.
[12] Ibid.
[13] 'Pakistan: Playing with Fire', *The Guardian*, 2 March 2011, http://www.guardian.co.uk/commentisfree/2011/mar/03/pakistan-fire-shahbaz-bhatti.

more generally.[14] Fundamental to this vision was the idea that the state, while based on Islamic principles, would be accepting of other faiths.[15] Jinnah saw the intense religious tension in India as not only inherently problematic but also a great hindrance to the country's progress, and he wanted Pakistan to rise above such strife.

This commitment was guaranteed in the Pakistani Constitution, which states in its Preamble, 'adequate provision shall be made for the minorities freely to profess and practice their religions and develop their cultures';[16] and Article 20 notes:

> Subject to law, public order and morality: (a) every citizen shall have the right to profess, practice and propagate his religion; and (b) every religious denomination and every sect thereof shall have the right to establish, maintain and manage its religious institutions.

Pakistan's commitment was also reflected in its advocacy for religious freedom at the international level, as it was Muhammad Zafarullah Khan, Pakistan's first foreign minister representative to the United Nations, who actively supported the adoption of Article 18 to the UDHR. Khan based his support of Article 18, which protects freedom of religion and conscience, on the Quranic injunction that there is no compulsion in religion.[17]

Simultaneous to these efforts to foster religious plurality, though, there was also a push by some Muslim fundamentalist groups, beginning in the 1950s, to turn Pakistan into a Sunni Islamic theocracy. In 1973, these efforts culminated in the Constitution's Repugnancy Clause, Article 227(1), which provides that: 'All existing laws shall be brought in conformity with the Injunctions of Islam as laid down in the Holy Quran and Sunnah, in this Part referred to as the Injunctions of Islam, and no law shall be enacted which is repugnant to such Injunctions.'[18] To ensure that the 'Injunctions of Islam' are followed, the Constitution further established the Islamic Council, a type of Islamic think-tank for Parliament and the Provincial Assemblies.[19] And finally, to seal the fate of the Ahmadis, a 1974 constitutional amendment declared Ahmadis non-Muslims,[20] making Pakistan the first Muslim majority country in the world to delineate who is Muslim or not in its Constitution.[21]

---

[14] Amjad Khan, 'Persecution of the Ahmadiyya Community in Pakistan: An Analysis Under International Law and International Relations', *Harvard Human Rights Journal* 16 (2003): 220–21.
[15] Ibid., 220–21.
[16] Preamble, Pakistan Constitution.
[17] Khan, 'Persecution of the Ahmadiyya', 221–2.
[18] Article 227 (1), Pakistan Constitution.
[19] Article 230 (1).
[20] Article 260, Pakistan's Constitution.
[21] Khan, 'Testimony of Amjad Mahmood Khan'.

Ahmadis in Pakistan

Mirza Ghulam Ahmad, born in Qadian, India in 1839, is the founder of the Ahmadiyya.[22] In 1889, Ahmad claimed to have received divine revelation, declaring that he, like the Prophet and the Caliphs, had the right to take the oath of allegiance from the faithful.[23] In 1891, he further claimed to be the messiah prophesied by the Prophet Muhammad.[24] This latter claim lies at the heart of the theological dispute between Ahmadis and the orthodox Muslim community, which believes that Prophet Muhammad was the last in the line of monotheistic prophets.

Ahmadis in Pakistan have faced persecution since at least 1953, when the first anti-Ahmadiyya riots erupted in Lahore.[25] From 1953 to 1974, many of Pakistan's religious clerics built up anti-Ahmadiyya sentiment by encouraging orthodox Muslims to ostracize Ahmadis.[26] In 1974, the government amended Pakistan's Constitution to specifically identify Ahmadis as non-Muslim.[27] And in the late 1970s and early 1980s, President Zia-ul-Haq, as part of his Islamization efforts, further entrenched inferior treatment of Ahmadis by creating separate voter registration for non-Muslims,[28] amending Pakistan's blasphemy laws to specifically target Ahmadis,[29] and requiring Ahmadis to use the derogatory term 'Qadiani' to identify their religion on passports and identity cards.[30]

Sections 295 and 298 of Pakistan's Penal Code contain the country's blasphemy laws. The British in India first enacted these blasphemy laws to 'protect religious feelings'.[31] They now prohibit, among other things, defilement of the Quran and denigrating language about Islamic personalities.[32] Blasphemy offenses are

---

[22] *Encyclopedia Britannica Online*, 'Ahmadiyya', http://www.britannica.com/EB checked/topic/10189/Ahmadiyyah.

[23] The oath of allegiance of the faithful is called 'bay'ah' in Arabic. It is an Islamic principle through which a person takes an oath of allegiance with the community leader to declare himself a part of a community.

[24] 'Pakistan: Massacre'.

[25] Aziz Ahmad Chaudhry, *The Promised Messiah and Mahdi* (New York: Islam International, 1996), 136.

[26] Nadeem Ahmad Siddiq, 'Enforced Apostasy: Zaheerudin v. State and the Official Persecution of the Ahmadiyya Community in Pakistan', *Law and Inequality* 14 (1995): 285–7.

[27] See Pak. Const. Pt XII, ch. 5 articles 260 (3) (a) and (b).

[28] See Barbara Crosette, 'Pakistan's Minorities Face Voting Restrictions', *New York Times*, 23 October 1990, http://www.nytimes.com/1990/10/23/world/pakistan-s-minorities-face-voting-restrictions.html.

[29] 'Pakistan: Massacre'.

[30] Khan, 'Testimony of Amjad Mahmood Khan'.

[31] 'Pakistan Blasphemy Law: Ending the Abuse of the Blasphemy Law', http://www.pakistanblasphemylaw.com/?page_id=15.

[32] See Pakistan Penal Code §§ 295B–295C.

punishable by fines, life imprisonment or death.³³ Section 295C, for example, punishes derogatory statements about Muhammad with the death penalty or life imprisonment and a fine.³⁴

Haq enacted Sections 298B and 298C, which target Ahmadis, in 1984 as part of Martial Law Ordinance XX. The Ordinance restricted the Ahmadiyya from calling themselves 'Muslim' orally or in writing, using Islamic terminology and engaging in public acts of worship.³⁵

These provisions have been regularly enforced.³⁶ Despite being a fraction of the 5 per cent religious minority population in Pakistan, they constitute 40 per cent of the arrests under the blasphemy laws.³⁷ Ahmadis also remain disenfranchised in Pakistan. Until 2002, non-Muslims and Ahmadis could only vote for minority candidates for minority seats in Parliament. In 2002, President Musharraf passed Chief Executive Order No. 7, eliminating the joint electoral system and allowing all Pakistani citizens to vote equally.³⁸ However, four months later, as a result of pressure by religious hardliners,³⁹ Musharraf issued Chief Executive Order No. 15 stating that the 'status of Ahmadis [was] ... to remain unchanged'.⁴⁰ Ahmadis can now vote only if they '(1) declare themselves to be a non-Muslim; (2) declare the founder of the Ahmadiyya Muslim Community to be an imposter; and (3) add their names to a separate supplementary list'.⁴¹

Ahmadis also face challenges while obtaining passports and identity cards. Pakistani passport forms request applicants to list their religious affiliation. 'Qadiani' is listed separate from 'Muslim'.⁴² If applicants indicate that they are Muslim, they must also sign a declaration that states: 'I consider Mirza Ghulam Ahmed Qadiani to be an imposter nabi [prophet] and also consider his followers, whether belonging to the Lahori or Qadiani group, to be non-Muslims'.⁴³ The

---

33 See Pakistan Penal Code §§ 295A–295C. § 295A.

34 Pakistan Penal Code § 295C.

35 Ibid., 288–89.

36 'Written Statement Submitted by the International Association for Religious Freedom, a Non-governmental Organization in General Consultative Status', *U.N. Human Rights Council*, 28 February 2012, .A/HRC/19/NGO/127.

37 Khan, 'Testimony of Amjad Mahmood Khan'.

38 Chief Executive Order No.7 of 2002, F. No. 2(4)/2002–Pub., http://www.nrb.gov.pk/publications/conduct_of_general_elections_2002.pdf.

39 Mahmood Ahmad and Amjad Mahmood Khan, 'Apartheid in Pakistan', *Washington Post*, 19 January 2011, http://onfaith.washingtonpost.com/onfaith/guestvoices/2011/01/apartheid_in_pakistan.html.

40 Chief Executive Order No. 15, F. No. 2(4)/2002–Pub., http://www.thepersecution.org/50years/jointelec.html.

41 Khan, 'Testimony of Amjad Mahmood Khan'. See also Ahmad and Khan, 'Apartheid in Pakistan'.

42 High Commission Consulate General of Pakistan Passport Application, http://www.pakmission.ca/Forms/Manual%20Passport%20Application.pdf.

43 Pakistan Passport Application.

National Database and Registration Authority's form for identity cards also has a category for 'Qadiani/Ahmadi', and next to 'Muslim' has asterisks with a statement similar to the one above.[44]

Ahmadis in court

Until the amendment of 1974 declaring them non-Muslim, the courts treated Ahmadis as religious minorities deserving of state protection. For example, in the 1969 case *Abdul Karim Shorish Kashmiri v The State of West Pakistan*, the court held that the Pakistani Constitution guarantees Ahmadis the same freedom to profess their religion as any other Pakistani citizen. The court also deemed the legal process insufficient to determine who is or is not Muslim, holding that litigants cannot legitimately ask civil courts to answer this question.[45] Most importantly, the court stated that Islam guarantees freedom of religion, and that persecution of religious minorities like the Ahmadis is unconscionable,[46] concluding that the treatment of Ahmadis reflects 'sad instances of religious persecution against which human conscience must revolt, if any decency is left in human affairs'.[47]

Even after the 1974 amendment, judicial treatment of Ahmadis continued to be fair. In 1978, the High Court of Lahore decided *Abdur Rahman Mobashir v. Amir Ali Shah Bokhari ('Mobashir')*. In this case the petitioners, encouraged by the amendment to Article 260, sought a permanent injunction to bar Ahmadis from engaging in religious practices associated with orthodox Islam.[48] Using concepts from intellectual property law, they argued that because the Constitution deemed them non-Muslims, Ahmadis had no right to call their places of worship 'masjid' (mosques), perform the call to prayer or perform their prayer in the traditional Islamic manner.[49] The Court denied the request,[50] holding that that there is no law or legal right which can be used to prevent Ahmadis from worshipping freely and calling their house of worship a 'masjid'.[51] The court also said that religious terms are not property, and are thus not subject to ownership, and do not fall within the purview of intellectual property law.

---

[44] See National Identity Card for Overseas Pakistanis Form, http://www.nadra.gov.pk/images/docs2/NICOP2.pdf.
[45] *Abdul Karim Shorish Kashmiri v. The State of West Pakistan* PLD 1969 (Lah.) 289 at 308.
[46] Ibid., 307.
[47] Ibid., 308.
[48] *Abdur Rahman Mobashir v. Amir Ali Shah Bokhari* PLD 1978 (Lah.) 113 at 126.
[49] Ibid., 126.
[50] Ibid., 126.
[51] Ibid., 126.

The court in *Mobashir* distinguished between moral and legal rights and emphasized that the state could enforce only the latter.[52] It noted that there was no cognizable injury to plaintiffs when Ahmadis 'use ... their old place of worship or ... offer their prayers' or make the call to prayer.[53] Rather, if the court granted the injunction, 'the injury ... [would] be suffered by the Qadianis who are being restrained from practicing their religion'.[54]

The courts' equitable treatment of Ahmadis ended with the enactment of Ordinance XX in 1983, which criminalized various forms of Ahmadi public worship.[55] In the 1985 case *Mujibur Rahman v. Government of Pakistan* the Federal Shariat Court, Pakistan's Islamic law court, which has the power to void laws that it finds to be in conflict with Islamic injunctions,[56] held that the Pakistani parliament did have the power to declare Ahmadis non-Muslim,[57] and that the restrictions Ordinance XX imposed on Ahmadis were consonant with Islam precisely because, in the court's view, Ahmadis are not Muslims.[58]

The court emphasized the importance of Ordinance XX, noting that although Article 260 of the Constitution had defined Ahmadis as non-Muslim since 1974, Ahmadis persisted in calling themselves Muslims. The court explained that Ordinance XX was needed to restrict this practice.[59] It went on to analyze the theological differences between Ahmadis and orthodox Muslims to support its holding that Ahmadis could not practice as Muslims and that Parliament was well within its rights to declare 'Qadianis' non-Muslims.[60]

The constitutionality of Ordinance XX was challenged in the 1993 Supreme Court case *Zaheerudin v. State*, brought by a group of Ahmadis appealing their convictions under Ordinance XX and Pakistan Penal Code Section 295(c). The appellants had been sentenced to a fine and imprisonment for wearing a badge with the Islamic declaration of faith ('There is no God but God, and Muhammad is the Messenger of God').[61] The court, in a 4-to-1 opinion, held that Ordinance XX did not violate religious freedom and was constitutional.

The court's rationale was based primarily on concerns about public order. According to the court, public religious expression by Ahmadis was offensive

---

[52] Ibid., 135 and 139.
[53] Ibid., 135 and 192–3.
[54] Ibid., 135 and 193.
[55] See Pakistan Constitution Pt XII, ch. 5 articles 260 (3)(b).
[56] Siddiq, 'Enforced Apostasy', 320. Federal Shariat Court decisions are not binding on Pakistan's Supreme Court, but they may be enforced through executive action.
[57] See *Mujibur Rehman v. Government of Pakistan*, 1985 S.D. Vol. II (Fed. Shariat Court) 382, 473 (Pak.).
[58] See *Rehman v. Pakistan*, 473; See also Martin Lau, 'The Case of Zaheer-ud-din v. The State and Its Impact on the Fundamental Right to Freedom of Religion', *Center of Islamic and Middle Eastern Law*, 9 April 2012, www.soas.ac.uk/cimel/materials/intro.html.
[59] *Rehman v Pakistan*, 382.
[60] Ibid., 387.
[61] Siddiq, 'Enforced Apostasy', 288.

to Pakistan's orthodox Muslim citizens and could lead these offended citizens to engage in violence.[62] The court reasoned that, since Ahmadi practices can elicit violent reactions, the Pakistani government had the power to restrict these practices. The court also held that Islamic terminology could not be used by Ahmadis because they are not Muslim. According to the court, Ahmadi use of these terms misleads people into thinking Ahmadis are Muslims, and this deception can legitimately be regulated by law. To support this conclusion, the court used trademark law from the US and other countries: 'Not only in Pakistan but throughout the world ... laws protect the use of words and phrases which have special connotations or meaning ... which[,] if used for other [purposes,] may amount to deceiving or misleading people'.[63]

The trademark argument first came up in 1978 in *Mobashir* with a favourable outcome for the Ahmadis. The court there explained, 'Our law does not in general recognize any exclusive right to the use of a name, personal or local. I may use a name ... as long as I do not use it to pass off my wares or business as being [another's], which is quite another matter'.[64] However, the court in *Zaheerudin* dismissed the *Mobashir* reasoning summarily, stating that Ordinance XX trumps all previous judicial decisions.[65]

The *Zaheerudin* court went on to misapply US trademark law – first and most fundamentally by assuming that trade and religion can be analogized and that religious terminology can be copyrighted. US federal trademark law states that 'religious prayers and names cannot be trademarked', so the very application of trademark law to the matter was inappropriate.[66]

The court encouraged the Ahmadis to coin their own terminology, reasoning that certain words are unique to, and somehow owned by, orthodox Muslims. However, some terms used by Muslims today originated in Christianity, undermining even the theological accuracy of the court's opinion.[67]

Moreover, the court misconstrued US religious freedom jurisprudence. The court cites the 1878 case *Reynolds v. US*,[68] which upheld a ban on polygamy despite religious objections, to support the proposition that, while laws cannot interfere with religious belief, they can legitimately interfere with religious practice.[69] What

---

[62] Amjad Mahmood Khan, 'Misuse and Abuse of Legal Argument by Analogy in Transjudicial Communication: The Case of Zaheerudin v. State', *Richmond Journal of Global Law & Business* 10 (2011): 507–9.
[63] *Zaheerudin v. State*, (1993) 26 SCMR (SC) 1718, at 19 (Pak.).
[64] Mobashir, 135 and 139.
[65] *Zaheerudin v. State*, (minority opinion) para. 21.
[66] Khan, 'Misuse and Abuse', 510.
[67] Ibid., 511. For example, in pre-Islamic Arabia, the term 'Allah', which Muslims use to refer to God, was also used by people who were not Muslim. 'Allah' is also used today by Christian and Jewish Arabs to refer to God.
[68] *Reynolds v. US*, 98 US 145 (1878).
[69] *Zaheerudin v. State*, 25.

the court fails to note however is that the statute in *Reynolds* did not explicitly target a religious group[70] the way Ordinance XX did with the Ahmadiyya.[71]

The court similarly misunderstands *Hamilton v. Regents of the University of California*.[72] In *Hamilton*, the US Supreme Court held that the government does not violate religious freedom when it makes military training compulsory on a university campus, despite students' religious objections, because such training is essential to the government duty to maintain peace and order.[73] Again, the law in question applied equally to all university students of a certain age[74] and did not explicitly target adherents of a particular set of religious beliefs. In fact, the Supreme Court in *Hamilton* underscores its belief in robust religious liberties: 'Undoubtedly [religious liberty] does include the right to entertain the beliefs, to adhere to the principles, and to teach the doctrines on which these students base their objections to the order prescribing military training'.[75]

The *Zaheerudin* court also misunderstood US law regarding the public order exception to religious freedom protection. The court stated that sections 298(b) and 298(c) of the Pakistani Penal Code allow restrictions on Ahmadi religious practice in order to maintain public order and safeguard the religious sentiments of Pakistan's majority Sunni population.[76] The court cited several US cases to support this proposition.[77] However, the court failed to strike the necessary balance between broad religious freedom rights and limits that are narrowly tailored to serve compelling government interests.[78]

Article 20 of the Pakistani Constitution protects the right to religious freedom – limited only by the fundamental rights of others or as needed by a state of emergency – in two realms: the internal process of belief and spirituality and the external expression of those beliefs.[79] The government is allowed to restrict only the latter, and even then only in limited circumstances when justified by public order and morality.

The court in *Zaheerudin* seizes on these exceptions. After going through a lengthy consideration of US cases that restrict religious expression and concluding that freedom of religion covers only those religious practices that the judiciary deems integral to a religion, the court considers – and misapplies – *Cantwell v. Connecticut*. There, two men proselytizing on the street were arrested for breach of the peace when passers-by were offended by the men's criticism of organized

---

[70] *Reynolds v. US* at 164.
[71] Ibid.,163–66.
[72] *Hamilton v. Regents of the University of California*, 293 US 245 (1934).
[73] *Zaheerudin v. State*, 30.
[74] *Hamilton v. Regents* at 256.
[75] Ibid., 262.
[76] Khan, 'Misuse and Abuse', 511.
[77] Siddiq, 'Enforced Apostasy', 288.
[78] See *Cantwell v. Connecticut*, 310 US 296, 307 (1940).
[79] *Zaheerudin v. State*, para. 9.

religion, particularly Roman Catholicism, and responded with hostility.[80] The *Zaheerudin* court focused on the *Cantwell* Court's acknowledgement that 'a state may by general and non-discriminatory legislation ... safeguard the peace, good order and comfort of the community, without unconstitutionally invading [upon religious] liberties'.[81] However, the *Zaheerudin* court failed to heed the qualifications set forth in *Cantwell*: 'A State may not, by statute, wholly deny the right to preach or to disseminate religious views'.[82]

Although *Cantwell* repeatedly cautioned against misuse of the public order argument to suppress a fundamental right, the *Zaheerudin* court cites *Cantwell* even as it 'wholly den[ies Ahmadis'] right to' religious expression.[83] Holding that in order to protect public order the state must protect orthodox Muslims from perceived insults to their religion, which could incite violence, the court justifies suppression of non-violent Ahmadi religious practice. The court's assumption that Ahmadis expressing their beliefs will *necessarily* be accompanied by violence on the part of offended orthodox Muslims overlooks the seemingly obvious alternative: that disorder is more effectively prevented when the state punishes the violent actors instead of the peaceful speakers.

Along with US law, the *Zaheerudin* court also grossly misconstrues international law. The public order exception in Pakistani law is based on similar principles in international law,[84] in particular the public order exception to the religious freedom guarantees in Article 18 of the ICCPR: 'Freedom to manifest one's religion or beliefs may be subject only to such limitations as are prescribed by law and are necessary to protect *public safety, order,* health, or morals or the fundamental rights and freedoms of others'.[85] General Comment 22 to Article 18, which elucidates the meaning of the Article, says with respect to the exceptions, 'Limitations imposed must be established by law and must not be applied in a manner that would vitiate the rights guaranteed in article 18'.[86] In other words, the exception can only be used in very limited circumstances.

Pakistan ostensibly subscribed to that philosophy. The *Zaheerudin* court referenced the ICCPR framework as a guidepost even before Pakistan was a signatory or party to the ICCPR, showing that Pakistan had, at some level,

---

[80] *Cantwell v. Connecticut* at 308–9.

[81] Ibid., 304.

[82] Ibid.

[83] Ibid., 304 (emphasis added).

[84] International Covenant on Civil and Political Rights, arts. 18, 27, G.A. Res. 2200A (XXI), U.N. GAOR 21st Session, (entered into force 1976), http://treaties.un.org/Pages/ViewDetails.aspx?src=TREATY&mtdsg_no=IV-4&chapter=4&lang=en#EndDec. Pakistan was a signatory of the ICCPR since 17 April 2008, but has recently ratified the convention.

[85] ICCPR, Article 18 (3) (emphasis added).

[86] Human Rights Committee, General Comment 22. Para. 8 Article 18 (48th session, 1993), U.N. Doc. CCPR/C/21/Rev.1/Add.4 (1993).

accepted it as legitimate.[87] Pakistani jurists also contributed to Pakistan's *opinio juris* stating that the ICCPR affirms human rights norms. The Chief Justice of Pakistan's Supreme Court, Muhammad Haleem, stated at a judicial colloquium that 'a matter is essentially within the domestic jurisdiction of the state only if it is not regulated by international law. ... The international human rights norms are in fact part of the constitutional expression of the liberties guaranteed at the national level'.[88] Pakistan's use of US court cases reflects a similar baseline acceptance of American jurisprudence as worthy of emulation.

Despite all of this, the *Zaheerudin* court uses the public order exception to protect violent responses to Ahmadiyya religious expression in exactly the manner ICCPR Article 18 prohibits. Rather than controlling violence from extremists, the court's decision gave the government carte blanche to bully religious minorities.[89] Impunity flourishes where there are no consequences for the criminals. Under Article 18, instead of penalizing non-violent actors, the law should control violent actors and regulate their behaviour by enforcing existing criminal laws against, for example, assault, battery, murder and arson. This is clearly a much more effective method of creating public order.

ICCPR Article 18 also allows limitations on religious freedom when such is 'necessary to protect ... the fundamental rights and freedoms of others'.[90] The *Zaheerudin* court used this exception the way it did the public order exception: by turning the very concept of human rights on its head. Under international law, individuals are guaranteed human rights simply by virtue of being human.[91] The *Zaheerudin* court, instead of protecting the *physical well being* of the minority, instead protects the *feelings* of the majority. However, there is no fundamental right not to be offended.

Similarly, Ordinance XX and the blasphemy laws protect *a religious belief system* ('Islam' as interpreted and defined by orthodox Muslims) from perceived threats rather than protecting *individuals*. For example, Section 295A protects 'the religion or the religious beliefs' instead of the people who profess the religion or religious beliefs. In practice, such provisions act as a form of thought control, empowering the state to determine which ideas are 'insulting' and which are not.

The *Zaheerudin* court also engages in religious inquiry, entangling itself in religious questions such as whether Ahmadis are Muslims or not. Given the court's reliance on American law, it is curious that it overlooked a fundamental tenet of US religious freedom jurisprudence: courts are strictly forbidden from considering religious questions. US law holds that civil courts cannot become

---

[87] See Khan, 'Persecution of the Ahmadiyya', 233.

[88] Ibid., 232–3.

[89] Asma Uddin, 'Indonesian Blasphemy Act Restricts Free Religious Expression', Huffington Post, 27 April 2010, http://www.huffingtonpost.com/asma-uddin/the-indonesian-constituti_b_554463.html.

[90] ICCPR, Article 18 (3).

[91] See Universal Declaration on Human Rights.

involved in religious questions, nor should they determine the importance of those questions to the religion.[92] Religious experts are presumably more competent in religious questions than civil judges. And competence aside, the very intrusion of civil authorities into religious matters can lead to precisely what happened in *Zaheerudin* – an imposition of one interpretation of the religion on members of the faith who may disagree with that interpretation.[93]

The *Zaheerudin* opinion reflects Pakistan's continuing and predominant legal and social approach to Ahmadis. Today, Ahmadis continue to be punished for the peaceful practice of their religion, while the government continues to look the other way when violent actors attack Ahmadis.

Pakistan's international obligations

Pakistan is a party to many significant international treaties and declarations that afford protection to religious minorities like the Ahmadiyya. In addition to the ICCPR, the UDHR[94] and the 1981 UN Declaration on the Elimination of All Forms of Religious Intolerance and of Discrimination Based on Religion or Belief[95] also protect religious freedom. States are expected by these documents to protect adherents of both majority and minority religions in their religious belief and in all of the myriad forms in which those beliefs are expressed.

The Declaration in particular grants adherents of minority religions the right to be free from the imposition of majority or state religions. While Article 18 of the ICCPR grants basic principles of freedom of religion and belief,[96] the Declaration adds to these protections by prohibiting discrimination based on intra-religious disagreement.[97] As with the UDHR and ICCPR, Pakistan violates the Declaration by passing and enforcing its draconian blasphemy laws and Ordinance XX, and by daily looking the other way as Ahmadis are persecuted by private actors.

In 1985, the U.N. Sub-Commission on Prevention of Discrimination and Protection of Minorities denounced Ordinance XX, asking for its immediate repeal and for the protection of Ahmadis under Resolution 1985/21.[98] The Sub-

---

[92] See *Watson v. Jones*, 80 US 679 (1871); *Presbyterian Church v. Mary Elizabeth Blue Hull Memorial Presbyterian Church*, 393 US 440 (1969).

[93] *Thomas v. Review Board of Indiana Employment Security Division*, 450 US 707, 717 (1981).

[94] UDHR, Article 18.

[95] Declaration on the Elimination of All Forms of Intolerance and of Discrimination Based on Religion or Belief, G.A. Res. 36/55, U.N. GAOR, 36th Session, Supp. No. 51, at 171, U.N. Doc. A/36/684 (1981).

[96] ICCPR, Article 18.

[97] Khan, 'Persecution of the Ahmadiyya', 234.

[98] Report of the Sub-Commission on Prevention of Discrimination and Protection of Minorities on its Thirty-Eighth Session, at 102 U.N.Doc.E/CN.4/1986/5 (1985/21, The situation in Pakistan).

Commission report says Ordinance XX violates the rights of religious minorities to practice their own religion, and denies them an effective legal remedy when their religious freedom is violated. Resolution 1985/21 rejects Pakistan's justification of Ordinance XX as necessary to public safety. Pakistan did not respond to the U.N.'s call for the repeal of Ordinance XX, but, in a related interview, General Zia-ul-Haq made his position clear: 'Ahmadis offend me because they consider themselves Muslims. ... Ordinance XX may violate human rights but I don't care'.[99] Today, Ordinance XX remains on the books.

In 1999, Pakistan was also at the forefront of an effort by the Organization of Islamic Cooperation (OIC) to pass a resolution in the Commission on Human Rights on the Defamation of Religions. Pakistan presented the draft resolution as an effort to have the Commission stand up against what the OIC deemed a campaign to defame Islam, which they argued could incite already increasing manifestations of intolerance towards Muslims to a degree similar to anti-Semitic violence of the past.[100]

The Defamation of Religions Resolution was heavily criticized as a cover for domestic blasphemy laws. Over the years, the Resolution began to lose popularity among delegates. In response, resolution 16/18 in March 2011 removed the defamation language completely. While 16/18 provides more balance in terms of equal treatment of all religions and condemning all forms of discrimination and violence against people of all religions, critics believe that the new resolution's use of words like 'intolerance' or 'incitement' may be code words for banning proselytism and conversion.

Looking to the future

There are multiple levels of reform that Pakistan must undertake in order to significantly alleviate anti-Ahmadi persecution. Ideally, oppressive laws must be re-written or repealed. Pakistan should repeal the blasphemy laws, Ordinance XX, and Article 260 of Pakistan's Constitution, which states that Ahmadis are non-Muslims. By repealing these laws, Pakistan would begin the process of ending official sanction of discriminatory Ahmadi targeting. Without laws on the books to justify their criminal behaviour, perpetrators of anti-Ahmadi violence could then expect punishment rather than validation of their actions.

This of course requires that law enforcement agencies enforce existing Pakistan law against, for example, assault and battery, arson, vandalism and so on. In order to stop the persecution of Ahmadis, the government must take steps to prosecute criminals engaging in hate crimes. As long as the government fails to hold criminals accountable and continues to bow to pressure from religious

---

[99] Siddiq, 'Enforced Apostasy', 243.
[100] Commission on Human Rights, Summary Record of the 61st Meeting, E/CN.4/1999/SR.61, para. 1–9.

extremists who perpetrate or encourage violence against religious minorities, Ahmadis will be unable to practice their religion in peace.

In addition, Pakistan should establish independent commissions to monitor and investigate complaints of discrimination or hate crimes against racial or religious minorities.[101] These commissions should be based on principles of respect and should help build within the judiciary and police force training on human rights and anti-discrimination policies.

Pakistan's government should ensure that religious minorities be able to take part in all aspects of public life. For Ahmadis, this means eliminating existing restrictions on their voting rights as well as the discriminatory classifications on passports and ID cards, which require them to self-identify as 'Qadianis' and non-Muslims. Pakistan may also consider an affirmative action programme to reverse the effects of discrimination against minorities or at least keep a method of monitoring discrimination in the workplace and elsewhere.

While these reforms reflect the ideal, the volatile socio-political situation in Pakistan and entrenched beliefs about the limits on religious freedom and free speech make it difficult, if not impossible, to actualize these ideas. Repealing Ordinance XX or the blasphemy laws, or eliminating discriminatory classifications on official documentation, is unlikely any time soon since both Pakistan's Supreme Court and Federal Shariat Court have ruled that these provisions are valid. The recent assassinations of Punjab Governor Salman Taseer and Minorities Minister Shahbaz Bhatti for their opposition to Pakistan's blasphemy laws, and the public celebration of those assassinations, reflect the deep-rooted violent and extremist ideology that allow for these laws to thrive in Pakistan.

One way that domestic litigation against the blasphemy laws can achieve more success would be by bringing a case with a Sunni Muslim plaintiff. A plaintiff who belongs to the majority Muslim group can help put the public's – and the judiciary's – focus on the abusive elements of such laws. That is, when a religious minority is prosecuted for blasphemy, the public is likely to be moved by emotions and its deep-seated need to 'protect' Islam from insult. A Sunni plaintiff would help eliminate these emotions, especially if the statement for which the plaintiff is being prosecuted involves primarily political or commercial rather than religious sentiments. Private citizens routinely misuse blasphemy allegations to intimidate their opponents in property or business disputes;[102] choosing a plaintiff from among these cases may potentially create case law that moves the discussion beyond that of religious insult.

Another, perhaps complementary, avenue to relief is to challenge these discriminatory laws at the international level. Pakistan should be forced to comply

---

[101] 'Religious Minorities in Pakistan', *Minority Rights Group International*, August 2002, www.unhcr.org/refworld/docid/469cbfc30.html.

[102] 'Blasphemy Laws Exposed: The Consequences of Criminalizing 'Defamation of Religions'', *Human Rights First*, March 2012, http://www.humanrightsfirst.org/wp-content/uploads/Blasphemy_Cases.pdf.

with the ICCPR, the International Convention on the Elimination of All Forms of Racial Discrimination (ICERD), and other international conventions to which it is a party. International laws and treaty bodies have the ability to call attention to problems and regulate them through reports and resolutions. The ICCPR and ICERD are treaty bodies with monitoring mechanisms. For example, the Human Rights Committee monitors state implementation of the ICCPR. A state party to the ICCPR is obliged every four years to report its compliance to the Committee, which examines the country report and writes its own report, listing any concerns its has about the country in its concluding observations.[103] Since Pakistan only became a party to the ICCPR in 2010, it has not yet been called to report to the Human Rights Committee.[104] But compliance mechanisms like these can be useful tools in forcing a country, like Pakistan, to acknowledge and address its human rights violations.

These laws can also be challenged on their procedural and substantive weaknesses. For example, the blasphemy laws have language that is overbroad or vague. Section 295C, which covers derogatory remarks about the Prophet Muhammad, fails to define what constitutes 'derogatory remarks' and is furthermore vague and immensely overbroad in describing what is punishable under the law – the statute punishes remarks made by 'imputation, innuendo, or insinuation, directly or indirectly'.[105] The failure to more specifically describe the actions subject to prosecution gives enforcing officials tremendous discretion in deciding how the statute will be enforced; indeed, different officials will apply the statute differently, based on their subjective prejudices, thus leaving Pakistani citizens vulnerable to the mere whims of law enforcement. Moreover, as discussed above, penal protections like these that protect ideas rather than individuals empower the state to define 'insulting' or 'derogatory' in line with its own religious interpretations.

The blasphemy laws should also be challenged as redundant; Pakistan's Penal Code and its property and torts laws already punish any valid offense regulated by the blasphemy laws. For example, Section 295 prohibits defilement of the Quran and the defilement and destruction of houses of worship.[106] Valid offenses under this provision include crimes like arson, vandalism and such. (Invalid ones include writing 'Muhammad' on a mosque's bathroom walls.[107]) However, other Pakistani

---

[103] 'FAQ: The Covenant on Civil & Political Rights (ICCPR)', *American Civil Liberties Union*, https://www.aclu.org/human-rights/faq-covenant-civil-political-rights-iccpr.
[104] See Human Rights Committee Sessions, http://www2.ohchr.org/english/bodies/hrc/sessions.htm.
[105] See Pakistan Penal Code § 295C.
[106] Ibid., § 295B.
[107] 'Four Ahmadi School Children and an Adult Frivolously Booked and Arrested by the Police on False Accusation of Blasphemy by Extremist Elements', *The Persecution*, 2 February 2009, http://www.thepersecution.org/case/case009.html.

laws already punish these offenses,[108] thus eviscerating the need for additional regulatory provisions, particularly those open to abuse.

There are also non-legal routes – such as calling media attention to the atrocities being committed under these laws and educating the community on religious liberty and the benefits of pluralism by reinforcing the founding ideals of Pakistan. This sort of media campaign may be particularly effective with Pakistan's youth, which today constitute the majority of the population.[109] Many of these youth are plugged into social media. Recent debacles related to the Pakistani government's ban on Facebook because of a Facebook page blaspheming the Prophet Muhammad help drive home to this segment of the population the abusive nature of these laws.[110]

Finally, and most fundamentally, because Pakistan's government is repeatedly bowing to pressure from extremist groups,[111] the root of this extremist opposition must be addressed. This can be done with the support of religious leaders who will counteract extremist messages that call for oppression of and hatred toward minority groups. Numerous modern Islamic scholars have elucidated the Islamic foundation for religious freedom.[112] Such arguments, based soundly in Islamic scripture and core religious texts, should be utilized, as religiously authentic arguments can go a long way in a deeply religious nation such as Pakistan.

Freedom of religion and belief was at the core of the foundation of Pakistan as a safe haven for Muslims, who were a minority in British India. To ignore the wishes of Jinnah and persecute religious minorities in Pakistan today relinquishes the principles Pakistan was founded on and created to uphold. Until Pakistan internalizes its commitment to freedom of religion instead of seeing it as a threat to the sanctity of Islam, and until it recognizes that restrictions on religious freedom only encourage extremist ideologies, a meaningful pluralist society cannot exist there.

---

[108] See, for example, Pakistan Penal Code § 503 on Criminal Intimidation; § 425 on Criminal Mischief; §§ 435–36 on Criminal Mischief by Fire or Explosive; or § 441 on Criminal Trespass; see also Pakistan Constitution, Article 20 on Freedom to Profess Religion and to Manage Religious Institutions.

[109] In 2007, youth under 25 years old made up 63 per cent of Pakistan's population. 'UNDP and the Youth: Pakistan', *United Nations Development Programme*, 25 May 2012, http://undp.org.pk/undp-and-the-youth.html.

[110] Asma Uddin, 'Pakistan's Facebook Ban Protects the Violent', *The Washington Post*, 21 May 2010, http://onfaith.washingtonpost.com/onfaith/panelists/asma_uddin/2010/05/pakistans_facebook_ban_protects_the_wrong_party.html.

[111] 'Pakistan: Playing with Fire'.

[112] See Abdullah Saeed, 'The Quranic Case Against Killing Apostates', *The Witherspoon Institute Public Discourse*, 25 February 2011, http://www.thepublicdiscourse.com/2011/02/2716; see also Mohammad Hashim Kamali, *Freedom of Expression in Islam*, (Cambridge: Islamic Text Society, 1997); and Abdullah Saeed and Hassan Saeed, *Freedom of Religion, Apostasy and Islam*, (Aldershot: Ashgate Pub Ltd., 2004).

Conclusion

Forty thousand people flooded the streets of Karachi in January 2011, praising as a hero the assassin who killed Salman Tasser for his opposition to the blasphemy laws.[113] The month prior, 24 Ahmadi graves were desecrated in Punjab.[114] And in March 2012, 5,000 people demonstrated to demolish the largest Ahmadi mosque in Rawalpindi.[115] While the government fails to act and the international community remains silent, the senseless killings and arrests of the Ahmadiyya continue. As one author says when describing the horrendous torture and murder of Abdul Qudoos, the Ahmadi teacher whose story introduced this chapter, 'A darkness has descended over us all; we may deem some amongst us to be non-Muslims[,] but in the process we have all become non-human. The nightmare is all too real. There has to come a time when we unite to speak with one voice. Otherwise there will be no awakening and there will certainly be no turning back'.[116]

---

[113] 'More than 40,000 Protest Blasphemy Law Change', Dawn, January 9, 2011, http://dawn.com/2011/01/09/more-than-20000-protest-blasphemy-law-change-police/.

[114] 'Pakistan Should Protect Ahmaddiya [sic] Community Against Threats of Violence', Amnesty International Press Release, 3 February 2012, http://www.amnesty.org/en/news/pakistan-should-protect-ahmaddiya-community-against-threats-violence-2012-02-02.

[115] Ibid.

[116] Ahmad, 'A Murder Most Foul'.

PART III
Atlantic Models – Religious Minorities, Diversity and the 'European West'

Chapter 7

Public Policies and Cults in European Case Law: Between Security, Non-discrimination and Public Information

Louis-Léon Christians

The legal approach to cults and what are sometimes called 'controversial religious movements' varies considerably across European countries,[1] ranging from – put simply – pronounced indifference in the Northwest to increasingly acute vigilance as one moves towards the Southeast.

The heart of European jurisprudence on freedom of religion is heavily built around complaints of so-called cults (consisting of about 20 per cent of judgments and decisions in the last 20 years). These petitioners have mostly succeeded, but court procedures are particularly cautious and always apply a proportionality test.

Standing out against the long flow of jurisprudence, a major turning point in European history concerning the regulation of cults arose in Recommendation 1412/1999 of the Parliamentary Assembly of the Council of Europe. Indeed, it explicitly united policy objectives previously perceived as conflicting, simultaneously addressing the need to better respond to illegal practices carried out on behalf of 'religious, esoteric or spiritual' groups at the same time 'encourag[ing] an approach to religious groups which will bring about understanding, tolerance, dialogue and resolution of conflicts; [and] to take firm measures against any action which is discriminatory or which marginalizes religious or spiritual minority groups'.[2] Recommendation 1412, however, is also an historic turning point for another reason. It continues: 'It is of prime importance to have reliable information

---

[1] In comparative European law, see for example the European Consortium for Church-State Research, *New Religious Movements and the Law in the European Union* (Milan: Giuffre, 1999), 390; Olivier Dord, 'Entre Laïcité et Exigences Européennes, Une Politique de Lutte Contre les Dérives Sectaires Est-elle Possible?', in *Laïcité, Liberté de Religion et Convention Européenne des Droits de L'homme*, ed. Gèrard Gonzales (Bruxelles: Bruylant, 2006), 223–49; Sabrina Pastorelli, 'The European Union and the New Religious Movements', *Religion, State and Society* 1–2 (2009): 193–206; Nathalie Luca, ed., *Quelles Régulations Pour les Nouveaux mouvements Religieux et les dérives sectaires dans l'Union Européenne?* (Marseille: Presses Universitaires d'Aix-Marseille (PUAM), 2011).

[2] Recommendation 1412/1999 Para. 10, sections vi–vii, http://assembly.coe.int/defaultE.asp.

on these groups that emanates neither exclusively from the sects themselves nor from associations set up to defend the victims of sects, and to circulate it widely among the general public, once those concerned have had the chance to comment on the objectivity of such information'.[3]

Here are summarized three sectarian public policies that the European Court of Human Rights has gradually imposed: (1) the suppression of illegal practices, (2) non-discrimination – particularly in the context of policy incentives, and more recently (3) the policy of informing the public.[4]

This chapter examines the balances and the limits imposed by the European Court with regard to each of these policies and concludes with some prospective remarks.

Repression of illegal practices

The model of cult repression is limited by conventional principles. It must respect the natural limits of a common law in which the importance of neutrality influences its justification and non-discrimination in its execution. The non-negligible positive outcomes to applicants show that the principles governing the common law cannot sanction everything. They are, however, a *favor minoritatis* guide that safeguards Europe's minorities.

In a decision of 29 August 1996, *Manoussakis v. Greece*, the Court – after admitting that 'States are entitled to verify whether a movement or association carries on, ostensibly in pursuit of religious aims, activities which are harmful to the population' – nevertheless noted that the magnitude and general direction of litigation on the matter 'seems to show a clear tendency on the part of the administrative and ecclesiastical authorities to use these provisions to restrict the activities of faiths outside the Orthodox Church'.[5] Greece was thus condemned.

The fact that the road to repression is closely marked does not mean that this *favor minoritatis* automatically establishes any immunity for minority groups. The distinction has always been supported by European jurisprudence between

---

[3] Ibid., para. 7; see also Pastorelli, 'New Religious Movements', 193–206; Nathalie Luca, ed., *Quelles régulations pour les nouveaux mouvements*.

[4] We do not consider here the cases of the private law of the family and especially the care of children where one parent is accused of belonging to a cult. The Court stated in *Hoffmann v. Austria*, ECtHR 12875/87 (1993) that the membership of a parent in a contested group could not *in itself* justify a withdrawal of care and specifically established that the interest of the child was the only criterion admissible. See also *Palau Martinez v. France*, ECtHR 64927/01 (2003); *FI v. France*, November 3, 2005; *Ismailova v. Russia*, ECtHR 37614/02 (2007); *Gineitienė v. Lithuania*, ECtHR 20739/05 (2010); *M. and C. v. Romania*, ECtHR 29032/04 (2011). We refer also to *Riera Blume v. Spain*, ECtHR 37680/97 (1999) in which the Court condemned Spain for letting parents arbitrarily kidnap their adult children for 'deprogramming'.

[5] *Manoussakis and others v. Greece*, ECtHR 18748/91 (1996).

the system of beliefs on the one hand and practices on the other, the latter being subject to more intrusive countermeasures. Moreover, Article 17 of the European Convention excludes any interpretation which intends to legitimize a 'right to engage in any activity or to perform any act aimed at the destruction of any of the rights and freedoms set forth herein or at their limitation to a greater extent than is provided for in the Convention'.[6]

This emphasis on the protection of socially contested movements, so long as they do not fall within the scope of Article 17, however, is at best a presumption rebuttable by the state by establishing that the state's alleged actions could reasonably be deemed necessary in a democratic society to achieve a legitimate purpose under the Convention.

To strengthen the repression of cults, new crimes against mental manipulation or psychological destabilization are emerging in various European countries (for example France [2001][7] and Belgium [2011][8]). Without formally targeting specific groups, these standards have been specifically created for the purpose of reaching them, as shown by the various works of national parliaments. The European Court has not yet had the opportunity to assess these new criminal offenses but has already established relevant founding principles of jurisprudence, for example in the notion of abusive proselytism, outlined in 1993 in the famous case of *Kokkinakis v. Greece,* which will permit the delineation of the fairly strict new offenses of manipulation and abuse of vulnerability. For the Court, improper proselytism 'may ... take the form of activities offering material or social advantages with a view to gaining new members for a Church or exerting improper pressure on people in distress or in need'.[9] Likewise, involving the use of violence or 'brainwashing', more generally, is not consistent with respect for the freedom of thought, conscience, and religion of others. The Court noted that

> Scrutiny of section 4 of Law no. 1363/1938 shows that the relevant criteria adopted by the Greek legislature are reconcilable with the foregoing if and in so

---

[6] Convention for the Protection of Human Rights and Fundamental Freedoms, Article 17, http://conventions.coe.int/treaty/en/Treaties/Html/005.htm.

[7] French law No. 2001–504 of June 12, 2001, known as the About-Picard law, 'attempts to reinforce the prevention and repression of sectarian movements, affecting human rights and fundamental freedoms'. See Patrice Rolland, 'Le phénomène sectaire au regard de la laïcité à la française', in *La laïcité. Une valeur d'aujourd'hui? Contestations et renégociations du modèle français,* eds Jean Bauduin and Phillipe Portier (Rennes: PURennes, 2001), 331–47.

[8] Article 442 quarter of the Belgian Penal Code (as amended by the Act of November 26, 2011 amending and supplementing the Criminal Code to criminalize the abuse of a person in position of weakness and expand the criminal protection of the vulnerable against abuse, Moniteur belge of 23 January 2012), with a special incrimination of a 'mise en état de sujétion psychologique'.

[9] *Kokkinakis v. Greece,* ECtHR 14307/88 (1993) section 48.

far as they are designed only to punish improper proselytism, which the Court does not have to define in the abstract in the present case.[10]

Finally, the Court related that the Greek courts had established 'the responsibility of the applicant on grounds that merely reproducing the terms of Article 4 did not sufficiently specify how the accused had attempted to convince his neighbour by abusive means. None of the facts they set out warrant[ed] it'. And that concluded the condemnation of Greece.

In another important decision, *Thlimmenos v. Greece*, 6 April 2000, the Court set an important new principle, an expanded version of the principle of non-discrimination in criminal matters. The Court considered that in principle the states have a legitimate interest in excluding some convicted offenders from the profession of (in effect) public accountant. However, it considered that,

> unlike other convictions for serious criminal offenses, a conviction for refusing on religious or philosophical ground to wear the military uniform cannot imply any dishonesty or moral turpitude likely to undermine the offender's ability to exercise this profession. Excluding the applicant on the ground that he was an unfit person was not, therefore, justified.[11]

The *Thlimmenos* case provides yet another lesson, many times subsequently confirmed and of great importance to minority groups: even when an exception to a law based on conscience could not legitimately be offered by a state, it still is appropriate that the criminal sanction that eventually punishes the conscientious violation not be excessive and take into account the nature of the origins of the offence.

Finally and more generally, the principle of the legality of criminal offenses and penalties pertaining to cults has also been reiterated by the Court. If we compare civil prosecution with criminal prosecution, we find a recent example in the decisions of *Jehovah's Witnesses v. France* of 30 June 2011 and 7 July 2012,[12] in which the Court condemned France for laying a tax penalty on the Jehovah's Witnesses in the amount of 59 million euros, because of the vagueness and ambiguity of the terms of the law that established the tax.

Non-discrimination and selection by policy incentives

A second type of European policy about cults consists not of crackdowns but of incentives, including public funding, which are accompanied by conditions similar to screening measures. Policies relating to registration or recognition are organized

---

[10] Ibid.
[11] *Thlimmenos v. Greece*, ECtHR 34369/97 (2000), sections 47 and 44.
[12] *Association Les Temoins de Jehovah v. France*, ECtHR 8916/05 (2012).

in many European countries. These incentive policies are considered optional by the Court: they are neither prohibited nor required. If, however, a state decides to implement such policies, the Court will retain control under the Convention. It is not the purpose of this paper to look at all the case law of the Court concerning these procedures, but only to show the scope of the Court's control with regard to policies dealing with cults, first generally, and then more specifically in relation to the principle of non-discrimination.

Three general principles emerge from the case law: (1) no essential rights to the exercise of religious freedom can be subject to a prior authorization scheme that would impose specific conditions, (2) a balance of proportionality must exist between the strictness of the conditions applied and the degree of benefit that results, but (3) in the delicate matter of church–state relationships, the Court grants this last category a wide margin of appreciation and allows only measures subject to high contextualization to control.

More specifically, the European Court recognizes that states can require in their policies of support or recognition that groups submit information to the state about themselves. Thus, for the Court, in a decision of March 3, 2009, *Lajda v. Czech Republic*,

> the submission of a document outlining the fundamental principles of a religion is necessary for the State to determine the authenticity of the organization whose goal is to acquire the status of Church, and see if this religion is not a threat to democratic society. Such a requirement can not be regarded as disproportionate.[13]

Or, according to a decision of 14 October 1999, *CR v. Switzerland*, 'National authorities ... cannot be criticized ... for adopting preventive measures without waiting for a commission of an offense because of the danger that could result in the applicant's pursuit of his business'.[14]

An important caveat should be reiterated here: *classified* confidential information cannot under any circumstances be used to oppose an individual or collective exercise of freedom of religion. The Court explained its reasoning in a decision of 12 February 2009, *Nolan and K. v. Russia*: a careful reading of Article 9 of the Convention states that unlike public safety, *national security* is not included in the list of purposes that may limit freedom of religion under Article 9. This, incidentally, is a peculiarity of Article 9: other articles in the Convention do not preclude national security from being on the list of admissible evidence.

---

[13] *Lajda v. Czech Republic*, ECtHR 20984/05 (2009).

[14] *CR v. Switzerland*, ECtHR 40130/98 (1999). This doctrinal information will be subject to certain verifications of their sincerity: 'The Court reiterates that an association's programme may in certain cases conceal objectives and intentions different from the ones it proclaims. To verify that it does not, the content of the programme must be compared with the actions of the association's leaders and the positions they embrace,' (*Moscovite Branch of the Salvation Army v. Russia*, ECtHR 72881/01 [2006]).

The activity of intelligence services is not invalidated in matters of cults, but they cannot restrict religious freedom, even if they might restrict the freedom of expression or association.[15]

The Court holds a strict line towards one principle in particular: non-discrimination. Only impartial guidance is admitted with regard to the selection techniques of incentive policies. A decision of 10 June 2010, *Jehovah's Witnesses v. Russia*, particularly shows the intensity of analysis conducted by the Court when legal consequences are in question. Faced with the case of the dissolution of a community of Jehovah's Witnesses, the Court's assessment of the accuracy of the information allegedly held by public authorities was thorough. The decision also explicitly states the principle: 'The State has a narrow margin of appreciation and must advance serious and compelling reasons for an interference with the choices that people may make in pursuance of the religious standard of behaviour within the sphere of their personal autonomy' (§ 119).[16] More than 50 pages long, the Court's opinion examines point by point all the data of the file, from the applicants' refusal to celebrate holidays and birthdays, to the rejection of blood transfusions, even touching upon the types of emotionality attributed to Jehovah's Witnesses.[17]

Public information policies

Given the limits of repressive or incentive-based policies, the management of information becomes an overriding and helpful element in new, mainly communicative public policies. Techniques for surveillance and vigilance concerning traditional criminal intelligence services are reinforced, and new information flows are created through the devices of the welfare state: the conditions attached to the granting of public benefits include new documentation requirements and monitoring. The most innovative element is decisively associated with the neoliberal state and its tension with the communicative state. In the neoliberal model, the state is the guarantor of an external, unfettered 'religious market', implying the availability of objective information to consumers by market players. Once this information is disseminated and acquired by 'informed consent', each individual is admonished as to his responsibilities. In the communicative model, the state is the guarantor of the freedom of public debate at the heart of civil society: it is through the free exchange of ideas that society will confront the risks to which it is susceptible. The communicative state itself thus becomes an actor in the civil debate, including ensuring the dissemination of specific information

But just how much public information is sufficient? And what method of diffusion will guarantee a peaceable society, serving both the prevention of risk and the avoidance of stereotypes?

---

[15] *Nolan and K. v. Russia*, ECtHR 2512/04 (2009).
[16] *Jehovah's Witnesses of Moscow and Others v. Russia*, ECtHR 302/02 (2010).
[17] Ibid.

At the outset, this issue is particularly intense when it comes to the consideration of cults, when various forms of vulnerability or mental manipulation are imputed to potential recipients of information. Interestingly, the question for debate is the *ambiguous condition of modern autonomy*.[18] Two visions of humanity are proposed and challenged: on one side, man has a weak conscience, is easily abused, which calls for his pragmatic protection by the civil community; on the other, man is deemed responsible and strong, self-assertive, wisely informed, and therefore is free to engage in the most diverse experiences, even free to waive certain fundamental rights.

Faced with this scientific and axiological confusion, the return to the autonomy of the individual seems to be a crucial concept. The European Court of Human Rights set forth a solemn reminder in its judgement of 10 June 2010, *Jehovah's Witnesses v. Russia*, that 'The ability to conduct one's life in a manner of one's own choosing includes the opportunity to pursue activities perceived to be of a physically harmful or dangerous nature for the individual concerned'. (§ 135) Likewise 'an interference may be justified [only] if the choices [of the group in question] are incompatible with the key principles underlying the Convention' (§ 119).[19]

The European framework could appear in many respects to be the 'laboratory' of a new rationality whose task is to precisely articulate the variety of traditions in the convergence required by the project of post-national democracy.

We already address the methods of *gathering information* that accompany the classical political state: on the one hand, the collection of information by monitoring and the vigilance associated with the repressive apparatus of the formal state, and on the other, collecting information as a condition of a physical or economic intervention of the welfare state.

It is also necessary to address the methods *of the control and diffusion of that information*: on the one hand, the positive obligation of the state to ensure an impartial freedom of expression to all stakeholders in the public debate held within civil society, and on the other hand, the specific features of the expressive state by which governments intervene to disseminate specific information within civil society. These various measures of public regulation of information flow obviously involve broader issues that do not limit themselves to the field of cults. It remains, however, that the regulation of information pertaining to cults remains closely tied to rights of freedom of religion, and to the specific jurisprudence which governs it, both in terms of non-discrimination and in terms of impartiality and state neutrality.

---

[18] Louis-Léon Christians et al. *Mouvements religieux contestés: Psychologie, droit et politiques de précaution* (Bruxelles: Gand, Academia Press, 2005), 216.

[19] *Jehovah's Witnesses of Moscow and Others v. Russia*, ECtHR 302/02 (2010). The position of the Court, however, becomes more complex when one sees the first examples of deviations against these 'key principles': polygamy, underage marriage, breach manifest by equality among groups (referring to the possibility of prohibiting the headscarf of students), or other 'choices' even if they are compelled by force or coercion (section 119).

Freedom of expression in the public debate

With regard to information policies, the role of the state is primarily to ensure freedom of expression horizontally to all members of civil society in public debate. Committed to this important guarantee of freedom of expression, the jurisprudence of the Court has not failed to capture the polemical nature of the debates about 'cults'. Religious freedom does not leave groups and beliefs immune to criticism. The largest latitude is granted to discussions that contribute to the public debate and are useful to the human condition. The Court notes several times: 'we must recognize that the issue of "cults" or "sects" is widely debated in European societies. This gives the evidence, as the Court has already noted ... a problem of general interest, which obliges a strict interpretation [of limitations that may be imposed on freedom of expression]'.[20] This means a high level of commentary should be permitted when it comes to the debates about cults. This approach is further reinforced by various remarks that the word 'cult' itself must be considered as a *value judgment* and not a judgment of fact.[21] Although the Court confirmed there has been a lack of objectivity in defining a 'cult', paradoxically, according to jurisprudential criteria, it suggests the concept should benefit from frequent usage, although there is no conclusive evidence that this is happening.

In accordance with its common law jurisprudence, the Court considers that special actors in public debate, including not just politicians but also victims' associations, should themselves indicate that they will not tolerate excessive criticism of the very groups that they denounce. The debate may become intemperate when carried on in public, but one should expect more professional treatment of the issues from specialized professional actors.

The decision *Paturel v. France* of 22 December 2005 provides an exemplary illustration. In limiting Mr Paturel's right to criticize a well-known victims' association, domestic courts had inferred bias and animosity towards Mr Paturel's membership in the Jehovah's Witnesses. It was as if his being a Jehovah's Witness depreciated his right to expression because he could not take part in an objective public debate about cults. It forces the question of whether the value of an argument can be linked to the life of its author. The Court's position was just the contrary. On the one hand, the biographical connection of argument and author could be read to oppose the European Convention, as noted in *Grand Orient of Italy and*

---

[20] *Paturel v. France*, ECtHR 54968/00 (2005), section 48, referring mutatis mutandis to *Riera Blume and Others v. Spain*, ECtHR 37680/97 (1999) –VII and Thoma, § 58.

[21] Ibid.; 'The materiality of the [statements of fact] may be proved, but [value judgments] do not lend themselves to demonstrate their accuracy. For value judgments, the obligation of proof is impossible to fulfil and infringes on freedom of opinion itself, the fundamental right guaranteed by Article 10[, though] a value judgment totally devoid of factual basis may be excessive.' *Jerusalem v. Austria*, ECtHR 26958/95 (2001), section 42, a case specifically related to a controversy about cults.

NF v. Italy, which condemned Italy for forcing Freemason judges and officials to disclose their membership. Even more importantly, according to the Court, if such membership or biographical information is disclosed, it cannot be used against a person to contradict his ideas or even to question his 'good faith'. The Court also observed that 'any reprimand [concerning biographies] could be equally directed at the plaintiff and the [victims' association] defendant, given its statutory purpose and activities, but also in the context of the heated debate which arises in the context of the litigation' (§ 45).[22]

Attempting a generalization, one could say that public debate can only be understood by incorporating each side's perspective. A kind of ratchet effect chills each stage that excludes participants. To avoid any bias and any attack on principle, suspected cults could therefore not be excluded from debates about cults, as seen in Recommendation 1412/1999. European jurisprudence only sets limits on extremes. The former European Commission restated this in its July 1980 decision in *Scientology v. Sweden*: 'Freedom of religion does not protect a particular creed or confession from all forms of criticism, unless it reaches such a level that it might endanger this freedom and the public authorities tolerate this behaviour'.[23]

In an important decision, *Raelian Movement v. Switzerland* of July 13, 2012, the Grand Chamber of the European Court of Human Rights showed that freedom of expression involving cults remains a complex issue. Regarding a religious movement's poster displayed in a government-owned area, the Chamber decided by a very slim majority (9 to 8) that a state had more leeway to restrict Raelian freedom of expression in government-controlled display areas than on private property. In reaching this conclusion, the Court noted two main arguments: first, it noted a weaker level of protection for speech intended to proselytize; second, it accepted the state had special responsibility where it was owner of the display area.

The Court found according to this first argument, that the Raelist poster merely referenced a website promoting the group, which sought mainly to draw public attention to the group's ideas and activities, its supposed religious connotations deriving from a message claimed to be transmitted by extra-terrestrials. The applicant association's website thus referred only incidentally to social or political ideas. The Court took the view that the type of speech in question was not political because the main aim of the website was to draw people to the cause of the applicant association and not to address matters of political debate in Switzerland. Even if

---

[22] *Grande Oriente d'Italia di Palazzo Giustiniani v. Italy*, ECtHR 35972/97 (2001).

[23] *Church of Scientology v. Sweden*, ECtHR 8282/78 (1980); see also *Universelles Leben e.V. v. Germany*, ECtHR 29745/96 (1996), citing *Kokkinakis v. Greece*, ECtHR 14307/88 (1993): 'A State may even legitimately consider it necessary to take measures aimed at repressing certain forms of conduct, including the imparting of information and ideas, judged incompatible with the respect for the freedom of thought, conscience and religion of others.'

the applicant association's speech falls outside the commercial advertising context – there was no inducement to buy a particular product – it was nevertheless closer to commercial speech than to political speech per se because of its proselytizing function. The State's margin of appreciation was therefore broad enough to impose the restriction.[24]

The second argument was based on the fact that no expression by the Raelian Movement was prohibited (website, leaflets in the street, etc.). Only the use of a public display area was denied, as otherwise one might be led to believe that the government indirectly approved the Raelian message. However, cloning, geniocracy and the sexual arousal of children – which were espoused by the Raelian movement – were contrary to Swiss public policy. Therefore,

> even though some of these reasons, taken separately, might not be capable of justifying the impugned refusal, the Court takes the view that the national authorities were reasonably entitled to consider, having regard to all the circumstances of the case, that it was indispensable to ban the campaign in question in order to protect health and morals, protect the rights of others and to prevent crime.[25]

The expressive state: the dissemination of information by the state

The European Court repeatedly emphasizes that, 'but for very exceptional cases, the right to freedom of religion as guaranteed under the Convention excludes any discretion on the part of the state to determine religious beliefs or the means used to express such beliefs are legitimate'.[26]

This area of absolute neutrality does not, however, affect the essence of the debate on cults, because the state generally comments not on doctrinal content, but on actual practices and the resulting likelihood of abuse. But between the absolute neutrality of the state towards the internal legitimacy of doctrines, and the almost absolute freedom of speech guaranteed to private actors in the public debate, how does one measure the extent of public authorities' right to speak? Is the state limited to strict obligations of neutrality and objectivity, or does the state itself enjoy the benefit of spontaneous freedom of speech?

The jurisprudence of the Court requires a fact-specific treatment of policies concerning public information about cults. The requirement of neutrality, formally seen as a bright line, can be modified by various weights of proportionality.

It should be noted first of all, regarding the theoretical qualification of groups, that the Court adopts a position of abstention not to benefit the beliefs held by the groups involved, but to benefit the nation-states. For example, the Court noted the

---

[24] *Mouvement Raelien Suisse v. Switzerland*, ECtHR 16354/06 (2012), section 62.
[25] Ibid., section 72. Eight dissident judges disagreed on this statement by the majority.
[26] *Obst v. Germany*, ECtHR 425/03 (2010), section 44.

controversial nature among member-states of the question of whether Scientology is a 'religion':

> In the absence of any European consensus on the religious nature of Scientology teachings, and being sensitive to the subsidiary nature of its role, the Court considers that it must rely on the position of the domestic authorities in the matter and determine the applicability of Article 9 of the Convention accordingly.[27]

The Court recognizes that states have a great ability to organize cult-awareness informational campaigns, either via state agencies or through publically-subsidized private associations.[28] In a decision dated November 27, 1996, *Universal Leben e.V. v. Germany*, evaluating the German-government brochure entitled 'Sogenannte Jugendsekten und Psycho-Gruppen in der Bundesrepublik Deutschland' (So-called Youth Sects and Psycho Groups in the Federal Republic of Germany), the former European Commission considered

> that a State, in fulfilling the functions assumed by it in the information of the public on matters of general concern, is entitled to convey, in an objective, but critical manner, information on religious communities and sects, if such information does not pursue aims of agitation or indoctrination endangering the freedom of religion.[29]

Exonerating Germany, the Commission held this publication had not created an arbitrary restriction on the applicants' religious freedom.

In the case *Keller v. Germany*, 4 March 1998, the former Commission examined a dossier warning against Scientology, produced by the education administration and directed at schools. It discovered, among other extracts, a cartoon ending with 'Scientology, No!' and various pejorative descriptions of the

---

[27] *Kimlya et al v. Russia*, ECtHR 76836/01 (2009) section 79, citing *Church of Scientology Moscow v. Russia*, ECtHR 18147/02 (2007), section 64.

[28] 'Given that assumption that the state cannot be held responsible for all actions taken by the associations which, given their status, it has granted the status of a public utility. The granting of this utility does not imply in any way a conversion into the public sphere, which only could implicate the state in respect of compliance with the Convention', *Gluchowski v. France*, ECtHR 44789/98 (1999).

[29] *Universelles Leben e.V. v. Germany*, ECtHR 29745/96 (1996); this objectivity is itself multidimensional. It is necessary but perhaps not sufficient to establish by reference to open scientific sources. The introduction of an adversarial documentary procedure was raised by Recommendation 1412/1999. Finally, the state administration can use its own experience and original resource expertise. On these points, for a Belgian criminological point of view, see Benjamine Mine, 'La régulation du 'phénomène sectaire' en Belgique: une mise à l'épreuve des hypothèses relatives aux transformations de la gouvernementalité dans les sociétés occidentales contemporaines', *Annales de droit de Louvain* (ADL) 2 (2009): 101–93.

movement. The Commission rejected the applicants' petition because no causal link was sufficiently established between the brochure and the negative attitudes of the neighbourhood and the local press towards the applicants.[30]

The Court reinforced this line of reasoning in a decision of 6 November 2001, *Jehovah's Witnesses against France* – a case involving two reports of 'parliamentary commissions of inquiry'. According to the applicant, although the reports of parliamentary commissions are, in principle, simple background documents that should have no legal effect, this was not the case regarding the Parliamentary Commission of 1995 (also called the Gest-Guyard report) and the Guyard-Brard report of 1999. The applicant exhibited itself as the subject of a series of administrative refusals and hostile attitudes: 'The official status of "cult" alone provided the brand and the stigma that justify the surveillance of the police and other authorities in the areas of law enforcement, society, tax and customs'.[31] Again, the Court's conclusion was based on the weak causal link between the parliamentary report and the administrative hostility: 'Even when reference is made, this reference is a simple dictum, which cannot in any circumstances be regarded as the ratio legis of the measure'.[32] Causation was denied *de jure*, even though the Court recognized *de facto* that parliamentary reports have been used by the government.

In a decision of 6 November 2008, *Leela Förderkreis e.v. v. Germany*,[33] the Court commented on preventive measures, namely informational brochures, concluding that they were 'consistent with [the state's] positive obligations under Article 1 of the Convention to secure the rights and freedoms of persons within their jurisdiction' (§ 99).[34] In this case, the Court also engaged in a thorough review of the state's informational campaign and the use of different pejorative names, contested by three associations of the Bhagwan movement. After years of national court cases, the German Constitutional Court had ordered the state to remove the terms 'destructive', 'pseudo-religious', and 'manipulating their members' from its official descriptions of Bhagwan associations. However, other expressions – 'cult', 'new religious movement', and 'psycho-cult', which the applicants had also petitioned the European Court to prohibit – were allowed to remain. The Court held that these terms do not violate the direct practice of religion, although it

---

[30] *Keller v. Germany*, ECtHR 36283/97 (1998).

[31] *The Christian Federation of Jehovah's Witnesses in France v. France*, ECtHR 53430/99 (2001).

[32] Ibid.

[33] *Leela Förderkreis E.v. and Others v. Germany*, ECtHR 58911/00 (2008); See also Gérard Gonzalez, 'Haro sur les 'sectes' mais ... pas trop!', *Revue trimestrielle des droits de l'homme* (2009): 553–68.

[34] It justified these information campaigns explaining that 'these obligations are not only related to interference, which could result from acts or omissions by state agents or occurring in public institutions, but also the interference caused to individuals within non-state institutions'.

acknowledged the possibility of *negative consequences* for the applicants, *without being able to immediately determine their nature and scope.*

For the Court, the goal of the government was to provide information that would contribute to a democratic debate in society on a matter of public interest and to draw attention to the dangers posed by groups commonly referred to as cults. Though this duty might, if pursued overzealously, infringe upon the rights of religious minorities, the court found that drawing a bright line to delineate appropriate and inappropriate state action would be impractical, and it was sufficient that the state's language be neutral even if it ended up negatively impacting the minority.[35]

The essence of the Court's argument in *Förderkreis* seems to emphasize the historical context of the case – namely that while the state's approach might not be appropriate today, at the time it was reasonable. The Court emphasized the highly sensitive nature of these questions *at the time of the facts* (§ 98). It also noted that the alleged terms, even if they had pejorative connotations, were at that time commonly applied almost indiscriminately to all non-traditional religious movements (100). The Court finally observed that since that time, and especially since the German parliamentary report of 1998, the Government had clearly refrained from using the term 'cult', and concluded that the disputed use of vocabulary did not (at least at the time when it was in use) exceed the limits of what a democratic state could be considered justified in using for the public interest.

This obviously raises the question of whether the Court suggests, since 2002, that advances in scientific knowledge regarding disputed religious groups and the evolution of public policy in this area have led to a stricter stance by the Court towards public information campaigns conducted today.

Conclusion

The European Court of Human Rights' jurisprudence has developed a pragmatic and balanced body of case law on the delicate issue of 'cults' following Recommendation 1412 (1999) of the Parliamentary Assembly of the Council of Europe.

Regulation of state public policies concerning information on religious minorities gives rise to complex legal issues. At first glance, any state that

---

[35] See paras. 89 and 90. Note that the literature has identified various counter-productive effects resulting from too formal controls, such as the 'objectivity' of scientific information underlying public policies. See, for example, Stephen M. Johnson, 'Junking the 'Junk Science' Law: Reforming the Information Quality Act', *Administrative Law Review* 58 (2006); Stephen M. Johnson 'Ruminations on Dissemination: Limits on Administrative and Judicial Review under the Information Quality Act', *Catholic University Law Review* 55 (2005–2006).

intervenes in the public debate seems to be subjecting itself to exceptionally high standards. It does not benefit in any case from the same freedoms as other stakeholders, and it is bound by stricter obligations, especially those of neutrality and objectivity. On the other hand, when information disseminated has actual negative consequences for religious minorities, the Court's demands on the state seem to be quite lenient. Fairly often, failure to provide proof of a causal link between the state's information and the disturbances of these groups' exercise of their freedom of religion allows the state to escape censure – and such proof has proven elusive.

Finally, in deciding cases that deal with information spread by states about religious minorities, the Court itself becomes an actor in the dissemination of this information. It necessarily contributes information, both normative and factual, that circulates through the whole of European society and contributes to its policy on cult issues.

Chapter 8
The French System against Sectarian Deviations

Hervé Machi

For nearly 25 years, the French state has strongly affirmed its will to protect victims from the deviant behaviour of sectarian movements. State action has been developed, step-by-step, as the result of parliamentary reports and the gradual development of various forms of organizations established by successive, democratically elected prime ministers, to combat the problems that might arise.

There is no legal definition of what constitutes a sect in French law, no more so than a definition of religion, whatever it is, old or new, minor or major. This is partly the result of the fact that, in virtue of its laic principles since the French Revolution, France has refused to define or to limit religious and spiritual phenomena, thereby avoiding the risk of infringing upon the absolute principle of freedom of belief.

I think it is appropriate to quote fundamental laws of France. So, I propose to go back more than 200 years, to focus on two articles of the *Declaration des droits de l'homme et du citoyen* (*Declaration of the Rights of Man and of the Citizen*), dated 1789. The first one is article X, which states: 'No one shall be disquieted on account of his opinions, including his religious views, provided their manifestation does not disturb the public order established by law.' The second is article XI, which states: 'The free communication of ideas and opinions is one of the most precious of the rights of man. Every citizen may, accordingly, speak, write, and print with freedom, but shall be responsible for such abuses of this freedom as shall be defined by law.' The *Declaration des droits de l'homme et du citoyen* is included in the Constitution of the Fifth Republic, established on 4 October 1958, Article 1 of which states, 'France shall be an indivisible, secular, democratic and social Republic … . It shall respect all beliefs'.

The Inter-ministerial Commission on Sects (MIVILUDES's predecessor) agreed as early as 1997 that 'it would not be facilitating the government's actions against aberrations of this nature, if it [the government] attempted to define and finalize a notion, whose very definition is in a constant state of evolution and is largely uncontrollable, in a text which would necessarily be limited, disregarding the legal and constitutional obstacles which this task would face'. It is relevant, more than 10 years later, to acknowledge the rightness of this statement: today, sectarian deviations have a greater presence in the fields of health, alternative therapies and personal development than they have within spiritual and religious contexts.

The lack of definition of 'sect' in no way detracts from the reality of the existence of the victims of the aberrations of certain sectarian movements, however. The notion of sectarian deviations is constantly evolving and the French approach is both pragmatic and supported by legal texts. In the absence of a legal definition of what constitutes a sect, the law represses any actions, in the specific context of mental control, that infringe upon human rights and fundamental freedoms which represent a threat to public order or which are against French laws and regulations.

In certain countries, activity in this field almost exclusively concerns the private sector. In France, there are numerous associations whose function is to aid victims and their families, but all political, legislative and executive leaders, whatever their parties, have judged that the government cannot escape its responsibilities and duties in regard to this matter. This is why the task of state institutions to struggle against sectarian deviations in all its forms is effectuated at different levels. The task of administrative executives is to implement adequate monitoring and prevention provisions. For example, the function of social workers is to identify dangers and to aid victims.

As for MIVILUDES – the Inter-ministerial Mission for Monitoring and Struggling Against Sectarian Deviations – it coordinates all the provisions implemented by the government at local, regional and ministerial levels, it provides information for the public and training for government officials, and it analyzes the evolution of the phenomenon on behalf of the prime minister. Since 28 November 2002, MIVILUDES, as indicated by its name, fulfils both a mission of vigilance – I mean the prevention and detection of potential sectarian risk – and a mission of struggle against recognized aberrations.

Lastly, the task of the judiciary, the guardian of freedoms, is to provide protection against all forms of physical or psychological subjection, and to continue in the tradition of respect for the law, from which no government, and no citizen, must be exempt.

This concerted and pragmatic government function, in the absence of any specific incrimination, exercises a dual protective role:

1. ensuring the freedom of belief
2. ensuring individual freedoms, especially those of the weak (that is, children, and, since 2001, people in a state of subjugation).

As a matter of principle, no judgement is made about the value or the sincerity of an ideological or spiritual commitment. This aside, however, not everything is allowed in the name of freedom of belief or religion, and it is the responsibility of the judge to provide reminders of those lines that cannot be crossed, either of an administrative or legal nature, and at a national or European level, with the European Court of Human Rights.

Let me provide some examples of judgements by civil or criminal jurisdictions that allow us to illustrate more precisely the concept of sectarian deviations. So far as the judgements of civil jurisdictions are concerned, this includes the conduct of individual members of sectarian movements, as well as individual conduct by itself (that is, not merely because of the fact that the individual belongs to such a movement) that can result in unfavourable judgements.

Belonging to a sectarian movement does not in itself constitute sufficient grounds for divorce, for example. It is only when the behaviour of one spouse deeply disrupts the life of the couple that the Family Tribunal Judge can deem that behaviour as a fault which makes the continuation of the relationship intolerable and thus award a divorce on these grounds.

The overzealous implementation of the movement's doctrine, whether it is of a religious or other nature, such as proselytizing, a demonstrable lack of concern about family and friends, violence and restrictions, are all gravely detrimental to family life, and as such are deemed incompatible with the continuation of family ties.

Similarly, if only one of the two parents belongs to a sectarian movement, this in itself does not constitute grounds for an unfavourable verdict against him or her with regards to the determination of the custody, visiting and access rights. It is the consequences of these choices and not the choices themselves which are subject to criticism when the child's stability is at risk. In the event of separation, if the practices of a parent have a strong potential to physically or psychologically traumatize the children, the Family Tribunal Judge can decide to award custody to the other parent and/or restrict visiting and access rights. For example, the Grenoble Court of Appeal reconfirmed the principle of religious freedom for a father and his daughter, subject to an opening of access to and participation in social networks.

Juvenile Court Judges are called upon when the health, safety or moral integrity of a minor is at risk, or when the conditions of his or her education, physical, emotional, intellectual or social development are greatly endangered. In this context, the magistrate can decide to implement educational provisions, such as the placement of the minor, or to provide educational monitoring within the family home.

According to articles 375 and subsequent provisions of the Civil Code, in addition to the deprivation of care and food, and cases of physical or sexual violence encountered in any groups, the parents' decision for their children to live in a 'closed world', where they are neither properly educated nor given any serious teaching at all, equally gives immediate cause for the public prosecutor to be informed and for the appropriate state representative to engage in legal proceedings. For example, in a verdict delivered in February 2000, the Court of Cassation confirmed a previous judgement which had ordered a mother to keep her children away from any members of her group, with the exception of herself and her partner, and to refrain from leaving French soil without written consent from the children's father. According to the Court of Cassation, the debated verdict did not directly infringe on many rights and freedoms, it merely subjected their exercise to certain conditions, purely for the wellbeing of the children.

The infraction of the French Common Law can often occur because the victim has already been psychologically broken down by the manipulation and by the psychological potency of a group or a person. Manipulation or psychological potency is the precursor to criminal action. The Common Law applies to a specific field characterized by constraint. The following offences are those which are the most frequently observed:

- Self-proclaimed therapeutic or healing groups expose themselves to breaches of the Public Health Code, particularly by practising medicine or providing pharmaceuticals illegally, which, in a worst-case scenario, can lead to manslaughter;
- Cases of destruction of property, fraud, abuse of trust, or deception with regards to substance, or false advertising are regularly reported in relation to certain movements offering personal development services;
- Personal attacks, physical violence, sexual abuse, the non-rendering of assistance to persons in danger and deprivation of care or food with respect to minors are most often observed among communities which withdraw into themselves and are resolutely cut off from the outside world;
- Infractions concerning educational obligations require special attention: these include charges against parents and directors of private institutions who have failed to fulfil their obligations regarding children; and
- The matter of failing to report crimes deserves particular attention as certain groups take this attitude with respect to the law and the justice system: by keeping quiet about any internal affairs which could have a negative impact on the group, the movements manipulate the system as often as possible to their own ends.

In 2001, Parliamentary officials voted to pass an amendment to the Law on the Exploitation of a State of Weakness, adding the state of subjection to the scope of this Law.[1] This 'About-Picard Law' (12 June 2001), aiming to prevent and suppress movements infringing on human rights and fundamental freedoms, is a general text which does not target sectarian movements as such (the expression is not included in the law). It applies to all legal and *de facto* legal persons. The new article 223–15–2 of the Penal Code condemns the fraudulent abuse of ignorance or weakness in minors or particularly vulnerable people (as a result of age, sickness or disability). It now also protects people subject to psychological or physical subjection, resulting from the strong or repeated application of pressure, or from the application of techniques aiming to alter their judgement and lead people to commit acts or abstain from acts which could have serious negative consequences for themselves.

---

[1] The full title of the law reads *Loi n° 2001-504 du 12 juin 2001 tendant à renforcer la prévention et la répression des mouvements sectaires portant atteinte aux Droits de l'Homme et aux libertés fondamentales* ('Law number 2001-504 of 12 June 2001 intended to reinforce the prevention and repression of sectarian [cultic] movements that infringe on human rights and on fundamental freedoms'.)

This, then, is a short description of the French state's system for monitoring and struggling against sectarian deviations. MIVILUDES has, further, provided some other recent legal or administrative advances, including the creation of a specific police force responsible for the handling of aberrant behaviour by sectarian movements (the CAIMADES), the legal regulation of the status of 'psychotherapists', and the provision of a better legal framework for all professional training centres.

Let me end with the results of a poll conducted in September 2010:

- For 66 per cent of the French people, sectarian movements are seen as a threat to democracy, and for 30 per cent, a threat to themselves;
- Twenty-five per cent of the French people have had some kind of contact with sectarian movements (which represents 15 million French people);
- Twenty per cent of the French people have close relatives who have been victims of sectarian deviations;
- Thirty-nine per cent of the French people consider that the French Government does what is necessary to struggle against sectarian deviations; for 44 per cent of them, the state response is not sufficient.

It would seem these figures totally justify the government function in this field.

Chapter 9
The French 'War on Cults' Revisited: Three Remarks on an On-going Controversy

Etienne Ollion

When it comes to human rights, few can claim as much experience as Asma Jahangir. Her father was a political dissident who spent years in Pakistani jails, and she was herself briefly imprisoned in 2007 for persistently criticizing President Pervez Musharraf's regime. As a Special Rapporteur on Freedom of Religion or Belief for the United Nations from 2004 to 2010, she repeatedly dealt with cases of persecution – even aggravated torture – across the world. It was consequently hard to ignore her remarks about France's policy regarding *sectes* ('cults')[1] when, in the opening paragraphs of a report, she expressly noted that:

> the Special Rapporteur considers that the policy of the Government may have contributed to a climate of general suspicion and intolerance towards the communities included in a list established further to a parliamentary report, and has negatively affected the right to freedom of religion or belief of some members of these communities or groups.[2]

Taking stock of the French legal and administrative provisions against so-called 'cults', the Special Rapporteur dedicated a large section of her report to this specific question before issuing a series of recommendations urging the French government to put an end to the 'undue limitation' of the 'right to freedom of religion or belief of members of these groups'.[3]

Jahangir's report was one of the many reactions that followed France's rapid organization of an extensive, state-sponsored policy of surveillance of minority groups labelled cults. By all standards, this regulatory attempt was unique among

---

[1] While it should appear clearly in the rest of the text, a remark is in order here. The use of the term cult without quotes does not mean that I endorse any of its multiple (and often contradictory) meanings. Rather than taking part in the struggle over the word's use, I am intent on studying it.

[2] Asma Jahangir, 'Civil and Political Rights, Including the Question of Religious Intolerance' (report, Special Rapporteur on Freedom of Religion or Belief, United Nations, Economic and Social Council, Commission on Human Rights, 2006), http://www.unhcr.org/refworld/publisher,UNCHR,,,441181fe0,0.html.

[3] Ibid., § 108.

democratic countries across the world. In 1995, an official report written by national representatives singled out a list of 173 'dangerous cults'. Just a few months later, a state agency was established specifically to coordinate similar efforts across all sectors of the administration. And within a few years, a series of laws were passed or modified to cope with what was now seen as a critical public issue. The most important law was a piece of legislation, unanimously adopted in 2001, explicitly aimed at curtailing 'mental manipulations'. The language of this policy, which received broad public support, bore witness to France's international singularity: only in France would a policy against cults receive a specific and widely used name: *la lutte contre les sectes* (which could translate as the 'War on Cults').

In a noticeable mirror effect, the anti-cult policy was as criticized abroad as it was lauded in France. It gave way to many a debate, pitting two clear-cut sides against one other. For proponents of strong state intervention, the French position was a determinate attempt to limit the influence of groups detrimental to personal and public liberties – a welcome intercession in the activities of pernicious entities. If anything, the argument went, the law should be reinforced to finally outlaw the most dangerous so-called cults. In contrast, these groups and their supporters relentlessly denounced what they saw as a vicious attack on religious freedom. Foes of the French 'War on Cults' decried the mounting discrimination the targeted groups were facing, and broadly called for greater tolerance. In their views, cults were not manipulative groups posing an immediate threat to society, but rather religious minorities stifled by an oppressive government.

The French debates closely resembled those that took place in all countries where these groups tried to establish themselves,[4] only with different timing, greater intensity and extended duration. While most cult controversies had taken place in the 1970s and early 1980s,[5] the French debate reached a peak in the early 2000s, as legislative activism was at its height. The debates regularly made the headlines of the national press, which – in a characteristic instance of French public and academic discussions dovetailing – called upon experts to weigh in on the controversy. No consensus was reached among specialists, and the debate remained polarized, mostly dividing between disciplinary boundaries. Anti-cult activists largely resorted to psychologists to back up their theory of cultic mind control, while the cult groups and their allies largely drew on social scientists to call into question what they saw as state-supported regulation of the religious sphere – some going so far as to call it a state-led Second Inquisition.

---

[4] For an early account of these controversies, see James A. Beckford, *Cult Controversies: The Societal Response to New Religious Movements* (London: Tavistock, 1985). For an overview of the debates, see Benjamin D. Zablocki and Thomas Robbins, *Misunderstanding Cults: Searching for Objectivity in a Controversial Field* (Toronto: University of Toronto Press, 2001).

[5] Notable exceptions include the tragedies of Waco's massacre and Tokyo's subway attacks, both of which occurred in the mid-1990s.

Rather than taking part directly in this on-going controversy, this chapter attempts to shed new light on some key aspects of the French 'War on Cults'.[6] Three aspects are studied in sequence: the intensity of the French response to cults; the question of whether cults and religions can be distinguished; and the impact of the state's intervention on the so-called cults themselves.

This intellectual detour is not so much meant to avoid the question as to sidestep some difficulties in which the classical approaches are steeped. Having discussed these three questions, I will then try to draw general conclusions from the aforementioned results.

The intensity of the policy

Since its inception, French anti-cult policy – and more generally the climate of suspicion surrounding groups labelled as cults – has been seen as singular. In a rare instance of consensus in this otherwise highly contentious field, both proponents and adversaries of state intervention have acknowledged – in praise or criticism – this national specificity. Two aspects of French anti-cult policy merit special attention: the extent of the measures taken, and the velocity of the response. Both set France apart among democratic countries.

An extended policy of surveillance

The most visible – and certainly the most frequently cited – element of governmental engagement in this domain is the French governmental agency in charge of coordinating public action against cults, now known as MIVILUDES.[7] First established in 1996, the agency was placed under the direct authority of the Prime Minister, a position that enabled its officials to request the help of all sectors of government. Through its various iterations over the years, the agency's practices have remained largely the same. MIVILUDES coordinates public action in areas including justice, education, health, sports, youth programmes, and homeland

---

[6] Unless mentioned otherwise, the material presented here is part of a recent research conducted amongst both proponents and foes of the French 'War on Cults'. For details, see Étienne Ollion, 'La secte sécularisée: Contribution à l'étude des processus de requalification conceptuels', *Genèses* 78 (2010): 25–47.

[7] The agency's name has changed several times. The first central state agency, created in January 1996, was called the *Observatoire de Lutte contre les sectes* (OLS, or 'Observatory to Fight Cults'). It was promptly replaced by a larger agency with extended powers, called *Mission Interministérielle de Lutte contre les Sectes* (MILS, or 'Inter-ministerial Agency to Fight Cults'). Following a change of political majority and some heated controversies between France and other countries on the topic, in 2002 the agency was renamed *Mission Interministérielle de Lutte contre les sectes*, or MIVILUDES (Inter-ministerial Agency to Monitor and Fight against Cultic Deviances). Despite the slight moderation the name seems to indicate, MIVILUDES has overall enforced the same policies as its predecessors.

security, just to name a few. Each area has a person (or more often a bureau) in charge of orchestrating public action, whether local or national in nature. MIVILUDES' widely advertised and multifaceted prevention initiative includes, among other things, anti-cult education at schools and in civil service training, with the main goal of raising awareness of the 'cult phenomenon'. MIVILUDES' action has been met with wide public support: at the beginning of 2000 an opinion poll showed that two-thirds of French people regarded cults as a major threat for 'democracy, their relatives, or for themselves'. Eighty-six per cent declared their support for measures that would prohibit some cults altogether.[8]

This massive and wide-ranging public support, both material and symbolic, differentiates France from any other democracy in the world. In the United States, the only attempts to pass anti-cult legislation (to say nothing of establishing an anti-cult agency) happened at the state level. None successfully gathered widespread support, and all were virtually forgotten by the early 1980s.[9] Most European countries reacted similarly, and despite the concerted efforts of a few grassroots anti-cult organizations, public authorities in most of Europe have taken little action against cults.[10] In Great Britain for instance, more public backing (namely, subsidies) has gone to the Information Network Focus on Religious Movements (INFORM, a charity founded by sociologist of religion Eileen Barker to provide neutral and objective information on 'new religious movements') than has gone to anti-cult organizations. Even in countries where the anti-cult movement has gained some momentum, the overall response was never as intense as in France. In Germany, most concern was focused on a single group (Scientology), while the action of Belgium's and Switzerland's specific public agencies (similar to France's in their design) has also remained limited.

No less remarkable – albeit more limited than the administrative regulations – have been the adaptations within the legislative sphere of this general surveillance. One law was explicitly conceived to severely limit the practices of cults: the About-Picard act,[11] passed in June 2001 as a tool to 'reinforce both prevention and repression of cults', defined as movements that 'posed a threat to Human Rights and to Fundamental Freedoms'. Although the final version, the result of protracted

---

[8] Opinion poll conducted in February 2000 and published in *La vie*, edition du 8 février 2000.

[9] For an overview of the opposition to cults in the USA, see David G. Bromley and Anson D. Shupe, *Strange Gods: the Great American Cult Scare* (Boston: Beacon Press, 1981); and David G. Bromley and Anson D. Shupe, 'Anti-cultism in the United States: Origins, Ideology and Organizational Development', *Social Compass* 42 (1995): 222–336.

[10] For an up-to-date and comprehensive overview of the situation in different countries, see Philipp C. Lucas and Thomas Robbins, *New Religious Movements in the Twenty-first Century: Legal, Political, and Social Challenges in Global Perspective* (London: Routledge Press, 2004).

[11] Named after the two representatives who presented it. The former was the head of the Parliamentary Commission on Cults, a newly created (1996) but quite active commission within the National Assembly.

debates between governmental bodies,[12] did not expressly mention 'cults', the text was clearly a response to the practices of these groups, and was presented as such. Its main provision holds that any organization that has been found guilty of certain misdemeanours twice could be disbanded and prevented from officially reorganizing.

Any summary of French anti-cult policy would be incomplete without mentioning one last element that both deepens and broadens what can be rightfully seen as a 'dispositive of surveillance', namely the broad public support enjoyed by non-governmental anti-cult organizations. The two main anti-cult organizations, UNADFI and CCMM,[13] have already received important public funding (over 350,000 Euros a year each after 2000). They were also granted official recognition in the mid-1990s – a legal provision that brought them both increased economic resources and greater public legitimacy. In that sense, the situation in France at the close of the twentieth century could rightfully be called 'exceptional'.[14]

The rapid establishment of the policy

The extent and depth of the anti-cult policy in France tend to conceal an interesting fact upon which neither its proponents (who try to emphasize the precocity of the action) nor its analysts and critics (who focus on its exceptionality) have really commented: the remarkable swiftness of its development. In fact, a close investigation of French cult policies over the last four decades reveals an important but understudied fact: rather than evolving slowly as a progressive creation, the current dispositive was established abruptly, and in a rather unforeseeable way.

Everywhere in the world, when anti-cult organizations were founded, their demands were met with some diffidence.[15] France in the 1970s was no different: in a rapidly changing society whose socio-religious scene was undergoing swift transformations,[16] cults were originally seen neither as problematic, nor really different from the numerous social experiments that were blossoming in those

---

[12] Patrice Rolland, 'La loi du 12 janvier 2001 contre les mouvements sectaires portant atteinte aux droits de l'Homme: Anatomie d'un débat législatif', *Archives de Sciences Sociales des Religions* 212, (2003): 149–66.

[13] The UNADFI [*Union Nationale des Associations de Défense de la Famille et de l'Individu*] is an umbrella organization coordinating grassroots chapters of the ADFI at the national level. The first ADFI chapter was established in 1974, and there are currently 28 chapters in all. The CCMM (*Centre Contre les Manipulations Mentales*), created by popular, award-winning author Roger Ikor after the cult-related death of his youngest son, was incorporated in 1982.

[14] Nathalie Luca, 'Quelles politiques pour les sectes? La spécificité française face à l'Europe occidentale', *Critique internationale* 17 (2002): 105–25.

[15] Beckford, *Cult Controversies*.

[16] See Danièle Hervieu-Léger, *Le pèlerin et le converti: la religion en mouvement* (Paris: Flammarion, 1999); and Denis Pelletier, *La crise catholique: Religion, société, politique en France (1965–1978)* (2002; repr., Paris: Petite bibliothèque Payot, 2005).

years.[17] An anecdote demonstrates this well: when early anti-cult ADFI volunteers had their first meeting with public officials in 1976, the interlocutor granted their request to commission psychiatrists – but to their greatest dismay he meant their services to be a help for parents to accept their children's involvement in cults, rather than as a countermeasure against brainwashing. Meanwhile, all through the late 1970s, various leaders of the then centre-right ruling coalition gave lengthy interviews in the journal of the controversial Unification Church.[18] Unsurprisingly, demands for public action against cults went largely unheeded.

This situation would continue for most of the following decade. State interventions were not non-existent, but remained limited and occasional at most, usually taking place in the immediate aftermath of highly publicized events relating to cults. For instance, the first Parliamentary investigation on cults in France followed the Guyana Massacre of November 1978, and the second – as well as the first public official document on the topic, the Vivien Report[19] – followed a failed attempt at deprogramming a 'Moonie' by her parents.[20] The Vivien report of 1983, often described as a turning point in the intervention of public authorities with cult activities, was actually not published until two years after its completion due to disagreements about its relevance among top government officials,[21] and was not followed by any measure for another 10 years. Actually, it was nothing more than a one-off action; its tone and recommendations appear moderate in light of subsequent texts.

But France's relatively indifferent approach to cults was to change abruptly in December 1995, following an unlikely combination of circumstances which saw a parliamentary report[22] on cults released on the eve of a mass murder-suicide in Switzerland by devotees of a mystical group called the *Ordre du Temple Solaire* ('Order of the Solar Temple'), or OTS. The media broadly covered the tragedy, partially because it took place during the holiday season, which is relatively low on front-page news. The unusual circumstances of the event also contributed to its popularity: after several hours of a widely publicized search, the adherents'

---

[17] Analyses of the media show that they were not separated from broader phenomena like communes and other types of social experiments. On communes in France, see Bernard Lacroix, *L'utopie communautaire: Histoire sociale d'une révolte* (1981; repr., Paris: PUF, 2006). On the analysis of the media, see Étienne Ollion, 'Les sectes mises en causes: Sociologie politique de la 'lutte contre les sectes' en France (1970–2010)' (PhD diss., CSO, 2012), 570.

[18] See the 'Interview' section in the monthly editions of *Le Nouvel Espoir* from 1976 onwards.

[19] Alain Vivien, *Les sectes en France: Expressions de la liberté morale ou facteurs de manipulations?* (Report to the Prime Minister, 1985).

[20] Commission Marchand (1978) and Commission Ravail (1980–1982).

[21] Alain Vivien, in discussion with the author, 7 November 2007.

[22] Alain Gest and Jacques Guyard, *Les sectes en France*, Parliamentary Report No. 2468 (1996).

charred bodies were finally discovered in a remote mountain clearing arranged in a star-like pattern.

What made the OTS tragedy a political turning point in France was not its sensational character, but its occurrence immediately following the release of the parliamentary report on cults. The collision of these two events gave way to an unprecedented and long-lasting media frenzy, with journalists' and politicians' interests coinciding to produce a large-scale media phenomenon of immense public interest. While journalists avidly looking for material welcomed the report as a resource, the national representatives who had sat on the Parliamentary Commission on cults saw this as an opportunity to publicize it – and themselves. The focus of both the media and the political spheres combined to their mutual reinforcement, putting the question of cults squarely at the centre of the country's attention.

The OTS incident remained a front-page story for weeks, forcing the government to act swiftly and decisively. While many had expressed doubts about the relevance of cults when the Commission began to work,[23] now its members were thrust into the limelight, giving countless press briefings and interviews. And whereas no real public measures against cults had been taken in the previous 10 years, an entire intergovernmental agency was established within four months after the tragedy, along with other official anti-cult positions within the administration. Even more remarkable was the new recognition and support given to anti-cult organizations that had hitherto been mostly distrusted or ignored – an indication of the radical reversal of the French administration's posture toward cults. For years before the incident, UNADFI, the leading anti-cult group, had requested official public interest status (*reconnaissance d'utilité publique*) from the government, which would grant it specific sources of funding and would legitimate its action in the eyes of many partners. The administration, on the recommendation of the Homeland Ministry, had repeatedly denied this request, the last refusal coming in August 1995.[24] Within months after the tragedy, however, UNADFI was officially recognized as a public interest group. Its public funding increased exponentially soon thereafter.

This unprecedented, enduring attention dedicated to cults after December 1995 led to the previously un-planned and un-imagined institutionalization of the anti-cult cause, which few could have predicted even months before its occurrence. Keeping in mind that the intervention of public authorities in France is as extensive as it is recent, let us now turn to another highly disputed issue: the controversial question of the difference – if any – between 'cult' and 'religion'.

---

[23] Jacques Guyard, in discussion with the author, 29 January 2008.
[24] Archives of the French Administration, Ministère de l'Intérieur 'Article 8, Dossier Associations Antisectes' (Centre des Archives Contemporaines, 1997–0154).

Cults vs religions in France

The intensity of France's anti-cult policy generated many a discussion. Observers were quick to draw a direct line between French socio-religious tradition and this policy, many pointing to the historically complex relationship France has with religion and analizing the situation as a more or less direct consequence of French *laïcité*.[25]

Central to these debates is the question of the religious nature of cults – a heated topic of debate worldwide since the beginning of the secular anti-cult movement. Emphasising the mind control techniques cults allegedly impose upon their followers, anti-cult groups categorically reject cults' religiosity. Cults, they insist, only claim to be religions in order to conceal the undue manipulation they impose on their followers, and to benefit from the protection such a status affords. Conversely, adherents and supporters of these movements claim they are unfairly discriminated against as 'religious minorities' or 'new religious movements'.

A close-up on the French case invites us to recast this debate. A quite remarkable – although rarely noticed – fact is that not all groups labelled as 'cults' in France nowadays have to do with religion. Along with those whose religiosity is contested (for example, Jehovah's Witnesses, Scientology, Soka Gakkaï, etc.), a large number of entities targeted by the French government under this policy are actually undeniably located outside of the religious field (for example, psychotherapists, alternative schools, paramilitary groups, etc.). Such groups do not claim to be religious at all. This present section highlights some elements that account for this secularization of anti-cult targets.

French secular anti-cult organizations, like those of many other countries, have claimed from the beginning that they are in no way anti-religious, that they dutifully respect freedom of religion, and that the groups they target cannot be accurately defined as religious. Evidence of this, they say, can be found in their definition of 'cult'. Instead of the original sense once promoted by a dominant religion (in this case, the Roman Catholic Church), which emphasizes religious differences (scriptures, practices, etc.), anti-cult organizations favour a new definition focused on the 'mental manipulation' cults purportedly use to control their followers. Drawing upon brainwashing theories first developed to account for rapid behavioural changes in U.S. prisoners of war,[26] they developed a new framework for thinking about cults: less than theology, this new approach emphasized psychology. In this sense, 'cultic behaviour' can be found equally both inside and outside of the religious sphere; cults are thus not necessarily religious groups.

---

[25] The term refers to the specific place given to religion within the public sphere in contemporary France. On laïcité, see Patrick Weil, *Politiques de la laïcité au XXe siècle* (Paris: Presses Universitaires de France, 2007).

[26] Dick Anthony and Massimo Introvigne, *Le lavage de cerveau, mythe ou réalité* (Paris: L'Harmattan, 2006).

This redefinition of cults was attempted in virtually every country. It had even been one of the major initiatives of the secular anti-cult movement of the 1970s. More aligned with the experiences of anti-cult volunteers – often family members of cult followers – this meaning was also more likely to garner external support for their cause. By presenting cults as groups where mind coercion enables all sorts of human rights violations, the anti-cult movement became a potentially quasi-universal cause in rapidly secularizing societies. This would have been impossible if cults were popularly thought of as religions.

Nowhere has this semantic subversion been so successful as in France.[27] Less than ten years after the creation of the first secular anti-cult organizations, most of France – experts, journalists, public officials and laypersons – subscribes to the new, psychological definition of 'cult'. This transformation had a significant impact on the movement. For one thing, it ensured a larger audience and greater support for the anti-cult movement. Long seen as a religious affair only, the fight against cults – reframed as a secular battle for human rights – became a potential cause not just for concerned relatives and religious authorities, but for every citizen. This is especially true of public officials. Whereas before the late 1970s officials and politicians were, in the words of Parliamentary Representative Alain Vivien, 'interested [in the topic], but reluctant to intervene in what were seen so far as religious affairs',[28] they became directly involved around the time the secular definition came into use.

This redefinition had another consequence, for the groups targeted also shifted somewhat along with the word's definition. The secularization of the meaning of 'cult' opened the way for the incrimination of groups unambiguously located outside of the religious sphere.[29] Deep ecology and paramilitary groups, commercial companies accused of scamming their customers, and a wealth of unlicensed psychologists joined followers of Reverend Moon, Krishna devotees and Scientologists on the list of accused groups. These clearly non-religious groups resisted the stigmatic label of cult, but could not fight to be recognized as minority religions like their companions in adversity had so incessantly done. And far from being only a few outliers, these explicitly non-religious groups made up the vast majority of the groups denounced by anti-cult organizations and government agencies as of the early 2000s. The growing concern for alternative

---

[27] A detailed account of the process of redefinition is presented in Ollion, 'La secte sécularisée'. On this aspect, see also Arnaud Esquerre, *La manipulation mentale: Une sociologie des sectes en France* (Paris: Fayard, 2009); and Véronique Altglas, 'Laïcité is as Laïcité does: Rethinking the French Cult Controversy', *Current Sociology* 58 (2010): 489–510.

[28] Alain Vivien, in discussion with the author, 7 November 2007.

[29] While the definition of what is religious should certainly not be limited to its institutional or official definition and its boundaries are certainly fluid, one would be hard-pressed to explain why some therapists were denounced as cults unless the secular definition was applied to them.

healing techniques, visible in different MIVILUDES reports during the 2000s, bears witness to this important change. Along with spiritual groups, the agency repeatedly warned of potential abuses by individual therapists and commercial companies – their common accusation being the use of mental manipulation techniques.

The adoption of the new meaning of 'cult' cannot be reduced to mere rebranding meant to disguise a legal and political assault on religion. The change in the definition brought a genuine change in anti-cult targets, although religious groups are still very much involved in the controversy. Here probably lies one of the main misunderstandings between proponents and opponents of the French policy. While the latter, focusing on groups fully recognized abroad as religious (Soka Gakkaï, Jehovah Witnesses, etc.), denounce what they regard as an egregious attack on religious minorities, the former emphasize their denunciation of non-religious groups as evidence of their unbiased focus on mind coercion techniques. Both positions have blind spots. On the one hand, it is untenable to say that opposition to cults is *only* another name for opposition to religious minorities. The fact that a majority of the groups targeted in the 2000s are non-religious clearly calls into question any explanation that analyzes the French 'War on Cults' through a purely religious lens. On the other hand, it is equally obvious that the system created to deal with cults has sometimes served to regulate religion. Without even entering the debate about the religiosity of controversial movements who see themselves as such, the fact that both the language and the tools of anti-cult policy were deployed in controversies waged within the Roman Catholic Church (about whether charismatic communities would be fully recognized by the Vatican)[30] illustrates the apparatus' potential to be used to ascertain the boundaries of legitimate religion. And these measures have been far from harmless to the groups subjected to anti-cult scrutiny, as we shall see now.

Effects of state intervention on minority groups

Whether religious or not, did the French 'War on Cults' have an effect on the groups placed, for a moment or for a decade, in the public eye? Well before A. Jahangir's vituperation against the 'climate of general suspicion and intolerance' that French authorities had purportedly favoured, complaints about the effects of their intervention were already countless. 'Cults' and their allies argued that, along with the popular support – material as well as moral – bestowed upon anti-

---

[30] Françoise Champion and Martine Cohen, 'Recompositions, décompositions: Le Renouveau charismatique et la nébuleuse mystique-ésotérique depuis les années soixante-dix', *Le Débat* 75 (1993): 81–96; Jean-Paul Sauzet, *Le Renouveau Charismatique: Les chrétiens du Nouvel-Age?* (Lyon: Golias, 1994); and Martine Cohen, 'Les charismatiques et la santé: offres religieuses de salut ou médecines parallèles?', in *Gestions religieuses de la santé*, eds Jacques Maître and Françoise Lautman (Paris: L'Harmattan, 1995).

cult organizations, the involvement of the state had led to their individual and collective stigmatization, and to increased discrimination in various aspects of their lives.

On countless occasions during my own research, cult members mentioned complex situations they had had to face due to their membership in one of these ill-reputed groups. From personal difficulties (in the workplace or in their relationships with their families) to verbal or even physical harassment, they made a direct link between the involvement of the public authorities and their troubles. Still, numerous and egregious as the cases presented were, the number of alternative explanations available made it impossible to establish a robust connection between state involvement and persecution. Instead, I sought out extensive data on the situation of a large and long-present group in an attempt to demonstrate causation. I turned to a long established group with a large membership: the Jehovah's Witnesses.

Investigating the effects of state intervention on minority groups

The case of the Jehovah's Witnesses

Early on in my research, the Jehovah's Witnesses appeared to offer a strategic opportunity for investigating the effects of state intervention on groups labelled as 'cults' in France. Several criteria were needed to conduct a study that would produce relevant and robust results: the group needed to have been designated a 'cult' for a long period of time; it needed to have chapters located in various regions (in order to be able to disambiguate a local effect from a national one); and it needed to have a large enough membership, for a relatively small sample would turn up results with limited statistical significance.

The Jehovah's Witnesses met each of these criteria. Well-established in France by the mid-1950s,[31] the group has undeniably been regarded as a cult since at least the mid-1990s and is the largest such group in the country, with chapters in virtually every medium- and large-sized French city.

Finally, the group itself keeps extensive data about its affairs,[32] including membership records, as well as a list of all acts of vandalism perpetrated against their places of worship, called 'Kingdom Halls'. The Witnesses had recorded these data systematically for insurance purposes in a central database, but had never really analyzed them. After some negotiations with group leaders in France, I was granted permission to do just that. In order to confirm the quality of the information, I randomly selected a series of events, and asked to consult the file

---

[31] The first chapter was actually established in 1904. See Philippe Barbey, *Les Témoins de Jéhovah: Pour un christianisme original* (Paris: L'Harmattan, 2003), 198.

[32] While at one time the state would have made such information publicly available, this is no longer common in France.

for each of them. All were correctly coded and I decided that the data were reliable enough to work with. After filtering the files (mostly to remove burglaries, which – much more than other acts of vandalism – cannot be distinguished from pure economic interest and would have been hard to interpret), the database contained almost 2,000 incidents of vandalism throughout France from 1990 to 2009.

Data about the group over the last 20 years offer evidence of the structuring role of the state on the daily life of groups labelled as cults. Variations in membership numbers constitute the first element of proof. Jehovah's Witnesses keep a yearly account of their members in France, specifically distinguishing between 'publishers' – baptized members who report at least one hour of preaching every month (a task expected from all teenaged and adult members) – and Memorial attendees, who participate yearly in the group's most important ritual celebration. Since attending the Memorial is less a commitment than is 'publishing', attendees can be seen as sympathizers, while publishers are more akin to active adherents.

Figure 9.1 shows that membership in France declined in both categories soon after 1995 – at the same time as the intense media coverage of the first Parliamentary report. The Witnesses' appearance on the infamous list of 'dangerous cults' probably accounts for this, as the stigma attached to belonging to a publicly condemned group certainly increased the social cost of adherence, deterring members as well as potential recruits. The same held true in the following decade: the overall climate of hostility deterred many a person to join or remain in the group, and each public indictment of cults led to a reduction in membership.

Another telling indicator of the impact of State intervention on minority groups is the degradation of places of worship. The data collected by the Jehovah's Witnesses once again reveal a clear correlation between major moments of public denunciation of cults by French authorities and increased acts of vandalism perpetrated on 'Kingdom Halls' across the country. Throughout France, increased building degradation followed the publication of each of the three Parliamentary reports – in 1995, 1999, and 2006 – each wave of vandalism more widespread than the last.[33] The reports' different treatment of the Witnesses could even account for the variations in the intensity of each. While in the 1995 report, Jehovah's Witnesses were merely one group on a list with 172 others, the 1999 report singled them out, along with Scientology, as one of the two most 'dangerous' cults. And in 2006, during the widely publicized, nationally televised commission hearings, the Witnesses aroused more controversy than any other group. Their case was discussed extensively, with some civil servants questioning whether the group should be classified as a cult at all while commission members and top officials adamantly defended the label.

Forced into the public eye due to the intense publicity of these reports and stigmatized because of the infamous label bestowed upon them, the Jehovah's Witnesses have faced a surge in hostility after each one. It should be pointed out

---

[33] Degradation reached its peak (so far) after the 2006 report, which precipitated over 180 acts of vandalism within a year.

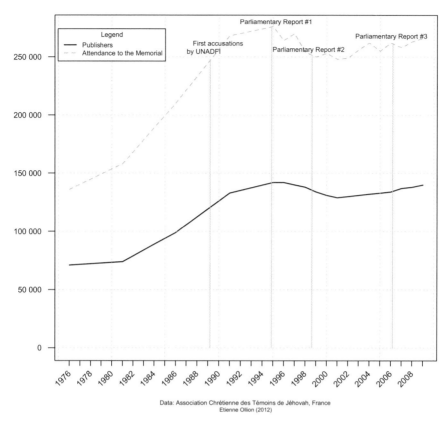

Figure 9.1 Variations in the membership of Jehovah's Witnesses: France, 1976–2009

that the correlation noted above does not imply in any way that public authorities called for, or even implicitly warranted, any act of vandalism. None did, and indeed several publicly condemned such acts. But the repeated official denunciation of the group did call the public's attention to the group and its followers, thereby attracting hostility – whose most extreme manifestation included building degradation.

The effect of state intervention on the life of the group went far beyond the various measures taken to limit their recruitment. Deliberately or not, the public authorities' actions fostered a climate of general hostility toward Jehovah's Witnesses. This probably holds true for all other groups concerned, as all have faced increased and multifaceted difficulties as the 'War on Cults' has developed.[34]

---

[34] Incidentally, the same conclusions could probably be drawn from a study of discrimination against Muslims (when equated with terrorists), gay people (when denied

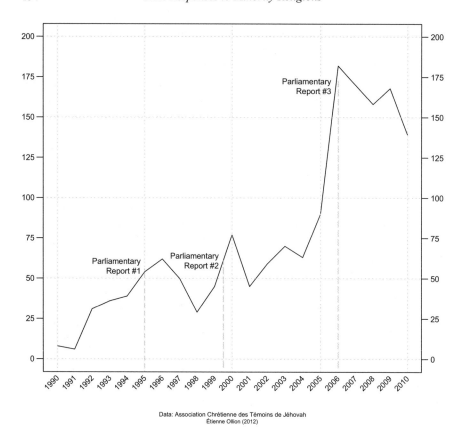

Data: Association Chrétienne des Témoins de Jéhovah
Étienne Ollion (2012)

Figure 9.2   Degradations in Jehovah's Witness places of worship: France, 1990–2009

Conclusion

This historical foray into the French 'War on Cults' is rich in lessons, both empirical and theoretical. For one thing, it offers a wealth of original data that shed new light on the origins and development of this controversy. Here I have discussed in detail three aspects: first, France's current policy against cults is exceptional in its intensity and extension, in many respects as a direct consequence of an unlikely combination of circumstances. If it had not been for the collision between a Parliamentary report and a graphic massacre, the policy would probably not have existed – and certainly would not have developed as it did. Second, and

---

equal rights) or any other minority. The power of *state nomination* – the ability to confer legitimacy, to draw boundaries between groups and to ascertain hierarchies – is probably no different.

probably most controversially, all cults cannot be neatly defined as 'minority religions' or 'new religious movements', as some of their supporters attempt to do. Some are explicitly located outside of the religious field – a proportion that in fact grew as opposition to cults intensified in France. In contemporary France, most of the groups labelled as cults are actually clearly located outside of the religious field. Finally, the policy of surveillance, which makes France unique among democratic nations, has had a strong impact on groups publicly labelled as cults. The multifaceted support France has offered to secular anti-cult organizations is only one aspect of the structuring role played by public authorities in this domain. By singling out certain groups and attracting public ire against them, public authorities actively participate in the stigmatization of these groups.

In turn, these empirical results are an invitation to revisit some of the most classic explanations of the French 'War on Cults'. Although it is often described as a radically secular (or secular-Catholic) reaction to religious minorities and a by-product of France's historically complex relationship with religion, the 'War on Cults' cannot be reduced to a religious dispute. As illustrated above, the controversy cuts through – and at the same time extends well beyond – the religious field. Alternative schools, individual psychotherapists, professional coaches and well-being specialists make up the majority of so-called 'cults'. Thus, the 'War on Cults' is probably best described more generally as a controversy over alternative ways of life in domains where state authorities have long exerted an important control in France (education, health, etc.). In this sense, the intensity of the French cult policy can be attributed to the state's constant patrolling of the practices of the self in a country where public authorities have long competed to establish their jurisdiction over personal and collective behaviours.[35]

---

[35] Such a view helps reconsider other recent controversies often analyzed as a consequence of *laïcité*. While it seems beyond dispute that part of the mobilizations against the *hijab* has to do with a certain level of unease with respect to Islam, the involvement of many left-wing, pro-diversity persons along with right-wing defenders of the Christian roots of France has probably more to do with some deeply entrenched beliefs about personal practices of the body (the veil as 'a constraint imposed on women') and public practices of the self (the veil as 'a communitarian practice') than with Islamophobia. If both aspects are sometimes intertwined in practice, a clearer understanding the dynamics that gave way to the unlikely coalitions, which in turn led to the passing of these laws, would gain from this analytic disambiguation.

Chapter 10
Switzerland and Religious Minorities: Legal, Political and Educational Responses

Brigitte Knobel

In Switzerland, about 10 per cent of the population – nearly 700,000 people – consider themselves members of a religious minority.[1] Although the Catholic Church and the Evangelical Reformed Church still dominate (with 42 per cent and 33 per cent of the population, respectively), the Swiss religious landscape has been characterized in recent decades by an increase in new religious communities, spurred by both immigration and by a growing interest toward non-traditional religions. These new communities form the majority of the 'religious minority' category that includes traditional religions such as Islam (4 per cent of the Swiss population), Orthodoxy (1.8 per cent), Hinduism (0.4 per cent), Buddhism (0.3 per cent), and Judaism (0.2 per cent), as well as new faith communities (new religious movements or 'cults') such as Evangelical revivalism (2.2 per cent), esotericism, neo-paganism, 'UFO religions' and New Age movements. The Swiss census classifies many religious minorities into the broad categories of 'other Christians' and 'other movements'. Therefore, there are no precise figures on the number of religious minorities.[2]

In Switzerland, in general, there has not been any violence nor any real conflict concerning religions, except for some anti-Semitic and, more recently, Islamophobic tensions among the population. According to a 2010 study by the European Social Survey (ESS), only about 1 per cent of the population feels discriminated against because of religious affiliation.

However, over the last 20 years, there have been about a dozen important or even tragic events involving religious minorities. For example, in 1994, 48 bodies, including six children, were found charred in two chalets located in the French-speaking part of Switzerland. They belonged to the esoteric organization called

---

[1] 2000 Census. Since 1850, the Swiss Confederation has organized a census every 10 years that includes a question on religious affiliation. The federal census has gradually been focused to include religious minorities. Thus the number of religious groups mentioned on census forms has expanded from three items in 1850 (Roman Catholic, Protestant, and Old Catholic) to the introduction of open category ('Other') in 1900 to the introduction of Judaism, Islam and Orthodoxy in 2000.

[2] Claude Bovay and Raphaël Broquet, *Le paysage religieux en Suisse* (Neuchâtel: Office fédéral de la statistique, 2004).

the Order of the Solar Temple.³ In 2002, various associations – including Swiss Animal Protection (SAP), the Society of Swiss Veterinarians, and some consumer organizations – induced the Federal Government to maintain the ban on the slaughter of animals in Jewish and Muslim rituals. In 2005 and 2007, synagogues in Lugano and Geneva, respectively, were victims of arson. In 2009, the Swiss voters adopted a popular initiative banning the construction of minarets.

Since as early as the Catholic-Protestant conflicts of the nineteenth century, the Federal State has developed legal measures and policies to manage and anticipate religious controversy. But Swiss state policy regarding religious minorities is particularly interesting today given the country's changing religious landscape. The goal of this chapter is to outline the legal, political and, in particular, educational measures Switzerland has taken in response to the presence of religious minorities.

Legal measures

Unlike the media or public opinion, Swiss law does not distinguish between majority religions, 'cults', and religious minorities, and therefore contains no specific protections for religious minorities. However, Switzerland has enacted a number of laws that protect believers and practitioners and regulate the status of its religious communities.

Freedom of belief and worship

In 1874, Switzerland adopted an article into its Constitution that guaranteed freedom of religion and worship. Over a century later, the new Federal Constitution of 1999 (Art. 15) expanded on this theme, introducing the right to freely choose or change one's religion – a sign that the state at least outwardly embraces religious plurality, as noted by Andrea Rota.⁴

Laws against religious discrimination

Switzerland has also taken legal steps to protect individuals against religious discrimination. Article 8 of the Constitution stipulates that: 'No one may be discriminated against, in particular on grounds of origin, race, gender, age,

---

[3] Other tragedies of the Order of the Solar Temple took place in 1994 in French-speaking Canada, in 1995 in France (Vercors), and in 1997 again in Canada, resulting in the deaths of 74 people, including children. These events inflicted a lasting impression on the public mind. See the study by Roland J. Campiche and Cyril Dépraz, *Quand les sectes affolent: Ordre du Temple Solaire, médias et fin du millénaire* (Genève: Labor et Fides, 1995).

[4] Andrea Rota, 'La régulation du champ religieux par l'Etat: Exemples du cas suisse', (Mémoire de licence, Faculté de lettres de l'Université de Fribourg (CH), 2007), 27–8.

language, social position, way of life, religious, ideological, or political convictions, or because of a physical, mental or psychological disability.'

Recognition: public law status

Although Swiss federal law does not distinguish between religions, 'cults' or religious minorities, the cantonal authorities, by contrast, differentiate between religious movements by granting public law status only to some of them. This status provides financial and social benefits – financing of places of worship, tax exemption, clerical access to prisons and hospitals, etc. – with the obligation to respect the democratic order and the beliefs of others. Until recently, only the Catholic and Evangelical Reformed churches enjoyed public law status. However, starting in the 1990s, the Jewish community obtained recognition in the cantons of Bern, Fribourg, Vaud, Basel-Stadt and St. Gallen. All the other religious minorities – including the largest, the Muslim community – have the status of private association or private foundation. It is interesting to note that obtaining public law status is opening up to other religious minorities. Currently, the constitutions of half of the cantons offer this possibility.[5] However, to date, no religious minority, except the Jewish community, has obtained this legal recognition.

Recognition: charitable status

Switzerland also offers charitable status, which allows some organizations tax exemption. Religious movements, including religious minorities, can obtain this status, but subject to some conditions. Geneva, for example, requires that a religious community be established in Geneva for 10 years, publish annual accounts, be organized as an association or foundation, provide social activities that benefit the entire population, defend widely recognized spiritual values, respect free will and freedom of belief and allow members to resign.

Jurisprudence

In Switzerland, many religious issues are handled on a case-by-case basis in the courts. Before 2008, for example, schools generally allowed religious exemptions for public school swimming classes based upon a Federal Court ruling from 1993. But in 2008 the Court issued a new judgment valuing integration, equal opportunity, and learning to swim above the observation of religious principles. Since then public schools have limited swimming exemptions.

---

[5] Vaud, Valais, Jura, Ticino, Zurich, Bern, Obwalden, Nidwalden, Glarus, Basel-Land, Schaffhausen, Appenzell Inner Rhodes and Aargau. See Sandro Cattacin et al., *Etat et religion en Suisse. Lutte pour la reconnaissance, formes de la reconnaissance* (Berne: commission fédérale contre le racisme (CFR), 2003).

Political measures

Responsibility of local authorities

In Switzerland, local authorities (cantons and municipalities) regulate religious groups. This policy is a legacy of the nineteenth century: in 1848, the new Swiss Confederation decided that local authorities were best qualified to end the Catholic–Protestant conflict that had existed since the Reformation.[6] Thus, there are no religious departments at the federal level. Each canton or municipality in Switzerland is required to negotiate with its religious communities on matters ranging from the management of cemeteries to proselytizing.[7]

Religious neutrality

A second measure taken in the nineteenth century was the principle of religious neutrality. To ease the tensions between Catholics and Protestants, the new Confederation decided not to take sides in religious conflicts while recognizing the peoples' freedom to practice their religion.[8] This policy, still in effect, prohibits public employees from displaying their religious affiliation or officially siding with one religion or the other in a conflict. A public school teacher, for example, is not allowed to wear religious symbols. In contrast, students – as members of the general public – have the right to display their belief, such as by wearing a veil. Religious neutrality is not legally defined in any legislation, but it is based upon the Swiss Constitution's definition of freedom of belief and the prohibition of any form of religious discrimination (Articles 8 and 15).

Expert reports

When tensions, conflicts, or tragedies arise, the authorities seek the advice of experts – lawyers, political scientists, religious scholars, etc. After much controversy concerning the Church of Scientology and especially the tragedy of the Order of the Solar Temple, state and political authorities issued four major reports on the new religious movement phenomenon. These reports highlight the threatening aspect of these movements, which are not, for that matter, considered as

---

[6] In 1847, the Catholic cantons and the Protestant cantons fought each other in a civil war known as the Sonderbund War.

[7] Because of this political system, there are 26 different models in Switzerland about how to manage religions. It is worth noting, however, that the federal vote banning the construction of minarets deviates from this decentralized policy; it remains to be seen whether this will become a trend.

[8] For further study of religious neutrality in Switzerland, see Claude Rouiller, 'Le principe de la neutralité confessionnelle relative. Réflexion sur la liberté de religion', *Pratique juridique actuelle* 8 (2003): 944–58.

religious minorities. As noted by Jean-Francois Mayer, by conceptualizing 'cults' as something entirely separate from 'religions', they create a differentiation that may seem discriminatory.[9] Moreover, these reports recommend non-repressive measures by focusing on the importance of educational measures.

The first report appeared in 1997 in Geneva. The Department of Justice and Police published the *Audit sur les dérives sectaires* (*Audit of Sectarian deviation*),[10] conducted by legal experts led by Francois Bellanger, which marked the first time the term 'sectarian deviation' was used to define illegal acts committed in the name of belief. The report analyzed the legal framework in different fields, such as child protection, labour laws or medical practices, and concluded that specific legislation addressing controversial religious movements was unnecessary, and that the current laws were sufficient to protect the population. The report did, however, emphasize the need for educational and preventive measures, recommending the creation of an independent information centre. In 1998, the Advisory Commission on the Protection of the State made a well-documented 135-page report on the Church of Scientology concluding that preventive monitoring was unnecessary.[11]

In 1999, the Control Committee of the National Council published a report[12] which asked the Federal Council to articulate its position on 'cults'. It marked the first time the term 'indoctrinating' was used to characterize certain groups in which might occur 'alteration of free will [which] can escalate to the complete loss of all autonomy'. In this report, the commission requested the Federal Council to create a public information agency, to improve the protection of children, to encourage academic research and to harmonize activities between public service administrations and cantons.

In response to this report, the Federal Council published a report[13] in 2000, which pronounced that it was not up to them to develop a policy on 'cults' because the cantons – not the Confederation – were the only authorities in religious matters. It stressed that first and foremost the Federal Council defends freedom of belief in accordance with international agreements (primarily the European Convention

---

[9] Jean-Francois Mayer, interview by Andrea Rota, 26 May 2006 in Rota, 'La régulation du champ religieux par l'Etat'.

[10] *Audit sur les dérives sectaires*, Rapport du groupe d'experts genevois au Département de Justice et Police et des Transports du canton de Genève, Rapport général et Rapport relatif aux mesures de droit administratif, Éditions Suzanne Hurter, Genève 1997.

[11] *La Scientologie en Suisse*, Report to the Advisory Commission for the protection of the State (July 1998).

[12] *'Sectes' ou mouvements endoctrinants en Suisse. La nécessité de l'action de l'État ou vers une politique fédérale en matière de 'sectes'.* (*'Cults' or Indoctrinating Movements in Switzerland: The Need for Action by the State, or a Federal Policy on 'Cults'*). Rapport de la CdG N, 1999.

[13] *'Sectes' et/ou mouvements endoctrinants en Suisse. Réponse du Conseil fédéral au rapport de la CdG-CN* (*'Cults' and/or Indoctrinating Movements in Switzerland: The Federal Council's Response to the Report of the Control Committee of the National Council*), 2000.

on Human Rights, as well as UN and OSCE agreements), and that it can only intervene if a group's activities infringe upon the rights of the individual or harm the state. It recommended caution in using the term 'cult' because its pejorative connotations are inconsistent with freedom of belief and noted that most groups are not dangerous. The Council did recognize, however, the need to strengthen interdisciplinary research and improve information sharing within the federal administration.

Since the late 1990s, federal authorities have published more than a dozen reports on Islam and Judaism. As opposed to the reports on 'cults', these publications note discrimination against Jews and Muslims, advising that measures must be put in place to integrate these communities, considered as religious minorities. For example, the Federal Commission against Racism (*Commission fédérale contre le racisme*, or CFR),[14] founded in 1995, has published seven reports related to the Muslim community and three related to the Jewish community. The CFR generally recommends pragmatism and tolerance toward minorities, highlighting the discriminatory nature of certain decisions (that is, the ban on ritual slaughter, the ban on Islamic veils, and so on). In 1998, the CFR published the report *L'antisémitisme en Suisse*15 (*Anti-Semitism in Switzerland*) regarding prejudice against the Jewish community incited by the debates on Switzerland's role in the Holocaust and the lawsuit filed by the World Jewish Congress to recover unclaimed Jewish assets from Swiss banks. Five years later, in 2003, the CFR published another report,[16] which called for easier access to public law status for religious minorities to equalize treatment among all communities. In its 2006 report,[17] the CFR denounced Islamophobia and asked the population, the administrations, businesses and the media to exercise more tolerance toward Muslims in Switzerland. In 2008 and 2009, the CFR published several press releases criticizing the initiative banning the construction of minarets.

The Federal Commission on Migration (FCM), founded in 2008, also published a report in 2010 called *Vie musulmane en Suisse* (*Muslim Life in Switzerland*), which recommended, among other things, that public authorities grant public law status to Muslim groups, facilitate their integration into the political sphere, and create a system for training imams in Switzerland.

---

[14] Switzerland created this service in 1995 following the signing of the International Convention on the Elimination of All Forms of Racial Discrimination in 1993. 'Commission fédérale contre le racisme', Confédération suisse, http://www.ekr.admin.ch/org/00316/index.html?lang=fr.

[15] *L'antisémitisme en Suisse*. Rapport sur les manifestations historiques et actuelles avec recommandations d'action, 1998.

[16] *Etat et religion en Suisse. Lutte pour la reconnaissance, formes de la reconnaissance* (*State and Religion in Switzerland*), 2003.

[17] *Les relations avec la minorité musulmane en Suisse (The Relationship with the Muslim minority in Switzerland)*, 2006.

National research program

In 2005, the Federal Council decided to allocate up to 10 million Swiss francs to a national research programme called 'Religion in Switzerland' (NRP 58). This programme aims to study the evolution of the religious landscape in Switzerland, to provide a tool to guide social and educational policies, and to encourage peaceful coexistence. Of the 28 projects selected for research since the programme's founding, eight have focused exclusively on Islam, three on Buddhism, one on Hinduism, one on Judaism and one on Orthodoxy. Only one project was focused on new spiritualties. Other projects have dealt with religious diversity generally. The research's findings have consistently resulted in the same recommendations: that the state consult more with religious minorities in decisions affecting them; that it participate in the training of imams; and that cantonal and federal authorities better inform the public about religious minorities, especially Islam.[18]

Educational measures

The Confederation and the cantons have also implemented several innovative educational measures over the past decade.

Creating an internet portal

In 2002, acceding the request of the Control Committee of the National Council, the Confederation created a public website called the *Réseau 'Mouvements endoctrinants'* (*'Indoctrinating Movements' Network*), which provides the addresses of the information and counsel centres existing in 21 Swiss cantons.[19] The site also allows visitors to read federal reports related to 'cults', but it does not provide information on more mainstream religious minorities such as Islam, Orthodoxy or Buddhism.

Teaching in public schools

In the early 2000s, some cantons begin to discuss replacing the denominational approach to religious education with a non-denominational approach, open to other religions and religious minorities present in Switzerland.[20] Since 2003, several cantons (Neuchâtel, Aargau, Fribourg, Zurich and Vaud) have introduced

---

[18] *Les religions en Suisse*. Portrait du Programme national de recherche PNR 58. Collectivités religieuses, Etat et société. Fond national suisse, 2007.

[19] 'Mouvements endoctrinants', Confédération suisse, http://www.bk.admin.ch/dokumentation/00492/index.html?lang=fr.

[20] In Switzerland, public education is the responsibility of the cantons.

religious history courses. Teachers Training Schools are also gradually integrating religious history studies into teacher training programs.[21]

The Information Centre on Beliefs (CIC)

In 2001, the cantons of Geneva, Vaud, Valais and Ticino committed to finance an information centre on beliefs (*Centre d'information sur les croyances*, or CIC). This was meant both to address the population's concerns after the disaster of the Solar Temple and to act as a preventative measure by providing neutral information on 'cults'. The lack of information in this area was highlighted in the 1997 *Audit sur les dérives sectaires*.[22] Currently, the CIC is the only Swiss institution of its kind that is entirely publicly funded.[23]

CIC: scope of activity

The CIC deals primarily with recently established religious movements, migrant communities, emerging religious groups, para-religious groups and spiritual therapies. It also addresses issues relating to sectarian deviation, religious laws and policies, and articles of worship. The CIC receives an average of 500 greatly varied requests per year. In 2011, the CIC was asked for information on over 220 different religious groups and themes.

CIC: features

As part of its mandate, the CIC provides the following services: public documentation and consultation; personal interview services; elaboration of files, research resources on religious movements, including access to relevant legal texts and resources from similar centres across Europe and North America;[24] testimony recording services; referrals for psychological, legal and social departments; and classes in schools and universities. The CIC also organizes public seminars and conferences on new religious movements.

---

[21] 'Didactiques de l'histoire et sciences des religions', *Haute école pédagogique Vaud*, 31 août 2012, http://www.hepl.ch/cms/accueil/formation/unites-enseignement-et-recherche/didactiques-sciences-humaines/didactiques/histoire-sciences-religions.html.

[22] 'Audit sur les dérives sectaires', in *Rapport général et Rapport relatif aux mesures de droit administratif* (Genève: Éditions Suzanne Hurter, 1997).

[23] There are currently four information centres in Switzerland: Basel Inforel (est. 1987), Relinfo (est. 1963), Geneva (est. 2002) and Infosekta (est. 1990) at Zürich. Only Infosekta receives grants from the canton and the city of Zurich (25 per cent of its budget in 2007).

[24] The CIC currently has records on over 700 topics; 780 specialized works; 80 judgements given by courts in Switzerland and abroad; and over 80 audio-visual materials, press reports organized by subject, and teaching materials for schools.

CIC working methods: a neutral approach

From the outset, the CIC adopted a policy of neutrality in order to avoid entanglement in the often sharp controversy that so often surrounds new religious movements and religious minorities. To this end it has developed four methodological principles: provide several points of view; employ the same approach with all groups; use neutral language; and use the methodological tools of social science.

The CIC disseminates documents that provide several views in order to allow readers to form their own opinion. Each file includes documentation from five different sources: the religious group itself (sacred books, leaflets, website, etc.); university studies; the media; victim advocacy groups; and domestic or foreign authorities (judgments, policies, legal documents, etc.). Files usually include both apologetic and critical documents, revealing internal dysfunction as well as external discrimination.

The principle of neutrality also obligates the CIC to apply the same approach with all religious groups, whether celebrated or controversial; traditional or newly created; majority or minority. This methodological principle assumes that any religious movement may malfunction or, conversely, may represent a social or psychological resource for certain people in certain circumstances.

The CIC is careful to use neutral language. It favours terms such as 'member' instead of 'follower', or 'lobbying' instead of 'infiltrating'. Likewise, the CIC does not use the pejorative and stigmatizing term 'cult', which implies something strange and dangerous, and it tends to understate the religious dimension of controversial groups.

To collect information from religious leaders, members, former group members or relatives, the CIC uses interview guides borrowed from social science. The CIC also makes these guides available for relatives or any other person who wants to meet religious groups and their leaders in order to know more about them.

CIC working methods: outreach work

To the extent possible, the CIC establishes direct contact, in the form of telephone interviews or field observations, with religious/spiritual organizations, including emerging and marginal groups. This indiscriminate, transparent outreach allows the CIC to become quickly informed of the creation or disappearance of organizations, of changes within certain groups, and of the presence of sectarian deviation.

CIC working methods: networking

The CIC coordinates with other information centres in Switzerland and other countries, especially France, Belgium, Britain, Canada and the USA. It also maintains contact with Swiss and international academia and victims advocacy groups, and has developed close collaborative ties to sociologists, religious historians, journalists, doctors, psychologists, lawyers and members of religious movements.

CIC working methods: a nuanced approach

The CIC's neutral posture does not prevent it from remaining vigilant to potential malfunctions or problems which can exist in any religious group. The CIC analyses three problematic situations:

- Illegal acts such as fraud, sexual abuse, the illegal practice of medicine, or discrimination.
- Problematic situations that are not illegal, such as the seclusion of a group; the domineering personality of a leader; the presence of internal conflicts; inadequately supervised ascetic practices (such as fasting or sleep deprivation); or discrimination against women, homosexuals, foreigners, or other religions.
- Practices which are socially disturbing, such as the style of dress required of members, initiatory practices, or the amount of time devoted to religious practice.

Each situation requires a different response. When necessary, the CIC advises concerned parties to consult a lawyer, to lodge a complaint or to enter into mediation. Sometimes, the CIC refers a situation to the competent authority, such as the police or the department of public health.

Who utilizes the CIC?

A diverse segment of the general public utilizes the CIC – not only concerned relatives or friends, but also teachers, students, journalists, executives, social workers, doctors, lawyers, employers and members of religious communities themselves.

People often contact the centre when a loved one converts to a religious group, as this can cause relationship problems. Television programmes focusing on the dangers of a certain group always generate calls. Many people still call the CIC because they stumble upon the French Parliamentary Commission's 1996 list of 'cults' on the Internet and become worried. Administrative services call CIC to obtain specialized information to help them make decisions regarding tax exemption, demonstrations on the public highway, advertising and even child custody. Finally, more and more religious groups themselves contact the CIC to research Swiss law, to receive help in drafting their articles, to research potential places of worship, and sometimes simply to take note of studies about their group.

Conclusion

Three observations can be made about the legal, political and educational approaches Swiss authorities have taken toward religious minorities. First, we note that although Switzerland has no specific policy regarding religious minorities, it is not indifferent toward them. Since the nineteenth century, authorities have put measures in place to guarantee religious neutrality and freedom of belief and worship. Second, we see that Swiss authorities have favoured educational measures over repressive methods. In the last ten years, the cantons have gradually introduced non-denominational religious instruction in schools, raising young people's awareness about different ways to believe and practice. The federal and cantonal authorities have funded several studies and also published, for a wide audience, many reports on Judaism and Islam. Finally, four cantons have funded independent information centres on beliefs, offering the public an array of objective information on the various religious minorities in Switzerland, especially new religious movements. With these and other educational measures, the authorities hope to relieve inter-cultural tension by increasing the public's understanding of new religious minorities.

Third, there is a gap between political authorities' views and the law. Swiss law does not distinguish between religion, 'cult' or religious minority. At least ostensibly, all religious groups are equal before the law. On the contrary, political authorities established, in an informal way, a hierarchical distinction between religious minorities from major religious traditions (Islam, Buddhism, Hinduism and so on) and new religious minorities, so called 'cults'. The religious minorities issued from major traditions are analyzed from the angle of the discriminations to which they are subject, while 'cults' are considered as a threat to the population and are not considered as religious minorities.

PART IV
Moving Eastward – Emerging Democracies and the Communist Legacy

Chapter 11
Recognition, Registration and Autonomy of Religious Groups: European Approaches and their Human Rights Implications

Jeroen Temperman

Introduction

The issue of freedom of association is inextricably linked with the freedoms enjoyed by organized religious groups. This chapter looks at European approaches to religious registration/recognition[1] and the related issue of religious autonomy while examining some of their human rights implications. The section on registration looks predominantly at Central and Eastern European states, as it is chiefly in those states that registration of religious organizations is regulated by means of elaborate – even intricate – laws on religious association. The section on church autonomy looks predominantly at Western European examples; although this issue gives rise to contentious human rights debates in virtually all parts of the world, Western European states in particular have recently sought to come to terms with this issue through complicated – and not completely transparent – domestic regulation.

Registration

The question, 'Why should legal recognition of religious groups be any different from regulations pertaining to other non-profit organizations?' is bound to embarrass any government that has adopted complex and burdensome religious registration regulations, for the answer can only serve to uncover double standards and prejudices vis-à-vis non-traditional and non-dominant religions. Neither the freedom of religion nor the freedom of association is absolute; accordingly, 'public order' arguments may warrant some regulation in this area. But to generally argue that public order in all cases requires stringent registration schemes is simply false. There are states that prove the opposite. There are states that no longer even have special laws on religious association in place. Rather, the issue is regulated by virtue of general civil code provisions on private associations. Moreover, there are

---

[1] Legal 'recognition' is a term somewhat broader than registration and is also added and used so as to cover the fact that within some jurisdictions registration is not required for legal personality.

states where all religious organizations, however organized, by whatever name, and whatever their precise organizational objectives, are automatically granted legal entity status – without leading to mayhem, dangers to the state or to society. What intricate registration schemes signal is that religion, and especially 'new religions' (or 'sects'), are a problem, and that the solution to this legal problem is more legislation, including registration laws. These laws – particularly the criteria they impose and the oftentimes arbitrary distinctions they make between the different religions present in a country – raise serious human rights concerns.

Moreover, states rarely make it clear exactly how burdensome membership requirements, duration of existence of an organization, or other criteria promote 'public order'. In sum, recognition of religious organizations is a policy area that would immensely benefit from deregulation. What exactly is the problem if only three persons wish to found a religion? And why is it an issue if a religion did not exist, say, 2,000 years ago, but emerged more recently? Some small or new religions may prove unsuccessful and will not survive long; others may be successful and gain many new adherents.

Deregulation here means essentially that states are to let the 'free market of religion' uninhibitedly determine these processes. Intricate registration schemes that determine membership or duration criteria for obtaining basic legal entity status, or that determine further conditions for receiving special privileges, throw the free market of religion off its natural balance: large or old religions are *a priori* supported – and thus given artificial incentives to remain large or grow larger – whereas small or new religions are *a priori* disadvantaged. This is not to say that proportionality may not be a criterion when it comes to allocating certain benefits or privileges; what is objectionable are the unfair discrepancies which result from artificial multi-tier registration systems and unreasonable requirements for basic legal entity status.

Two common forms of state discrimination against religious groups are: (1) denial of basic recognition as a legal entity by the state (and the basic rights that come with this status); and (2) denial of additional privileges of a financial or other nature (this mechanism is often interwoven with the issue of the status of religious groups).

As to the first issue, status as a legal entity and the basic rights and protections connected with that status are generally indispensable for any religious organization nowadays. Clearly the most objectionable policy in this context is proactively outlawing a certain religion or denomination on account of the religion in question being considered 'heretical', 'dangerous', or otherwise undesirable. Short of banning and actively persecuting a religion or belief are those measures that pose unreasonable registration requirements for basic legal recognition that certain groups simply cannot meet.

State practice shows, as to the second issue, that state funding for certain privileges (for example, tax exemptions) drastically impacts the ability of religious groups to function. In some countries, such funding may be dependent on mere legal recognition as a religious or ideological organization. In others, all or some privileges may be dependent on being recognized as a *special category* of religious organization – and may thus hinge on further requirements. There is no clear-cut right for organized religions to be funded by the state at all; however, if the state does decide to provide funding or support to religion, it follows from the equality principle that it must adopt an equitable approach and not discriminate against certain groups.

Objectionable registration policies may manifest themselves in the following ways: numerical requirements, presence requirements and *sui generis* requirements.[2]

Numerical requirements

As regards the base-level recognition of legal entity status, it can be argued that numerical requirements are hardly ever legitimate. After all, the Human Rights Committee has considered that the right to freedom of religion or belief

> is not limited in its application to traditional religions or to religions and beliefs with institutional characteristics or practices analogous to those of traditional religions. The Committee therefore views with concern any tendency to discriminate against any religion or belief for any reason, including the fact that they are newly established, or represent religious minorities that may be the subject of hostility on the part of a predominant religious community.[3]

---

[2] Cf. W. Cole Durham, 'Facilitating Freedom of Religion or Belief through Religious Association Law', in *Facilitating Freedom of Religion or Belief: A Deskbook*, eds T. Lindholm, W.C. Durham and B. Tahzib-Lie (Leiden: Martinus Nijhoff Publishers, 2004).

[3] Human Rights Committee, General Comment No. 22, para. 2. Examples of cases in which the Human Rights Committee found this principle breached in the specific context of religious associations include: Human Rights Committee, *Sister Immaculate Joseph and 80 Teaching Sisters of the Holy Cross of the Third Order of Saint Francis in Menzingen of Sri Lanka v. Sri Lanka*, Communication No. 1249/2004, UN Doc. CCPR/C/85/D/1249/2004 (2005), Views of 21 October 2005 (the refusal to acknowledge/register this order amounted to a violation of Art. 18 in conjunction with Art. 26 of the ICCPR); and Human Rights Committee, *Sergei Malakhovsky and Alexander Pikul v. Belarus*, Communication No. 1207/2003, UN Doc. CCPR/C/84/D/1207/2003 [2005], Views of 26 July 2005. It is worth noting that at the European level, the ECHR has provided a comprehensive set of benchmarks on the issue of recognition/registration/religious autonomy in its case law.

For dealing with different aspects of recognition/registration, see ECtHR, *Metropolitan Church of Bessarabia and Others v. Moldova*, Application no. 45701/99, Decision of December 13, 2001; ECtHR, *Hasan and Chaush v. Bulgaria*, Application no. 30985/96, Decision of 26 October 2000; ECtHR, *Moscow Branch of the Salvation Army v. Russia*, Application No. 72881/01, Decision of 5 October 2006; ECtHR, *Church of Scientology Moscow v. Russia*, Application No. 18147/02, Decision of 5 April 2007; ECtHR, *Biserica Adevărat Ortodoxă din Moldova and Others v. Moldova*, Application No. 952/03, Decision of 27 February 2007; and ECtHR, *Svyato-Mykhaylivska Parafiya v. Ukraine*, Application

Thus, the key question is what is reasonable and what is unreasonable in this context. A minimum membership criterion of 20,000 persons, as is the case in Slovakia, is clearly unreasonable.[4] This registration criterion has been dismissed as being 'among the most restrictive of any democratic state in the entire world'.[5] But what if 'only' a couple of dozen people are required? Again, the most convincing argument in this context asks why numerical requirements for religious organizations should be any different from regular civil non-profit associations covered by domestic association laws. The only thing that numerical requirements achieve is that smaller religious communities fail to gain legal recognition and the benefits connected with legal personality – not necessarily that they cease to exist. 'Public order' is not necessarily served by numerical requirements. Although in theory registration authorities may face more work if the threshold for registration is lowered, human rights law does not hold the avoidance of a higher workload as grounds for limiting fundamental rights. Also, states with flexible recognition schemes show no signs of being overwhelmed by a deluge of registration claims.[6]

Nevertheless, many states pose unreasonable numerical requirements – some clearly more unreasonable than others – for acquiring base-level legal entity status (for example, Armenia: 200 members; Belarus: 20; Bosnia and Herzegovina: 300; Croatia: 500; Czech Republic: 300; Estonia: 12; Hungary: 100; Latvia: 10; Lithuania: 15; Macedonia: 50; Moldova: 10; Poland: 100; Romania: 300; Russia: 10; Serbia: approximately 75; and Ukraine: 10).[7]

No. 77703/01, Decision of 14 June 2007. The Court reasons, *inter alia*, that basic legal-entity status is indispensable for religious organizations and that the state (as 'neutral and impartial organizer of the different religions') may, consequently, not raise such legal obstacles as to prevent certain religious groups from acquiring legal recognition. In some cases (*for example* ECtHR, *Religionsgemeinschaft der Zeugen Jehovas and Others v. Austria*, Application No. 40825/98, Decision of 31 July 2008), the Court went further than that, arguing that those multi-tier systems that distinguish between different religious groups (on the basis of their traditional ties to the country or numerically, etc.) so as to grant them different privileges are also at odds with the state duty to remain neutral and impartial in exercising its regulatory power in the sphere of religious freedom and in its relations with different religions, denominations and beliefs. See also ECtHR, *Verein der Freunde der Christengemeinschaft and Others v. Austria*, Application No. 76581/01, Decision of 26 February 2009.

[4] Sec. 11 of the Law on the Freedom of Religious Belief and on the Status of Churches and Religious Societies, Law No. 308/1991 (1991), as amended by Law No. 192/1992 (effective 1 June 1992), and by Law No. 394/2000 Coll. (2000) (effective since January 1, 2001).

[5] Peter Mulík, 'Church and State in Slovakia', in *Law and Religion in Post-Communist Europe*, eds Ferrari and Durham (Leuven: Peeters, 2003), 320. These regulations have also been criticized by the Human Rights Committee: A/52/40 vol. I (1997) 58 at para. 382 (Slovakia).

[6] One can take the US or the Netherlands as examples.

[7] See Jeroen Temperman, *State-Religion Relationships and Human Rights Law* (Leiden/Boston: Martinus Nijhoff Publishers, 2010), particularly Chapter 8, for a more detailed analysis of the relevant laws.

Some states pose numerical requirements for acquiring a *special status* entitling the group in question to privileges beyond those attached to mere legal recognition (for example, Austria: approximately 16,500 members, to qualify as a 'state recognized religion').[8]

Duration requirements

'Presence' or 'duration' requirements that a given religion exist in a state for a certain number of years[9] are equally illegitimate. Although the Human Rights Committee has stated that traditional and newly-founded religions should be treated equally, minimum duration requirements can nonetheless be found in several states. Generally, minimum duration requirements must be met in order to be granted a special, more privileged, or protected status: Austria (20 years to qualify as an upper-tier 'state recognized religion'); Belarus (20 years to qualify as a 'religious association'); Czech Republic (10 years to qualify as religious society with 'special powers'); Lithuania (25 years to qualify as a recognized religion); Romania (12 years to qualify as a 'state recognized denomination'); Russia (15 years to qualify as a 'religious organization'); and Portugal (30 years to qualify as a religious community that is 'settled in the country').

Although imposing duration requirements for special privileges – rather than for any official recognition whatsoever – may be more subtle, it constitutes discrimination nonetheless. Those multi-tier schemes posing particularly high minimum duration requirements for upper-tier status are designed to safeguard the historical prerogatives of traditional religions; in most of the Eastern European examples above, that means the national Orthodox Church. Granted, it only makes sense for the state to allocate certain financial privileges proportionally. However, multi-tier systems do something else entirely: they fix *a priori* which religions will 'hit the jackpot' and which are destined to be deprived of state support because they are too small or too new, thus needlessly unsettling the free market of religion. The argument that only multi-tier registration systems are manageable – and thus that public order concerns warrant this arrangement – cannot be substantiated, as ample proof to the contrary exists. More often than not, multi-tier systems are not the result of administrative laziness, but are expressly designed to protect traditional and dominant churches and hamper new ones. Dominant churches are often consulted during the drafting of religious association laws, with codified numerical or duration requirements being the direct result.[10]

---

[8] Sec. 11, para. 2, of the 1998 Austrian law requires an adherence of '2 persons per thousand Austrians'. This has been deemed discriminatory by the Human Rights Committee: A/54/40 vol. I (1999) 42 at para. 192.

[9] See also Durham, 'Facilitating Freedom of Religion', 388–90, analysing 'minimum duration requirements'.

[10] This holds true for instance for the compromises on numerical requirements enshrined in the Bosnian or recently revised Hungarian laws on religious association.

As mentioned before, 'public order' hardly requires any of this. Other grounds of limitation, notably 'morals', also do not in any way justify such discriminatory policies. The point that one religious tradition is historically interwoven with the fabric of a state while newly emerging or newly arriving beliefs are not does not constitute a persuasive argument from a human rights perspective. Note also that the Human Rights Committee has explained 'that the concept of morals derives from many social, philosophical and religious traditions; consequently, limitations on the freedom to manifest a religion or belief for the purpose of protecting morals must be based on principles not deriving exclusively from a single tradition'.[11]

Sui generis *illegitimate registration requirements*

Furthermore, registration requirements may be considered illegitimate if they are excessively burdensome or leave too much discretion to the authorities.[12] The requirement that official registration be obtained at both national and local levels (as in Kazakhstan and Russia, for instance) appears to be excessively burdensome.[13] Similarly, the demand that religious organizations in Russia annually provide registration authorities with data on their religious activities and notify them of their wish to continue these activities (failure of which may result in the suspension or dissolution of the organization) seems excessively burdensome as well.[14]

Even absent presence or duration requirements, other qualitative criteria may make discrimination against newly established religions inevitable. Armenian registration law, for instance, demands that a religious association be 'based on any historically canonized Holy Scriptures'.[15] Belarusian religious association law, too, seems to require special proof of the merits of newly emerging religions:

> A religious community confessing a faith previously unknown in the Republic of Belarus must include in its application information about its teachings and worship practices, including information about the history and origin of the religion practiced by the community, forms and methods of its activities, attitudes toward marriage and family, education, fulfilment of state responsibilities, receipt of medical treatment by followers of the given religion, and other meaningful information in response to inquiries of the State Governance Body on Religious Affairs.[16]

---

[11] Human Rights Committee, General Comment No. 22, para. 8.
[12] Cf. Durham, 'Facilitating Freedom of Religion', 392–9.
[13] Under the 1992 Kazakh Law and under the 1997 Russian Law respectively.
[14] Art. 10, para. 9 and subsequent final provisions, of the 1997 Russian Law.
[15] Art. 5, para. b, of the Law on the Freedom of Conscience and Religious Organizations of 17 June 1991 (amended 1997 and 2001). It is furthermore provided that its doctrine must form 'part of the international contemporary religious-ecclesiastical communities' (para. c).
[16] Art. 17 of the 2002 Belarusian Law; the timeframe for reviewing the application is, moreover, in the case of new religions extended to six months (normally one month).

So-called 'one [national] church per religion' rules also foster abuse and discrimination. In Latvia, for instance, congregations of the same denomination may establish only one national religious association in the country.[17] This clause has effectively prevented both the Confessional Lutheran Church and the Autonomous True Orthodox Church from being recognized as a church at the national level in Latvia.[18]

Religious autonomy

The focus of this section is on how far religious autonomy may reach under international law. This question is especially complicated in the context of *equality law*: how far may the state push its equality agenda at the expense of religious autonomy? Religious organizations and the state may disagree on equality issues such as:

- appointment of religious officials
- other employment issues, especially hiring and firing
- membership
- services.

Under relevant international human rights standards, how do states optimally maximize religious autonomy without condoning discrimination? And where the two conflict, what balance should be struck?

Appointment of religious officials

Of these four issues, the appointment of religious officials is by far the most straightforward, as international human rights law has clearly settled this matter. The 1981 UN Religious Tolerance Declaration expressly recognizes 'the freedom to train, appoint, elect or designate by succession appropriate leaders called for by the requirements and standards of any religion or belief'.[19] The European Court of Human Rights has also affirmed that the state is not to unduly meddle with the appointment of religious leaders; this should be an exclusive church prerogative.[20] Thus, collective freedom of religion, in addition to religious association rights, categorically trump any non-discrimination concerns in this area. This should mean that the state must tolerate appointment practices which it might consider

---

[17] Art. 7, para. 3, of the 1995 Latvian Law.

[18] For a criticism of this type of rule, see Ringold Balodis, 'Church and State in Latvia', in *Law and Religion in Post-Communist Europe*, eds S. Ferrari and W.C. Durham (Leuven: Peeters, 2003), 153–5.

[19] Article 6g of the UN Religious Tolerance Declaration (1981).

[20] *Serif v. Greece*, Application No. 38178/97, Decision of 14 December 1999.

misogynistic or homophobic; and in most of Europe, states do not overtly interfere in appointment matters. Paradoxically, constitutionally privileged religious groups – namely, 'official', 'state' or 'established' churches – are often most at the mercy of the state in this area, whether directly or indirectly: either state authorities formally appoint church leaders, or Parliament must officially approve church nominations.

One other salient point to make here is that state interference in church appointment also takes place in secular European states with no established religion, albeit in more unexpected areas. For example, a 2010 US State Department report observes that in the Netherlands, 'the government of Turkey exercises influence within the country's Turkish Muslim community through its religious affairs directorate, the *Diyanet*, which is permitted to appoint imams for most of the more than 200 Turkish mosques in the country'.[21]

Other employment settings

In other employment areas where the link between the position and the religion is more remote, human rights law is somewhat more unsettled. Religious autonomy claims in this area have at times been respected by human rights monitoring bodies, but an international jurisprudential rule is not yet clearly discernible. The two leading cases before the European Court of Human Rights involved the dismissals of a Mormon public affairs official (*Obst v. Germany*)[22] and a Catholic organist (*Schüth v. Germany*)[23] for extramarital affairs. In *Obst* the Court found in favour of church autonomy, deeming that the courts had properly acted within the 'margin of appreciation' of the European Convention on Human Rights in weighing Obst's employment opportunities against the Church's adherence to its religious ethos. On the same day, however, the European Court ruled in *Schüth* that the state had breached the Convention. The difference between the two decisions seems to be that in the latter case the domestic authorities failed, according to the European Court, to make a fair and comprehensive assessment of all relevant and conflicting interests, particularly those of the individual employer.[24] The decision shows that church autonomy does not automatically trump all other interests. Implicitly,

---

[21] Bureau of Democracy, Human Rights, and Labor, *International Religious Freedom Report 2010*, November 2010, Netherlands entry, http://www.state.gov/j/drl/rls/irf/2010/148969.htm.

[22] *Obst v. Germany*, Application No. 425/03, Decision of 23 September 2010.

[23] *Schüth v. Germany*, Application No 1620/03, Decision of 23 September 2010.

[24] See for more extensive analyses of these and other relevant cases, Ian Leigh, 'Balancing Religious Autonomy and Other Human Rights under the European Convention', *Oxford Journal of Law and Religion* (2012): 1–17; and Carolyn Evans, 'Religious Autonomy and Secular Employment Standards: Developments in the European Court of Human Rights' (conference paper presented at the International Center for Law and Religion Studies, 2010), http://iclrs.org/index.php?pageId=2&linkId=152&contentId=412&blurbId=1060.

the Court hints at two critical factors: (1) Employment arrangements may make compliance with the religious ethos of an organization a contractual obligation for certain positions; and (2) the state must look at the particulars of the case to assess whether the 'damage' inflicted upon the organization by 'unorthodox behavior' warrants more or less freedom from state oversight. This is problematic because church autonomy is typically granted precisely so that secular authorities not be called upon to adjudicate spiritual matters. Another unsettled area of European jurisprudence involves sexual orientation. Putting it bluntly, what if Obst had been dismissed for coming out of the closet rather than for adultery?[25] We will return to that question below.

Employment in religious schools constitutes its own special jurisprudential category because many states recognize education as a particularly important service. May a school take disciplinary steps against a teacher who deviates from its religious orthodoxy? This issue was put before the Human Rights Committee in *Delgado Páez v. Columbia*.[26] Delgado Páez was a religion and ethics teacher at a secondary school in Leticia, Colombia. As an advocate of 'liberation theology', his views on these subjects differed from those of local ecclesiastical and educational authorities, resulting eventually in his resignation.[27] The Human Rights Committee concluded that requiring Mr Delgado to teach the traditional Catholic religion did not violate his right to freedom of expression, religion or belief.[28] This case reinforces religious autonomy, seemingly establishing that anyone who voluntarily becomes an employee of a denominational school may be required to abide by this organization's ethos.[29]

---

[25] See *Lillian Ladele and Gary McFarlane v. United Kingdom*, Application Nos. 51671/10 and 36516/10, lodged on 27 August 2010 and 24 June 2010: a variation on that theme will shortly be decided by the ECHR (civil servants refusing to register same-sex partnerships), albeit it in the form of an individual conscientious objection claim rather than a church autonomy claim, thus making it less relevant for our current purposes. It is the fact that dismissals here have occurred in the public sphere that makes that type of case fundamentally different.

[26] *William Eduardo Delgado Páez v. Colombia*, Communication No. 195/1985, UN Doc. CCPR/C/39/D/195/1985, Views of July 12, 1990.

[27] Ibid., para. 2.1–2.10, for the particulars of the case.

[28] Ibid., para. 5.7–5.9. The Committee did ultimately establish a violation of Art. 25, para. c, of the ICCPR as it considered that the constant harassment and the threats against his person (in respect of which the state party had failed to provide protection) made the author's continuation in public service teaching impossible (para. 5.9) (something that clearly was specific to this case).

[29] Some states have laws in place to guarantee this. See Art. 60, para. 5b, of the UK School Standards and Framework Act 1998 (c. 31), which deals with schools with a religious character and provides that 'regard may be had, in connection with the termination of the employment of any teacher at the school, to any conduct on his part which is incompatible with the precepts, or with the upholding of the tenets, of the religion or religious denomination so specified'.

Though fact-specific assessments are necessary in this area, they make clear rules difficult to identify regarding how far religious autonomy stretches. This affects not only *dismissals*, but also *hiring*. To what extent may a school hire – or decline to hire – personnel because of their religious affiliation? European state practice, informed by EU Regulations, has started to set out some 'general solutions' to this issue. An EU Council Directive entitled 'Employment Framework Directive' of 2000 indicates two types of possible exceptions to equality law in employment matters:

- 'genuine occupational requirements' exceptions[30]
- preservation of 'institutional religious ethos' exceptions.[31]

If religious affiliation is essential to appropriately carrying out the tasks and responsibilities of a certain job, it may be made a precondition for obtaining that job. These are 'genuine occupational requirements' (*bona fide* requirements in US legal practice and literature). An occupational requirement is only 'genuine' if there is a legitimate link between the nature of the work and the religious affiliation in question. An employer's simple preference for someone of a certain religion would clearly not suffice, nor would an employer's prejudice against a certain religion. Thus, only certain positions include a genuine occupational requirement. Actual ecclesiastical positions, naturally, fall within this category (again, freedom of religion norms directly protect the right of religious groups to freely appointment their religious leaders).

Relatively recent British legislation, largely intended to implement the 'Employment Framework Directive',[32] shows an attempt to find that balance.[33] Similar genuine occupational requirement schemes can be found in the laws of many other European states.[34]

---

[30] 'Exception' is arguably a misnomer, given that in genuine occupational requirement cases differential treatment based upon religion is, in the first place, perfectly 'objective and reasonable' (in equality law jargon), is not discrimination, and therefore requires no exception.

[31] Council Directive 2000/78/EC ('EU Employment Framework Directive') of 27 November 2000.

[32] Art. 4, para. 1, of Council Directive 2000/78/EC ('Employment Framework Directive') of 27 November 2000.

[33] Art. 7, para. 2, of the Employment Equality (Religion or Belief) Regulations, No. 1660/2003, of 26 June 2003. The Regulations do not apply to Northern Ireland, which long since has its own similar regulations in place (Fair Employment and Treatment Order of 1998).

[34] For example, Austria, Belgium, Bulgaria, Cyprus, Czech Republic, Denmark, Finland, Germany, Greece, Hungary, Ireland, Italy, Latvia, Luxembourg, Malta, Norway, Poland, Portugal and Slovakia. For an extensive discussion and analysis, see Temperman, *State-Religion Relationships*, 265–8.

Only ecclesiastical jobs would automatically justify posing religion as an occupational requirement. The 'easy cases' which certainly do not merit a religious requirement involve such positions as cleaning personnel, janitors, secretarial personnel, catering staff, etc.[35] Positions in between these two extremes – such as the mentioned church organist – naturally are the most difficult to judge, especially for the state, which is poorly situated to make close assessments. Some might suggest, furthermore, that even if the state were competent to make such judgments, religious autonomy should prevent the state from interfering at all.

A number of European states have judged that, in order to accommodate organizations that wish to maintain their 'religious identity', certain types of employers merit greater flexibility in their hiring policies. This is the 'religious ethos exception'. In addition to the UK,[36] a number of other European states have religious ethos exemption schemes in place.[37] However, because the 'Employment Framework Directive' *approves* religious ethos exceptions but does not *impose* them,[38] European practice in this regard varies.

The Directive defines the scope of religious autonomy, making very clear not only what forms of differential treatment are to be tolerated but also what forms are not. It provides that religious ethos exemption schemes 'should not justify discrimination on another ground [besides religion or belief]'.[39] Thus, religiously-motivated 'multi-dimensional discrimination', such as gender or sexual-orientation discrimination, is impermissible despite its connection to an employer's religious beliefs. Some states, however, have ignored this restriction.

Membership

Turning to the next question, we now consider whether religious organizations may make distinctions between people on the basis of religion in the area of membership criteria. Membership would seem to be an internal issue *par excellence*, with state interference at odds with organizational autonomy rights and freedom of religion generally. Some states make this explicit, like the United Kingdom, where the Equality Act expressly authorizes religious organizations and charities to restrict membership based upon religion or belief.[40]

---

[35] As far as the latter position is concerned, it is not unimaginable that knowledge of certain religious dietary needs, such as familiarity with *halal* or *kosher* food, can be posed as a requirement for certain positions within certain institutions.

[36] Art. 7, para. 3, of the Employment Equality Regulations (ibid.).

[37] For example, Austria, Belgium, Bulgaria, Cyprus, Denmark, Germany, Greece, Hungary, Ireland, Italy, Latvia, Luxembourg, Malta, Netherlands, Poland, Slovakia, and Spain. For an extensive discussion and analysis, see Temperman, *State-Religion Relationships*, 268–72.

[38] Art. 4, para. 2, of Council Directive 2000/78/EC of 27 November 2000.

[39] Art. 4, para. 2, of the Employment Framework Directive.

[40] See Art. 57 and 60 of the Equality Act of 2006, Law c.3/2006. However, this does not apply to organizations whose sole or main purpose is commercial, despite their formally

Accommodation of organizational autonomy is far-reaching in this area, and may even trump equal *political* rights. Take for instance the case of *Arenz v. Germany* before the Human Rights Committee.[41] Mr Paul Arenz was excluded from the the German Christian Democratic Party (CDU) because he was a Scientologist. The Human Rights Committee agreed with the German courts that the state may not dictate how religious organizations, including political parties, choose their members. Thus, the right to participate in public affairs does not seem to include an absolute right to join one's political party of choice – the underlying rationale being, perhaps, that the *residual right* to found one's own party is always available.

However, *multi-dimensional* discrimination appears to transgress the limits of religious autonomy. The Committee on the Elimination of Discrimination against Women (CEDAW) has repeatedly criticized the Netherlands' reluctance to take action (for example, in the form of freezing its public funding) against the SGP, an orthodox Protestant political party founded in 1918 which until very recently restricted party membership to men, allegedly on biblical grounds. Clearly, Christian women have a residual right here: they could found their own political party. However, CEDAW argues that the Reformed Protestant Party (Staatkundig Gereformeerde Partij, SGP)'s policy violates the Covenant and must be changed.

Thus, it appears that differential treatment based purely on grounds of religion can be considered objective and reasonable, whereas religiously-motivated discrimination against women or homosexuals is increasingly considered to be *objective-yet-not-reasonable*. The approach taken internationally appears to be a matter of principle above anything. These monitoring bodies are not so naïve as to think that their actions will eradicate discriminatory practices; rather, they signal that they do not want to see states *pro-actively accommodating or indeed encouraging* such practices.

Services

A related issue arises when religious organizations seek to limit their services to members only. UK law explicitly allows this,[42] and it is generally unproblematic except where the service rendered has no *public alternative*. For example, in states where education has traditionally been provided exclusively by religious institutions, permitting them to render this service exclusively to their adherents may cause access issues. If the state fails in its positive duty to provide sufficient non-denominational schools, it may be actively – albeit perhaps inadvertently – contributing to religious segregation. The Committee on Economic, Social and Cultural Rights, for instance, observed that public schools in Northern Ireland are:

---

religious nature.

[41] Human Rights Committee, *Paul Arenz et al v. Germany*, Communication No. 1138/2002, UN Doc. CCPR/C/80/D/1138/2002 (2004), Views of March 24, 2004.

[42] See Art. 57, para. 3, and Art. 58 of the Equality Act of 2006, Law c.3/2006.

heavily segregated, with most Protestants attending Protestant schools and most Catholics attending Catholic schools and only approximately 2 per cent of the school population attending integrated schools. The ... current government policy, which appears to consist of a willingness to consider the conversion of existing Protestant or Catholic schools into integrated schools if it is the wish of the majority in a given school, is ineffective and likely to preserve the status quo.[43]

The Human Rights Committee similarly reproached Ireland recently, observing that:

the vast majority of Ireland's primary schools are privately run denominational schools that have adopted a religious integrated curriculum thus depriving many parents and children who so wish to have access to secular primary education. ... The State party should increase its efforts to ensure that non-denominational primary education is widely available in all regions of the State party, in view of the increasingly diverse and multi-ethnic composition of the population of the State party.[44]

If the state fails to provide non-denominational education, various educational and religious rights are almost inevitably infringed.[45] Ireland's Equality Act allows denominational schools, which are virtually all Catholic, to refuse admission to pupils who do not adhere to their denomination in order to preserve the religious 'ethos of the school'.[46] Such a system fosters serious human rights concerns for various reasons. First, no appropriate form of education may be available to children whose parents do not belong to a majority religion. Furthermore, because those parents might prefer their children to receive any education, religious differences notwithstanding, over none at all, they might feel compelled to *become* affiliated, for example, by means of conversion or baptizing their children to meet enrolment requirements.[47]

Guidelines published by the Office for Democratic Institutions and Human Rights, part of the Organization for Security and Cooperation in Europe, quite

---

[43] E/1998/22 (1997) 56 at para. 301 (UK); reiterated in 2002: E/2003/22 (2002) 39 at para. 226 and 245 (UK).

[44] CCPR/C/IRL/CO/3 (2008), para. 2 [Ireland].

[45] See Alison Mawhinney, *Submission to the Human Rights Committee with Respect to the Third Periodic Report of Ireland* [NGO Information], March 2008; this shadow report is a response to UN GAOR, Hum. Rts. Comm., UN Doc. CCPR/C/IRL/3, para. 409–11.

[46] Art. 7, para. 3c of the [Irish] Equal Status Act, No. 8/2000.

[47] Alison Mawhinney, *Submission to the Human Rights Committee*, at 2, 4. Both problems are reported in the mentioned shadow report; similar concerns have been raised by the Committee on the Elimination of Racial Discrimination in its Conclusion Observations: A/60/18 (2005), para. 142 [Ireland].

sensibly and convincingly argue that the legitimacy of restrictions on services depends on whether there are solely religious or also *public* services at stake: 'Although differential treatment may be permissible, it is appropriate to draw attention to the competing values of religious autonomy for institutions and the right of citizens to be free from discrimination on the grounds of religion, especially when the employers receive public financing or tax deductions for their activities.'[48]

More problematic, again, would appear to be religiously-motivated restrictions on the grounds of sex or sexual preference, such as Catholic adoption agencies refusing to place children with homosexual couples. While it is uncomplicated enough, most of the time, for human rights monitors to accept restrictive criteria as 'reasonable', it is much harder for them to endorse what they perceive as homophobic or misogynistic attitudes.

Concluding reflections

A number of states design and implement religious association laws not to facilitate religious freedom but rather to control the practice of religion, often actively discriminating against minority religions, including those they consider dangerous or otherwise undesirable sects. Deregulation is the key to removing these injustices. Before that, however, states must stop seeing organized religion as a 'problem' policy area in desperate need of ever more elaborate – and more burdensome – rules and regulations. States adopting, reviewing, revising and reforming religious association laws would be well-advised to consult human rights organizations, and if they consult religious organizations, to ensure that all groups present in the country – large and small – are heeded. All too often, human rights based reforms in religious association laws breed meagre – and occasionally downright counter-productive – results. One plausible explanation for this can be found in the *persecution paradox*. There is perhaps something inherent to established religion (in the wide sense of the word) – and to human nature – that resists reform. Durham and Scharffs explain this inherent trap:

> A flagrant flaw of human nature, which has been too often historically demonstrated, is the tendency of a majority group to abuse its power to the detriment and suffering of minority peoples. An unhappy irony occurs when these persecutors, emboldened by the strength of their numbers, have themselves previously suffered the pains of persecution.[49]

---

[48] OSCE/ODIHR, *Guidelines for Review of Legislation Pertaining to Religion or Belief* (prepared by ODIHR's Advisory Panel of Experts on Freedom of Religion or Belief in consultation with the Council of Europe's Venice Commission, June–July 2004), 15–16.

[49] W. Cole Durham Jr. and Brett G. Scharffs, *Law and Religion: National, International, Comparative Perspectives* (Austin: Wolters Kluwer/Aspen Publishers, 2010), 4–5.

Thus, it seems only too 'natural' that majority churches – most of whom suffered persecution as a minority sect at some point – want to maintain their precious and painstakingly acquired dominance at others' expense. States ought to prevent that.

Bright-line rules governing the delicate interplay between religious autonomy and equal rights have not yet fully crystalized. States recently seem to have developed an increased understanding for organized religion's need to enforce its ethos internally, provided any differential treatment is exclusively religion-based. When other characteristics – such as sexual orientation or gender – are implicated, autonomy is not quite the trump card religious organizations would like it to be. Because groups on both sides of the controversy have been traditionally discriminated against, decision-makers feel morally justified whichever side they take.

Chapter 12
The State, New Religious Movements, and Legislation on Religion: A Case Study of Three Baltic States

Ringo Ringvee

The relationship between the state and NRMs in the legal framework is influenced by various factors and has different consequences to all parties involved. This chapter will consider the legal concerns of religious associations in general and NRMs in particular in the Baltic States – Estonia, Latvia, and Lithuania. These three countries share a common recent history under Soviet rule from 1940 until 1991, when they re-established their independence. However, despite their similarities, these societies have different religious histories and are remarkably distinct from one another religiously. These differences are reflected in the legislative sphere, as each country's approach to church–state relations will show.

Three Baltic states – similarities and differences

Estonia, Latvia and Lithuania share a distinctive geographical area in Northeastern Europe, and their histories have much in common. The present day Estonia and Latvia were ruled in turn by the Teutonic Order; Danish, Swedish, and Polish kings; and – from the eighteenth century onward – by Russian tsars until their independence in 1918. Lithuania, on the other hand, formed part of a powerful political union with Poland starting in the sixteenth century, which lasted until it, like its neighbours, became part of the Russian Empire in the eighteenth century. It, too, gained independence from Russia in 1918. After the Second World War all three nations became part of the Soviet Union until its collapse.[1]

Despite their common recent history, the Baltic States' cultural identities and traditions – including their religiosity – are surprisingly diverse. Present day Latvia and Estonia became Christianized by the thirteenth century, and from the sixteenth century onward were Lutheran territories. Lithuania, on the other hand, was Christianized by the Roman Catholic Church as late as the fifteenth

---

[1] For the history of the Baltic States, see Andrejs Plakans, *A Concise History of the Baltic States* (Cambridge: Cambridge University Press, 2011); and Andres Kasekamp, *A History of the Baltic States* (Basingstoke: Palgrave Macmillan, 2010).

century, and unlike the other Baltic States, its national identity remains closely related to its majority Catholic identity.[2] In the nineteenth century the Catholic clergy in Lithuania – most of whom were native Lithuanians – greatly influenced the Lithuanian national awakening process, resulting in a distinctly Catholic Lithuanian nation.[3] During contemporaneous national awakenings in Estonia and Latvia, on the other hand, most clergy were not natives, but Germans. Thus, although the Lutheran tradition, especially the Herrnhut movement, set the stage for the awakening, the largely foreign Church participated little in the nationalist movement. Thus, Lutheran Latvia and Estonia lack Lithuania's connection between national and religious identities.[4] Nevertheless, the Lutheran Church retained its position in both countries as a form of civil religion. According to censuses from the 1930s, 77.6 per cent of the Estonian population and 55.1 per cent of the Latvian population identified themselves as Lutherans.

There were several social changes both in Latvia and in Estonia during the Soviet period that weakened the resilience of religion. Forced collectivization, rapid urbanization and industrialization, accompanied by immigration from the other parts of the Soviet Union, ate away at religion's influence. The Soviet atheist policy was successful in estranging the population from religion in the traditionally Lutheran territories of the Soviet bloc – Estonia, Latvia and Eastern Germany[5] – and the traditional Lutheran churches of these countries also fared poorly in the 1990s, struggling to adjust to the new consumer-oriented free market religious economy.[6] The same was true of the Lithuanian Catholic Church, although perhaps to a lesser extent. The ethnic composition of Lithuania did not change as much as in Latvia or Estonia under Soviet rule, and Lithuanians were thus able to largely retain their Catholic identity.

---

[2] See also Vilma Žaltuskaite, 'Catholicism and Nationalism in the Views of the Younger Generation of Lithuanian Clergy in the Late Nineteenth and Early Twentieth Centuries', *Lithuanian Historical Studies*, 5 (2000): 113–30.

[3] Arunas Streikus, 'The History of Religion in Lithuania since the Nineteenth Century', in *Religious Diversity in Post–Soviet Society: Ethnographies of Catholic Hegemony*, eds Milda Ališauskiene and Ingo W. Schröder (Aldershot: Ashgate, 2012), 37–8.

[4] Juris Dreifelds, 'Religion in Latvia: From Atrophy to Rebirth', in *Religion and Political Change in Europe: Past and Present*, ed. Ausma Cimdina (Pisa: Edizioni Plus: Università di Pisa, 2003), 242–3. For comparative analysis of the national movements in Estonia and Latvia see Toivo U. Raun, 'The Latvian and Estonian National Movements, 1860–1914', *The Slavonic and East European Review* 64 (1986): 66–80.

[5] On Eastern Germany, see Detlef Pollack and Olaf Müller, 'Religiousness in Central and Eastern Europe: Towards Individualization?', in *Religions, Churches and Religiosity in Post-Communist Europe*, ed. Irena Borowik (Krakow: Nomos, 2006), 23–8.

[6] Frans Hoppenbrouwers, 'Romancing Freedom: Church and Society in the Baltic States Since the End of Communism', *Religion, State and Society* 27 (1999): 161. See also Mikko Ketola, 'The Baltic Churches in the Process of Transformation and Consolidation of Democracy since 1985', *Kirchliche Zeitgeschichte* 1, (2007): 66–80.

While all religions welcomed the abolition of Soviet restrictions, the traditional majority churches considered the new market economy and the consequent increase in religious pluralism as threats to their traditional values and society. The Catholic Church in Lithuania and the Lutheran churches in Latvia and Estonia had no experience with the religious market – they had never had to do missionary work, for instance.[7] Thus, since the early 1990s, the traditional churches' membership has steadily decreased.[8]

Today, religiosity differs in each Baltic state, as shown by a Eurobarometer survey from 2005. Forty-nine per cent of respondents in Lithuania claimed to believe in God, compared to 37 per cent in Latvia and 16 per cent in Estonia. Interestingly, the same survey found that only 36 per cent of Lithuanians believed in 'a spirit or life force', compared to 49 per cent of Latvians and 54 per cent of Estonians.[9] According to a Gallup survey from 2009, religion was considered 'important' or 'very important' in daily life by 42 per cent of respondents in Lithuania, 39 per cent in Latvia and 17 per cent in Estonia.[10] According to a 2001 population census, 90 per cent of Lithuanians considered themselves religiously affiliated, while in Estonia less than 33 per cent said the same in a 2000 census.[11] In Lithuania 79 per cent of the population identified themselves as Catholics, with the Orthodox Church a distant second with 4.1 per cent.[12] In Estonia, on the other hand, Lutherans – the largest denomination – made up just 13.6 per cent of the population, followed by the internally divided Orthodox community with 12.8 per cent.[13] Latvia has not measured religiosity in its population censuses. The membership numbers provided annually by the Latvian Ministry of Justice place Latvia's devoutness somewhere between Lithuania and Estonia. In 2008 there were 450,506 Lutherans and 500,000 Catholics in Latvia according to the

---

[7] Ingo Schröder, 'The Elusive Religious Field in Lithuania', in *Religious Diversity in Post-Soviet Society: Ethnographies of Catholic Hegemony*, eds Milda Ališauskiene and Ingo Schröder (Aldershot: Ashgate, 2012), 86.

[8] Milda Ališauskiene, 'The Manifestation and Development of New Religions in Lithuania: Case Study of the Art of Living Foundation' (summary of doctoral dissertation, Vytautus Magnus University, 2009), 18. Lea Altnurme, 'Changes in Mythic Patterns in Estonian Religious Life Stories', *Social Compass* 58 (2011): 79.

[9] 'Social Values, Science and Technology', Special Eurobarometer 225/Wave 63.1 Report, http://ec.europa.eu/public_opinion/archives/ebs/ebs_225_report_en.pdf.

[10] 'Religion', Gallup Global Reports, 2009, http://www.gallup.com/poll/128210/Gallup-Global-Reports.aspx.

[11] The results concerning question of religious affiliation in population censuses conducted in 2012 will be published in 2013.

[12] 'Sociodemographic Characteristics', Department of Statistics to the Government of the Republic of Lithuania; Lithuanian Department of Statistics Webpage, http://db.stat.gov.lt/sips/Database/cen_en/p71en/demography/demography.asp.

[13] '2000 Population Census Data', Estonian Statistics Office Webpage, http://pub.stat.ee/px-web.2001/I_Databas/Population_census/PHC2000/16Religious_affiliation/16Religious_affiliation.asp.

statistics presented by the churches themselves. According to a survey from 2003, 25 per cent of Latvian respondents identified themselves as Lutheran, 25 per cent as Catholic and 21 per cent as Orthodox.[14]

In all the Baltic States the adherents of NRMs form a small minority in the general population. Most of them – like most denominations operating in the Baltic States today – arrived there after Soviet dissolution. Globalization, including the curiosity (and sensationalism) of the tabloid media, has made 'new spirituality' part of the Baltic States' mass culture and informs popular discourse regarding NRMs in the Baltic States.[15] Nikandrs Gills has described Latvia's national sentiment concerning NRMs in the 1990s as 'moral panic'.[16] Milda Ališauskiene has noted that in Lithuania the general population has little personal contact with NRMs, and the same seems to be true in both Estonia and Latvia.[17] As such, the role of the media as the sole information provider becomes crucial as they are often relied upon not only by ordinary citizens but also by political decision makers.

Legislation on religion

The constitutions of all three Baltic States guarantee freedom of religion or belief both on individual as well as on collective levels, following the principles of the European Convention for the Protection of Human Rights and Fundamental Freedoms. The Estonian Constitution, adopted by national referendum in 1992, states in Article 40 that Estonia has no state church and declares freedom of religion or belief.[18] The Constitution of Lithuania, also adopted by national referendum in 1992, stipulates in Article 26 that freedom of thought, conscience and religion shall not be restricted. Article 43 adds that there shall be no state religion in Lithuania. However, it continues, 'The State shall recognize the churches and religious organizations that are traditional in Lithuania, whereas other churches and religious organizations shall be recognized provided that they have support in society and their teaching and practices are not in conflict with the law and public morals'.[19] In 1992 the Latvian Parliament restored the pre-Soviet Latvian

---

[14] 'Religious Belonging and Religious Demography: Latvia', statistics by Ringolds Balodis, 2008, http://www.eurel.info/spip.php?rubrique402&lang=en.

[15] Ališauskiene, 'The Manifestation and Development of New Religions in Lithuania', 13. This was noted also by MIVILUDES in its 2007 report. See 'Interministerial Mission of Vigilance and Combat against Sectarian Aberrations Report to the Prime Minister', MIVILUDES 2007, http://www.miviludes.gouv.fr/publications-de-la-miviludes/rapports-annuels/rapport-annuel-2007.

[16] Gills, *Jehovas liecinieki Latvija* (Riga: Filozofijas un sociologijas instituts, 2008), 164.

[17] Ališauskiene, 'The Manifestation and Development of New Religions in Lithuania', 18.

[18] Constitution of the Republic of Estonia, http://www.president.ee/en/republic-of-estonia/the-constitution/index.html.

[19] The Constitution of the Republic of Lithuania, http://www3.lrs.lt/home/Konstitucija/Constitution.htm.

Constitution from 1922. However, religious freedom issues had been dealt with in a separate legal act, the Constitutional Law about the Rights and Obligations of the Citizen and Person, adopted in 1991. In 1998, the Latvian Parliament amended the Constitution by adding Chapter VII to replace this law. Article 99 of the Latvian Constitution stipulates that the church shall be separate from the state.[20]

All three Baltic States have adopted special laws which define religious associations as a specific form of non-profit organization. Legal entity status guarantees collective religious freedom and gives certain privileges to religious associations – most commonly tax exemptions, but also such benefits as state-funded denominational religious education in public schools, the right to conduct civilly valid marriages, and confessional privileges. In all three Baltic States religious communities are entitled to register as legal entities. If the community does not consider legal status necessary for their activities they may exist without official recognition as a religious entity. However, in certain situations lack of status or having regular non-profit association status may hinder a group's ability to practice its religion. For example, in June 2000 the Lithuanian Ministry of Justice warned the 'Collegiate Association for the Research of Principles' to discontinue proselytizing as they were registered under the Law on Public Organizations and not as an organization with religious objectives that ought to become a legal entity under the Law on Religious Organizations. Registration requirements for religious associations are highly susceptible to abuse, and many regimes, including some in the Baltic States, use them to discriminate against disfavoured groups, including NRMs.[21]

Drafting religious association laws is often a long process that reflects the influences of various interest groups. The general trend in post-Soviet societies has been for so-called traditional majority churches to attempt, during the reconstruction process, to re-establish social dominance and/or regain privileges from the pre-Soviet period, and the Baltic States have been no exception.[22] The Roman Catholic Church's efforts on this front have been the most successful of any religion present in the Baltic States. As a 'traditional' religious organization, the Church is protected by the Lithuanian Constitution, and in Latvia and Estonia special statutes regulate relations between the government and the Vatican.

---

[20] The Constitution of the Republic of Latvia, http://www.humanrights.lv/doc/latlik/satver~1.htm.

[21] W. Cole Durham, Jr, 'Facilitating Freedom of Religion or Belief through Religious Association Laws', in *Facilitating Freedom of Religion or Belief: A Deskbook*, eds Tore Lindholm, W. Cole Durham, Jr, and Bahia G. Tahzib-Lie (Leiden: Martinus Nijhoff Publishers, 2004), 321–30.

[22] Ales Crnic, 'New Religions in 'New Europe'', *Journal of Church and State* 3 (2007): 551.

Legislation on religion in Lithuania

Lithuania was the first of the Baltic States to draft legislation on religious communities, starting even before the dissolution of the Soviet Union. A first draft from 1989 guaranteed freedom of religion and considered all religious associations equal before the law. However, the 1992 Constitution of Lithuania merely indicates that the state shall recognize 'traditional' churches and religious associations.

This idea of a distinction between traditional and non-traditional religions was introduced in 1992 with the second draft of the Law on Religious Communities and Associations, which – when it was finally adopted in 1995 – established the so-called European model of a multi-tiered system of religious associations.[23] Article 5 of the Law considered the nine religious communities in Lithuania with a history of at least 300 years – Roman Catholic (the most privileged religious association in Lithuania[24]), Greek Catholic, Evangelical Lutheran, Evangelical Reformed, Russian Orthodox, Old Believers, Jewish, Sunni Muslim and Karaite – as traditional parts of the country's historical and cultural heritage.[25]

In 2001 the Law on Religious Communities and Associations was amended to provide state funding for educational institutions run by traditional religions, most of which are Catholic. Non-traditional religions may also apply for such financial support. Critics have condemned this kind of favouritism, although the Lithuanian Constitutional Court has upheld traditional churches' privileged status.[26] Religions that have existed for more than 25 years in Lithuania may gain state recognition if they are considered to have public support and serve an important role in Lithuania's society, spiritual heritage, and culture. Various benefits accompany recognition, including the right to provide religious education in public schools.[27] The Lithuanian Parliament makes the final decision regarding state recognition,

---

[23] Valstybės *Žinios* 1995, No 89-1985, 'Religinių bendruomeniųir bendrijų įstatymas'. For Lithuanian legislative acts see www.litex.lt. On the dynamics of the change in the drafting process of the Lithuanian law on religious associations see Donatas Glodenis, 'Legislation on Religion and the Challenge of Pluralism in Lithuania', *Religija . lt*, 1 July 2005, http://en.religija.lt/content/legislation-religion-and-challenge-pluralism-lithuania.

[24] Donatas Glodenis, 'Administrative and Financial Matters in the Area of Religious Freedom and Religious Communities: Case of Lithuania', in *Legal Aspects of Religious Freedom*, ed. Drago Cepar (Ljubljana: Office of the Government of the Republic of Slovenia for Religious Communities, 2008), 400. In addition to other privileges, it is, for example, exempt from all taxes.

[25] Ruta iliukaite and Donatas Glodenis, 'State and Church in Lithuania', in *State and Church in the Baltic States: 2001*, ed. Ringolds Balodis (Riga: Religijas Brivibas Asociacija, 2001), 76; and Glodenis, *Legislation on Religion*.

[26] Jolanta Kuznecoviene, 'Church and State in Lithuania', in *Law and Religion in Post-Communist Europe*, eds Silvio Ferrari and W. Cole Durham, Jr (Leuven, Paris, Dudley, MA: Peeters, 2003), 186–93.

[27] Glodenis, 'Challenge of Pluralism in Lithuania'.

which often has less to do with legal criteria than with historical–cultural considerations.[28] Several religious associations have been denied state recognition in Lithuania. Probably the most well known is the United Methodist Church, which has applied several times since 2001 without success.[29] The pagan Romuva community was also denied recognition in 2002, allegedly because of pressure from the Roman Catholic Church.[30] However, in 2001 the Evangelical Baptist Union of Lithuania, and in 2008 the Seventh-day Adventist Church, became state-recognized religions. In 2002 Lithuania started the drafting process for a new law on religious communities, during which there have been proposals to raise the recognition requirement from 25 years to 50 years.[31]

Groups that do not qualify for state recognition, including NRMs, may still apply to become registered religious communities. Few groups are denied registration, though there have been exceptions. Perhaps the most well known is the Osho Ojas Meditation Centre, which the Ministry of Justice refused to register in 1997, 1998 and 2003. The Ministry repeatedly questioned whether the Centre was religious at all and objected to its morals (before becoming a member, applicants had to produce a valid AIDS certificate issued at least three months previously).[32] The Centre subsequently argued its case in court and finally gained registration in 2005.[33]

Legislation on religion in Latvia

Although Lithuania was the first of the Baltic States to draft new legislation on religion, Latvia was the first to implement such legislation. In 1990, shortly before officially

---

[28] Irena Vaišvilaite, 'Tradicinių ir kitų religinių bendruomenių perskyra Lietuvoje', in *Religija ir Teise Pilietineje Visuomeneje*, ed. Danute Petrauskiene (Vilnius: Juistitia, 2001), 128; and Glodenis, 'Challenge of Pluralism in Lithuania'.

[29] See Žiliukaite and Glodenis, 'State and Church in Lithuania'; and IRFR Lithuania 2004, 'International Religious Freedom Report 2004', US Department of State, Bureau of Democracy, Human Rights, and Labour, http://www.state.gov/g/drl/rls/irf/2004/35468.htm. Also other communities like the New Apostolic Church, Pentecostals, and the Seventh-day Adventists have applied or reportedly planned to apply for this status.

[30] Michael Strmiska and Vilius Dundzila, 'Romuva: Lithuanian Paganism in Lithuania and America', in *Modern Paganism in World Cultures: Comparative Perspectives*, ed. Michael Strmiska (Santa Barbara, CA: ABC-Clio, 2005), 250; and IRFR Lithuania 2004.

[31] Glodenis, 'Administrative and Financial Matters', 398.

[32] Solveiga Krumina-Konkova, 'New Religious Minorities in the Baltic States', in *New Religious Movements in the 21st Century: Legal, Political, and Social Challenges in Global Perspective*, eds Phillip Lucas and Thomas Robbins (New York & London: Routledge, 2004), 121.

[33] Milda Ališauskiene, 'Freedom of Religion in the Baltic States', in *Spaces and Borders: Current Research on Religion in Central and Eastern Europe*, eds András Máté-Tóth and Cosima Rughiniș (Berlin/Boston: Walter de Gruyter, 2011), 141.

re-establishing independence, the Supreme Council of the Republic of Latvia adopted a law 'On Religious Organizations'.[34] The law was amended in 1991 with an important change to Article 5 stipulating that an organization applying for legal recognition as a religious organization must endure a three-year waiting period before the Ministry of Justice issues its decision.[35] This requirement was abolished in 1995 in Parliament's new Law on Religious Organizations.[36] However, it required new religious communities to re-register annually for the first 10 years of their existence, after which they would be granted permanent registration. Only groups with at least 10 members qualified for recognition. The 1995 Law has since gone through several amendments. One of the most important, in 2002, raised the required number of founding members from 10 to 20. Another amendment allowed churches and congregational unions to regulate their relations with the state through separate laws,[37] thus guaranteeing one of the most important privileges enjoyed by the Catholic Church to other religions, as in the pre-Soviet period.[38] Latvia signed special agreements with the Lutheran, Orthodox, Baptist, Adventist, Methodist and Old Believers churches[39] in 2004; with the Latvian Old-Believer Pomora Church,[40] Seventh-day Adventist Union,[41] Union of Latvian Baptists,[42] United Methodist Church[43] and Riga Jewish Religious Union[44] in 2007; and with the Evangelical Lutheran Church[45] and the Orthodox Church[46] in 2008.

---

[34] 'Likums 'Par reliģiskajām organizācijām'', Latvijas Republikas Augstākās Padomes un Valdības Ziņotājs, No.40, 1990.

[35] 'Par grozijumiem un papildinajumiem Letvijas Republikas likuma Likums 'Par reliģiskajām organizācijām'', Latvijas Republikas Augstākās Padomes un Valdības Ziņotājs, No.29/30, 1991.

[36] Latvijas Vēstnesis 146 (429) 26.09.1995 Reliģisko organizāciju likums. For Latvian legislative acts see www.likumi.lv.

[37] Latvias Vēstnesis 138 (2713), 26.09.2002. Grozījumi Reliģisko organizāciju likumā.

[38] Latvias Vēstnesis 137 (2712), 25.09.2002, *The Agreement between the republic of Latvia and the Holy See, November 8, 2000.*

[39] Jekaterina Macuka, 'Administrative and Financial Matters in the Area of Religious Freedom and Religious Communities in Latvia', in *Legal Aspects of Religious Freedom*, ed. Drago Cepar (Ljubljana: Office of the Government of the Republic of Slovenia for Religious Communities, 2008), 388.

[40] Latvias Vēstnesis 98 (3674), 20.06.2007, Latvijas Vecticībnieku Pomoras Baznīcas likums.

[41] Latvias Vēstnesis 93 (3669), 12.06.2007, Septītās Dienas Adventistu Latvijas draudžu savienības likums.

[42] Latvias Vēstnesis 86 (3662), 30.05.2007. Latvijas Baptistu Draudžu Savienības likums (Latvian Baptist Union Law).

[43] Latvias Vēstnesis 91 (3667), 07.06.2007. Latvijas Apvienotās Metodistu Baznīcas likums.

[44] Latvias Vēstnesis 98 (3674), 20.06.2007, Rīgas ebreju reliģiskās draudzes likums.

[45] Latvias Vēstnesis 188 (3972), 03.12.2008. Latvijas evaņģēliski luteriskās Baznīcas likums.

[46] Latvias Vēstnesis 188 (3972), 03.12.2008. Latvijas Pareizticīgās Baznīcas likums.

Though there is no legal definition for 'traditional religion' in Latvia, these religions could be considered 'traditional', as they have special privileges like the right to conduct civilly valid marriages. Some of them (Lutherans, Orthodox, Catholics, Old Believers and Baptists) may additionally provide teachers for state funded denominational religious education.[47] The Latvian Law on Religious Organizations and Associations from 1995 stipulates that state-funded religious education in public schools may be taught only by representatives of Evangelical Lutheran, Roman Catholic, Orthodox, Old Believer, Baptist and Jewish religions.[48] However, Latvia, like all three Baltic States, allows registered religious associations – including NRMs – to open private schools.

This does nothing to help non-traditional churches obtain registration. Perhaps none had a more tortuous – albeit ultimately successful – journey than the Jehovah's Witnesses. In 1993 the Witnesses applied to become registered as a religious association, contending that they had existed in Latvia in the 1930s as the International Bible Students Association, and thus should not to be subject to the three-year waiting period required of new religions. The Ministry of Justice disagreed, and the Jehovah's Witnesses took their case to court, eventually reaching the Latvian Supreme Court, which ruled in the Ministry's favour in 1995.[49] The next year the Witnesses' application was again denied, this time because the Ministry of Justice found them in violation of paragraph 11 of the Law on Religious Organizations: 'A religious organization is not registered if its activities pose a threat to the state security, public peace and order, [or the] health and morality of other persons, [or] if it propagates the ideas of religious intolerance and hatred'.[50] In July 1996 the Witnesses sued the Ministry for violating their Constitutional right to freedom of religion.[51] They dropped the case the following year, and finally became registered a year later.

Other churches have experienced similar difficulties. The Christian Science Church, which had already applied three times (in 1997, 1999 and 2001) without success, was finally registered as a religious organization in 2002 despite alleged opposition from the Latvian Medical Association.[52] Traditional churches have successfully lobbied for a 'one confession, one church' policy which, although

---

[47] Macuka, 'Administrative and Financial Matters', 387–8.

[48] On religious education in Latvia see Anta Filipsone, 'Time of Uncertain Conversions: Religious Education in Public Schools of the Post-Soviet Latvia', *Religious Education* 100 (2005): 52–66.

[49] Nikandrs Gills, 'Jehovah's Witnesses in Latvia in the 20th Century' (Paper presented at CESNUR 1998, Turin), http://www.cesnur.org/testi/bryn/br_gills.htm.

[50] Gills, 'Jehovah's Witnesses in Latvia'; Nikandrs Gills, 'Jehovah's Witnesses in the Social and Cultural Context of Contemporary Latvia' (Paper presented at CESNUR's 14th international conference, Riga, Latvia, 2000), http://www.cesnur.org/conferences/riga2000/gills.htm#Anchor-47857; and Gills, 'Jehovas Liecinieki Latvija', 155.

[51] Gills, 'Jehovas Liecinieki Latvija', 155–6.

[52] Krumina-Konkova, 'New Religious Minorities in the Baltic States', 121; Crnic, 'New Religions in 'New Europe'', 535.

intended to merely prevent religious schisms during the Latvian property reform,[53] makes it impossible for the Latvian Free Orthodox Church, for example, to register because the Latvian Orthodox Church already existed as a registered legal entity. Applications from the Confessional Lutheran Church and the independent Old Believers community were similarly denied. The Church of Scientology, present in Latvia since 2002[54] (indeed, Dianetics Centres have been operating in Latvia since the 1990s), has yet to receive recognition despite persistent efforts. Scientologists applied for registration as a religious association for the first time in 2006. The application was denied as the Ministry of Justice considered Scientology to be non-compliant to the Law on Religious Organizations.[55] In 2009 Scientology applied for the second time to become a registered religious association. However, according to the Ministry of Justice, Scientology could not to be considered a religion because it included elements of medicine.[56] In 2010 Scientology's application was once again denied, this time because the Ministry considered that Scientology had a negative impact on society.[57]

Legislation on religion in Estonia

From 1990 to 1993, religious organizations in Estonia obtained legal entity status by registering under the Law of Civic Associations. The drafting of a new law specific to religious associations started in 1991 under the leadership of the Religious Affairs Department at the Ministry of Culture, which stressed the importance of equal treatment of religious bodies. In 1993 the Estonian Parliament adopted the Churches and Congregations Act, establishing a neoliberal policy on religion.[58] Under the Act, groups register through the Ministry of the Interior rather than the Ministry of Culture. All religious groups applying for legal entity status

---

[53] Ringolds Balodis, *State and Church Relationship: Theory and Latvian State Experience. Summary of Presented Promotion* (Riga: Religijas Brivibas Asociacija, 2001), 46.

[54] Anita Stašulane, 'New Religious Movements in Latvia', *Soter* 32, (2009): 115.

[55] 'Interministerial Mission of Vigilance', 164.

[56] IRFR Latvia 2009, 'International and Religious Freedom Report 2009', US Department of State, Bureau of Democracy, Human Rights, and Labor, http://www.state.gov/j/drl/rls/irf/2009/127319.htm.

[57] IRFR Latvia 2010, 'International Religious Freedom Report 2010, Latvia', US Department of State, Bureau of Democracy, Human Rights, and Labor, http://www.state.gov/j/drl/rls/irf/2010/148951.htm.

[58] Riigi Teataja RT I 1993, 30, 510, *Kirikute ja koguduste seadus,* (Churches and Congregations Act). Estonian legal texts are available on www.riigiteataja.ee. On the impact of neoliberal governance on religion in Estonia see Ringo Ringvee, 'Regulating Religion in a Neoliberal Context: The Transformation of Estonia', in *Religion in the Neoliberal Age – Political Economy and Modes of Governance*, eds Tuomas Martikainen and François Gauthier (Aldershot: Ashgate, 2013): 143–60.

have the same requirements for registration (for example, at least 12 founding members) and the associations registered under the law enjoy the same privileges, such as tax benefits. Additionally, a 2001 amendment in the Family Law allows all registered religious associations to apply for the right to conduct civilly valid marriages.[59] Religious education in public schools is non-denominational and voluntary for all pupils. Registered religious associations, like other non-profit organizations, have the right to establish private schools.

Although there has been no official distinction between religions in Estonia, the government does maintain a close relationship with the Estonian Evangelical Lutheran Church. Furthermore, in 2002 the government signed a protocol of mutual interests with the Estonian Council of Churches, an ecumenical organization that represents the vast majority of Christians in Estonia.[60] Minority religions not belonging to the Council of Churches have criticized this move – especially the House of Taara and Native Religions, which represents indigenous neo-pagan groups.[61]

Despite the lack of difficult or discriminatory registration procedures, at least one group – Satanists – has nevertheless had problems getting their registration approved in Estonia. News of the registration efforts of the Church of Satan in Estonia started to spread in 1999 and prompted Parliament to consider limitations on religious freedom. The application was finally rejected in 2005 because, according to the Court's decision, Satanism was intended to unite criminally-minded people and could be dangerous to mentally unstable persons. Critics of the decision declared it to be politically motivated but considered appeal futile.[62] The Satanist group subsequently tried to become registered as a regular non-profit association, but this effort, too, was met with rejection.

---

[59] Riigi Teataja RT I 2001, 53, 307, Perekonnaseaduse muutmise seadus.

[60] The Estonian Council of Churches had 10 members in 2012: Estonian Evangelical Lutheran Church, Estonian Orthodox Church, Estonian Orthodox Church of Moscow Patriarchate, Roman Catholic Church, Union of Evangelical Christian and Baptist Churches, Estonian Conference of Seventh-day Adventist Church, Estonian Methodist Church, Estonian Christian Pentecostal Church, Estonian Congregation of the Armenian Church and Estonian Charismatic-Episcopalian Church. Sometimes the member churches of the Council are considered as traditional churches in Estonian context. However, in this approach it is interesting to see in the member list Charismatic Episcopalian Church, which was founded in the early 1990s in the United States, and arrived to Estonia in 1996. See also Huub Vogelaar, 'Ecumenical Relationships in Estonia', *Exchange: A Journal of Missiological and Ecumenical Research* 37 (2008): 190–219.

[61] On the relations between mainstream and minority religions in Estonia see Triin Vakker and Priit Rohtmets, 'Estonia: Relations between Christian and Non-Christian Religious Organizations and the State of Religious Freedom', *Religion, State and Society* 36 (2008): 45–53.

[62] On the case see Ringo Ringvee, 'Satanism in Estonia', in *Contemporary Religious Satanism: A Critical Anthology*, ed. J. Aagard Petersen (Aldershot: Ashgate Publishing, 2009): 129–40.

NRMs and the Baltic States

NRMs started to emerge in Estonia, Latvia and Lithuania in the late 1980s. Some were groups that had been banned or persecuted during the Soviet period, like the Jehovah's Witnesses or the Hare Krishna movement. The majority of the groups, however, were entirely new to the local religious landscape, including new Christian Charismatic movements, the Latter-day Saints (Mormons), Transcendental Meditation practitioners and followers of new Eastern gurus like Sathya Sai Baba.

Ethnic-based neo-pagan movements, such as Romuva in Lithuania, Dievturiba in Latvia, and Maausk and the Taara faith in Estonia, also appeared. These groups oppose Christianity, which they consider a foreign religion imposed on their native ancestors by the Crusades starting in the thirteenth century. They claim to represent the indigenous traditions of their countries' native people. Dievturiba and Maausk, which are similar to one another in many ways,[63] have particularly nativist views. The philosophy embodied in the slogan, 'Everybody who feels him– or herself Latvian is Dievturis' could easily apply to the Estonian followers of Maausk.[64] In all three countries these groups have appealed mostly to younger demographics.[65]

Thanks in part to the abrupt arrival of these and other groups, the religious situation in the Baltic States evolved rapidly during the late 1980s and early 1990s, often leading to confusion on the individual, collective and institutional levels.[66] New governmental institutions' reactions toward NRMs varied in different Baltic States, with those in Estonia and Lithuania generally being more liberal than in Latvia, where NRMs' legal status has long been a point of conflict. One reason for this may be that in Latvia, churches are more politically involved than in Estonia and Lithuania. Latvia's First Party (Latvijas Prima Partija), for example, has been an important political force closely associated with mainstream Latvian churches.[67] Furthermore, in each of the Baltic States, international politics –

---

[63] Both consider the term 'neopagan' pejorative and insulting, both represent high levels of individualistic approach to traditions, and there are also other similarities between the two; On Latvian *Dievturis* see Anita Stašulane, 'New Religious Movements in Latvia', *Soter* 32 (2009): 119–20.

[64] Solveiga Krumina-Konkova, 'New Religions in Latvia', *Nova Religio* 3 (1999): 130.

[65] Ibid., 122.

[66] Lea Altnurme, *Kristlusest oma Usuni: Uurimus Muutustest Eestlaste Religioossuses 20. Sajandi II Poolel. Kristlusest oma usuni* (Tartu: Tartu University Press, 2005), 80–3; Ringo Ringvee, *Riik ja Religioon Nõukogudejärgses Eestis 1991–2008*, (Tartu: Tartu University Press, 2011), 40; and Ringolds Balodis, 'Recent Developments of Latvian Model of Church and State Relationship: Constitutional Changes without Revising the Constitution', *Jurisprudenciija/Jurisprudence* 3 (2009): 11.

[67] Valdis Tēraudkalns, 'Religion and Politics in Latvia in the Beginning of 21st Century', *Religion in Eastern Europe* 21 (2011): 12–14.

notably the United States' promotion of religious freedom in the early 1990s and the French approach to sectarian movements in the beginning of the twenty-first century – have affected the attitudes of politicians concerning NRMs.

The anti-cult movement reached the Baltic States starting in the 1990s, and picked up steam in the beginning of the twenty-first century with the rise of state-sponsored anti-cult activities.[68] In 2001, 'destructive' sects were discussed in a parliamentary constitutional commission in Estonia. Parliament subsequently adopted the Churches and Congregations Act, which denied registration to religious associations headquartered outside of Estonia. Various religious organizations – including the Estonian Council of Churches – protested against the Act, and the president of Estonia refused to sign it; thus the Parliament adopted an amended version of it a year later in 2002.[69] In December 2001, the Lithuanian Parliament received a draft of proposed legislation called 'On Barring the Activities of Sects', which was severely critiqued by Parliament's legal departments and was eventually rejected.[70] In all the Baltic States, traditional religious organizations have spoken out against some NRMs, with varying results. For example, in May 2005 the Lithuanian Council of Bishops of the Roman Catholic Church raised concerns about 'shamanism' and objected to municipal funding of public 'tai chi' classes in Vilnius.[71]

In 2001, amid parliamentarians' calls for increased control of 'sects' or cults, Lithuania followed the Council of Europe's recommendation No. 1412 of 1999, establishing a commission to monitor the activities of religious, esoteric or spiritual groups. The commission has monitored how these groups spread their teachings, including through educational institutions, and launched investigations on various topics ranging from the alleged involvement of Satanists in the desecration of cemeteries to 'magic and the occult on television' to offers of 'magical services' by psychics and astrologers. Lithuanian Parliament also established a Working Group on Issues of Spiritual and Religious Groups in 2004 to respond to complaints from

---

[68] 'Литва перенимает у Франции опыт пресечения деятельности религиозных сект', *BNS News*, 13 December 2012, www.bns.ee; See also 'French Government's 'Anti-Cult Missionaries' Try to Export Anti-Cultism into Lithuania', *WorldWide Religious News*, 17 August 2009, http://www.wwrn.org/article.php?idd=14058&sec=55&con=41.

[69] Riigi Teataja RT I 2002, 24, 135. Kirikute ja koguduste seadus (Churches and Congregations Act). See also Ringo Ringvee, 'Dialogue or Confrontation? New Religious Movements, Mainstream Religions and the State in Secular Estonia', *International Journal for the Study of New Religions* 3 (2012): 93–116.

[70] IRFR Lithuania 2002, 'International Religious Freedom Report 2002', US Department of State, Bureau of Democracy, Human Rights, and Labor, http://www.state.gov/j/drl/rls/irf/2002/13946.htm; and IRFR Lithuania 2003, 'International Religious Freedom Report 2003', US Department of State, Bureau of Democracy, Human Rights, and Labor, http://www.state.gov/j/drl/rls/irf/2003/24419.htm.

[71] On the Commission's investigations see IRFR Lithuania 2005, 'International Religious Freedom Report 2004', US Department of State, Bureau of Democracy, Human Rights, and Labor, http://www.state.gov/g/drl/rls/irf/2005/51565.htm.

people whose relatives had allegedly been harmed by religious cults. The Group reviewed legislation regulating activities of religious groups and announced its intentions to introduce tougher registration requirements.[72] At the same time a similar legal body, the New Religions Consultative Council, was founded in Latvia to inform the government on NRM-related issues. The Council, however, has had little impact, and does not have decision-making authority.[73] Estonia has no special agencies concerned with NRMs. And despite the presence of anti-cult initiatives in all of the Baltic States – mostly driven by the mass media and dominant churches – it should be mentioned that no long-lasting or influential anti-cult organization has been established.[74]

In the 1990s conscientious objection from military service became a hot topic in all three Baltic States. In Latvia, alternative service was available from 1990 until 1997, when the Law on Compulsory Military Service removed that option.[75] An amendment to the Law in 2000 exempted Jehovah's Witnesses, along with clerics and clerical students, from military service.[76] In 2007 Latvian defence forces became fully contract-based, abolishing compulsory military service entirely. In Lithuania, before a fully contract-based military was introduced in 2008, authorities allowed conscientious objection on the basis of Article 139 of the Lithuanian Constitution: 'Citizens of the Republic of Lithuania are obliged to serve in the national defence service or to perform alternative service in the manner established by law'.[77] In 1996 the Jehovah's Witnesses and the Estonian Defence Ministry reached a resolution concerning alternative service, and twelve Witnesses served for the first time in the Rescue Company rather than as combat troops. Currently the primary alternative to military service is assisting the disabled.

The Baltic States and the ECtHR

The Baltic States have each had distinct experiences with the ECtHR regarding violations of Article 9 of the European Convention on Human Rights, which protects religious freedom.[78] Estonia has avoided any litigation before the Court

---

[72] IRFR Lithuania 2005.

[73] Ališauskienė, 'Freedom of Religion in the Baltic States', 144.

[74] Krumina-Konkova, 'New Religious Minorities', 126; and Ališauskienė, 'The Manifestation and Development of New Religions in Lithuania', 13.

[75] Latvias Vēstnesis 60 (775), 27.02.1997. Militārā dienesta likums (Law on Compulsory Military Service).

[76] Nikandrs Gills, 'Jehovah's Witnesses: New Problems with Military Service in Latvia', CESNUR, 24 September 1999, http://www.cesnur.org/testi/gills2.htm; and Gills, 'Jehovah's Witnesses in the Social and Cultural Context of Contemporary Latvia'.

[77] Valstybės Žinios 1996, 1062427, 'Karo prievolės įstatymas'.

[78] On the ECtHR on Lithuania and Latvia website, see Religion and Law Consortium, http://www.religlaw.org/portal.country.php?pageId=22.

altogether. Lithuania has had just one case brought against it: *Gineitiené v. Lithuania*, a child custody case the Court dismissed in 2010 involving a follower of the Indian spiritual guru Osho. Latvia has had three Article 9 cases brought against it, all involving NRMs. In 2008 the ECtHR held in *Perry v. Latvia* that the state had violated the Convention by withdrawing a residence permit from the leader of a newly-registered Christian congregation in 2001. In 2009 the ECtHR held in *Mirolubovs v. Latvia* that the state had violated a religious community's autonomy by becoming involved in an internal dispute. Finally, in 2012 the Court held in *Kovalkovs v. Latvia* that there was no violation of the Convention where the state set limitations on Hare Krishna followers' religious practices in prison.

Conclusion

Legislation on religion differs in each of the Baltic States, due mainly to historical, political and social factors. But in all three Baltic States, governmental policy toward NRMs has been influenced by lobbying from interest groups. Whether foreign or domestic, political or religious, their success has varied depending on the particular time and place in which they operated. In unchurched and secular Estonia, where since the early 1990s the religious climate has mirrored the neoliberal free market economy, religion in any form has been insignificant in political life. There, religion is considered a personal and private matter, and the government has shown little concern with either control over or special treatment of religious groups. In all the Baltic States, but especially Latvia and Lithuania, where religion has more civic relevance, traditional majority churches understandably have more political influence than NRMs, particularly in Catholic Lithuania, where the dominant church has deep connections to the national identity. Though this does not inevitably mean discrimination against NRMs, it probably contributes to the government's wariness toward them, as seen in Latvia's relatively unaccommodating registration procedures. Despite their inconvenience, though, these and other Baltic-States policies toward religion are not unrealistic, and even where dominant religions may interfere with minorities, religious freedom is protected both by legislation and its practical application in all of the Baltic States.

Chapter 13
With Fear and Favour: Minority Religions and the Post-Soviet Russian State

Marat Shterin

Introduction

The treatment of religious minorities in post-Soviet Russia has been in the spotlight of many international, governmental and non-governmental organizations and has been subject to numerous judicial proceedings at national courts and the European Court of Human Rights.[1] Taken together, the resulting reports and legal documents portray a pretty gruesome picture of increasingly restrictive legislation, continuous attempts to 'liquidate' a range of religious associations, and local administrations' frequent — almost commonplace — arbitrary action against religious minorities, such as dispossession of property, disruption of religious meetings and refusal of entry to coreligionists from abroad.

Taking a long view, our pessimism over the current state of affairs can be either mitigated (if we look back to the Soviet times) or augmented (if we fear current trends are likely to continue). In contrast to the Soviet period, the country now enjoys a Constitution with strong provisions for religious freedom and equality, and its religious life remains diverse and thriving. However, this situation can be best described as precarious and uncertain; despite Russia's constitutional provisions, the state and its agencies display a great deal of arbitrariness in dealing with religious minorities, which often find themselves in limbo concerning the scope of their freedoms and their prospects for protecting them.

There is little doubt the emergence of a dazzlingly diverse 'religious market' in the early 1990s — after centuries of state protection for the dominant Russian Orthodox Church and, subsequently, seven decades of state-imposed secularism and official atheism — was in itself an immense challenge for Russia.[2] In both situations the state was ultimately in charge of defining the boundaries — social, legal, political and even geographical — between religious minorities and the rest of society, and did so under the premise of protecting the best interests of the

---

[1] See annual religious freedom reports by the Moscow Sova Centre, http://www.sova-center.ru/en/misuse/reports-analyses; and Forum18, http://www.forum18.org/.

[2] Catherine Wanner and Mark Steinberg, 'Reclaiming the Sacred', in *Religion, Morality, and Community*, eds Mark Steinberg and Catherine Wanner (Bloomington and Indianapolis: Indiana University Press, 2009), 1–20.

'majority'. Many successive generations were raised on the idea that the state was meant to express and enforce the views of the majority.[3] Thus, in a post-Soviet society with limited experience in managing religious diversity, the presence of religious minorities and the concept of state responsibility for their rights became a daunting challenge. Nevertheless, it was in this context that Russia's incipient civil society with its fledgling liberal democratic structures enabled religious minorities to express their grievances and challenge the state in courts of law, political debates and public forums.

We should, no doubt, recognize the complexity of these kinds of challenges for the post-Soviet state and society in general. In addition, Russia's enormous ethnic and religious diversity further complicate the issue. Using an admittedly approximate typology, we can identify minority groupings as follows: those in which religion is seen as linked to ethnicity (for example, Muslim Tatars, Baskhirs and Chechens; Buddhist Kalmyks; and Jews); those ethnically Russian but identified by adherence to a shared, non-Orthodox religion (for example, Baptists, Pentecostals, Seventh Day Adventists, and Jehovah's Witnesses); and newer groups formed by first-generation members, referred to as NRMs in this volume. NRMs will be at the centre of my analysis, precisely because their emergence in post-Soviet Russia has brought the state's response to minority religions into sharpest relief.

Furthermore, the country's geographical diversity and its recent rapid social and political change impart additional dynamics, complexity, tension and conflict to the relationship between minorities and the state. For example, while Muslims as a whole are a religious minority in the Russian Federation, as ethnic groups some of them represent a majority in their historic homelands. This has provided a basis for their claiming more cultural autonomy or even political independence, as has been the case in Tatarstan in the Volga region or, most famously, in Chechnya and Dagestan in the Northern Caucasus.[4] On the other hand, in all these regions, new movements have emerged from inside the traditional Muslim milieus and formed distinctive minority communities (for example, Salafis) that, arguably, exhibit certain characteristics commonly associated with NRMs.[5] Likewise, 'new' Pagans in the Middle Volga regions renounced the historic Orthodox Christianity of their ethnic groups (namely, Mari and Udmurt) as imposed on them by the

---

[3] Eileen Barker, 'State-imposed Secularism: Yet Another Dimension?', in *Secularization and Social Integration: Papers in Honor of Karel Dobbelaere*, eds Rudi Laermans, Bryan R. Wilson and Jaak Billiet (Leuven, Belgium: Leuven University Press, 1998), 191–210.

[4] Roland Dannreuther and Luke eds., *Russia and Islam: State, Society and Radicalism* (London and New York: Routledge, 2010).

[5] Marat Shterin and Akhmet Yarlykapov, 'Reconsidering Radicalisation and Terrorism: The New Muslims Movement in Kabardino-Balkaria and Its Path to Violence', *Religion, State, and Society* 39 (2011): 89–113.

Russian majority and claimed more political autonomy on the basis of their cultural distinctiveness.⁶

What follows is that, in post-Soviet Russia, religious minority status is grafted onto a variety of cultural and political issues that many in the wider society, including state agencies, may see as threats requiring strict state regulation. We therefore need to look into how these anxieties and respective regulatory measures are 'socially constructed', that is, how they reflect both state agents' historical legacy and their current concerns, interests, and knowledge of religious minorities.

Historical legacy

Some deterministic accounts go as far as to derive Russia's legacy of state treatment of religious minorities directly from the cultural dominance of the Russian Orthodox Church, which apparently cannot accommodate – theologically or organizationally – any kind of institutionalized diversity, be it economic markets, political democracy or cultural pluralism.⁷ This view imagines a monolithic tradition consisting inseparably of the Russian Orthodox faith, Russia's geographic territory and the Russian people, within which religious minorities could not find any legitimate place as equal citizens and would forever have to defend themselves against suspicions of cultural contamination, spiritual erosion and outright treason against the state. Interestingly, such views mirror the apologetic perspective, often associated with Russian nationalism, which maintains that a primordial symbiosis (*symphonia*) of church and state, presumably inherited from the Byzantine tradition, gives Russia its political uniqueness and spiritual advantage over Western societies.⁸

Contrary to these views, Bryan Turner points out that in religiously diverse societies, *all* states, whether liberal or authoritarian, must of necessity manage 'tensions between competing religious traditions', including attempts by dominant religions to have a definitive say in the regulation of religious minorities. Historically, dominant religions have acquired considerable 'symbolic capital' through their involvement in nation building, which modern states have to take into account as they tackle the subsequent growth of religious diversity and the increasing prominence of religious minorities.⁹

---

⁶ David Lewis, *After Atheism: Religion and Ethnicity in Russia and Central Asia* (London: Curzon Press, 2000).

⁷ Dumitru Minzarari, 'The Interaction between Orthodox Church and State in Post-Soviet Russia', in *Spaces and Borders: Current Research on Religion in Central and Eastern Europe*, eds Andras Mate-Toth and Cosima Rughinis (Berlin: De Gruyter, 2011), 103–116.

⁸ See for example Natalya Narochnitskaya, *Russkiy Mir* (Moscow: Aleteya, 2008).

⁹ Bryan Turner, *Religion and Modern Society: Citizenship, Secularisation and the State* (Cambridge: Cambridge University Press, 2011), 175.

While the available space does not permit a more detailed analysis, the history of Russia's treatment of religious minorities displays many features that can be found elsewhere in Europe.[10] As in most European countries, the church and state collaborated in creating the early Russian nation-state from the fifteenth to the seventeenth centuries; in the eyes of the Muscovite rulers, Russia could only be an Orthodox state. Peter the Great (1682–1725) modernized the country on the European model, making the monarch head of both the state and the church. Within this vision of the nation as a uniform faith community, accommodating schismatic and other sectarian movements was considered counterproductive to state goals.[11]

Much of Russia's legacy in state management of minority religions also comes from its imperial past. Its expansion into predominantly non-Orthodox lands led to an immense ethno-religious diversity and presented a challenge to the dominance of one faith. Like other empires, Russia initially attempted Christianization, followed by more expedient and 'enlightened' policies of accommodating heterodoxy within its borders, such as those adopted by Catherine the Great in the late eighteenth century.[12] Michael Walzer refers to this type of policy as 'toleration', whereby the state accommodates certain established (mainly ethno-religious) groups and their authorities, but not 'free-floating men and women', that is, voluntary communities based on personal choice.[13] It was the fast-growing 'communities of the converted' such as Baptists, Evangelical Christians, Jehovah's Witnesses and Pentecostals that caused the most anxiety among officials of the late Imperial Russia (1860s–1917).[14] Toleration for these communities came only when, after years of oppression, democratic ideas and movements gained traction in wider Russian society. It does not seem coincidental that the foundations of both Russia's parliamentary democracy and religious freedom were established amidst the first democratic revolution (1905), when Tsar Nicolas II issued an edict on religious toleration and a manifesto on the establishment of the State Duma (Parliament).

However, the turning point in the state's treatment of religious minorities in Russia was the 1917 Bolshevik Revolution and the 'construction of communism' in the subsequent decades. The very notion of religious minority was inimical to the majoritarian ideology of the *Soviet people* as a single civic community of citizens with a shared communist ideology, morality and culture; any articulation of religiously defined difference was seen as socially unacceptable and politically

---

[10] Grace Davie, *Religion in Modern Europe: a Memory Mutates* (Oxford: Oxford University Press, 2000).

[11] The most considerable and consequential schism occurred in the seventeenth century and gave rise to the Old Believers movement, which eventually spawned a number of different denominations.

[12] Robert Geraci and Michael Khodarkovsky, *Of Religion and Empire: Missions, Conversion, and Tolerance in Tsarist Russia* (Ithaca: Cornell University Press, 2000).

[13] Michael Walzer, *On Toleration* (New Haven and London: Yale University, 1997).

[14] Catherine Wanner, *Communities of the Converted, Ukrainians and Global Evangelicalism* (Ithaca and London: Cornell University Press, 2007), 23–6.

subversive.[15] At certain points, the Soviet state made limited compromises with the leadership of the Orthodox Church, the Moscow Patriarchate (MP), and, to a lesser extent, surviving Islamic and Jewish leaders, but never with Baptists, Jehovah's Witnesses or underground Muslims or Jews, whose committed communities were not readily amenable to the state's direct control.[16]

The new 'religious market' and competition for souls

The reformist 1990s created a new political, legal, social and philosophical environment for the relationship between the state and religious minorities. In particular, the 1990 Law on the Freedom of Worship and the 1993 Constitution strictly prohibited establishment of a state religion and government intervention in the free exercise of religion by individuals and groups (and vice versa), and guaranteed freedom of conscience and the right to choose and practice religion individually or collectively.[17] This was accompanied by changes in the Russian judicial system, which provided legitimate avenues for religious associations and individuals to seek legal redress for their grievances in domestic and international law courts, including the ECtHR. In addition, abolishing state control of the mass media and other means of cultural production enabled minority groups and their members to seek social acceptability and respectability through the use of printed and electronic public forums.

Bolstered by these changes, a thriving religious market emerged, involving an ever-increasing diversity of religious groups and other associations based on a variety of beliefs, practices and affiliations.[18] In the post-Soviet society, however, the new 'war for souls' was not limited to competing offers of salvation, spiritual wellbeing or life-enhancing techniques; it also involved alternative claims on the very basis of individual identity and affiliation as society moved away from the Soviet 'communal apartment', in which individual differences were subsumed and suppressed under the overarching and state-imposed concept of 'Soviet people'.[19]

---

[15] While initially favouring religious minorities as opponents of the old regime, from the late 1920s, the Bolsheviks began to target them as the main opponents of the militant, state-imposed atheism.

[16] Pedra Sabrina Ramet, *Religion and Nationalism in Soviet and East European Politics* (Duke: Duke University Press, 1988); Wanner, *Communities of the Converted*, 1–20.

[17] See Cole Durham and Lauren Homer, 'Russia's 1997 Law on Freedom of Conscience and Religious Associations: Analytical Appraisal', *Emory Law Review* 12 (1998): 101–246.

[18] On the post-Soviet religious scene, see John Witte Jr and Michael Bourdeaux, eds, *Proselytism and Orthodoxy in Russia: The New War for Souls* (New York: Maryknoll, 1999).

[19] Yuri Slezkine, 'The USSR as a Communal Apartment, or How a Socialist State Promoted Ethnic Particularism', *Slavic Review* 53 (1994): 414–52; Marat Shterin, 'Religion

It was a time when 'ethno-religious' and religious entrepreneurs were competing to bring their faiths to the centre of newly defined and emerging social groupings: nation, ethnicity and voluntary associations. Moreover, the competition occurred not only between religious traditions but also between different strands within them.[20]

In any society, religious competition takes place in a concrete social space that includes cultural, legal and political dimensions, with competitors trying to justify or seek certain privileges or simply legitimize their presence. Post-communist societies are particularly interesting in this regard. After decades of oppression under the old regime their new liberal constitutions tend to create seemingly optimal conditions for equal enjoyment of religious freedom. But, as John Anderson observes, historic or 'traditional' religions in post-communist states have often sought to justify privilege by demanding 'proper recognition' of their contributions to society and by pointing to the supposedly harmful effects caused by their competitors during a moment of social flux, uncertainty and instability.[21]

In its most significant post-Soviet declaration, the MP revealed its claim to dominance by suggesting that 'when a nation ... represents an entirely or predominantly mono-confessional Christian Orthodox community, it in some sense can be seen as a single faith community ...'.[22] That the church does see itself as coterminous with the Russian nation is clear from a number of pronouncements by its current leader, Patriarch Kirill.[23] This self-understanding leads to the demand for privileged treatment by the state as the majority church.[24] It has to be noted that, while in tension with the Constitution, such a claim per se does not necessarily lead to discriminatory attitudes and policies; in theory, and even in some Western European practice, recognition of a dominant church and recognition of minorities' rights to profess, spread and live according to their faiths need not be mutually exclusive. The problem, however, is that the church sees the entire nation, defined mainly in ethnic terms as representing the Russian majority, and smaller ethnic groups under its jurisdiction as its 'canonical territory', that is, its 'reserved domain'

After Atheism: Moving Away from the Communal Flat', in *Challenging Religion*, eds James Beckford and James Richardson (London: Routledge, 2004), 56–69.

[20] For vivid descriptions of religious competition in different parts of post-soviet Russia, see Witte and Bourdeaux, *Proselytism and Orthodoxy*; and Marjorie Mandelstam Balzer, 'Whose Steeple Is Higher? Religious Competition in Siberia', *Religion State and Society* 33 (2005): 57–70.

[21] John Anderson, *Liberty in Transitional Societies: The Politics of Religion* (Cambridge: Cambridge University Press, 2003).

[22] 'Osnovy Sotsial'noi Kontseptsii Russkoy Pravoslavnoi Tserkvi', in *O Sotsial'noi Kontseptsii Russkogo Pravoslavia*, ed. Mikhail Mchedlov (Moskva: Respublika, 2002), 259.

[23] Alexander Verkhovsky, 'Russian Approaches to Radicalism and Extremism as Applied to Nationalism and Religion', in *Russia and Islam: State, Society and Radicalism*, eds Roland Dannreuther and Luke March (London and New York: Routledge, 2010), 26–43.

[24] 'Osnovy Sotsial'noi Kontseptsii', 274.

for missionary and other work.²⁵ By implication, this stance either relegates all other religions into their historic ethnic enclaves, tolerated on the condition of non-proselytizing, or altogether denies the right of newer religions to proliferate within Russian borders, thus evoking the Russian imperial past. Among other things, this has been the main reason for the MP's vehement objection to Roman Catholic proselytism, in particular during the 1990s and early 2000s.²⁶ The intolerance and tension is further augmented when the church singles out certain religions as particularly threatening to the Russian nation and the wellbeing of all Russian citizens.

On their part, the leaders of Russia's ethnic minority religions were perfectly happy to accept the Orthodox Church's privileged position, providing their own representative role was recognized by the state. Apart from their official pronouncements, Jewish rabbis and leading Muslim imams have on many occasions intimated to me their general concerns about proselytism by newer Christian groups and by newer strains within their own traditions. Likewise, the more established non-Orthodox Christian groups have publicly complained, especially during the 1990s, about the influx of Baptists, Evangelicals and Pentecostals from abroad.

NRMs, for their part, could not lay claim to Russia's cultural history to establish their legitimacy. Instead, their members formed alternative communities based on personal choice and commitments beyond national and ethnic ties. This fact alone made them the quintessential representation of an 'alien' threat to the stability of the nation and its constituent ethnic groups.

Cult controversies

While the Moscow Patriarchate was undoubtedly the most influential player in defining the status and portrayal of minority religions, it could not unilaterally blackball unwelcome religions purely on theological grounds in a secular, democratic and constitutional society. It needed other rationales – and allies to promote them – that would represent grounds for action by state agencies.

I have argued elsewhere that the causes of public anxieties about NRMs in Russia were not entirely dissimilar to those in Western societies and other post-communist countries of Eastern and Central Europe.²⁷ As elsewhere, the first anti-

---

²⁵ Sergey Filatov and Roman Lunkin, 'My Father's House Has Many Mansions: Ethnic Minorities in the Russian Orthodox Church', *Religion, State, and Society* 38 (2010): 361–78.

²⁶ Zoe Knox, *Russian Society and the Orthodox Church: Religion in Russia After Communism* (London and New York: Routledge, 2005), 172–6.

²⁷ See Marat Shterin and James Richardson, 'Effects of the Western Anti-Cult Movement on Development of Laws Concerning Religion in Post-Communist Russia', *Journal of Church and State* 42 (2000): 247–72; on the Western and post-Communist societies, see James Beckford, *Cult Controversies: Societal Responses to New Religious*

cult groups were formed by parents worried about their offspring leaving the family to settle in separate communities, adhering to 'strange' beliefs and practices, and committing themselves to follow charismatic leaders in outlandish causes.[28] In the early 1990s, however, these concerns were further exacerbated in Russia by the frenetic proselytizing of one NRM in particular, the home-grown Great White Brotherhood, whose members covered every possible public space all over Russia and Ukraine with grim images of their leader, Maria-Devi Christos, and attempted to stage her 'death and resurrection' in November 1993 in Kiev.[29] The fact that these and similar events in Russia coincided with the mass media coverage of a series of tragic events involving NRMs around the world – notably the Waco siege of the Branch Davidians (1993), Aum Shinrikyo's sarin gas attack on the Tokyo subway (1995), and the Solar Temple massacres in Switzerland, France and Canada (1995 and 1997) – further fuelled the 'cult controversy' in Russia.[30]

Ironically, the state's efforts to protect Russia's people and culture were informed by images of 'cults', and the threats they represented – including their supposed use of brainwashing and mind-control techniques – that originated in the Western anti-cult movement.[31] In the 1990s, Western Evangelical missionaries in Russia set up at least five anti-cult centres and disseminated tens of thousands of books and pamphlets. The main purveyor of these Western anti-cult representations of NRMs was affiliated, perhaps somewhat ironically, with the MP. As a Soviet expatriate in the US, Alexander Dvorkin had established connections with Western anti-cultists before returning to Moscow and setting up the St Ireneus of Lyons Information and Consultation Center (SILICC) in 1993. The Centre was hosted and funded by the MP, and most of Dvorkin's credibility and clout initially derived from his affiliation with both the church and Western anti-cultism.[32] He adroitly

---

Movements (London and New York: Tavistock Publications, 1985); Eileen Barker, *New Religious Movements: A Practical Introduction* (London: HMSO, 1989); and Irena Borowik, ed., *Religions, Churches, and Religiosity in Post-Communist Europe* (Krakow: Nomos, 2006), 119–252.

[28] Numerically speaking, NRMs represented only a relatively small section of the new Russian religious market. By my estimates, in the late 1990s, the total membership in 'newer' NRMs never exceeded between 30,000 and 40,000; if we add 'older' NRMs, such as Jehovah's Witnesses and Latter-Day Saints (the Mormons), and newer Pentecostal groups, we can talk about 300,000 to 400,000 members (approximately 0.2–0.3 per cent of the population).

[29] Eliot Borenstein, 'Articles of Faith: The Media Response to Maria Devi Khristos', *Religion* 25 (1995): 249–66; Marat Shterin, 'New Religious Movements in Changing Russia', in *Cambridge Companion to New Religious Movements,* eds Olav Hammer and Michael Rotstein (Cambridge: Cambridge University Press, 2012), 286–302.

[30] See, David Bromley and Gordon Melton, eds *Cults, Religions, and Violence* (Cambridge: Cambridge University Press, 2002).

[31] Shterin and Richardson, 'Western Anti-Cult Movement'.

[32] Marat Shterin and James Richardson, 'The Yakunin vs Dvorkin Trial and the Emerging Religious Pluralism in Russia', *Religion in Eastern Europe* 22 (2002): 1–38;

adjusted his Western rhetoric to long-standing Russian symbolism and post-Soviet sensibilities: thus, 'destructive cults' became 'totalitarian sects' organized as criminal mafias posing a threat not just to individual wellbeing and free will, but to the fledgling Russian democracy itself.[33] Through SILICC, information about 'destructive cults' and 'totalitarian sects' was widely disseminated within church circles and in the wider society, including to state officials.[34] The handbook *New Religious Organizations of Destructive and Occult Character*, which largely drew on Dvorkin's approach, was published in 1997 by the Missionary Department of the Russian Orthodox Church and became a standard source of knowledge about NRMs among local and federal officials, including law enforcement agencies.[35]

Many other anti-cult voices also had nationalistic overtones. In a lawsuit in St Petersburg, one parental committee complained about 'the Moonies' (the Unification Church) destroying 'the genetic fund of the Russian nation', while some academics from the Russian Academy of Civil Service claimed that the influx of cults in Russia was part and parcel of long-reaching Western plans for geopolitical expansion. In the late 1990s and into the 2000s, this kind of rhetoric became increasingly salient with the changes in the country's political environment, with many pointing to 'cults and sects' as an extremist threat to national identity and security.[36]

The post-Soviet state

No modern state can afford to neglect possible threats to national security, social cohesion, public order and individual wellbeing, and religious diversity – especially religious innovation – has often been regarded as just that by at least some agencies and officials in every modern state.[37] However, the ways in which states and their constituent parts scrutinize and respond to such prospects differ

---

Emily Baran, 'Negotiating the Limits of Religious Pluralism in Post-Soviet Russia: The Anticult Movement in the Russian Orthodox Church, 1990–2004', *Russian Review* 65 (2006): 637–56.

[33] Alexander Dvorkin, *Sekty Protiv Tserkvi* (Moscow: Moscow Patriarchate, 2000).

[34] As a revealing case of connections between anti-cult activists and state officials, in 2009 Dvorkin was appointed as Chair of the Committee of Religious Studies Experts for the Russian Ministry of Justice. The then Minister Alexander Konovalov was Dvorkin's former student at the St Tikhon Orthodox Spiritual Institute in Moscow.

[35] Missionerskyi Otdel, *Novye Religioznye Organizatsii Destruktivnogo i Okkul'tnogo Kharaktera* (Belgorod: Moskovsky Patriarkhate, 1997).

[36] Quoted in Marat Shterin, 'Cult Controversies in England and Russia: A Sociological Comparison', (PhD diss., London School of Economics and Political Science, 2002), 218–19, 326.

[37] Steve Bruce, *Politics and Religion* (Cambridge: Polity, 2003), 161–204.

considerably.[38] Moreover, research overwhelmingly suggests that state responses do not necessarily reflect actual threats from NRMs; rather, they are often driven by the mere perception of the public and of state agencies, which is frequently constructed by highly vocal concerned groups (anti-cultists, mental health and legal professionals, the mass media, academics and so on).[39] The prospects for NRMs to have a say in public policy-making depends on a variety of factors, including (broadly speaking) historical legacy, overall current anxieties and concerns, operation of the state system, and the specific interests of those acting on behalf of the state. As such, a brief comment on the post-Soviet state of affairs would be useful for the current discussion.

The post-Soviet political elites have failed to create an efficient state based on functioning democratic institutions and the rule of law. Instead, they have developed a political system largely dependent on personal patronage and informal connections, which is fraught with a high degree of arbitrariness and hence uncertainty. This system has proved to be detrimental to the development of a civil society that could speak and act efficiently on behalf of, and be accountable to, its citizens. Instead, political and economic power is concentrated in the hands of a few groups, whose status and prosperity depend on their personal loyalty to those at the helm of the state.[40] Despite these problems, the earlier post-Soviet period (the so-called 'Yeltsin regime'), a time of substantial political flux, accommodated a variety of social and cultural expressions and allowed civil society institutions, such as human rights and religious freedom advocacy groups, to operate with a considerable degree of freedom.

In contrast, the so-called 'Putin regime' of the 2000s provided increasingly limited space for political opposition and ideological alternatives, and involved increasing control over the mass media, electoral processes and just about anything else that could potentially jeopardize the ruling elite's dominance. Instead, a political doctrine of distinctive 'sovereign democracy' was promoted, based on a presumed unity of the government and the governed and organically linked to the 'Russian civilization'. The regime's heightened sensitivity to internal dissent and external influence – and its propensity to construct threatening representations of the same – was a corollary of this.[41] Not coincidentally, the beginning of Putin's presidency was marked with publication of the new *Doctrine of National Security of the Russian Federation* (2000), which specifically referred to the concept

---

[38] Philip Lucas and Thomas Robbins, eds., *New Religious Movements in the 21st Century: Legal, Political, and Social Challenges in Global Perspective* (New York: Routledge, 2004).

[39] Beckford, *Cult Controversies*; Eileen Barker, 'The Social Scientific Study of Religion? You Must Be Joking!' *Journal for the Scientific Study of Religion* 34 (1995): 287–310.

[40] Marie Mendras, *Russian Politics: The Paradox of a Weak State* (London: Hurst & Company, 2012), 257–76.

[41] See for example Mendras, *Russian Politics*.

of 'spiritual security', understood as protection against threats to the national 'spiritual unity' from internal and external influences.[42] In real terms, it meant protection of the status quo of the Orthodox Church's 'reserved domain' and of the enclaves of 'traditional religions'.

It is not hard to see the affinity between the doctrine of 'distinctive civilization' and the church's claim on the exclusive religious representation of the Russian nation. In addition, a range of reciprocal interests draws the post-Soviet ruling elite and the church towards each other. Weakened by malfunctioning democratic institutions, the ruling elite seeks to enhance its legitimacy through the historically rooted church's support. These links enable the church, on the other hand, to enjoy the opportunities provided by proximity to economic and political power.[43] This trend considerably escalated during the 2000s, and today the Church's leaders routinely glorify Putin's presidency, with some pronouncements arguably amounting to a sacralization of his power.

The implications of this situation for 'non-traditional' religious minorities are clear. Ultimately, their claim to legitimacy is based on their constitutionally recognized rights, the legal protection guaranteed thereby, and support from civil society – precisely the areas that have proven to be particularly vulnerable to the arbitrariness of the 'Putin regime'. While these problems did not start with Putin – defending NRMs' rights through the Russian legal system, which lacked judicial autonomy from government structures and influential lobbyists, has been a problem throughout the post-Soviet era[44] – this trend has solidified under his leadership. Furthermore, extra-legal means of governance have been increasingly salient during the entire period.[45] In addition, the political climate of popular support for Putin's presidency, along with a shrinking and suppressed civil society, has been hardly conducive to *un*popular religious minorities finding advocates for their constitutional rights. In fact, those NRMs that have persisted in challenging discriminatory policies have largely stood alone as some of the few remaining oppositional actors in civil society.

The 'securitization of Islam'

As Marie Mandras points out, after the tumultuous 1990s, Putin's regime was widely perceived as presiding over a time of economic growth and relative political

---

[42] See, Julie Elkner, 'Spiritual Security in Putin's Russia', *History and Policy*, January 2005, http://www.historyandpolicy.org/papers/policy-paper-26.html.

[43] Nikolai Mitrokhin, *Russkaya Pravoslavnaja Tserkov'* (Moscow: Novoe Literaturnoe Obozrenie, 2004).

[44] Shterin and Richardson, 'Yakunin vs Dvorkin'; Marat Shterin, 'Legislating on Religion in the Face of Uncertainty', in *Law and Informal Practices: Post-Communist Society*, eds John Gallighan and Marina Kurkchiyan, (Oxford: Oxford University Press, 2002), 113–33.

[45] Mendras, *Russian Politics*, 257–80.

stability, which, among other things, included the 'pacification' of Chechnya after two wars (1994–96 and 1999–2000). However, this period was also marked by horrific terrorist attacks in Moscow and other Russian cities and general instability in the predominantly Muslim regions of the Northern Caucasus. Combined with the ramifications of the 'War on Terror' declared by the US government in 2001, this contributed to the securitization of the official approaches to Islam and, to some extent, religious issues in general.[46]

While focusing mainly on the 'Islamist threat', the mass media and public debates of the 2000s often failed to distinguish between the religion of Islam, Islamist politics and Islamist terrorism, instead often presuming that all Russian Muslim communities were vulnerable to violent radicalization. As in many other countries, the loose and imprecise use of the notion of radicalization came very close to that of 'brainwashing' popularized by the anti-cult movement, in that it tended to present committed Islamic observance, in particular within new groups, as resulting from special indoctrination techniques. Young Muslims forming new communities – whether based on Salafi, Hizb-ut-Tahrir's or Said Nursi's teachings – or even young women wearing the Islamic headscarf, became suspected of involvement in global terrorist networks. Thus, the government faced the enormous challenge of addressing the real terrorist threat while avoiding anti-Islamism, given that at least eight per cent of Russian citizens were Muslims with deep roots in the country's history and society.

The mechanics of discrimination

Like its counterparts elsewhere, the post-Soviet state has at its disposal a variety of means to regulate and control minority religions, though in so doing it may have different interests and powers. In addition, different state agencies and groups within them may vary considerably in their understandings of what issues need to be addressed and how. The following discussion will indicate that in the security-driven legislation of the 2000s, law enforcement agencies, such as the increasingly influential police and security services, have been particularly prominent in oppressive actions against certain religious minorities.

Legislation was the subject of fierce debates in the 1990s, with an alliance of anti-cult activists led by Alexander Dvorkin, the MP, and nationalist politicians lobbying for amending the 1990 Law to include provisions favouring the Orthodox Church and other 'traditional religions' while restricting newer and 'foreign' faiths.[47] Between 1993 and 1997, anti-cult pressure was most severe on the provincial level, with about a third of them adopting local anti-missionary

---

[46] Verkhovsky, 'Russian Approaches to Radicalism', 26–43.
[47] Durham and Homer, 'Russia's 1997 Law'; Shterin, 'Legislating on Religion'.

and anti-cult laws.[48] But soon the federal government that initially met anti-cult pressure with much reluctance also gave in to a more anti-Western and nationalistic Duma. In September 1997, President Yeltsin signed, after some dithering, the new Law on Freedom of Conscience and Religious Associations. It retained the basic provisions for religious freedom but also contained a number of restrictions on registration for new religious associations, and listed numerous grounds for 'liquidating' religious associations (that is, removing their legal entity status). Its preamble rhetorically acknowledged the special status of Russia's historic religions, in particular the Russian Orthodox Church. Luckily, in the late 1990s the severity of the law's implementation was somewhat mitigated by several Constitutional Court rulings in favour of religious minorities.[49]

In the 2000s, however, much of the restrictive regulation was based on legislation indirectly related to minority groups. Most prominently, the 2002 Law on Combating Extremist Activity contained very broad and vague definitions, such as 'stirring up of social, racial, ethnic or religious discord', or claiming ethnic, racial or religious superiority – without linking any of these to violence.[50] In addition, according to the Law, the courts were to establish the facts of extremist activity primarily based on the opinions of state-appointed experts, which further increased the likelihood of arbitrary application. For instance, in many actual cases court-appointed experts have been known opponents of minority groups, including anti-cultists, who interpreted religious pronouncements as straightforward injunctions without proper historical, cultural and social contextualization. The Law also stipulated creation of the Federal List of Extremist Literature, which currently contains over 1200 items, including *Awake!* and *Watchtower* of the Jehovah's Witnesses, books by the prominent Turkish theologian Said Nursi, and *Bhagavad-Gita as It Is*, a key text of the worldwide Hare Krishna movement. As the law makes possession of materials from the List a criminal offence, a number of religious minorities have been and can be potentially affected.

The broad formulations and applications of these and other laws indicate that they can be used as a tool for arbitrarily suppression of any form of deviation from state approved social, political and cultural activities, including the beliefs and practices of religious minorities. In particular, Jehovah's Witnesses have been

---

[48] Marat Shterin and James Richardson, 'Local Laws on Religion in Russia: Precursors of Russia's National Law', *Journal of Church and State* 40 (1998): 319–42

[49] James Richardson and Marat Shterin, 'Constitutional Courts in Post-Communist Russia and Hungary: How Do They Treat Religion?', *Religion, State, and Society* 36 (2008): 251–67.

[50] Verkhovski, 'Inappropriate Enforcement', in *Xenophobia, Freedom of Conscience, and Anti-Extremism in Russia in 2011*, eds Vera Alperovich, Olga Sibireva, Alexander Verkhovski and Natalia Yudina (Moscow: Sova Center, 2012), 108–15; see also *The Institute on Religion and Public Policy Report: Analysis on Russia's New 'Extremist Activity Law'*, 2 August 2012, http://www.religionandpolicy.org/reports/the-institute-country-reports-and-legislative-analysis/europe-and-eurasia/russia/analysis-on-russia-s-new-extremist-activity-law-2012/.

the target of both church-sponsored anti-cult activities and discriminatory actions by law-enforcement agencies.[51] In a landmark case in Moscow, which lasted with interruptions over four years (1999–2003), the judge applied the 1997 law to rule that the Jehovah's Witnesses' local community was to be 'liquidated' for its extremism. Since 2009, a sustained campaign has been carried out against the Jehovah's Witnesses by law enforcement agencies in dozens of Russian regions, with local communities 'liquidated', publications put on the Federal List of Extremist Literature, individual members detained and their homes searched by the police and security services. In 2011, the Department of Internal Affairs of the Moscow region designed a special programme to counter Jehovah's Witnesses' 'extremism', which included comprehensive surveillance of their leadership and activities, including fingerprinting, police checks at places of worship and the monitoring of bank accounts. Revealingly, the programme was called the Apostate, pointing to the ways in which religious bias and prejudice can affect the perceptions and actions of Russian law-enforcement agencies.

Although we do not have any evidence that the federal government has elaborated a comprehensive policy against any particular religion, the arbitrariness of the legislation and its implementation makes any religious minority community vulnerable. Foreign origins, distinctive beliefs and practices, active missionary activities, or conflict with the Moscow Patriarchate or with the official leadership of other 'traditional religions' can all contribute to discrimination or even outright persecution. Today, newer Protestant communities, such as Pentecostals, have become the main targets of discriminatory actions by local administrations and law enforcement agencies in many regions, such as Orenburg, Amur and Khanty-Mansiysk. Their charges are remarkably similar to those levied against 'cults' and 'sects'; for instance, causing psychological harm through 'non-traditional' practices (for example, 'speaking in tongues') or 'destroying Russian national mentality', grafted on to the ubiquitous anti-extremist rhetoric. Interestingly, Alexander Dvorkin's anti-cult expertise has been enlisted in legal cases involving new Pentecostals. On many occasions, security services and local administrations have come up with 'recommendations' to ban minority communities after consulting a local Orthodox priest or on the basis of their 'anti-state and anti-Christian orientation', as was the case with the Jehovah's Witnesses in the town of Ozersk in Chelyabinsk region.[52] In the predominantly Muslim regions of Tatarstan and Dagestan local laws designed to combat Islamist extremism were adopted, though they have been applied mainly to counter local

---

[51] Emily Baran, 'Contested Victims: Jehovah's Witnesses and the Russian Orthodox Church, 1990 to 2004', *Religion, State and Society* 35 (2007): 261–78; Zoe Knox, 'Religious Freedom in Russia: The Putin Years', in *Religion, Community, and Morality*, eds Steinberg and Wanner, 298–302; Olga Sibireva, 'Freedom of Conscience in Russia: Restrictions and Challenges in 2011', in *Xenophobia, Freedom of Conscience and Anti-Extremism in Russia*, eds Alperovich et al., 62–86.

[52] Ibid., 81.

Salafi communities. Furthermore, security services have intervened in conflicts between the Moscow Patriarchate and Russian Orthodox communities outside its jurisdiction, such as the Russian Orthodox Church Abroad.[53] Finally, in many Russian regions anti-extremist legislation has been used against the Church of Scientology, with books by its founder Ron Hubbard being put on the Federal List of Extremist Literature.[54]

Several other legislative changes of the 2000s have also had a direct bearing on religious minorities. For instance, in its current form, the law on non-commercial and non-governmental organizations contains provisions causing a number of difficulties for groups with financial and organizational links abroad, as it involves cumbersome procedures and often insurmountable obstacles for obtaining visas and receiving sponsorship. The most recent flurry of legislation on 'state treason' and 'foreign agents' may have similar effects, as it is designed to curtail and control links between Russian groups and individuals with connections with organizations abroad. At the same time, some of the new laws can affect minority religions by excluding them from state protection; for instance the new draft law on 'Insulting Citizens' Religious Views and Feelings and Desecration of Objects of Religious Worship and Pilgrimage and Places of Religious Rites and Ceremonies' limits its application only to 'Russia's traditional religions'.

As elsewhere, state control of minority religions can include extra-legal actions, such as creating obstacles to registration (for example, for the Unification Church, Scientology, Jehovah's Witnesses and some new Muslim groups), restricting the availability of land for places of worship (such as for building a temple by the Krishna Movement in Moscow, or mosques in Astrakhan and Moscow), or obstructing charitable work (for example, that of many new Protestant groups in various regions). In Russia, implementation of these means of control is facilitated by lack of accountability for executive authorities that can often act out of overriding 'state interests' rather than according to the law. Reports by Russian human rights monitoring organizations, such as Moscow-based Sova-centre and Forum 18, document dozens of such actions by local authorities at various levels. In addition, official bodies continue to issue 'black lists', such as 'Foreign Organizations of Destructive Creeds', published by the Ministry of Education of the Republic of Bashkortostan (2011), which includes, among others, Jehovah's Witnesses, Scientologists, Mormons, Baptists and Pentecostals.[55]

Authorities are usually reluctant to intervene when religious minorities complain about infringement of their rights, such as acts of vandalism, defamation, and even death threats. Most cases brought by state prosecutors against groups

---

[53] Ibid., 82.
[54] On the implementation of the anti-extremist legislation against the Church of Scientology and its wider political implications, see an interview with Attorney Galina Krylova, http://www.portal-credo.ru/site/?act=authority&id=1619.
[55] Sibireva, 'Freedom of Conscience', 79.

such as Jehovah's Witnesses, Scientology, new Pentecostal churches, or even the Salvation Army, have tended to succeed in local courts while those filed by the minority groups against state agencies tend to fail.

Conclusion

Post-Soviet Russia has become a site of immense religious diversity characterized by many of the tensions and controversies that can be found elsewhere. Nothing in the preceding examination has suggested that the post-Soviet state has an institutional interest in suppressing particular religious minorities. It has, however, shown little concern for institutional protections of their rights. Religious minorities' vulnerability to the arbitrary actions of certain state agencies is largely a function of the vulnerabilities of the post-Soviet state itself. Having been initially constituted as a liberal democratic state, it has become controlled by political elites with little appreciation of its foundational principles of religious freedom and equality. The legitimacy of these elites has been largely dependent on the support of influential social actors, such as the leadership of the dominant church and, to a lesser extent, of other 'traditional religions' that have a vested interest in maintaining their privileged position in society at the expense of many religious minorities. (In this respect, I am sceptical that constitutional acknowledgement of the privileged position of the 'traditional religions', which has been proposed by some Western legal scholars, would redress the balance between the social and legal reality without jeopardizing minority rights.[56]) The state has also manifested its vulnerability in its fear of challenges from civil society and its tight grip on the legal system. This, in turn, has given considerable clout to law enforcement agencies that have used increasingly restrictive legislation in an often-unrestricted manner. Religious minorities' opportunities to defend their rights have thus been considerably reduced.

We should not overlook, however, that the post-Soviet political regimes have at least formally operated within a constitutional framework that tends to restrict the scope of their discriminatory policies. This did provide Russia's religious minorities with certain means to seek and, in certain cases, achieve justice within the domestic legal system and through the European Court of Human Rights.[57] The story remains unfinished and its unfolding ultimately depends on the evolution of Russia's democratic institutions and civil society.

---

[56] Dora Hallinan, 'Orthodox Pluralism: Contours of Freedom of Religion in the Russian Federation and Strasbourg Jurisprudence', *Review of Central and Eastern European Law* 37 (2012): 293–346; Giovanni Codevilla, 'Relations between Church and State in Russia Today', *Religion, State, and Society* 36 (2008): 113–37.

[57] Sibireva, 'Freedom of Conscience in Russia'; James Richardson and John Shoemaker, 'The European Court of Human Rights, Minority Religions, and the Social Construction of Religious Freedom', in *The Centrality of Religion in Social Life: Essays in Honour of James A. Beckford* (Aldershot: Ashgate, 2010), 103–16.

Chapter 14
China's Responses to Minority Religions

Ping Xiong

Religious development and minority religions in China

Historical background

China is a country with a long history of religious practice. The history of the five major religions being practiced in China now can be traced back for centuries.[1] Taoism, which originated in China, was established as a religion around 25–220 AD in the late Eastern Han Dynasty. Buddhism was introduced from India as early as the first century and gained continuing popularity in China. Christianity did not reach China until the seventh century AD and then disappeared for hundreds of years until it was re-introduced at the end of the Ming dynasty in the sixteenth century. Islam can be dated back to a mission in 651. Some also consider that Confucianism should be seen as a kind of religion.[2]

In addition to these well-known main religions, some minority religions were also practiced in China over a period of more than 400 years. Some were introduced from outside of China, such as the Bahá'í Faith,[3] Mormonism, Judaism,[4] Manichaeism,[5] Hinduism, and Zoroastrianism. Others were indigenous Chinese folk religions such as Heaven worship, while non-Han ethnic groups practiced such as faiths as Moz, White Stone Religion,[6] Dongbaism and Bön. With this historic context in mind, this chapter will lay out the current situation regarding the Chinese law governing religious minorities, followed by the case study of the plight of Falun Gong in modern China.

---

[1] Eric Kolodner, 'Religious Rights in China: A Comparison of International Human Rights Law and Chinese Domestic Legislation', *Human Rights Quarterly* 16 (1994): 462–4.

[2] See Michael Dillon, *Religious Minorities and China* (London: Minority Rights Group International, 2001), 10.

[3] Graham Hassall, 'Bahá'í Communities by Country: Research Notes', last modified 2000, http://bahai-library.com/hassall_bahai_communities_country. Hassall provides four periods when the Bahá'í Faith was introduced into China.

[4] Xu Xin, 'Judaism in China', in *Studies in World's Religions* 2 (2000). Xin comments that Judaism entered into China during the Tang Dynasty.

[5] Samuel Nan-Chiang Lieu, 'Manichaeism in Central Asia and China', in *Nag Hammadi and Manichaean Studies* 45 (1998): 231–9.

[6] Ming Xu, 'Qiang People's Worship of White-stone Godess [J]', *Journal of Southwest Institute for Ethnic Groups* 3 (1999).

The present situation

Upon the establishment of the People's Republic of China (PRC), the Communist Party of China, which controlled the government and was the authoritative source of acceptable policy positions on all matters, adopted the Marxist-Leninist view towards religion.[7] According to Kolodner, the Marxist-Leninist perspective views religion as a product of history and claims that religion will disappear 'when socioeconomic and cultural conditions have improved to the extent that people no longer require this "opiate"'.[8] Kolodner argues that the dominance of state orthodoxy informed by the Marxist-Leninist position and the underlying influence of traditional Confucian perspectives, cultural practices and attitudes, can together be seen as an obstacle to freedom of religion in China.[9] It is also argued that China can be seen as a traditional society with a collectivist emphasis upon the responsibility of a person as a member of society rather than an emphasis upon the individual and the rights of the individual and that this cultural perspective runs counter to the idea of an individual liberty to pursue religious freedom.[10].

However, when the PRC was formed some established religions were tolerated in China in order to preserve some aspects of the social status quo. The Chinese government recognized five traditional religions, namely Buddhism, Taoism, Islam, Catholicism and Protestantism, and established a system to control the institutions of the religions it recognized.

The Chinese government affords protection to the five officially sanctioned religions through five separate organizations: the Buddhist Association of China, the Chinese Taoist Association, the Islamic Association of China, the Protestant Three-Self Patriotic Movement and the Chinese Patriotic Catholic Association. This protection is extended only to what is called 'normal religious activity', generally understood to refer to religions that submit to state control via the State Administration for Religious Affairs.

However, since China's adoption of the open door policy in 1978, China has become a more open society tolerating more civil differences and disputes with some lessening of compulsory collective orthodoxy.[11] Even where orthodoxy is officially required, some *de facto* tolerance of divergent practice exists. An example can be seen in the rise of the 'house church' movement where Chinese Christians who preferred to worship outside the state-controlled religious movements began to meet in unregistered house churches which mushroomed throughout the country. This religious phenomenon is tolerated to some degree but not encouraged.[12] At the same

---

[7] Kolodner, 'Religious Rights in China', 465–6.
[8] Ibid., 466–7.
[9] Ibid., 462–3.
[10] Ibid., 466.
[11] Vicki Waye and Ping Xiong, 'The Relationship between Mediation and Judicial Proceedings in China', *Asian Journal of Comparative Law* 6 (2011): 35.
[12] Kolodner, 'Religious Rights in China', 467.

time a great diversity of new religious movements are developing across China. The majority of them are indigenous, and some are totally new, whilst others were already active before the communist revolution in 1949. These religions, however, are spreading quietly and have not been officially recognized in China.

Nowadays in China, according to official statistics, there are altogether more than 100,000,000 believers and this number is considered to be growing rapidly. China also has more than 300,000 clerics, more than 3,000 religious bodies, and more than 85,000 places for religious activities.[13]

Religion administration in China under the current legal framework

Religion administration and religious bodies

The legal framework in China for the protection of freedom of religion includes the laws promulgated by the People's Congress or the Standing Committee of the People's Congress, and administrative regulations promulgated by the State Council as well as the implementation rules of the various ministries.

The most important law is the Constitution of the PRC (amended in 2004), which protects both freedom of religion of citizens,[14] and the equal voting rights of citizens who are of different religious beliefs.[15] Article 36 of the Constitution provides,

> Citizens of the People's Republic of China enjoy freedom of religious belief.
>
> No State organ, public organization or individual may compel citizens to believe in, or not to believe in, any religion; nor may they discriminate against citizens who believe in, or do not believe in, any religion.
>
> The State protects normal religious activities. No one may make use of religion to engage in activities that disrupt public order, impair the health of citizens or interfere with the educational system of the State.
>
> Religious bodies and religious affairs are not subject to any foreign domination.

---

[13] The statistics are from the website of the State Administration for Religious Affairs of PRC.
[14] Article 36 of the Constitution of PRC.
[15] Article 34 of the Constitution of PRC provides, 'All citizens of the People's Republic of China who have reached the age of 18 have the right to vote and stand for election, regardless of ethnic status, race, sex, occupation, family background, religious belief, education, property status or length of residence, except persons deprived of political rights according to law'.

Protection of freedom of religion can also be found in other laws, such as the Law of the PRC of China on Regional National Autonomy (amended in 2001); the General Rules of Civil Law (1986); the Law of Education; the Labour Law; the Compulsory Education Law; the Law on the Election of Deputies of National People's Congress; the Organic Law of the Rural Residents Committees of PRC; and the Law of Advertisement. These laws protect the property of religious bodies, the separation between religion and education, the equal educational opportunities of the citizens with different religious backgrounds, the respect for the customs and religious beliefs of each ethnic groups, the equal opportunity of citizens for employment and the non-discrimination against any religion in 'advertizement'.

Two important rules and regulations especially relevant for foreign religious bodies include the Regulations on Religious Affairs (2005, State Council of PRC) and the Rules for the Implementation of the Provisions on the Administration of Religious Activities of Aliens within the Territory of the People's Republic of China (2000, State Administration for Religious Affairs).

One of the main characteristics of the law of China relating to freedom of religion is its controlling nature, as the government tries to administer almost every aspect of religious activity in order to maintain control over religious bodies, persons and practices.

A fundamental first principle in the Chinese government's policy perspective on the concept and practice of freedom of religion is that religion should not act as a tool to disrupt public order in China.[16] The Chinese government is suspicious of the possibility of foreign domination of the religious activities of the Chinese population,[17] because of China's past history of foreign bullying in the nineteenth century. In the White Paper on Freedom of Religious Belief in China issued by the State Council of the PRC on 16 October 1997, the government articulated its concerns about the foreign connection of religions.[18] It pointed out that the policy to establish religion independently was a historical choice of Chinese religious believers during anti-colonization and anti-imperialism struggles. The paper stated that western imperialists and colonists used the Roman Catholic and Protestant Churches as tools to invade China. It listed several examples, including opium smuggling by some foreign missionaries, foreign missionaries' assisting and spying for the Eight-Nation Alliance during their invasion in 1900, foreign missionaries participating in plotting and drafting some unequal treaties between China and western powers, and several cases involving foreign missionaries who evaded the administration of Chinese justice because of their extraterritorial jurisdictional privilege.

Secondly, in order to ensure that religious activity does not pose a threat to public order and stability, the Chinese government administers the establishment,

---

[16] Paragraph 3 of Article 36 of the Constitution of PRC.
[17] Paragraph 4 of Article 36 of the Constitution of PRC.
[18] See State Council of the PRC, 'White Paper – Freedom of Religious Belief in China' (1997), section 4, http://www.china-embassy.org/eng/zt/zjxy/t36492.htm.

alteration and cancellation of registration of religious bodies. According to the Regulations on Religious Affairs, a religious body is regarded as an association and therefore is subject to the Regulations on Registration Administration of Associations.[19] Usually, the Ministry of Civil Affairs or the local authorities in charge of civil affairs handle this kind of registration.[20] Despite the theoretical freedom to seek registration for a new religious institution, registration is exceptionally difficult. Registration requires approval from the Department for Religious Affairs at the state or local level,[21] but in practice the Department for Religious Affairs usually will not approve it, meaning that this kind of registration is highly unlikely, if not impossible. The five recognized religious bodies[22] constitute exceptions, because they all are members of the National Committee of the Chinese People's Political Consultative Conference (CPPCC),[23] and according to Chinese law, any association, if a member of the CPPCC, is able to have the registration requirement waived.[24] One implication of this is that minority religious bodies will not have a chance to be registered as a religious body to practice their religions in China. It is true that according to the PRC Administrative Review Law (1999), an administrative decision, including a decision to refuse an application for registration of an institution, is subject to review by the relevant administrative organ,[25] and according to the PRC Administrative Procedure Law (1990) can also

---

[19] Article 6 of the Regulations on Religious Affairs provides, 'The establishment, alteration, or cancellation of registration, of a religious body shall be registered in accordance with the provisions of the Regulations on Registration Administration of Associations'.

[20] Article 6 of the Regulations on Registration Administration of Associations (1998).

[21] See Article 3 of the Circular of the Implementation of the Measures for the Administration of the Registration of Religious Bodies (6 May 1991, the Ministry of Civil Affairs and the State Administration for Religious Affairs).

[22] The five recognized religious bodies are the Buddhist Association of China, the Chinese Taoist Association, the Islamic Association of China, the Protestant Three-Self Patriotic Movement and the Chinese Patriotic Catholic Association.

[23] According to the Articles of Association of the CPPCC, the object and purpose of the CPPCC is to establish the broadest patriotic united front by uniting people. Article 2 of the Articles of Association of the CPPCC provides that the function of the CPPCC is to have political consultation with the Communist Party on important issues before any big decision is made, to conduct democratic supervision to supervise or criticise the implementation of the Constitution, laws and regulations, and to participate in and discuss political matters which are the most important political, economic, social or cultural issues among the people.

[24] See Article 3 of the Regulations on the Administration of the Registration of Associations (October 25, 1998, the State Council of PRC).

[25] 'Any citizen, legal person, or any other organization may, according to this Law, apply for administrative review under any of the circumstances as follows: ... (8) holding that the administrative organ have failed to issue a certificate, such as a permit, license, credit certificate, or credential, or examine and approve and register related items according to laws, for which it/he considers itself/themselves legally qualified'. PRC Administrative

be challenged before a court.[26] Despite this possibility so far there have been no such challenges.

Where it is intended to establish or operate an institution for religious education an application should be made to the religious affairs department of the State Council by a national religious body or to the provincial department for religious affairs if the religious body is only a provincial religious body.[27]

Thirdly, the Chinese government administers all sites for the conduct of religious activities. The building of any temple, church, monastery or mosque is subject to the approval of the religious department of the government at county level.[28] The system of control applies also to preparations for establishing such a site, so approval should be sought before any such activity can take place.[29] The religious affairs department has the right to supervise and inspect the site to make sure that the activities conducted there are in compliance with the laws and regulations of the PRC.[30]

Fourthly, the Chinese government administers the personnel of religious bodies. According to the Regulation, any appointment of religious personnel or any vacating or leaving of chief religious posts shall be reported to the religious affairs department at, or above, county level.[31]

In summary, through the administration of the incorporation of religious bodies, the establishment of religious sites for religious activities and the appointment and retirement of religious personnel, the government maintains a network of control to make sure that the activities conducted by various religious bodies are lawful.

Religion administration and activities of foreigners

China's past history with foreign powers and the activities of foreigners in China during the nineteenth century, which was marked by oppressive and unjustifiable foreign exploitation and bullying, has deeply coloured the Chinese government's attitude towards the activities of foreigners and foreign institutions or organizations in modern China. Upon the establishment of the independent, sovereign PRC, the government began to oversee freedom of religion and the activities of many foreign religious bodies in China.

Review Law (1999), Article 6, http://www.fdi.gov.cn/pub/FDI_EN/Laws/law_en_info.jsp?docid=87754.

[26] Article 11 of the PRC Administrative Procedure Law (1990) provides, 'The people's courts shall accept suits brought by citizens, legal persons or other organizations against any of the following specific administrative acts: ... (4) refusal by an administrative organ to issue a permit or license, which one considers oneself legally qualified to apply for, or its failure to respond to the application'.

[27] Article 8 of the Regulations on Religious Affairs.
[28] Article 13 of the Regulations on Religious Affairs.
[29] Ibid.
[30] Article 19 of the Regulations on Religious Affairs.
[31] Articles 27 and 28 of the Regulations on Religious Affairs.

In 2000, the State Administration for Religious Affairs issued the Rules for the Implementation of the Provisions on the Administration of Religious Activities of Aliens within the Territory of the People's Republic of China to regulate foreigners' religious activities. This administration includes the following aspects.

Under the rules pertaining to religious activities, foreign religious personnel may preach and expound their scripture at lawfully registered sites for religious activities but only after being invited by Chinese religious bodies that are recognized at or above the province, autonomous region or municipality levels under the direct administration of the Central government. Foreigners who are not officially recognized as religious personnel require an invitation and approval at or above these same levels, also under the direct administration of the Central government, before they may preach and expound scripture at the registered sites.[32] This usually means that any foreign religious body wishing to conduct religious activities in China needs to have an established relationship with a contacting Chinese religious body. These relationships are generally regarded by the authorities as friendly contacts and a form of cultural and academic exchanges. Moreover, any exchange or friendly contact between religious bodies other than the five officially recognized religions and a Chinese government or a Chinese religious body will be subject to approval by the State Administration for Religious Affairs (SARA).[33] A Chinese contacting unit has to apply to the SARA. Then, if the foreign religious body is lawful, having a good record in its home country, and if it is assessed to be friendly to China, SARA may grant permission.[34] While the conditions for permission are reasonable, such activities are closely controlled, reflecting a widespread suspicion by authorities.

Religious bodies often desire to produce and distribute religious material and publications. However, foreign religious bodies are prohibited from bringing into China or importing their religious printed matter, or audio-visual products or other articles if the amount exceeds that which can be regarded as sufficient for reasonable personal use. If the contents of these religious publications are considered to be detrimental to Chinese national security and the public interests of Chinese society, they are strictly prohibited.[35] This means that foreign missionaries and other religious people cannot distribute pamphlets or brochures freely anywhere in China, and that any publication made by a foreign religious body will be subject to censorship.

---

[32] Article 6 of the Rules.

[33] This can be found at Item 367 of the Decision of the State Council on Establishing Administrative Approval System for Issues Necessary to be Reserved for Administrative Approval (State Council of PRC, 2004).

[34] See the Approval for the Exchange or Friendly Contact Activity between any Religious Body Other Than the Ones from the Five Officially Recognized Religions, and a Chinese Government or a Chinese Religious Body (SARA, 2007).

[35] Article 12 of the Rules.

Chinese nationals going abroad to study or to train to qualify as religious personnel, or who issue invitations to foreigners to come to China to study at Chinese religious institutions, require approval from the national religious bodies, and the application and approval, if granted, will be recorded at the State Administration for Religious Affairs.[36] A foreigner teaching at a Chinese religious institution is subject to specific provisions issued by the SARA.[37]

Missionaries seeking new converts have often spread religion and religious ideas and teachings in China; however, the Chinese government has enacted controls and limits especially on foreign missionaries and thus the following activities may be prohibited:

1. appointing religious personnel among Chinese citizens
2. developing religious followers among Chinese citizens
3. preaching and expounding the scripture at the sites for religious activities without permission
4. preaching and expounding the scripture or conducting religious gathering activities at the places outside the lawfully registered sites for religious activities
5. conducting religious activities in which Chinese citizens are admitted to participate at the temporary sites for religious activities, except that the Chinese religious personnel are invited to preside the religious activities
6. producing or selling religious books and journals, religious audio-visual products, religious electronic goods or other religious articles
7. distributing religious promotion materials
8. other missionary activities.

In sum, although foreign religious activities may be permitted if regarded as cultural or academic exchange provided they are assessed as opposing no threat to Chinese public stability, the Chinese laws relating to administration of foreign religious activities provide a very close level of assessment and control.

Responses to religion extremes

Falun Gong – a case study

The Chinese government considers that the stability of the State and maintenance of a stable cooperative society are matters of prime importance. Because religious belief, religious doctrine and practice can be powerful forces in society, it is not surprising that the Chinese government maintains a close watch upon all activities

---

[36] Articles 13, 14 of the Rules.
[37] See Methods of Engaging Foreign Professionals by Religious Institution.

of a religious nature.[38] It particularly wants to prevent the rise of any radical or extreme religious activity, which may prove disruptive to what the government regards as appropriate social and political activity.

The on-going antipathy between the Chinese government and the movement known as the Falun Gong is so well known that it naturally invites discussion. The Falun Gong is officially regarded by the Chinese government and the governmental system at all levels as a kind of 'evil cult'.

The Falun Gong was founded in 1992 by Li Hongzhi, known as the Master Li. The movement practices breathing or body energy exercises and which are claimed to cultivate the mind and thoughts and the body of practising believers.[39] In the beginning the Chinese government tolerated the Falun Gong, because it was considered to enjoy a 'seemingly benign' existence.[40]

This situation, however, changed in 1999 when 10,000 Falun Gong followers protested an academic journal article published by an academician from the Chinese Academy of Social Science. The article, highly critical of Falun Gong practices, was addressed as a warning to teenagers about the supposed harmful nature of the Falun Gong. The Falun Gong followers gathered outside the *Zhongnanhai* compound, the headquarters of the Chinese government, on 25 April 1999. Although the government was restrained and refrained from any aggressive actions against the demonstrators initially, and the demonstrators also 'stayed motionless, calm and seated on the sidewalk' and eventually returned home until their case was presented to the government,[41] the government became concerned that the Falun Gong constituted a potential or real threat and started to take actions against the group.

The response of the government to the Falun Gong group included a propaganda campaign to win public support and the issuance of a series of legislative decisions and interpretations in October 1999 to legalize the actions the government intended to take against the Falun Gong group. Then came the 'evil cult' declaration, followed by several criminal trials initiated by Chinese judicial organs.

In November 1999, the Hainan Province reported the first trial.[42] Then, more significantly, in December 1999, the Beijing First Procuratorate charged four Falun Gong group leaders with a number of crimes arising from their practices. The

---

[38] See Anne S.Y. Cheung, 'In Search of a Theory of Cult and Freedom of Religion in China: The Case of Falun Gong', *Pacific Rim Law & Policy Journal* 13 (2004): 13–14. The author points out that 'the danger of religious groups to the political order is particularly worrisome because spiritual leaders and religious beliefs have played powerful roles in mobilizing rebel forces'.

[39] See www.falundafa.org.

[40] Cheung, 'In Search of a Theory of Cult and Freedom of Religion in China', 21–2.

[41] Seth Faison, 'Cult's Followers Rally in Beijing', *New York Times*, 26 April 1999, quoted in Kelly A. Thomas, 'Falun Gong: An Analysis of China's National Security Concerns', *Pacific Rim Law & Policy Journal* 10 (2000): 475–6.

[42] Ibid., 480.

charges were that the Falun Gong leaders had been destroying the implementation of laws, organizing or using an evil cult, were illegally holding and disclosing state secrets, and were illegally organizing assembly to disrupt public order. The four people were sentenced to prison terms varying from five to 11 years.

The Judgment of the Beijing First Intermediate People's Court (1999)[43] illustrates the crimes that they were found to have committed. The charges of organizing or using the evil cult and destroying the implementation of laws were found to be proved through the defendants' activities of developing and controlling members of the group and organizing the Falun Gong cult itself; organizing, planning and instructing an assembly of cult members to assault state organs and disrupt social order; and amassing wealth by utilizing the Falun Gong to illegally publish and issue evil cult publications.

The charges of organizing and using the Falun Gong evil cult to disseminate superstition to cause the death of others were found to be proved by the examples of the death of a number of Falun Gong members who, because of their beliefs in the doctrines and teaching of the Falun Gung, refused to seek or accept medical treatment. These deaths were considered to be a form of suicide encouraged or promoted by the organization. The charges of illegally holding or stealing state secrets were found proved, the judgment stating that the Falun Gong evil cult collected top secret documents which it included in its publications to be disseminated to the public, although neither the names nor the content of the documents were set out in the judgment.

The criminalization of Falun Gong activities raises some questions: What is an 'evil cult'? Should wilful and conscious refusal of medical treatment, even in the face of likely death, where that decision is based upon an article of religious belief or faith be regarded as a form of self-harm by an adult and then be categorized or regarded as a criminal offence on the part of the body teaching such beliefs?

Laws relating to evil cults in China

The term 'cult' is a term of judgment and opprobrium. What categorizes a group of believers or practitioners as a cult rather than as a general religious organization? According to Cheung, there are seven characteristics that should be considered in forming a judgment that a group constitutes a cult.[44] The group will be characterized by:

1. Relatively newly-formed groups that present a distinct alternative to dominant patterns, and perceive themselves as elitist societies;
2. Strong authoritarian and charismatic leadership, in which the founding leader is often self-appointed and not accountable to the members;

---

[43] See the Judgment of the Beijing First Intermediate People's Court (1999) Yi Zhong Xing Chu Zi No. 2075.

[44] Cheung, 'In Search of a Theory of Cult and Freedom of Religion in China', 9–10.

3   Aggressive proselytizing methods and use of psychological methods to recruit and indoctrinate its members;
4   Systematic inducement of powerful experiences and fulfilment of members' needs;
5   A strong sense of 'insiders' and 'outsiders' and high degree of conformity and commitment amongst members;
6   A tendency to see themselves as legitimated by a long tradition of wisdom of practice of which they are the current manifestation;
7   A lack of benefit to members or the society from the wealth gathered by such groups.

While these factors seems suggestive and valuable in making an assessment, and the presence of a number of these characteristics in an organization tend toward the possibility that it can be adjudged to be a cult, there is then the further question of what is to be regarded as an 'evil' cult.

Article 300 of the Criminal Law of the PRC (adopted in 1979, revised in 1997) provides for criminal sanctions against any activities relating to an evil cult.[45] This article has three paragraphs and provides laws to punish any person or organization that 'forms or uses superstitious sects or secret societies or evil religious organizations or uses superstition' to undermine laws, cheat people, cause death, rape a woman or to swindle money. These are all recognized criminal activities and perhaps any person or organization committing, encouraging or teaching such practices could be termed 'evil'. Regardless, the article does not provide an explicit and detailed definition of the term 'evil cult'.

After the Falun Gong incidents, on 30 October 1999 the Standing Committee of the People's Congress of the PRC issued its decision 'Regarding the Ban, Prevention and Punishment of Evil Cult Activities (1999)' (the Decision). The Decision has a preamble and three paragraphs, and states its purpose as 'to maintain social stability, to protect the interests of the people, and to safeguard the smooth advancement of the reform and opening up and the construction of the modernization of socialism'. In November 1999, the Supreme People's Court of

---

[45]   Article 300 of the Criminal Law (revised in 1997) provides, 'Whoever forms or uses superstitious sects or secret societies or evil religious organizations or uses superstition to undermine the implementation of the laws and administrative rules and regulations of the State shall be sentenced to fixed-term imprisonment of not less than three years but not more than seven years; if the circumstances are especially serious, he shall be sentenced to fixed-term imprisonment of not less than seven years. Whoever forms or uses superstitious sects or secret societies or evil religious organizations or uses superstition to cheat another person, and causes death to the person shall be punished in accordance with the provisions of the preceding paragraph. Whoever forms or uses superstitious sects or secret societies or evil religious organizations or uses superstition to rape a woman or swindle money or property shall be convicted and punished in accordance with the provisions of Articles 236 and Article 266 of this Law respectively'.

the People's Republic of China (SPC) notified all Chinese courts to implement the National People's Congress (NPC) interpretation regarding evil cults.

In order to define what is meant by evil cult, the SPC and the Supreme People's Procuratorate of the PRC (SPP) together issued the Interpretation of Several Issues on Specific Law Application in Handling the Cases Involving Organizing and Using Evil Cults to Commit Crimes (1999), (the Interpretation) in October 1999. This Interpretation consists of nine articles.

Article 1 of the Interpretation defines 'evil cult' as 'an illegal organization which is established under the disguise of religion, breathing energy exercise, or other names, to deify the leaders of such organization, to bewitch or deceive others by utilizing the means of creating or distributing superstition or evil doctrines, to develop and control the members, and to endanger the society'.

This Interpretation further clarifies the three paragraphs of article 300 of the Criminal Law (revised in 1997). The first paragraph of article 300 of the Criminal Law, which refers to undermining the law and regulations by using superstitious sects or secret societies or evil religious organizations, is illustrated in Article 2 of the Interpretation which includes gathering of people to assault state organs or other working units; illegal assembly, procession or demonstration; inciting, cheating or organizing others not to fulfil the members' legal obligations; resuming or creating an evil cult after the organization has been outlawed; and publishing or printing or photocopying or issuing publications with the content of an evil cult.[46] These then are crimes relating to the disruption of public orders.

Articles 3 and 4 of the Interpretation further clarify the second paragraph of article 300. They refer to organizing and using an evil cult to create or distribute superstitions and evil doctrines, or to cheat members or others, to go on hunger strike, autotomy (cutting part of the body by oneself), autosadism, or causing (or contributing to the cause of) the death of the members or others by obstructing patients from obtaining normal medical treatment.[47] This crime can be regarded as homicide or murder.[48]

Articles 5 and 6 of the Interpretation clarify that raping a woman or a girl or swindling money are to be punished as crimes under the Criminal Law.

Article 7 of the Interpretation clarifies the criminality of organizing or utilizing an evil cult to divide or undermine the unity of the state, to overthrow the socialist system or to endanger public security and declares all of these activities punishable.

With the development of digital technology, in 2001 the SPC and the SPP together issued the Interpretation of Several Issues on Specific Law Application in Handling the Cases Involving Organizing and Using Evil Cult to Commit Crimes II (2001) (the Interpretation II) to provide more detail concerning activities that involve the making and dissemination of material with 'evil cult content' through the medium of the internet or other electronic media. According to Interpretation II, the making

---

[46] Article 2 of the Interpretation.
[47] Article 3 of the Interpretation.
[48] Article 4 of the Interpretation.

and dissemination of such material can include the making and dissemination of the master copy of any DVD, CD and VCD and the using of the Internet.[49] Later in 2002, the SPC and SPP also issued the Explanation of the Several Issues arising from the Interpretation II (the Explanation) to give a more detailed explanation of these activities.[50] In addition, Interpretation II added more specific crimes relating to the activities of evil cults, including criminal sanctions against the crimes of defamation or humiliation, and unlawful theft of state secrets provided in the Criminal Law.

Understanding of the law relating to evil cult

Through this kind of legal framework, the law in China imposes very severe sanctions against organizations that are found to be evil cults. In examining how the criminal law is being applied here, it is useful to consider the political foundation of criminal law in China. The Criminal Law (1997) is a revision of the former Criminal Law (1979), which was used, according to Chen, to stabilize the revolution after the establishment of the PRC. The old Criminal Law (1979) was also used 'to uphold the Marxism-Leninism-Mao Zedong thought as the guiding ideology and perhaps was used as an important weapon for class struggle, aimed primarily at attacking counter-revolutionaries and other criminals who seriously undermined social order and socialist construction'.[51] It reflected the social context at the time when the law was made. Clearly, 'the counter revolutionary [view] is more a political ... than a legal concept'.[52] The revised Criminal Law of 1997 generally takes a formalistic approach and 'signals the stabilisation of a revolution'. It is, however, according to Chen, still a failure as it does not address fundamental problems of the law while it retains most of the counter revolutionary crimes provisions while only changing their label.[53] This historical and political ideology is reflected in the way the state has formulated the law to respond to the challenges perceived to arise from the activities of Falun Gong. When a cult is regarded as a threat to the government and poses potential harm to the communist party regime, China may use the criminal law to suppress it. This has especially been true since the Falun Gong events. As one view puts it, the Standing Committee of the National People's Congress 'colored the terms' of the 1997 Criminal Law to reflect their official stance on the Falun Gong.[54]

---

[49] Article 1 of the Interpretation II.
[50] See Article I of the Explanation (2002). According to these two documents, any making or circulation of materials with evil cult content by using Internet, CD, DVD other BP will also be regarded as the crimes prescribed in article 300 of the Criminal Law.
[51] Jianfu Chen, *Chinese Law: Towards an Understanding of Chinese Law, Its Nature, and Development*, vol. 3 (The Hague: Martinus Nijhoff, 1999), 174.
[52] Ibid., 185.
[53] Ibid., 196.
[54] Cheung, 'In Search of a Theory of Cult and Freedom of Religion in China', 24.

As stated above, the Chinese government is concerned about foreigners exercising control over religious activities, and this kind of fear has also been reinforced in its response to the evil cult. A similar kind of suspicion informs the response to new cults or new religious movements. The leaders and members of cults can be thought of as 'outsiders', as not being part of the collective communist society, and as posing a potential threat to its stability. This categorization of 'outsider' is especially reinforced when the organization reaches beyond China to actually include foreigners.

While Article 36 of the Constitution of the PRC provides for freedom of religion, with the limitation that the religious institutions, teachings and practices must not be dominated by foreigners, Liu Peng pointed out that China's socialist ideology is founded on 'opposition to imperialism, including cultural or religious imperialism'.[55] This kind of ideology was also reflected in the laws against evil cults, especially when the Falun Gong was found, with its expansion, to have attracted tens of millions of followers extending from the PRC to the United States, Canada, Australia and Europe.[56] In the Explanation II, Article 8 punishes an evil cult for its activities 'to steal, spy, bribe to obtain, and unlawfully provide state secrets'.[57] This echoes the fear of the government that more foreign connection will lead to the activity of spying by the evil cults.

The set of laws also punishes any evil cult which obstructs its members from getting normal medical treatment or deceives its members into harming themselves or encourages them to refuse to get normal medical treatment. This raises the issue of 'whether the government can interfere with adults who choose to harm themselves and/or who refuse medical treatment'.[58] This is a very controversial issue. Some international human rights bodies considered the question extremely difficult and were reluctant to accept the view that freedom to self-harm, or doctrines that inhibit choice to seek normal medical treatment could be regarded as within the scope of the concept of religious freedom and autonomy of the believers.[59] Evans is of the view that 'the state may only intervene to protect a person who is in immediate danger'.[60] The law in China takes a further step and prohibits any such behaviour that may cause serious physical harm leading to death and signals how seriously it considers the offence by imposing the death

---

[55] Liu Peng, 'Unreconciled Differences: The Staying Power of Religion', 151, cited in Lison Harris, 'God and Caesar in China: Policy Implications of Church-State Tensions', *Hong Kong Law Journal* 35 (2005): 532–3.

[56] Cheung, 'In Search of a Theory of Cult and Freedom of Religion in China', 22.

[57] Article 8 of the Explanation II.

[58] Carolyn Evans, 'Chinese Law and the International Protection of Religious Freedom', *Journal of Church and State* 44 (2002): 769.

[59] Ibid., 770. For example, the author pointed out that the European Commission on Human Rights held that a state could require Sikhs to wear motorcycle helmets even though this meant that they were unable to wear a turban.

[60] Ibid.

penalty against the leaders of any guilty evil cults.⁶¹ This reflects China's very firm stand against organizations that can be categorized as evil cults and the intention of the government to eradicate such organizations and systematic practices.

Minority religion administration in the future

China's present legal framework is to administer religion to assure that everything remains under control and free from foreign domination. This characteristic of Chinese law is related to its history and is still developing. China is a country with a long history of unity as one country, a unification which required an authoritative government during feudal times.

The current legal framework demonstrates that, although the Chinese Constitution provides for freedom of religion, it still lacks a set of laws to ensure the specific implementation of this freedom. Currently, there are only regulations issued by the State Council and provisions or measures issued by SARA or other relevant ministries available to administer religious affairs. These, however, are specific implementing administrative rules made by the government or governmental agencies at the lower level of Chinese law, and are far from satisfactory to protect or facilitate freedom of religion on a national scale.⁶² The lack of higher-level laws directly made by the legislature, the People's Congress, to reinforce freedom of religion and actively safeguard reasonable practical implementation, could lead one to suspect that the constitutional right of freedom of religion is little more than lip service.

China is trying to build a civil society underpinned by the rule of law.⁶³ It is important and necessary within this transformative process for China to seek to administer religious affairs according to the requirements and processes of the rule of law.

It has been suggested by Liu Peng that a crucial step towards the future of the administration of religious freedom is to make a law on religion and to introduce legal personality for religious bodies.⁶⁴ This would mean that the law establish that a religious body have the legal attributes of a legal person and provide a framework to administer religious affairs rather than relying on current lower-level laws, regulations and provisions, to administer religious affairs.

---

⁶¹ Article 3 of the Explanation (1999).
⁶² China is a signatory of International Covenant on Civil and Political Rights, and the Chinese Constitution provides for 'freedom of religion' in Article 36.
⁶³ For example, some academics discussed China's progress towards rule of law. See Randall Peerenboom, 'Globalization, Path Dependency and the Limits of Law: Administrative Law Reform and Rule of Law in the People's Republic of China', *Berkeley Journal of International Law* 19 (2001): 162.
⁶⁴ See Peng Liu, *My Humble Opinion on Establishing a 'Religious Body Legal Person'* (Pu Shi Institute for Social Science Internal Publication, Beijing, 2012) 56–70.

The waiver of the requirement of registration of the five recognized religious bodies has established a *de facto* inequality for many other religious bodies, and this is especially unfair to new or minority religious bodies. It may be argued that part of the underlying implications of freedom of religion, is that it requires a state to 'uphold a policy of denominational equality and non-discrimination towards all religious groups'.[65]

The creation of a religious body legal personality would accord any religious body the legal status of a civil subject and would give each one equal status to engage in civil activities in society, permitting, for example, the purchasing of property. This could also be the most efficient way to administer religious affairs in China. Once a religious body can obtain the status of a religious legal person, it can then establish its branches in the same way that any other company does. This can then provide a lawful basis for the government to recognize new religious bodies, and allow new religions, especially minority religions, to become established in China. Through the rule of law China can better fulfil its duty to religious freedom.

---

[65] Cheung, 'In Search of a Theory of Cult and Freedom of Religion in China', 6.

PART V
Minority Religions in Non-European Democracies: Canadian and South African Models

Chapter 15
Expanding the Scope of Regulation: Some Reflections on Religious Minorities in Canada

Lori G. Beaman[1]

Introduction

Religious freedom is frequently written about as though it were a clearly defined generic category of analysis. Indeed, this volume focuses on state responses to religious minorities, invoking this idea of religious freedom while also assuming that the state's realm is demarcated in a manner that makes it possible to coherently discuss its interactions with religious minorities. Quite often the theory of the state responding to religious minorities relies upon the possibility of state neutrality or separation from religion. This chapter presents the idea that not only is the meaning of religious freedom not always shared by those who use it, but the matter is even further complicated by the unevenness with which we might, as social scientists, analyze it in a range of spheres. Moreover, the state cannot be easily distinguished from other realms of life, especially religion. Every nation-state has its own religious history that almost inevitably involves the intertwining of religion in state affairs and social institutions. The challenge is to recognize the ways in which this entanglement impacts the position of religious minorities. In a seemingly paradoxical move, I propose to differentiate the realms in which religious freedom operates and to de-differentiate the idea of the state from society. This move potentially allows us to see the core 'problematic' of this volume from a new vantage point. The point of all of this is to retell the story of religious freedom as one that is not simply about the state or the law, but about contests and collaborations among a variety of actors in a number of realms.

---

[1] The author thanks Morgan Hunter who provided both editorial and research assistance for this chapter, and also the Social Sciences and Humanities Research Council of Canada for its financial support for this project.

Realms of religious freedom

In seeking to exercise religious freedom, groups and individuals sometimes come into conflict with other individuals, groups, and/or the state. Thus, for example, Jehovah's Witnesses who proselytize door to door, or hand out pamphlets in parks may find that both individuals they encounter as well as municipal regulations work at cross-purposes to their desire to spread the word. This may be further complicated by the story of the individual Witness, who, for example, has a spouse (or ex-spouse) who does not want him or her to take their child on the proselytizing mission. To frame this merely as an issue of state regulation of religious minorities is to miss a great deal of the interactions that converge to determine whether the Witnesses are able to exercise their religious freedom. To be sure, the state plays an important role in the regulation of public religion, but there are often alliances and oppositions outside of what we normally consider the state that facilitate or inhibit the exercise of religious freedom. Analyses of religious freedom tend to focus either on the macro level (such as broad guarantees like that found in section 2(a) of the Canadian Charter of Rights and Freedoms) or micro level (such as individual stories, most often made visible through legal cases) of society. Both approaches offer hints about both how religious freedom is imagined and how it plays out 'on the ground' in any given context.[2] However, constitutional guarantees tell us little about religious majorities or minorities, a state's religious history, or about the ways in which the religion that is being protected (or not) is imagined. For instance, in some states freedom of religion may actually in practice mean freedom of *protestant* religion.[3] Similarly, cases can tell us about individual stories, and perhaps hint at the direction the broad constitutional guarantees might go, but they may not offer much in the way of big picture assessments of religious freedom. The focus of this paper is on possible realms of religious freedom and the ways that they might intersect in a given situation.

The inspiration for this closer examination of the ways in which religious freedom plays out in different realms is drawn from Linda Woodhead's work on the notion of domains of public religion. She argues that two models of public religion have dominated academic and wider discourse. They are the European model, which essentially divides life into the realms of the public and the private and locates religion in the latter, and the US American model, which sorts life into the realms of state, civil society and private life, with religion residing in the latter two. In response to the limitations of these models, which both rely on their own time-space contingencies and their links to ideology, Woodhead has formulated an approach that locates religion in various realms of social life – as it actually exists.

---

[2] Section 2(a) reads, 'Everyone has the following fundamental freedoms: *(a)* freedom of conscience and religion'.

[3] Winnifred Sullivan, *The Impossibility of Religious Freedom* (Princeton, NJ: Princeton University Press, 2005); and Winnifred Sullivan, *Prison Religion: Faith Reformers and the Constitution* (Princeton, NJ: Princeton University Press, 2009).

The most serious limitation of previous models, argues Woodhead, is that neither model can account for changes in a religious landscape that sees a decline in so-called traditional religion, a rise in the presence of 'other' world religions, and an increase in 'alternative' spiritualties and fuzzy religion. Her proposed scheme attempts to blur the boundaries between the neat divisions previously used, and introduces an approach that employs a 'broader model of the different domains of society in which religion is entangled'.[4] She diagrams her model, as she perceives it in the United Kingdom, as follows:

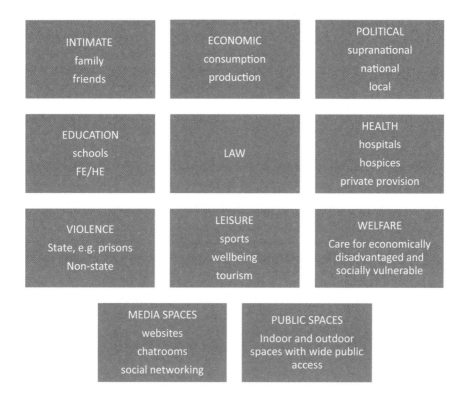

Figure 15.1   Domains of public religion (UK)[5]

---

[4] Linda Woodhead, 'Accommodating Religion in the Public Sphere: Looking Beyond Existing Models' (paper presented at Religare International Seminar – Religious Communities and State Support, Sophia, Bulgaria, 20 October 2011).

[5] Used with permission, Linda Woodhead, 19 February 2013.

One of the key limitations of schemes that differentiate various realms of social life for any number of reasons is that they tend to become entities in themselves, with boundaries that were perhaps initially imagined as fluid becoming solid containers that must be defended against breaches. Society becomes an automaton that functions very nicely on its own without, apparently, any human input. This is a classic problem for social science and one that has only been successfully challenged by a move to cultural analysis, which comes with its own set of problems. Woodhead also insists that the boundaries between these categories are blurred and shifting. My own weak attempt to resolve this problem of impermeable boundaries is not innovative, but simply insists on the permeability of the categories proposed, and a desire that they be recognized as such – merely heuristic. My hope is that the discussion that follows will demonstrate my commitment to that fluid approach.

One of the advantages of imagining religious freedom in this configuration is that it pushes state and civil responses into one framework, forcing a reconciliation or consideration of the ways in which these responses differ. Further, the realms of religious freedom might be used as an analytical tool in a couple of ways: first, to ask questions about the various ways that states and civil actors regulate religious freedom in those realms. We might, for example – as Bäckström, Davie, Edgardh and Pettersson have done[6] – explore the various ways in which religion and the state collaborate on the provision of welfare by asking which religious actors participate in welfare provision, and so on. We might examine the ways in which they are constrained in those contexts, and how they imagine their missions to be carried out. We might ask, for example, whether they express their service in 'god language', whether they want to do so, and whether they feel constrained from doing so. We might further inquire about those who receive such services: do members of minority religious groups feel forced to receive welfare services with religious strings attached? Similar exploration could be undertaken in the realm of health care. In many states the institutional history of health care is tied to majoritarian religion. For example, many hospitals in Canada have Roman Catholic origins and links to religious orders that continue to this day.

Systematic investigations that consider realms of social life and engage in a detailed explication of the links between state and civil actors might enable us to do a cross-national comparison that is much more nuanced than much of the comparative research on religious freedom in which we are presently engaged. We might, for example, ask questions about the realm of education: are religious symbols permitted in public schools? Seemingly a simple enough question, but one that inevitably leads to complex analysis. Or, is education about religion present in public schools? Who controls its content? Who teaches it? On what basis is it offered? This sort of analysis could allow us to construct a complex

---

[6] See Anders Bäckström, Grace Davie, Ninna Edgardh, and Per Pettersson, *Welfare and Religion in 21st Century Europe*, vol. 1, *Configuring the Connections* (Aldershot: Ashgate, 2011).

picture of religious freedom that might account for variability across realms, or at the very least identify such variability.

The second way in which such a schema might be used is to begin with a specific issue to examine the ways in which it plays out in various realms. Such a bottom-up query might begin, for example, with the response to Fundamentalist Latter-day Saints (FLDS, Fundamentalist Mormons) living in Bountiful, British Columbia. We could locate this in the realm of intimate relations, which we might imagine as perhaps the realm most insulated from state and public intervention. However, some in the FLDS community practice polygamy, which attracts criminal prosecution in Canada. Although other intimate family arrangements in Canada include multiple partners, whether polyamorous or adulterous, polygamous FLDS are targeted for special state attention. This response has important historical elements that can be traced to the founding of Canada as a nation-state and its relations with its American neighbours.[7] Although important, the state response to this religious minority is only part of the story in relation to FLDS' religious freedom. If we shift our analysis to the media we could analyze media coverage to assess, for example, whether the FLDS are negatively or positively portrayed. Negative media response may generate negative public pressure, which in turn creates a call by the public to *do something*. We might also ask questions about health. The research of Angela Campbell has shown that FLDS women have developed their own birthing services because of the scrutiny they felt when using public health care facilities.[8] Specifically, they risked moral judgment from their care-givers as well as difficulties in completing state birth registration information in ways that would not put their families at risk of prosecution. A query into economic activity, on the other hand, might reveal that FLDS relations with the surrounding community are quite amicable, with non-FLDS describing them as good neighbours who contribute to the economic wellbeing of the community. This ease of relationship arguably acted as a shield against prosecution for quite some time. Nevertheless, Reference re: Section 293 of the Criminal Code, the reference case to British Columbia's Supreme Court on the constitutionality of the polygamy prohibition in the Criminal Code, revealed the importance of non-government or state actors – for example, feminist organizations, other religious groups, and even international lobbies – that became part of the public and court discourse, framed the issues, and in essence supported the provisions against polygamy.[9] There, the political realm included not only state but also lobby activity, illustrating yet another wrinkle in how religious freedom can be shaped vis-à-vis a given issue.

We might therefore reconfigure the realms diagram in this instance like this:

---

[7] See Sarah Carter, *The Importance of Being Monogamous: Marriage and Nation Building in Western Canada to 1913* (Edmonton: University of Alberta Press, 2008).

[8] Angela Campbell, 'Bountiful Voices', *Osgoode Hall Law Review* 47 (2009): 183–234.

[9] Reference re: Section 293 of the Criminal Code of Canada, 2011 BCSC 1588.

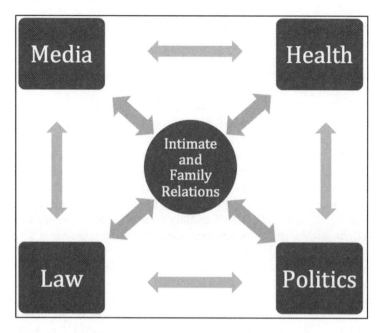

Figure 15.2   Regulating polygamy

Finally, in thinking about a scheme to assess state responses to religious minorities we may also want to ask a broader question focused on groups rather than realms: Which groups attract state attention and action? For example, Jehovah's Witnesses seem to serve as a litmus test for various countries' commitment to religious freedom; their unique beliefs and practices inevitably attract some sort of state attention. In the North American context it is for the refusal of blood transfusions by minors;[10] in South Korea it is for their commitment to pacifism; and in India it is for their proselytization. The next question is, what is the level of this attention? Is it municipal in nature, consisting, for example, of bylaws that purport to impose neutral laws on property use but in practice disproportionately impact a particular religious minority? Or is it a provincial or state response, like Bill 94 in Quebec that would regulate face covering in order to receive public services?[11] What we do with this information is vital, for on its own it tells us very little.

---

[10]   See *A. C. v. Manitoba (Director of Child and Family Services)*, [2009] 2 S.C.R. 181; and *B. H. v. Alberta (Director of Child Welfare)*, [2002] A.B.Q.B. 898.

[11]   'Quebec Will Require Bare Face for Service', *CBC NEWS*, 24 March 2010, http://www.cbc.ca/news/canada/montreal/story/2010/03/24/quebec-reasonable-accommodation-law.html.

In asking which groups attract state attention and action, it seems imperative that we be aware of the activity of other realms. We might consider whether state action is accompanied by increased media attention or whether there is increased academic interest or analysis. For example, when the minister of citizenship and immigration declares that Muslim women will not be permitted to take the oath of citizenship wearing a *niqab*, state action is only one small part of a much broader context. Why has the attire of Muslim women come to attract so much attention? What does the media coverage consist of? What other issues in the news are associated with Muslims (for example, polygamy, honour killing, etc.)? How has the recent burst of academic activity around Muslims – however 'well intentioned' – problematized Islam? Ultimately, how does this confluence of state, media and academia impact Muslims' lives day-to-day in Canada? What is the international context in which some of this activity might be understood? These questions, which implicate both state and non-state actors and various realms of social life, allow a more robust consideration of the issues presented, and might encourage us to examine the global persecution of particular religious groups.

Although I have linked the state regulation of religion to religious freedom, I am not proposing a checklist of factors upon which to assess particular countries' performance. A number of such schemes exist, probably most famously the US Office of International Religious Freedom's annual report identifying a list of countries of concern. The 2012 list, for example, included India for its anti-conversion laws. Grim and Finke measure religious freedom by analyzing three scales based on reports created by the State Department – government regulation of religion, government favouritism of religion and social regulation of religion[12] – and breaking them down into smaller components. Because their data set is generated by US embassies, it does not measure the United States itself.[13] In his 147 variable assessment of religious freedom, Jonathan Fox begins by examining whether a country has an established religion.[14] This of course ensures that the United States will almost always score well, though its lack of a state religion is rather debatable.[15] Data in Fox's study relied on media reports, law reports and

---

[12] The social regulation of religion index created by Grim and Finke looks at responses to religion from outside the government and within the general population. Their measures include questions about the public's attitude toward non-traditional religions, conversions and proselytization, as well as questions of whether existing religions shut out new religions or whether there are social movements within the country that are opposed to certain religions.

[13] Brian J. Grim and Roger Finke, 'International Religion Indexes: Government Regulation, Government Favouritism, and Social Regulations of Religion', *Interdisciplinary Journal of Research on Religion* 2 (2006): 1–40.

[14] Jonathan Fox, 'Religion and State Codebook', *The Religion and State Project*, http://www.thearda.com/ras/downloads/.

[15] See Sullivan, *The Impossibility of Religious Freedom*; and Sullivan, *Prison Religion*.

academic discussions.[16] Although each of these sources can offer some insight about how religious minorities are regulated, they also raise concerns about how religious freedom is assessed. For example, in the Bouchard Taylor commission report, the authors note that of the 21 responses to religious diversity that received the most media attention, 15 had what Bouchard and Taylor describe as 'significant distortions'.[17] These cases, which all involved religious minorities, significantly shaped public notions of how the government should respond to growing concerns about 'too much accommodation' of religious groups.

The most serious limitation of these various measures of religious freedom is their focus on the state. As I am arguing here, the regulation of religious minorities does not reside solely – indeed, sometimes not even primarily – in the state. Non-state actors play a vitally important role in the social and cultural contexts in which religious groups exist. A second limitation of the 'measures of religious freedom' approaches is their reliance on unexamined assumptions about religious freedom: for example, that an 'established religion' (terminology largely generated in and relevant to the United States) ensures a less religious freedom than separation of church and state.

One important contribution to the sort of analysis that offers better insight into the complexity of the regulation of religious minorities is the edited collection *Regulating Religion: Case Studies from Around the Globe* by James T. Richardson.[18] Although the collection focuses on the state, and more particularly on law, the contributors consider the social realms within which religious minorities are regulated. For example, James Beckford considers the historical and cultural context of laïcité in his discussion of new religious movements in France. This discussion brings to the fore the importance of understanding narratives of 'who we are' when examining how religious minorities are regulated, or perhaps *not* regulated. Religious freedom is thus understood as a much more complex issue than simply constitutional regulation and state intervention.

In her discussion of religious freedom, Elizabeth Hurd, a scholar of international relations, argues that the United States in particular has, in the name of liberal democracy, attempted to export a particular version of religious freedom that has at its core the notion that belief is the defining characteristic of religion. Hurd takes this approach to task, arguing that

---

[16] For an analysis of religious discrimination across states see Yasemin Akbaba, 'Who Discriminates More? Comparing Religious Discrimination in Western Democracies, Asia and the Middle East', *Civil Wars* 11, (2009): 321–58, who uses data from both the US State Department reports and Fox's data set.

[17] Gérard Bouchard and Charles Taylor, 'Building the Future: A Time for Reconciliation', *Commission de Consultation sur les pratiques d'accommodement reliées aux différences culturelles* (Québec: Québec Government Printing Office, 2008), 69.

[18] James R. Richardson, ed., *Regulating Religion: Case Studies from Around the Globe* (New York: Kluwer Academic, 2004).

Inasmuch as the protection and enforcement of religious freedom hinges upon, and even sanctifies, a religious psychology that relies on the notion of an autonomous subject who chooses beliefs, and then enacts them, such projects privilege particular kinds of religious subjectivity while disabling others.[19]

Clearly, the way we think about religion is especially important, and we as scholars need to be cautious about our choice of analytical frameworks in thinking about state regulation. As Hurd notes:

In its strongest forms, the story of international religious freedom globalizes the secular state's power over the individual. Appearing as a guarantee of the worth of the individual's own desires, it is actually a story of telling people who they are, what to do and how to be. It privileges particular ways of doing and being as deserving special protection by the state or associations thereof, leaving others behind. Like other categories, it singles out authorized representatives of believers (and less frequently non-believers) for legal protection, reinforcing divisions and hierarchies within and between communities.[20]

A consideration of religious minorities in context, existing within a web of social relations that includes state and civil actors – including religious actors – is therefore vital. So too is seeing religious minorities themselves as actors. Exploring resistance and subversion can reveal important ways that groups exercise agency and reshape power relations.

Instead of focusing on a more narrowly conceptualized notion of state regulation of religious minorities, I am concerned with the way social institutions and various realms of social life impact the lives of religious minorities. I am not interested in judging specific countries to be more or less hospitable to religious minorities; this seems to me an unproductive contest of cultural superiority rather than a serious consideration of religious minorities and the control, state or otherwise, of their activities. This is not to say that state treatment of religious minorities within the borders of nation states should not be considered, but handing out report cards on religious freedom obscures issues that can sometimes only be understood by asking broader questions. Why, for example, does Christian proselytizing attract violent responses in some countries where Christians have not formed part of the historic majority? What are the similarities and differences between state responses to new religious movements? Are there transnational media responses to particular religious groups? Are there lobby groups who target particular religious groups across national borders?

---

[19] Elizabeth Shakman Hurd, 'Believing in Religious Freedom', *The Immanent Frame*, http://blogs.ssrc.org/tif/2012/03/01/believing-in-religious-freedom/.
[20] Ibid.

Reconsidering the regulation of religious minorities in Canada

Within this broader framework, if one were to ask about state regulation of religious minorities in Canada, the answer would be complex. Focusing on the legal aspect, which is the area I work in most, I would say that until recently the Canadian context has been generally positive. And I would guess that we likely would score quite high on any of the standard 'religious freedom' tests, which rely a great deal on legal standards and regulations. The Canadian Charter of Rights and Freedoms guarantees freedom of conscience and religion, but historically religious freedom has been endorsed through case law, most notably early cases involving Jehovah's Witnesses.[21] Recent case law also supports a robust interpretation of religious freedom, and in one instance the Court has intervened to override a contract to protect an Orthodox Jewish man from what the Court characterizes as a privileging of aesthetics over religious freedom.[22] The Court takes a similarly broad approach in *Multani* when it affirms the right of a Sikh schoolboy to wear his *kirpan* to school.[23]

However, one of the Court's most recent decisions on religious freedom – the *Hutterian Brethren* case – offers cause for worry among religious minorities in Canada. Rather than analyze this case specifically, I would like to step somewhat outside of law and reposition the analysis to consider the ways in which various realms of social life contribute to its result. In part, this requires that we move into the world of the Brethren and their needs as a religious minority. To be sure, the law plays an important role in this example, as it is regulation that brings the Hutterian Brethren to the attention of the state, and the Supreme Court that fails to protect the Brethren from the effects of that regulation. However, various factors outside of law or the state frame the Hutterian Brethren's ability to live life according to their religious beliefs. Thus, a review of the complex web of social and economic relations in which they found themselves enmeshed will offer a richer analysis, illustrating the ways in which the regulation of religious minorities fluctuates over time, often for reasons completely unrelated to the group itself. In other words, while some groups attract regulation specifically targeted at their activities, others – like the Hutterian Brethren – simply find themselves in the wrong place at the wrong time.

The Hutterian Brethren fled persecution in Europe and the US and immigrated to Canada in the early 1900s. Their communal lifestyle is intimately linked with their religious commitment. Property is shared and communally held, and intimate life – the world of family and friends – is organized around this core principle.[24]

---

[21] See *Boucher v. the King*, [1949] 96 C.C.C. 48; *Saumur v. City of Québec*, [1953] 2 S.C.R. 299.

[22] *Syndicat Northcrest v. Amselem*, [2004] 2 S.C.R. 551.

[23] *Multani v. Commission scolaire Marguerite-Bourgeoys*, [2006] 1 S.C.R. 256.

[24] The commitment to this form of family and communal living is evidenced in *Lakeside Colony of Hutterian Brethren v. Hofer*, [1992] 3 S.C.R. 165. See Alvin Esau, *The*

Although families have their own private spaces, day-to-day life is inextricably bound up in social activities with family and friends who share this devotion. Although largely self-sufficient, they do participate in the broader economic sphere as both consumers and producers. Indeed, they are known for their highly economically successful agriculture-based activities. Moreover, since most Hutterites are educated at only a very basic level, they must obtain health care and other professional services outside of the colony. Even this cursory review reveals how religion affects not only intimate and family life, but community involvement as well.

Conflict arose when the province of Alberta changed a law to require that driver's licence holders have their photographs taken on renewal.[25] The Hutterian Brethren believe that the Second Commandment prohibits them from having their photographs taken.[26] But failure to receive a driver's licence would prevent them from engaging in commercial activity, which in turn would threaten their ability to continue as a communal group. The Supreme Court held that the requirement to have photographs on driver's licences was a reasonable limit on religious freedom justified by the security regime put in place by the province of Alberta, ostensibly to prevent identity theft.

The Court suggested that the Brethren could simply hire drivers. But taking care of each other through, for example, driving a fellow colony member to a medical appointment is part of the Brethren's commitment to communal living and to loving their fellow human beings. Thus, hiring outsiders rather than relying upon one another would be inappropriate. The holistic nature of this religious commitment affects all spheres of public life.

The *Hutterian Brethren* case demonstrated, as Benjamin L. Berger has argued, that strictly legal consideration in isolation is poorly suited for sustained conversation about religious diversity and equality. The Court could seemingly only imagine the Hutterian Brethren as economic actors who make decisions on a cost-benefit basis, and not as a community of religious actors.[27] This failure

---

Courts and the Colonies: The Litigation of Hutterite Church Disputes (Vancouver: UBC Press, 2005), for an excellent and detailed description of the case and the communal lives of the Brethren.

[25] Until 2003 the registrar of motor vehicles had the power to grant exceptions to the requirement for a photograph on driver's licenses (which had been the practice since 1974).

[26] Like all religious groups, the Brethren are not homogeneous, and thus not all Hutterian Brethren interpret the Second Commandment in this way. This raises a problem often faced by religious minorities and indeed by those who claim orthodoxy. We see this in current debates questioning the 'religiousness' of the *niqab*. The extra challenge for groups following these practices is that challenge comes not only from those outside of their religious group, but from within as well. The Fundamentalist Latter-day Saints are another example in that 'mainstream' Latter-day Saints reject the worldly practice of polygamy.

[27] Benjamin L. Berger, 'Polygamy and the Predicament of Contemporary Criminal Law', in *Polygamy's Wrongs? The Social Family in the Culture of Rights*, ed. Gillian Calder and Lori G. Beaman (Vancouver: UBC Press, Forthcoming).

of imagination has serious implications for religious minorities generally, and does not bode well for other cases that bring religious minorities into the legal realm. If the law can only understand religion as individualized practice-belief that rationally proceeds on a cost-benefit analysis, it excludes religion as group-based, passionate or committed. It also ignores how embedded religion is in other realms of social life.

Furthermore, as I have attempted to argue throughout this chapter, law is not the only domain of regulation. Woven through the realms of social life are shifting currents that feed on each other to create unassailable and interlinking vortexes. Thus, the logic of securitization that permeates the *Hutterian Brethren* decision has infiltrated other realms of social life such that it has become a logic unto itself. The minority of the Court attempts, unsuccessfully, to displace the weight of securitization, which forms the lynchpin of the decision:

> Seven hundred thousand Albertans are without a driver's licence. That means that 700,000 Albertans have no photograph in the system that can be checked by facial recognition technology. While adding approximately 250 licence holders to the database will reduce some opportunity for identity theft, it is hard to see how it will make a significant impact on preventing it when there are already several hundred thousand unlicensed and therefore unphotographed Albertans. Since there are so many others who are not in the database, the benefit of adding the photographs of the few Hutterites who wish to drive would be marginal.[28]

The notion that regulatory regimes exist for the safety of society and that we must all comply with them works outside of the specific realm of the state or the law. Likewise, the notion that religious actors, particularly religious minorities, are requesting an exemption, an exception, or special treatment also has currency outside of these realms.

The *Hutterian Brethren* case is framed by the realm of the political, in which we see state actors promulgating a climate of fear (requiring increased security measures) coupled with a promotion of 'Canadian values' that is especially hostile to the religious 'Other' (most often imagined as Muslim). Their religiously motivated commitment to group living brings the Hutterian Brethren into conflict with an increasingly dominant rhetoric of individualization and freedom of choice, which reflects a particular version of economic rationalization. The intimate and family relations chosen by the Hutterian Brethren also place them in opposition to 'normal' family and community life. Law and the state are not the lone arbiter here, nor the single regulator. This decision could only occur because securitization, fear of the religious 'Other', and a neoliberal, cost-benefit logic came together to regulate against the Hutterian Brethren.

---

[28] *Alberta v. Hutterian Brethren of Wilson Colony* [2009], 2 S.C.R. 567 at par. 158.

Conclusion

This discussion may seem like a bit of an odd way to reflect on the state regulation of religious minorities in Canada. In part it is inspired by my involvement as an expert witness in *Reference re: Section 293 of the Criminal Code of Canada*, in which the Supreme Court of British Columbia upheld a law forbidding the practice of polygamy, including in a religious context. During the process of that case it seemed to me that there was much more going on than what could be easily described as state regulation of religion, and that it was indeed often very difficult to sort out where state began and ended. This entanglement of interests had profound effects on how the public viewed the members of the FLDS, how feminist groups discussed them and how the media reported the happenings of the trial and its results. It seemed to me that the desire expressed by the court in its decision to protect monogamy was not a legal matter, but an intertwining of historical and cultural factors that the idea of state regulation of religion cannot encompass. I was astounded by the emotion embedded in every discussion of the issue: fear, hostility and anxiety were consistent themes, reminding me of the importance of emotion in thinking about religious minorities.[29]

What does this tell us about the regulation of religious minorities in Canada, and elsewhere for that matter? We might read the story of the Hutterian Brethren, or of the FLDS, as one of government overregulation and the law's complicity. But how is it, for example, that a judge can cite the protection of monogamy as a state goal? Or that a court can accept that there is only one way to protect citizens from identity theft? The answers require a broad consideration of regulation that explicates the various realms within which religion operates. Entangled in these stories, for example, are realms of intimacy and family life that link to religious commitment and which contrast with normative ideals that circulate about how families look, what Canadian values are and what it means to be a citizen. Regulation does not reside in the state, but more broadly, in everyday life and its social realms.

---

[29] For an excellent scholarly work on the sociology of religious emotion, see O. Riis and L. Woodhead, *A Sociology of Religious Emotion* (New York: Oxford University Press, 2010).

Chapter 16
The Constitutional Protection of Religious Practices in Canada

Richard Moon[1]

The Canadian courts formerly described freedom of conscience and religion under section 2(a) of the Canadian Charter of Rights and Freedoms as the liberty to hold, and live in accordance with, spiritual and other fundamental beliefs without state interference.[2] Under this definition, freedom of religion – understood as a liberty – precluded the state from compelling an individual to engage in a religious practice and from restricting an individual's religious practice without a legitimate public reason. In later judgments, however, there has been a discernible alteration in the courts' reading of section 2(a). The wrong addressed shifted from coercion to exclusion, while the interest protected shifted from liberty to equality.[3] Under this new interpretation, the state must not support or prefer the practices of one religious group over those of another, nor restrict the practices of a religious group unless necessary to protect a compelling public interest. Thus religion, or at least religious questions, are excluded and insulated from politics.[4]

---

[1] For a fuller account of the arguments presented here, see Richard Moon, 'Freedom of Religion under the Charter of Rights: The Limits of State Neutrality', *UBC Law Review* 45 (2012): 1.

[2] *R. v. Big M Drug Mart Ltd.*, [1985] 1 S.C.R. 295; Canadian Charter of Rights and Freedoms, Part 1 of the Constitution Act, 1982, being Schedule B to the Canada Act, 1982, c. 11 (UK).

[3] I have described this shift in Richard Moon, 'Liberty, Neutrality and Inclusion: Religious Freedom under the Canadian Charter of Rights and Freedoms', *Brandeis Law Journal* 41 (2003): 563.

[4] The requirement of state neutrality was most recently affirmed by Madame Justice Deschamps, writing for the majority of the Supreme Court of Canada in *S.L. v. Commission scolaire des Chenes*, [2012] S.C.C. 7, para. 10: 'Religious neutrality is now seen by many Western states as a legitimate means of creating a free space in which citizens of various beliefs can exercise their individual rights'. Deschamps observes at para. 17 that the 'Canadian courts have held that the state sponsorship of one religious tradition amounts to discrimination against others'. The concurring judgment of J. LeBel expresses a similar view at para. 54: 'Moreover, in the modern Canadian political system, the state in principle takes a position of neutrality. And it is barred from enacting private legislation that favours one religion over another'. The state may, however, provide even-handed support to different religious communities or practices.

Yet this requirement of state neutrality towards religion cannot be, and has not been, consistently enforced by the Canadian courts. The problem is not simply that religious beliefs involve claims about what is true and right, which must be viewed as a matter of judgment that is open to contest and revision within the sphere of community debate; the more fundamental difficulty with the requirement of state neutrality is that religious beliefs sometimes have public implications. State neutrality is possible only if religion can be treated as simply a private matter – separable from the civic concerns addressed by the state. Religious belief systems, however, often have something to say about the way we should treat others and about the kind of society we should work to create. Because religious beliefs sometimes address civic concerns and are often difficult to distinguish from non-religious beliefs, they cannot be fully excluded or insulated from political decision-making.

The difficulty in enforcing state neutrality towards religion is apparent in the Canadian courts' section 2(a) judgments dealing with both state support for religious practice and state restriction on such practice. The courts' ban on state support or preference for the practices of a particular religion has been tempered by a recognition that religious practices have shaped the traditions and rituals of the community and cannot simply be erased from civic life or completely ignored in the formulation of public policy.[5] More significantly, the Canadian courts have indicated that legislators may draw on their religious values when determining public policy and should not be expected to leave their religious values at 'the boardroom door'.[6] The state is thus prohibited from supporting particular religious *practices* but permitted to affirm religious *values*. The Canadian courts, however, offer no guide for distinguishing between the two. It appears that a religiously-motivated action will be regarded by the courts as a 'practice' (a matter of religious worship towards which the state must remain neutral) if it relates simply to the individual's spiritual life and does not address civic matters. A religious belief that addresses civic matters – the rights or welfare of others in the community – will be viewed as a 'value' that may be debated on its merits and either supported or rejected by the state. In other words, the neutrality requirement applies only to the spiritual or 'personal' (non-civic) elements of religious belief – the proper form of worship or the individual's relationship to the divine – and not to its civic or 'public' dimensions. However, the location of the line between the 'civic' and 'private' elements of a religious belief system will reflect prevailing (and contestable) views about religious worship, human welfare, civic justice and the proper scope of political action.

In this chapter, however, I want to focus on another dimension of religious freedom: the insulation of religious practice from state restriction. The Canadian courts have said that under section 1 (the limitations provision of the Charter)

---

[5] See, for example, *R. v. Edwards Books*, [1986] 2 S.C.R. 713, in which a provincial Sunday closing law was upheld by the Supreme Court of Canada.

[6] *Chamberlain v. Surrey School District No. 36*, [2002] 4 S.C.R. 710, para. 19.

the state must justify any law that restricts a religious practice, but the courts have adopted a weak standard of justification.[7] The courts do not engage in any real balancing of competing claims (the state's policy versus the individual's religious practice) and have required the state to accommodate a religious practice only when the practice does not directly conflict with civic interests. In other words, the state will be required to make space for the religious practice by adjusting the means it has adopted to advance a particular public purpose only when this will have no significant impact on the realization of that purpose. When a religious belief or action addresses matters of civic interest, the courts will treat it as a 'political' position subject to legal restriction that may be rejected or accepted in the political process. While formally the courts have adopted an equality-rights approach to the restriction of religious practices under section 2(a), viewing religion as a cultural identity that should be treated with equal respect, in practice they have treated religion as a personal practice in which the individual should be free to engage unless it interferes with the rights or interests of others.

The Canadian courts' accommodation of religious practice

According to the Canadian courts, the Charter right to freedom of religion is breached any time the state restricts a religious practice in a non-trivial way. Even when a law advances a legitimate public purpose, such as the prevention of drug use, cruelty to animals or violence in the schoolyard, under section 1 the state ostensibly must justify the law's non-trivial interference with a religious practice.[8]

Yet despite the courts' formal declaration that the state must justify any non-trivial restriction of a religious practice (or reasonably accommodate the practice), they have given this requirement little substance and appear willing to uphold a legal restriction if it has a legitimate objective (that is, anything other than the suppression of an erroneous religious practice) that would be noticeably compromised if an exception was made. In other words, even though the courts have structured their approach to section 2(a) so that it has the form of an equality right (that draws on human rights code and Charter equality jurisprudence), they have adopted in practice a very weak standard of justification under section 1 so that the right protects only a limited form of liberty. Because space is limited, I

---

[7] Section 1 of the Charter provides that the listed rights may be subject to limits that are 'prescribed by law', 'reasonable', and 'demonstrably justified'. In R. v Oakes, [1986] 1 S.C.R. 103, the Supreme Court of Canada established a multi-part test for determining whether a restriction is justified.

[8] In the recent judgment of *Alberta v. Hutterian Brethren of Wilson Colony*, [2009] 2 S.C.R. 567, Justice McLachlin said that a law that restricts a religious practice will be upheld only if it satisfies the *Oakes* test.

will discuss only two of the most important Supreme Court of Canada judgments that illustrate this.[9]

In *Syndicat Northcrest v. Amselem* the Supreme Court of Canada held that a condominium association's refusal to permit Orthodox Jewish unit-owners to construct *succahs* on their balconies as part of the Jewish festival of *Succot* breached their freedom of religion under the Quebec Charter of Human Rights and Freedoms.[10] Because the restriction on religious practice was imposed by a non-state actor, the Canadian Charter of Rights was not applicable. However, the majority judgment of Justice Iacobucci was clear that 'the principles ... applicable in cases where an individual alleges that his or her freedom of religion is infringed under the Quebec Charter' are also applicable to a claim under section 2(a) of the Canadian Charter of Rights and Freedoms.[11]

In holding that the condominium association had violated the appellants' freedom of religion, Justice Iacobucci made two significant determinations concerning the scope of the freedom. First, he held that a spiritual practice or

---

[9] A number of other Supreme Court of Canada judgments might have been examined here, including: *Trinity Western University v. B.C. College of Teachers*, [2001] 1 S.C.R. 772 (The decision of a regulatory body to not accredit the teacher training programme of a private religious college because of its affirmed anti-gay views was unconstitutional. The Court found no evidence that graduates of the programme had committed acts of discrimination in the public school system.); *Multani v. Commission scolaire Marguerite-Bourgeoys*, [2006] 1 S.C.R. 256 (A Sikh boy was permitted to wear a *kirpan* [a ceremonial dagger required to be worn by baptized Sikhs] to school despite a ban on weapons. The Court held that a kirpan was a religious symbol and, being a weapon in form only, represented no real threat to school safety.); *R. v. Jones*, [1986] 2 S.C.R. 284 (Mr Jones should not be exempted from the requirement that he apply to the Alberta education authorities for permission to homeschool his children.); *B.(R.) v. Children's Aid Society of Metropolitan Toronto*, [1995] 1 S.C.R. 315 (The state was justified in overriding the parents' right to make decisions about the medical treatment of their infant child.); *Young v. Young*, [1993] 4 S.C.R. 3 (The 'best interests of the child' test in custody/access decisions did not breach section 2(a), or was a justified restriction under § 1.); *A.C. v. Manitoba (Director of Child and Family Services)*, [2009] 2 S.C.R. 181 (The 'best interests of the child' test in cases concerning medical treatment of an older minor did not breach the *Charter*, particularly if the assessment of the minor's best interests took into account her religious views.); *S.L. v. Commission scolaire des Chenes* (A group of Roman Catholic parents sought to have their children excused from a required 'ethics and religions' course in public school. The Court accepted that the parents had a sincere religious objection to their children being taught a 'relativistic' view of religion but found no evidence to show that the course advanced such a view of religion.).

[10] *Syndicat Northcrest v. Amselem*, [2004] 2 S.C.R. 551; Quebec Charter of Human Rights and Freedoms, R.S.Q., ch. C-12 (1976). The condominium bylaws – to which all unit owners formally agreed prior to purchasing or occupying their particular unit – prohibited decorations, alterations, and constructions on their balconies. However, the bylaws also provided that an individual owner might apply to the condominium association for an exemption from this general prohibition.

[11] *Amselem*, para. 37.

belief will fall within the protection of section 2(a) even though it is idiosyncratic and not part of an established or widely-held religious belief system. Second, a practice will be protected under section 2(a) even though it is not regarded as obligatory by the individual claimant. Freedom of religion protects practices that have spiritual significance for the individual, 'subjectively connecting' her or him to the divine.[12] And so, even though not all of the appellants in this case regarded the practice of erecting a *succah* on their property as a religious obligation, the practice was protected because it had spiritual significance for them. According to Justice Iacobucci, the court should consider the sincerity of an individual's belief but not its validity – neither its objective truth, nor the extent of its acceptance within the particular religious group. It was not for the courts, he said, to decide what is required by a particular belief system or which interpretation of that system is correct.

However, Justice Iacobucci did more than merely acknowledge that religious beliefs are contestable and that there is (at least from a civic perspective) no single authentic version of Judaism. He went further, saying, 'religious belief is intensely personal and can easily vary from one individual to another'.[13] Freedom of religion, he said, is a matter of 'personal choice and individual autonomy and freedom'.[14] But this seems too narrow a view of religious adherence. Religion may be viewed through two lenses alternatively or simultaneously – as both a personal commitment and a cultural practice. It is a shared belief system; a tradition that may be understood and followed by individual adherents in a personal or particular way. Justice Iacobucci's focus in *Amselem* on individual belief rather than community practice may have contributed to a weak standard of accommodation in later cases. There are two reasons for this: first, the potentially broad scope of protection makes it impractical to impose on the state a significant duty to accommodate; second, the focus on individual belief raises the question of why religious beliefs should be treated differently from other beliefs.[15]

In *Amselem*, Justice Iacobucci held that preventing the appellants from erecting *succahs* on their balconies amounted to a non-trivial interference with their religious practice. He further held that the condominium association had not established the need for restriction under the limitations provision of the Quebec

---

[12] Ibid., para. 47.
[13] Ibid., para. 54.
[14] Ibid., para. 40.
[15] The Court opted for a subjective test to avoid being drawn into disputes about the proper interpretation of a religious doctrine or tradition – see Richard Moon, 'Religious Commitment and Identity: *Syndicat Northcrest v. Amselem*', *Supreme Court Law Review* 29 (2005): 201, which also argues that the Court's ambivalence about religious adherence (as either personal judgment or cultural identity) manifests itself in a series of doctrinal tensions concerning the scope of religious freedom (whether it protects all deeply held views or beliefs or only *religious* beliefs and practices) and the nature of the wrong it addresses (whether it simply prohibits coercive state action or whether it goes further and prohibits the state from supporting or favouring a particular religious belief system).

Charter. He regarded the association's interest in the aesthetic appearance of the building as a minor or local concern, and noted that only a small number of *succahs* would be erected for nine days in the year. Moreover, the association could require that the *succahs* be constructed so as to blend in, as much as possible, with the general appearance of the building. Iacobucci concluded: 'In the final analysis ... the alleged intrusions or deleterious effects on the respondent's rights or interests under the circumstances are, at best, minimal and thus cannot be reasonably considered as imposing valid limits on the exercise of the appellant's religious freedom'.[16]

The more recent case of *Alberta v. Wilson Colony of Hutterian Brethren* involved a challenge to the regulations in Alberta dealing with drivers' licenses, which were amended in 2003 to require that all license holders be photographed. The license holder's photo would appear on his or her license and be included in a facial recognition data bank maintained by the province.[17] Prior to this change, the regulations had permitted the Registrar of Motor Vehicles to grant an exemption to an individual who, for religious reasons, objected to having his or her photo taken. Members of the Hutterian Brethren of Wilson Colony, who believed that the Second Commandment prohibited the making of photographic images, had been exempted from the photo requirement under the old regulations, but were required under the new law to be photographed before a license would be issued. The Colony members argued that the photo requirement breached their section 2(a) Charter rights and could not be justified under section 1. They claimed that no one from the Colony would be able to obtain a driver's licence and that this would affect the Colony's ability to purchase goods and sell produce, activities that were necessary to the maintenance of its agrarian and communal way of life.

The majority judgment of Chief Justice McLachlin accepted that the photo requirement breached the section 2(a) rights of the Wilson Colony members, but found that the breach was justified under section 1. Chief Justice McLachlin insisted that 'reasonable accommodation analysis' is not appropriate when the court is considering whether a *law* that restricts a religious practice is justified under section 1.[18] According to Chief Justice McLachlin, 'a law's constitutionality under section 1 of the *Charter* is determined not by whether it is responsive to the unique needs of every individual claimant, but rather by whether its infringement

---

[16] *Amselem*, para. 84.

[17] Driver's licences in Alberta are governed by the Traffic Safety Act, R.S.A., ch. T-6 (2000).

[18] In repudiating the 'reasonable accommodation' analysis, McLachlin makes what is sometimes referred to as a 'floodgates' argument: there were very few claimants in this case; had they been granted an exemption, the impact on government policy would have been minor. But McLachlin seems concerned about the possibility of more claimants coming forward later. It is unreasonable, she says, to expect the state to respond to, or anticipate, every possible claim for religious exemption.

of Charter rights is directed at an important objective and is proportionate in its overall impact'.[19]

Chief Justice McLachlin found that the purpose behind the photo requirement (reducing the risk of identity theft by ensuring the integrity of the driver's licence system) was pressing and substantial. The inclusion of driver's licence photos in a digital data bank would 'ensure that each licence in the system is connected to a single individual and that no individual has more than one licence', which in turn would help to prevent the fraudulent acquisition of driver's licences.[20] Chief Justice McLachlin also accepted that requiring all licence holders in the province to have their photo included in a digital photo bank would advance the government's objective more effectively 'than would an exemption for an as yet undetermined number of religious objectors'.[21] In her view any form of exemption from the requirement would detract from the system's effectiveness. Furthermore, she considered that the costs of the regulation did 'not seriously affect the claimants' right to pursue their religion [or] negate the choice that lies at the heart of freedom of religion'.[22] She noted that the photo requirement does not compel the Colony members to have their photos taken and that the Colony members could hire others to do their necessary driving, and although she acknowledged that relying on outsiders might detract from the community's traditional self-sufficiency, she concluded that the benefit of the law outweighed its negative impact on religious practice. Chief Justice McLachlin distinguished the claim in *Wilson Colony* from that in other cases 'where the incidental and unintended effect of the law is to deprive the adherent of a meaningful choice as to the religious practice'.[23] The unanswered question is, when is a legal constraint so significant that it removes meaningful choice? The answer to this may depend on whether or not section 2(a) is seen as a form of equality right that is concerned with preventing the marginalization of minority religious groups.

Reasonable accommodation and balancing

The Canadian courts' weak standard of justification for the restriction of religious practices reflects the practical concern identified by Chief Justice McLachlin in the

---

[19] *Wilson Colony*, para. 69. Despite her formal rejection of reasonable accommodation analysis, McLachlin does ask at the final step of the *Oakes* test whether an exception to the law should be made for the members of the Colony. However, she effectively rules this out as an option when she says that the claimants for exemption are potentially unlimited and that a court cannot know in advance how many individuals might have a sincere religious objection to having their photo taken.
[20] Ibid., para. 42.
[21] Ibid., para. 80.
[22] Ibid., para. 99.
[23] Ibid., para. 96.

Wilson Colony case: given the innumerable ways in which religion may conflict with law, a duty to accommodate would severely limit the state's ability to act in the public interest. The weak standard also more fundamentally reflects the courts' uncertainty about whether religious beliefs and practices differ from other beliefs and practices in a way that justifies their insulation from political decision-making. More particularly, it reflects the courts' ambivalence about whether religion should be viewed as a personal commitment that should be protected as a matter of liberty or as a cultural identity that should be treated with equal respect by the state. The problem with the latter is that religious beliefs involve truth claims, some of which have political significance. When the religious beliefs or practices of an individual or group affect the welfare of others, they cannot be treated with equal respect or insulated from political action. Even if the state seeks to avoid passing judgment, at least directly, on the truth or falsity of a spiritual belief, it must sometimes pursue goals that are inconsistent with particular religious practices or values.

Law and religious practice may conflict in a variety of ways. This conflict may be described as indirect when the religious practice conflicts with the means chosen to advance a public purpose and not with the purpose itself.[24] For example, the government may have decided on a particular route for a new highway, only to discover that its preferred route runs through an area that is sacred to an aboriginal group.[25] In such a case it may be possible for the state to advance its purpose in a different way, through different means, so that it does not interfere (at least to the same degree) with the religious practice or interest. It may be said in such a case that law-makers should take into account the interests and circumstances of different religious groups in the community and design the law so as to avoid unnecessary conflict. (Indeed, it may reasonably be asked whether the state would enact such a law were the religious practices of a more politically influential group similarly affected.[26]) It is important to recognize that even in the case of what might be described as an indirect conflict between law and religion, the adoption of different means will often detract to some extent from the law's ability to advance a particular policy. In the example given, an alternative route might add to construction costs or detract from ideal road conditions. In the case of an indirect or incidental conflict between law and religious practice, 'reasonable accommodation' might be the appropriate response. 'Reasonable accommodation' analysis asks whether the law, and more specifically the means it employs to advance its purpose, can be adjusted without significantly

---

[24] Though I have drawn a distinction here between direct and indirect restrictions, I recognize that these categories might more accurately be seen as part of a continuum.

[25] Such a claim was rejected in the U.S. Supreme Court judgment of *Lyng v. Northwest Indian Cemetery Protective Association*, 485 U.S. 439 (1988).

[26] *See* Christopher L. Eisgruber and Lawrence G. Sager, *Freedom of Religion and the Constitution* (Cambridge, MA: Harvard Univ. Press, 2010). Note, however, that the authors mistakenly believe that this test can be applied in a way that does not depend on the special character of religion.

compromising that purpose so that it does not interfere to the same extent with the religious practice. When applying this test and determining whether a religious practice should be accommodated, there may be disagreement about the extent to which government policy should be compromised. (I would note here that the Canadian courts have not been willing to require the state to compromise its policies in any significant way.)

Sometimes, though, the law pursues a policy that is directly at odds with a religious practice such that the conflict between law and religion is more direct, making a 'reasonable accommodation' approach unsuitable. In such a case the conflict cannot be avoided or reduced by simply requiring the state to adjust the means it has chosen to advance its civic purpose. If law-makers have decided, for example, that corporal punishment of children is wrong and should be banned or that sexual orientation discrimination is wrong and ought to be prohibited, how is a court to decide whether an exception to these requirements should be granted to a religious individual who believes that corporal punishment is mandated by God? The issue for the court is not whether physical discipline is effective or whether the value or utility of physical discipline outweighs its physical and emotional harm to children, nor whether parents should have the right to make judgments about the welfare of their children without state interference (If that question were resolved in favour of parental autonomy, the ban would be entirely struck down.). In other words, the court is not questioning the public norm and considering whether physical discipline is in fact sometimes right or justified. Instead, the issue is whether some parents – *religious* parents – should be exempted from an otherwise justified ban on physical discipline because they believe that God has mandated them to discipline their children in a way that the law has forbidden. The court must decide whether there is a legitimate place in society for a particular normative view – a view that the legislature has rejected.

In such a case the court's task is not to decide the proper balance or trade-off between competing interests or values (in accordance with the ordinary justification process under section 1 of the Charter); instead, it is to determine whether a religious individual or group should be exempted from the law. But if, as a democratic community, we have decided that a particular activity should be restricted as harmful, or a particular policy should be supported in the public interest, why should the issue be revisited for an individual or group that holds a different view on religious grounds? From a secular/civic perspective a particular religious practice has no intrinsic value; indeed, it is said that the court should take no position concerning its validity. When possible, the state should of course avoid forcing an individual to choose between following her or his conscience and obeying the law. However, the importance of the religious practice to the individual cannot alone justify the creation of an exemption to a democratically-mandated norm. Then again, the exemption of a religious practice may simply acknowledge that political decision-makers are fallible, and that some respect should be paid to the responses of different religious communities to fundamental moral issues. Governments recognize, after all, that if religious adherents are required to act contrary to what they believe, they may become alienated from the political order and perhaps even engage in civil disobedience. Preventing this marginalization of minority groups may indeed be the overarching reason for accommodation. In their interpretation of religious freedom, the Canadian courts have drawn on equality and anti-discrimination case law, which focuses on the relative status of identity groups within the larger political community.[27]

The state's willingness to treat a particular practice as part of the 'private' sphere, thus exempting a religious individual or group from a particular legal standard or public norm, may depend on two related considerations. The first is whether the practice has an impact on the rights or interests of others in the community, or whether instead it can be considered a matter personal to the individual or internal to the religious group. This distinction is by no means clear-cut and there is plenty of room for disagreement about the civic or private character of a religious practice. For example, while the education of children may be seen principally as the concern of parents, there is also a public interest in how children are educated. The community may also have some responsibility to children to ensure they are properly educated.[28]

The second consideration is whether membership in the religious group is voluntary. The internal operations of a group will be exempted from public norms, such as anti-discrimination rules, only if individual members are free to exit the group. Where this is the case, the assumption is that those who choose to be members of the group do not require protection from intra-group oppression. In this short discussion I can do nothing more than observe that the 'voluntariness' of group membership is a relative matter. An individual's identity may be tied in a deep way to his or her religious group, so that exiting from the group is difficult even when there are few material barriers. In other words, the individual's exit from his or her religious community may be difficult for precisely the same reason that community autonomy is important: because religious community plays a central role as a source of meaning and significance in the individual member's life and identity.

The difficulty of determining when an exemption should be granted is apparent in the case of paternalistic laws. A religious exemption might seem appropriate in the case of a law that precludes individuals from engaging in 'risky' activities that are required by their faith: for example, an exemption for Sikh men from a law that requires everyone to wear a helmet when riding a motorcycle. Paternalistic laws are intended to protect individuals from their own bad decisions. A commitment to religious freedom may at least limit the state's power to treat 'self-regarding' religious practices as unwise – as something against which the individual needs to

---

[27] The seminal Canadian 'effects discrimination' case is *Ontario Human Rights Commission v. Simpsons-Sears,* [1985] 2 S.C.R. 536.

[28] Another example involves the performance by a religious authority of a marriage ceremony that has civic effect. This is generally viewed as a private matter, even though it has civic or legal consequences.

be protected. Yet, even in the case of apparently paternalistic laws, the Canadian courts have been hesitant to recognize exceptions – in other words, to treat the practice as a private matter.[29] This reluctance appears to be based on a realization that no law is purely a paternalistic intrusion into a private matter, and that any time an individual is injured there will be an impact on others, including friends and family members, employers, co-workers, and of course the general community, which must cover the injured person's medical costs.

Conclusion

The Canadian courts have held that section 2(a) of the Charter is breached any time the state restricts a religious practice in a non-trivial way. According to the courts, the state must justify the restriction under section 1 of the Charter. This is said to involve a balancing of competing interests – the individual's freedom to practice his or her religion weighed against the state's responsibility to advance the public good. Yet despite their formal commitment to 'reasonable accommodation' or 'proportionality', the Canadian courts have been unwilling to require the state to compromise its policies in any significant way.

The conflict between religious practice and state law is often a conflict between different normative views. The court must decide not whether the state has properly balanced competing values or interests, but instead whether a religious individual or group should be exempted from a particular public norm and permitted to live in accordance with their different normative view. At issue in the 'religious accommodation' cases is the line between the political sphere, where government action is justified, and the private sphere, where religious practice is protected. The courts may sometimes draw the line in a way that exempts a religious practice from the application of an otherwise justified law. In this way they may create some 'private' space for religious practice without directly challenging the state's authority to govern in the public interest and establish public norms. A religious practice will be accommodated only if it can be seen as sufficiently private – not impacting the rights and interests of others in any significant way. Accommodation, though, will not be extended to beliefs or practices that explicitly address civic matters – the rights or welfare of others in the community – and are directly at odds with democratically adopted public policies. When religious beliefs address civic

---

[29] See, for example, *R. v. Badesha*, [2008] O.N.C.J. 94. In March 2008 an Ontario judge ruled that exempting Sikh men from motorcycle helmet laws would put undue hardship on the province's safety regulations. Sikhism forbids male adherents from covering their turbans with any other head coverings, including helmets. Courts in British Columbia, Manitoba, the U.K., Hong Kong and India had previously reached the opposite decision on the same issue. See also 'Judge Rules Against Sikh Challenge of Helmet Law', *CBC NEWS*, 6 March 2008, http://www.cbc.ca/news/canada/toronto/story/2008/03/06/helmet-sikh.html.

matters they will be treated as political judgments that may be rejected or accepted in the political process. While the courts appear, at least formally, to adopt an equality-rights approach to the restriction of religious practices under section 2(a), viewing religion as a cultural identity that should be treated with equal respect, in practice they seem to treat religion as a personal practice in which the individual should be free to engage unless it interferes with the rights or interests of others.

Yet it is important to recognize that religious freedom in these cases is not just the residue of legitimate state action. While the courts do not engage in anything that could properly be described as the 'balancing' of competing public and religious interests, they have sometimes sought to create space for religious practices at the margins of law by adjusting the boundary between private liberty and civic action. In some cases, accommodation may be granted to religious practices that conflict indirectly with the law. There, the court may require the state to compromise, in a minor way, its pursuit of a particular objective to make space for a religious practice. In other cases, there may be a more direct conflict between a religious practice and a public norm. There, the court will require the state to accommodate a religious individual or group only if this will have no tangible impact on others in the community. Because there is no principled way for the courts to determine the appropriate 'balance' between democratically selected public values or purposes and the spiritual beliefs or practices of a religious individual or community, the insulation of religion from public decision-making is generally minor and pragmatic in the Canadian courts.

Chapter 17
Religious Minorities' Right to Self-Determination

Johan D. van der Vyver

Leyla Şahin was a Muslim student at Istanbul University in Turkey who was excluded from classes because she wore a headscarf, as required by her Muslim faith. A Turkish law banned the wearing of headscarves in all universities and official government buildings, basing the proscription on the fact that Turkey is a secular state. In 1998, Leyla filed a complaint under the European system for the protection of human rights and fundamental freedoms.[1] Ultimately, the Grand Chamber of the European Court of Human Rights decided in favour of Turkey. It decided that the headscarf ban was based on the constitutional principles of secularism and equality, and consequently did not constitute a violation of the European Convention for the Protection of Human Rights and Fundamental Freedoms. The Grand Chamber further decided that her suspension from the university for refusing to remove the headscarf did not amount to a violation of the European Convention.[2] Ms Şahin subsequently left Turkey and is now living in Vienna.

The case of Leyla Şahin is one of many instances that reflect insensitivity toward the faith-based practices of religious groups. *Şahin v. Turkey* is notable because although Islam is the dominant religion in Turkey, its dress code was nevertheless undermined for the sake of secularism and equality concerns. Much more common, however, is discrimination against religious minorities.

Religious minorities are clearly marginalized in countries with a constitutional commitment to a particular religion. Several Muslim states testify in their constitutions to the overriding sovereignty of Allah (Pakistan and the Islamic State of Iran), or proclaim Islam to be the official state religion (Afghanistan, Algeria, Bahrain, Bangladesh, the Islamic Republic of the Comores, Egypt, Jordan, Kuwait, Libya, Malaysia, Maldives, Mauritania, Morocco, Qatar, Saudi Arabia, Somalia, Syria, Tunisia, the United Arab Emirates, and Yemen). Israel proclaims itself to be a Jewish state. The Evangelical Lutheran Church is an established church in Denmark, Iceland and Norway. The Eastern Orthodox Church of Christ is singled out as the 'prevailing religion' in Greece and the

---

[1] *Leyla Şahin v. Turkey*, Appl. No. 44774/98 ECtHR (2005).
[2] See also *Kurtulmuş v. Turkey*, Appl. No. 65500/01 ECtHR (2006); *Köse & Others v. Turkey*, Appl. No. 26625/02 ECtHR (2006).

'traditional religion' in Bulgaria. The Church of England is the established church in England, and the Presbyterian Church enjoys the same status in Scotland. Buddhism is the official religion in Laos and Sri Lanka. The Roman Catholic Church is an established church or is afforded special constitutional recognition in Argentina, Bolivia, Costa Rica, El Salvador, Guatemala, Liechtenstein, Malta, Monaco, Panama, Paraguay and Peru.

In the Preamble to the Constitution of Papua New Guinea the people proclaim 'our noble tradition and the Christian principles that are ours now'. Russia's Law on Freedom of Conscience and Religious Associations, enacted in 1997, recognizes in its Preamble 'the special contribution of Orthodoxy to the history of Russia and to the development of Russia's spirituality and culture' and promises respect for 'Christianity, Islam, Buddhism, Judaism and other religions and creeds which constitute an inseparable part of the historical heritage of Russia's people'.[3] The Fundamental Law of Hungary, that country's constitution, which entered into force on 25 April 2011, recognizes in its Preamble 'the role of Christianity in preserving nationhood'. In Poland it is commonly said: 'To be Polish is to be Catholic'.

Many countries restrict the participation of religious minorities in public affairs by requiring the registration of religious institutions and applying strict criteria for such registration. In Russia, a local religious organization must be established by no fewer than ten citizens of the Russian Federation.[4] In Poland, the Law on Guarantees Regarding the Freedom of Conscience and Belief of 17 May 1989 requires at least 15 Polish citizens to endorse an application for registration, a prerequisite for 'the right to create churches and other religious unions'.[5] In Slovakia, at least 20,000 signatures must endorse an application for registration of a church.[6]

In Austria, the Federal Law concerning the Legal Status of Religious Belief Communities, enacted in 1998, prescribes stringent requirements for a religious institution to enjoy the status of a 'state-recognized' religious community.[7] It must, for example, have existed in Austria for a period of at least 20 years – ten of them as a 'legally recognized' religious community – and must have

---

[3] *See* Giovanni Barberini, 'Religious Freedom in the Process of Democratization of Central and Eastern European States', in *Law and Religion in Post-Communist Europe 7*, eds. Silvio Ferrari and W. Cole Durham Jr (Leuven: Peeters Publishers, 2003), 14.

[4] Russian Federation, Law on Freedom of Conscience and Religious Associations, arts. 8(3), 9(1) (1997), trans. Lawrence Uzzell, in *Emory International Law Review* 12 (1998): 656–714.

[5] Law on Guarantees Regarding the Freedom of Conscience and Belief, art. 30, reprinted in *Law and Religion in Post-Communist Europe*, 213–31.

[6] Slovak National Council, Collection of Laws of the Czech and Slovak Federative Republic, Law No. 192/1992; see also Law No. 308 (1991) regulating registration procedures.

[7] Religiöses Bekenntnisgemeinschaftengesetz (Federal Law concerning the Legal Status of Religious Belief Communities) Bundesgesetzblatt (BGBL) No. 19/1998.

a following of at least two people per thousand of the population (between 16,000 and 17,000 adherents).[8] This legislation has paved the way for reducing state-recognized religions from 12 to probably no more than four. It should be noted, though, that religious communities, including those not qualified for recognition under the 1998 Law, can be afforded recognition by special legislation or an administrative decree. The Catholic Church, the Protestant Church and the Orthodox Church are thus 'historically recognized',[9] and statutory recognition has also been granted to the Israelite Religious Society,[10] Islam[11] and the Coptic Orthodox Church.[12] On 7 May 2009, the Jehovah's Witnesses became a recognized religious society through an executive order of the Federal Secretary. Religions not recognized by the government are denied certain benefits, including the right to levy taxes, to conduct religious classes in public schools, to receive state subsidies for their private schools and to broadcast radio services. Discrimination in Austria against unregistered religious minorities has been criticized in several decisions of the European Court of Human Rights.[13]

In Hungary, the Law on the Right to Freedom of Conscience and Religion, and on the Legal Status of Churches, Religious Denominations and Religious Communities, adopted by Parliament on 11 July 2011,[14] likewise laid down stringent requirements for the registration of churches, including proof that the church applying for registration 'operated for at least twenty years in an organized way in Hungary'.[15] This means in effect that all but 14 of the more than 350 religious groups that were previously registered in Hungary no longer qualify for registration, including the Methodist Church, Pentecostal groups and Muslim

---

[8] Ibid., sec. 11.

[9] The legal status of the Catholic Church was regulated by the 1934 Konkordat (Concordat) Bundesgesetzblatt (BGBl) No. 2/1934; the Protestant Church by the 1961 Protestantengesetz (Protestant Act) Bundesgesetzblatt (BGBl) No. 182/1961; and the Orthodox Church by the 1967 Orthodoxengesetz (Orthodox Act) Bundesgesetzblatt (BGBl) No. 229/1967.

[10] By the 1890 Israelitengesetz (Israelite Act) Reichsgesetzblatt (RGBl) No. 57/1890.

[11] By the 1912 Islamgesetz (Islam Act) Reichsgesetzblatt (RGBl) No. 159/1912.

[12] By the 2003 Bundesgesetz über äußere Rechtsverhältnisse der Orientalisch-Orthodoxen Kirchen in Österreich (Federal law on external legal relations of the Oriental Orthodox Church in Austria) Bundesgesetzblatt (BGBl) No. 20/2003.

[13] See *Zeugen Jehovas & Others v. Austria*, Appl. No. 40826/98 ECtHR (2008); *Freunde der Christengemeinschaft & Others v. Austria*, Appl. No. 76581/01 ECtHR (2009); *Gütl v. Austria*, Appl. No. 49686/99 ECtHR (2009); *Löffelmann v. Austria*, Appl. No. 42967/98 ECtHR (2009); *Lang v. Austria*, Appl. No. 28648/03 ECtHR (2009).

[14] 2011. évi C. törvény a lelkiismereti és vallásszabadság jogáról, valamint az egyházak, vallásfelekezetek és vallási közösségek jogállásáról (Act C of 2011 on the Freedom of conscience and religion, and on the legal status of churches, denominations and religious communities).

[15] Ibid., art. 14(3)(a).

religious communities.[16] In Hungary, churches must be registered in order to: be recognized as legal persons;[17] receive tax exemptions and similar benefits;[18] perform pedagogical, educational, healthcare, charity, cultural and sports activities; and engage in family, child or youth protection programmes.[19]

Persecution of religious minorities is all too commonplace in many countries: the Tamil minority in Sri Lanka; Tibetan Buddhists and Falun Gong practitioners in China;[20] the Ahmadis in Pakistan; and the Copts in Sudan have all been victims. Following a referendum held on 29 November 2009, an article was inserted in the Constitution of Switzerland that prohibits the construction of minarets – that is, a high tower attached to a mosque from which a *muezzin* (crier) calls Muslim people to prayer.[21] In several countries, endorsement of a particular religion by the state has led to violence.

The failure of national systems to provide protection to the interests of religious minorities within their jurisdiction, or minorities' mere perception of being marginalized, is an important contributing cause for such groups' tireless aspirations toward the establishment of homogenous states, as in the cases of the Maoists in Nepal; the Muslim communities of Kashmir and Kosovo; the Basques in Northern Spain; the Hindu factions in Sri Lanka; the Catholic minority in Northern Ireland; the Kurds in Iraq and Turkey; people of Macedonian extraction in Florina (Northern Greece); and many others. On 17 February 2008, a substantial majority of the Assembly of Kosovo, dominated by (Muslim) Kosovar Albanians, adopted a unilateral declaration of independence from Serbia. On 9 July 2011, a civil war between the Muslim north and the non-Muslim south of Sudan that had lasted for several decades culminated in the secession of Southern Sudan as the final stage in a six-year peace agreement between the two religiously-defined regions of the country.

Nepal may also be cited here as a case in point. At its creation in 1768 as a unified state and until not so long ago, Nepal was proclaimed to be a Hindu state and was constitutionally structured as a monarchy. This state of affairs was formally endorsed by its very first meaningful constitution, adopted in 1990. Dissatisfaction with the constitution prompted a Maoist insurgency, plunging the country into a decade-long civil war which brought about approximately 17,500

---

[16] The churches, religious denominations and religious communities recognized by the Hungarian parliament are confined to the Catholic Church, the Hungarian Reformed Church, the Evangelical-Lutheran Church, three Jewish denominations, five factions of the Orthodox Church, the Unitarian Church in Hungary, the Baptist Union of Hungary and the Faith Church. See ibid., Melléklet (Annex).

[17] Ibid., sec. 11(1), read with sec. 7(4).

[18] Ibid., sec. 20(5).

[19] Ibid., sec. 12(1).

[20] In China there are only five recognized religions: Protestantism, Catholicism, Buddhism, Taoism and Islam.

[21] Constitution fédérale (Cst) (Constitution) Apr. 18, 1999, RO 101, art. 72, para. 3.

casualties before concluding in 2005 with a 12-point peace agreement. An interim constitution was put in place, and the King was forced to abdicate in 2008 (he is now an ordinary citizen of the country and his palace has been converted into a museum). The first president, Dr Ram Baran Yadav, was sworn in on 23 July 2008 under the current interim constitution. A Constitutional Assembly was established to draft a final constitution that would address, and seek to overcome, the causes of unrest in the country, including religious tension. Although approximately 80 per cent of Nepalese are Hindus, the establishment of Hinduism as a state religion will clearly not be reinstated under a new constitutional dispensation.

Regulating the rights of religious minorities

The different mechanisms for dealing with group rivalries in highly polarized communities can perhaps be classified into three distinct categories:

1. segregate the rival groups from one another
2. create homogeneity by uniting the people under the umbrella of a single ethnic, religious or linguistic identity
3. promote the right of self-determination for ethnic, religious or linguistic communities.

Segregation

Separating oneself from 'the hostile Other' is a distinct attribute of, for example, Orthodox Judaism. Orthodox Judaism does not espouse turning the other cheek, a decree from the New Testament. Instead, the Talmud makes the maintenance of peace and security conditional upon the construction of a fence that would separate those who belong from their enemies. This approach was also favoured by the Constituent Assembly of Nepal.

A major cause of concern in Nepal is the polarization of its diverse ethnic and religious population. Although the vast majority of Nepal is Hindu, there are influential Buddhist and Muslim minorities, and the ethnic composition of the population reflects no fewer than 91 different language groups. The Constituent Assembly initially proposed a federal system of government based on the religious and ethnic composition of the Nepalese population as a means of securing internal peace in the years to come, but this proposed 'solution' to accommodate religious and ethnic conflict in the country seems untenable. Complete territorial segregation of religious and ethnic varieties in any political community is almost impossible to orchestrate, and consigning regional powers of government to religious or linguistic factions could be a recipe for disaster. We know from the gruesome experiences of the former Yugoslavia that attempts to create religiously or ethnically homogenous states can lead to profound animosity toward the Other in one's midst, and may culminate in a policy of 'ethnic cleansing' that could include brutal acts of genocide. On 15 May 2012, the Constituent Assembly of Nepal finally decided to settle for 11 federal states, but decided that the boundaries of the states will be determined by a future commission.

Religious homogeneity

Instead of dividing conflicting groups into distinct territorial regions within the body politic, an alternative strategy would be to eliminate the group-related foundation that might lead to conflict within a political community.

Turkey, Greece and France may be singled out as members of the European community that are not favourably disposed toward accommodating the ethnic or religious practices of distinct factions within their respective communities. We have already referred to the case of Leyla Şahin, which exemplifies the policy of secularism and equality in the Turkish legal system and its detrimental effect on religious traditions.

Greece also is particularly unaccommodating to the claim of a distinct identity of people of Macedonian extraction in Florina, and has been forced to defend itself before the European Court of Human Rights for sanctioning rigid, and indeed prohibitive, conditions restricting the activities of faith communities outside the Greek Orthodox Church,[22] including restrictions placed on the evangelical activities of Jehovah's Witnesses[23] and the Pentecostal Church.[24]

On 15 March 2004, President Jacques Chirac of France signed into law an amendment to the French Code of Education that prohibits, as a principle of the separation of church and state, 'the wearing of symbols or garb which shows religious affiliation in public primary and secondary schools',[25] and on 11 April 2011, a French law entered into force banning the covering of one's face in public,[26] which was clearly intended to outlaw the wearing of a burqa by Muslim women.

Outside of Europe, a trend toward promoting homogeneity is also reflected in Article 15(3)(c) of the Nigerian Constitution, which obliges the state to encourage inter-marriage between members of different religious and tribal communities for the purpose of 'promoting national integration'.[27] This has proven ineffective,

---

[22] *Manoussakis & Others v. Greece*, Appl. No. 18748/91 ECtHR (1996).

[23] *Kokkinakis v. Greece*, Appl. No. 14307/88 ECtHR (1993).

[24] *Larissis & Others v. Greece*, Appl. Nos. 23372/94; 26377/94; 26378/94 ECtHR (1998).

[25] Loi no. 2004-228 du 15 mars 2004 encadrant, en application du principe de laïcité, le port de signes ou de tenues manifestant une appurtenance religieuse dans les écoles, colleges et lycées publics (Law No. 2004-228 of Mar. 15, 2004 concerning, as an application of the principle of the separation of church and state, the wearing of symbols or garb which show religious affiliation in public primary and secondary schools).

[26] Loi interdisant la dissimulation du visage dans l'espace public (Act prohibiting concealment of the face in public spaces) (14 Sept. 2011).

[27] Art. 15(3)(c) of the Constitution of the Federal Republic of Nigeria (1999).

however, as the Nigerian people are as divided today as they ever were – perhaps even more so.

In 2002, several predominantly Muslim provinces in northern Nigeria formally adopted Islamic Sharia law, including Islamic criminal law, as part of their legal system. As of 2012, nine provinces altogether have instituted Sharia.[28] The imposition of Sharia penalties, which by international standards include cruel and inhuman punishments, attracted media attention (and condemnation) from many parts of the world when in March 2002, a Sharia court sentenced Amina Lawal, a 30-year-old woman, to death by stoning because she was expecting a child out of wedlock. The sentence was set aside in 2004 by the Sharia Court of Appeal based on the rule against retroactive criminal sanctions because the law incorporating Islamic law was enacted after she had become pregnant. However, the case was widely publicized as a reminder of Sharia's unbecoming – and, in Nigeria, unconstitutional – penalties, and of the sharp divide between the northern Islamic communities and the predominantly Christian population of the rest of Nigeria. The country has been disrupted now for several months by religious violence orchestrated by a radical Muslim group, the Boko Haram, which has cost the lives of several hundred Nigerians and left more than 10,000 people displaced. The violence has also caused severe damage to government buildings and Christian places of worship. The Nigerian situation shows that attempts to create religious homogeneity, either through constitutional directives or terrorist interventions, are profoundly counter-productive.

* * *

How, then, should religiously-based rivalries within the body politic be regulated to secure peace and freedom of religion? Perhaps the answer can be found in the case of a teenage South African girl of Hindu extraction, Sunali Pillay.

Sunali gained entry into the Durban Girls' High School – one of the most prestigious state schools in South Africa – where she received an excellent education. When she reached a certain stage of maturity, a golden stud was inserted in her nose, which is a Hindu custom indicating that a girl has become eligible for marriage. This brought her into conflict with school authorities. The school's code of conduct, signed by her parents as a condition for Sunali's admission to Girls' High, prohibited the wearing of any jewellery except earrings, and then only under strict conditions meticulously specified in the code. Sunali's mother explained to the school authorities that her daughter did not wear the nose stud as a fashion statement, but in deference to an age-old tradition of her Hindu community. The school management nevertheless refused to grant Sunali an exemption from its dress code. A discrimination complaint was thereupon filed by Mrs Pillay in the equality court, which ruled in favour of the school.[29] However, when the matter

---

[28] Zamfara, Kano, Sokoto, Katsina, Bauchi, Borno, Jigawa, Kebbi, and Yobe.
[29] *Pillay v. MEC for Education: KwaZulu-Natal & Others*, 2006 (6) SA 363 (EqC).

eventually came before the Constitutional Court of South Africa, it ruled that the school authorities' refusal to grant Sunali an exemption from the jewellery provision in the school's code of conduct amounted to unreasonable discrimination and was therefore unlawful.[30]

Post-apartheid South Africa abandoned territorial segregation as a supposed recipe for the peaceful co-existence of racial and ethnic groups, and did not attempt to promote homogeneity within the ranks of its nation. It instead opted for a system designed to promote national unity on the basis of the internationally acclaimed right to self-determination of peoples – as exemplified by the case of Sunali Pillay.

Religious minorities' right to self-determination

Religious minorities, as well as ethnic and linguistic minorities, constitute 'peoples' and, under the norms of contemporary international law, are entitled to a right to self-determination. The right to self-determination of ethnic, religious and linguistic communities entails, respectively, 'the right to enjoy their own culture, to profess and practice their own religion, and to use their own language, in private and in public, freely and without interference or any form of discrimination'.[31]

The right to self-determination of religious minorities involves more than merely an accommodating disposition toward particular sectional beliefs and practices. By virtue of the right to self-determination, governments are required to secure, through their respective constitutional and legal systems, the interests of distinct sections of the population that constitute a people, including religious minorities. The Declaration on the Rights of Persons Belonging to National or Ethnic, Religious and Linguistic Minorities clearly spells out that obligation: to protect – and encourage conditions for the promotion of – the group identities of concerned minorities under the jurisdiction of the duty-bound state (arts. 1(1) and 4(2)); to afford to minorities the special competence to participate effectively in decisions pertinent to the group to which they belong (art. 2(3)); to not discriminate in any way against any person on the basis of his or her group identity (art. 3); and in fact to take action to secure their equal treatment by and before the law (art. 4(1)). The Declaration further provides:

---

[30] *MEC for Education: KwaZulu-Natal & Others v. Pillay & Others*, 2008 (1) SA 474 (CC).

[31] Declaration on the Rights of Persons Belonging to National or Ethnic, Religious and Linguistic Minorities, art. 2.1, G.A. Res.47/136 of Dec. 18, 1992, 47 U.N. GAOR Supp. (No. 49), at 210, U.N. Doc. A/Res/47/135 (1992); see also Covenant on Civil and Political Rights, art. 27, G.A. Res. 2200 (XXI) of Dec. 16, 1966, 21 U.N. GAOR Supp. (No. 16) at 52, U.N. Doc. A/6316, 999 U.N.T.S. 171.

States shall take measures to create favourable conditions to enable persons belonging to minorities to express their characteristics and to develop their culture, language, religion, traditions and customs, except where specific practices are in violation of national law and contrary to international standards.[32]

The Council of Europe's Framework Convention for the Protection of National Minorities[33] articulates minority rights in much the same vein. It guarantees equality before the law and equal protection of the laws (art. 4(1)); state parties promise to provide 'the conditions necessary for persons belonging to national minorities to maintain and develop their culture, and to preserve the essential elements of their identity, namely their religion, language, traditions and cultural heritage' (art. 5(1)); and the right of a person belonging to a national minority 'to manifest his or her religion or belief and to establish religious institutions, organizations and associations' (art. 8).

Limitations to the right of self-determination

It must be emphasized that the right to self-determination of ethnic, religious and linguistic groups (1) is not an unlimited right, and (2) does not include a right to political independence. The Declaration on the Rights of Persons Belonging to National or Ethnic, Religious and Linguistic Minorities excludes from the right of self-determination specific practices of an ethnic, religious or linguistic community that violate the national laws of their country or are contrary to international standards. For instance, practices such as female genital mutilation (FGM) cannot be justified on the basis of the right to self-determination for religious communities. FGM amounts to sexually defined physical mutilation of extreme severity and with irreversible consequences. Its practice is almost exclusively inspired by male interests (namely, the prolonged sexual pleasure of the male partner). As such it constitutes sex- and gender-based discrimination of the worst kind, and since it is mostly executed while the victim is an infant, it also implicates the rights of children. The United Nations' Declaration on the Elimination of Violence against Women (1993) describes FGM as an instance of 'violence against women'.[34]

The killing of persons suspected of witchcraft, or ritual murders, which are fairly common practices in some African communities, likewise cannot be tolerated, even if such acts are justified for their perpetrators by the belief that they would ward off an existing or imminent evil force.

---

[32] Declaration on the Rights of Persons Belonging to National or Ethnic, Religious and Linguistic Minorities, article 4(2).

[33] European Framework Convention for the Protection of National Minorities, 1995 E.T.S. 157, reprinted in 34 I.L.M. 35 (1995).

[34] Declaration on the Elimination of Violence against Women, art. 2(a), U.N. GA Res. 48/104 of 20 Dec. 1993, U.N. Doc. A/RES/48/104 (1993).

Self-determination and a right to secession

The right of ethnic, religious and linguistic communities to self-determination does not include a right to secession – not even in instances where political authorities act in breach of a minority's legitimate expectations. The United Nations' Declaration on the Rights of Persons Belonging to National or Ethnic, Religious and Linguistic Minorities accordingly proclaims that its provisions must not be taken to contradict the principles of the United Nations pertaining to the 'sovereign equality, territorial integrity and political independence of States'.[35] The United Nations' 2007 Declaration on the Rights of Indigenous Peoples also proclaims that the right of self-determination for indigenous peoples must not be construed as 'authorizing or encouraging any action that would dismember or impair, totally or in part, the territorial integrity or political unity of sovereign and independent States'.[36] In the Framework Convention for the Protection of National Minorities, the Council of Europe proclaimed:

> Nothing in the present framework Convention shall be interpreted as implying any right to engage in any activity or perform any act contrary to the fundamental principles of international law and in particular of the sovereign equality, territorial integrity and political independence of States.[37]

There are many compelling reasons why the destruction of existing political communities harbouring a plural society should be avoided: (1) a multiplicity of economically non-viable states will further contribute to a decline of the living standards in the world community; (2) the notion that people sharing a common culture, language or religion would also be politically compatible is clearly a myth, and disillusionment after the event might provoke profound resentment and conflict; (3) the movement of people within plural societies across territorial divides has greatly destroyed ethnic, cultural and religious homogeneity in regions where it might have existed in earlier times, and consequently the demarcation of borders that would be inclusive of the sectional demography which secessionists seek to establish is in most cases quite impossible; (4) affording political relevance to ethnic, cultural or religious affiliation not only carries the potential for repression of minority groups within the nation, but also affords no political standing whatsoever to persons who, on account of mixed parentage or marriage, cannot be identified with any particular faction of the group-conscious community, nor to those who – for whatever reason – do not wish to be identified under any particular ethnic, cultural, or religious label; (5) in consequence of the above, an ethnically, culturally or religiously defined state will more often than not create

---

[35] Declaration on the Rights of Persons Belonging to National or Ethnic, Religious and Linguistic Minorities, article 8.4.
[36] Ibid., art. 46(1).
[37] Framework Convention for the Protection of National Minorities, article 21.

its own 'minorities problem', which would almost invariably result in profound discrimination – or worse still, a strategy of 'ethnic cleansing' – against those who do not belong.

The South African model

The Constitution of the Republic of South Africa, Act 108 of 1996, can in general be described, as far as religion and religious diversity are concerned, as one of profound toleration and accommodation: it allocates to church institutions the rights in the Bill of Rights to the extent required by the nature of the right and the nature of the church as a legal person (sec. 8(4)); it guarantees the free exercise of religion (sec. 15(1)); and it sanctions freedom of assembly (sec. 17) and freedom of association (sec. 18).

Of special importance in the context of the present overview is the constitutional protection of the right to self-determination for ethnic, religious and linguistic communities (secs. 31 and 235). In order to enhance that right, the Constitution makes provision for a Commission for the Promotion and Protection of the Rights of Cultural, Religious and Linguistic Communities.[38] The Constitution thus encourages the maintenance of, and pride in, the ethnic, religious and linguistic group identities of the country's diverse population. The constitutional preamble accordingly expresses the belief that all who live in South Africa are 'united in our diversity'. In its substantive provisions, the Constitution proclaims 11 official languages (sec. 8(1)), calls on the State 'to take practical and positive measures to elevate the status and advance the use of ... [the indigenous languages of our people]' (sec. 8(2)), and affords to everyone 'the right to use the language and to participate in the cultural life of their choice' (sec. 30). As far as accommodating the interests of religious communities is concerned, the Constitution envisioned the establishment, by means of national legislation, of a Pan South African Language Board charged, *inter alia*, with promoting and ensuring respect for 'Arabic, Hebrew, Sanskrit and other languages used for religious purposes in South Africa' (sec. 6(5)(b)(ii)).

The Constitutional Court has on several occasions emphasized the vital importance of religion as a component of South Africa's constitutional democracy. In *Christian Education South Africa v. Minister of Education*, Justice Albie Sachs had this to say:

> There can be no doubt that the right to freedom of religion, belief and opinion in an open and democratic society contemplated by the Constitution is important. The right to believe or not to believe, and to act or not to act according to his or her beliefs or non-beliefs, is one of the key ingredients of any person's

---

[38] Sections 181(1)(c) and 185–6; see also the Commission for the Promotion and Protection of the Rights of Cultural, Religious and Linguistic Communities Act 19 of 2002.

dignity. Yet freedom of religion goes beyond protecting the inviolability of the individual conscience. For many believers, their relationship with God or creation is central to all their activities. It concerns their capacity to relate in an intensely meaningful fashion to their sense of themselves, their community and their universe. For millions in all walks of life, religion provides support and nurture and a framework for individual and social stability and growth. Religious belief has the capacity to awake concepts of self-worth and human dignity which form the cornerstone of human rights. It affects the believer's view of society and founds the distinction between right and wrong. It expresses itself in the affirmation and continuity of powerful traditions that frequently have an ancient character transcending historical epochs and national boundaries.[39]

Religion is not only an important component of a person's day-to-day life and inherent human dignity; being religious is also of vital importance *to the state*. Delivering a unanimous decision of the Constitutional Court in another matter, Justice Sachs noted the many difficulties attending 'the relationship foreshadowed by the Constitution between the sacred and the secular',[40] and went on to say:

Religious bodies play a large and important part in public life, through schools, hospitals and poverty relief programmes. They command ethical behaviour from their members and bear witness to the exercise of power by State and private agencies; they promote music, art and theatre; they provide halls for community activities, and conduct a great variety of social activities for their members and the general public. They are part of the fabric of public life, and constitute active elements of the diverse and pluralistic nation contemplated by the Constitution. Religion is not just a question of belief or doctrine. It is part of the people's temper and culture, and for many believers a significant part of their way of life. Religious organizations constitute important sectors of national life and accordingly have a right to express themselves to government and the courts on the great issues of the day. They are active participants in public affairs fully entitled to have their say with regard to the way law is made and applied.[41]

Concluding Observations

The South African nation comprises perhaps the most diverse plural composition in the entire world and is furthermore notorious for the polarization of factions of

---

[39] *Christian Education South Africa v. Minister of Education*, 2000 (4) SA 757; 2000 (10) BCLR 1051, para. 36 (CC).
[40] *Minister of Home Affairs v. Fourie; Lesbian and Gay Equality Project v. Minister of Home Affairs*, 2006 (1) SA 524; 2006 (3) BCLR 355, para. 89 (CC).
[41] Ibid., at para. 93.

the population. Dealing with group rivalries and orchestrating reconciliation are central to social engineering within that troubled land.

The drafters of the South African Constitution rejected both the segregation of rival ethnic, religious and linguistic communities and the promotion of cultural, religious or linguistic homogeneity within the nation as means of counteracting group-related tensions in the country's social construct. Instead, they opted for creating – in the celebrated words of Archbishop Desmond Tutu – 'a rainbow nation'. Accordingly, as far as religious diversity is concerned, the post-apartheid constitutional dispensation seeks to promote pride in one's denominational affiliation. It encourages citizens to be faithful to their membership in the Catholic, Methodist, Dutch Reformed or Zion Christian Church, and to find comfort in being a member of the Muslim, Hindu or Buddhist community.

Pride in one's particular religious affiliation does not elevate one to a superior status in the community. The respect of others for your religious persuasion and spiritual values demands full respect for the religious and spiritual predilections of others. The constitutional principle that applies in this regard has been reduced to perhaps the most basic moral directive for a 'new South Africa': *ubuntu* or *botho*, 'an idea based on deep respect for the [inner] humanity of another'.[42] *Ubuntu* translates into 'humaneness' and constitutes 'part of our *rainbow* heritage'.[43] It stands in sharp contrast to 'dehumanising and degrading the individual'.[44] Justice Albie Sachs on occasion referred to *ubunthu-batho* in the sense of 'civility' as 'a precondition for the good functioning of contemporary democratic societies' and noted that 'civility in a constitutional sense involves more than just courtesy and good manners.... It presupposes tolerance for those with whom one disagrees and respect for the dignity of those with whom one is in dispute'.[45]

The Constitution therefore subjects the freedom of expression to limitations, which limitations include a prohibition of the 'advocacy of hatred that is based on race, ethnicity, gender or religion, and that constitutes incitement to cause harm'.[46] Under the Promotion of Equality and Prevention of Unfair Discrimination Act, 'no person may publish, propagate, advocate or communicate words ... against any person, that could reasonably be construed to demonstrate a clear intention to (a) be hurtful; (b) be harmful or to incite harm; [or] (c) promote or propagate hatred'.[47] South African law therefore does not uphold the almost incontestable sanctity of freedom of speech, as does the American constitutional system. In South African

---

[42] *Dikoko v. Mokhatla*, 2006 (6) SA 235, 2007 1 B.C.L.R. 1, para. 68 (CC); *see also id.*, at para. 69.

[43] *S v. Makwanyane*, 1995 (3) SA 391, para. 308 (CC) (J. Mokgoro).

[44] Ibid., at para. 250 (J. Lange).

[45] *Masetlha v. President of the RSA & Another*, 2008 (1) SA 566, 2008 1 B.C.L.R. 1, para. 238 (CC).

[46] 1996 S.A. Const., sec. 16(2)(c).

[47] Promotion of Equality and Prevention of Unfair Discrimination Act 4 of 2000, sec. 19(1).

law, 'certain expressions do not deserve constitutional protection because they have the potential to impinge adversely on the dignity of others and cause harm'.[48] In South Africa, 'the right to freedom of expression is not a pre-eminent freedom ranking above all others';[49] in this respect it 'differs fundamentally from the balance struck in the United States',[50] where freedom of speech constitutes the basic norm – a *Grundnorm* – of the entire rights regime.[51]

The 'new South Africa' is instead founded on zero tolerance for words and conduct that are offensive to others. Depicting members of a particular population groups as 'hotnot', 'kaffir', 'rooinek', 'boer' or 'coolie' is therefore strictly forbidden since such names 'have for decades been used to bring people of different races into contempt'.[52] Refusing to serve a Muslim client wearing a fez in a business enterprise open to the public constitutes unbecoming discrimination based on religion.[53] The media are under legal constraint not to publish cartoons depicting the Prophet Mohammed as a terrorist (those that first appeared in a Danish newspaper) because they 'advocate hatred and stereotyping of Muslims'.[54]

As noted by Chief Justice Lange, 'The process of reconciliation is an on-going one which requires give and take from all sides'.[55] 'Our democracy is still fragile', said Judge Bertelsmann, adding that, 'Participants in the political and socio-political discourse must remain sensitive to the feelings and perceptions of other South Africans when words were used that were common during the struggle days, but may be experienced as harmful by fellow inhabitants of South Africa today.'[56]

Perhaps the most salient component of the right to self-determination as a means of accommodating the needs of religious minorities is its inherent decree of providing protection to one's own religious beliefs and rituals, and – as exemplified by the South African experiment – demanding respect for the spiritual convictions and religious practices of others.

---

[48] *Du Toit v. Minister for Safety and Security*, 2009 (6) SA 128, para. 32 (CC).

[49] S v. Mamabolo (E. TV & Others Intervening), 2001 (3) SA 409, 2001 5 B.C.L.R. 449, para. 41 (CC).

[50] Ibid., at para. 40.

[51] Johan D. van der Vyver, 'Constitutional Protection of Children and Young Persons', in *The Law of Children and Young Persons in South Africa 265*, ed. J.A. Robinson (Durban: Butterworths, 1997), 282; Johan D. van der Vyver, 'Limitations of Freedom of Religion or Belief: International Law Perspectives', *Emory International Law Review* 19 (2005): 508.

[52] Decision of the Broadcasting Complaints Commission in P Johnson v. 94.7 Highveld Stereo, Case No. 07/2002 (2002).

[53] *Woodways CC v. Moosa Vallie*, Case No. A251/05 (H.C. Western Cape) (2009).

[54] *Jamait-Ul-Ulama of Transvaal v. Johncom Media Investment Ltd & Others*, Case No. 1127/06 (W.L.D.) (2006).

[55] *Du Toit v. Minister of Safety and Security*, 2009 (6) SA 128, para. 28 (CC); see also *Agriforum & Another v. Malema & Another*, 2011 (6) SA 240), para. 11 (Eq.C).

[56] *Agriforum v. Malema*, 2010 (5) SA 235 (GNP).

Bibliography

Abiad, N. *Sharia, Muslim States and International Human Rights Treaty Obligations: A Comparative Study*. London: British Institute of International and Comparative Law, 2008.

Abrahamian, E. *A History of Modern Iran*. Cambridge, UK: Cambridge University Press, 2008.

Akbaba, Y. 'Who Discriminates More? Comparing Religious Discrimination in Western Democracies, Asia and the Middle East'. *Civil Wars* 11 (2009): 321–58.

Alfredsson, G. 'A Frame with an Incomplete Painting: Comparison of the Framework Convention for the Protection of National Minorities with International Standards and Monitoring Procedures'. *International Journal of Minority and Group Rights* 7 (2000): 291–304.

Ališauskiene, M. 'Freedom of Religion in the Baltic States'. In *Spaces and Borders: Current Research on Religion in Central and Eastern Europe*, edited by A. Máté-Tóth and C. Rughiniş, 133–50. Berlin/Boston: Walter de Gruyter, 2011.

Ališauskiene, M. 'The Manifestation and Development of New Religions in Lithuania: Case Study of the Art of Living Foundation'. Summary of Doctoral Dissertation, Vytautas Magnus University, 2009.

Altglas, V. 'Laïcité is What Laïcité Does: Rethinking the French Cult Controversy'. *Current Sociology* 58 (2010): 489–510.

Altnurme, L. 'Changes in Mythic Patterns in Estonian Religious Life Stories'. *Social Compass* 58 (2010): 77–94.

Altnurme, L. *Kristlusest oma usuni: Uurimus muutustest eestlaste religioossuses 20. sajandi II poolel* [From Christianity to own belief: A study about the changes in the religiosity of Estonians in the second half of the 20th century]. Tartu, Estonia: Tartu University Press, 2005.

Anderson, J. *Liberty in Transitional Societies: The Politics of Religion*. New York: Cambridge University Press, 2003.

Anderson, L. 'Religion and State in Libya: The Politics of Identity'. *Annals of the American Academy of Political and Social Science* 483 (1986): 69–70.

Anthony, D. and M. Introvigne. *Le lavage de cerveau, mythe ou réalité*. Paris: L'Harmattan, 2006.

Bäckström, A., et al. *Welfare and Religion in 21st Century Europe. Volume 1: Configuring the Connections*. Aldershot, UK: Ashgate, 2010.

Balodis, R. 'Church and State in Latvia'. In *Law and Religion in Post-Communist Europe*, edited by S. Ferrari and W.C. Durham, 141–75. Leuven, Belgium: Peeters, 2003.

Balodis, R. 'Recent Developments of Latvian Model of Church and State Relationship: Constitutional Changes without Revising the Constitution'. *Jurisprudenciija/Jurisprudence* 3 (2009): 7–19.

Balodis, R. *State and Church Relationship: Theory and Latvian State Experience: Summary of Presented Promotion*. Riga, Latvia: Religijas Brivibas Asociacija, 2001.

Balzer, M.M. 'Whose Steeple Is Higher? Religious Competition in Siberia'. *Religion, State and Society* 33 (2005): 57–70.

Baran, E. 'Contested Victims: Jehovah's Witnesses and the Russian Orthodox Church, 1990 to 2004'. *Religion, State and Society* 35 (2007): 261–78.

Baran, E. 'Negotiating the Limits of Religious Pluralism in Post-Soviet Russia: The Anticult Movement in the Russian Orthodox Church, 1990–2004'. *Russian Review* 65 (2006): 637–56.

Barberini, G. 'Religious Freedom in the Process of Democratization of Central and Eastern European States'. In *Law and Religion in Post-Communist Europe*, edited by S. Ferrari and W.C. Durham, 15–19. Leuven, Belgium: Peeters, 2003.

Barbey, P. *Les Témoins de Jéhovah: Pour un christianisme original*. Paris: L'Harmattan, 2003.

Barker, E. *New Religious Movements: A Practical Introduction*. London: HMSO, 1989.

Barker, E. 'The Social Scientific Study of Religion? You Must Be Joking!' *Journal for the Scientific Study of Religion* 34 (1995): 287–310.

Bauman, Z. *Modernity and Holocaust*. Cambridge, UK: Polity, 1989.

Beaman, L.G. 'Religious Freedom and Neoliberalism: From Harm to Cost-Benefit'. In *Religion in the Neoliberal Age: Political Economy and Modes of Governance*, edited by Toumas Martikainen and François Gauthier. Farnham, UK: Ashgate, 2013.

Beckford, J.A. *Cult Controversies: the Societal Response to New Religious Movements*. London Tavistock, 1985.

Bellanger, F. 'Le statut des minorités religieuses en Suisse'. *Archive des Sciences sociales des Religions* (2003): 87–99.

Berger, B.L. 'Polygamy and the Predicament of Contemporary Criminal Law'. In *Polygamy's Wrongs? The Social Family in the Culture of Rights*, edited by Gillian Calder and Lori G. Beaman. Vancouver, BC: University of British Columbia Press, forthcoming.

Blitt, R.C. 'Defamation of Religion: Rumors of Its Death Are Greatly Exaggerated'. *Case Western Reserve Law Review* 62 (Winter 2011): 347–97.

Borenstein, E. 'Articles of Faith: The Media Response to Maria Devi Khristos'. *Religion* 25 (1995): 249–66.

Borowik, I., ed. *Religions, Churches, and Religiosity in Post-Communist Europe*. Krakow, Poland: Nomos, 2006.

Bouchard, G. and C. Taylor. 'Building the Future: A Time for Reconciliation'. *Commission de Consultation sur les pratiques d'accommodement reliées aux*

différences culturelles. Québec, QC: Québec Government Printing Office, 2008.
Bowker, J., ed. *Oxford Dictionary of World Religions.* Oxford: Oxford University Press, 1997.
Bromley, D.G. and A.D. Shupe. 'Anti-cultism in the United States: Origins, Ideology and Organizational Development'. *Social Compass* 42 (1995): 222–36.
Bromley, D.G. and A.D. Shupe. *Strange Gods: the Great American Cult Scare.* Boston: Beacon Press, 1981.
Brubaker, R. *Ethnicity without Groups.* Cambridge, MA: Harvard University Press, 2004.
Bruce, S. *Politics and Religion.* Cambridge, UK: Polity, 2003.
Campbell, A. 'Bountiful Voices'. *Osgoode Hall Law Review* 47 (2009): 183–234.
Carter, S. *The Importance of Being Monogamous: Marriage and Nation Building in Western Canada to 1913.* Edmonton, AB: University of Alberta Press, 2008.
Champion, F. and M. Cohen. 'Recompositions, décompositions: Le Renouveau charismatique et la nébuleuse mystique-ésotérique depuis les années soixante-dix'. *Le Débat* 75 (May-August 1993): 81–96.
Chaudry, A.A. *The Promised Messiah and Mahdi.* Tilford, Surrey, UK: Islam International Publications, 1996.
Chen, J. *Chinese Law: Towards an Understanding of Chinese Law, Its Nature, and Development.* The Hague, Netherlands: Kluwer Law International, 1999.
Cheung, A.S.Y. 'In Search of a Theory of Cult and Freedom of Religion in China: The Case of Falun Gong'. *Pacific Rim Law & Policy Journal* 13 (2004): 1–30.
Codevilla, G. 'Relations between Church and State in Russia Today'. *Religion, State, and Society* 36 (2008): 113–37.
Cohen, M. 'Les charismatiques et la santé: offres religieuses de salut ou médecines parallèles?' In *Gestions religieuses de la santé,* edited by J. Maître and F. Lautman. Paris: L'Harmattan, 1995.
Coleman-Norton, P.R., ed. *Roman State and Christian Church: A Collection of Legal Documents to AD 535.* Vol. 1. London: S.P.C.K., 1966.
Côté, P. 'Québec and Reasonable Accommodation: Uses and Misuses of Public Consultation'. In *Religion and Diversity in Canada,* edited by Lori G. Beaman and Solange Lefebvre, 41–66. Leiden, Netherlands: Brill, 2008.
Cotran, E. and A.O. Sherif, eds. *Democracy, the Rule of Law and Islam.* London: Kluwer Law International, 1999.
Črnič, A. 'New Religions in New Europe'. *Journal of Church and State* 3 (2007): 517–51.
Crouch, M. 'Implementing the Regulation on Places of Worship in Indonesia: New Problems, Local Politics and Court Action'. *Asian Studies Review* 34 (2010): 403–19.
Crouch, M. 'Law and Religion in Indonesia: The Constitutional Court and the Blasphemy Law'. *Asian Journal of Comparative Law* 7 (2012): 1–46.
Dannreuther, R. and L. March, eds. *Russia and Islam: State, Society and Radicalism.* London: Routledge, 2010.

Davidson, C.R. 'Reform and Repression in Mubarak's Egypt'. *The Fletcher Forum of World Affairs Journal* 24 (2000): 75–98.
Davie, G. *Religion in Modern Europe: a Memory Mutates*. Oxford: Oxford University Press, 2000.
De Jong, C.D. *The Freedom of Thought, Conscience and Religion or Belief in the United Nations (1946–1992)*. Antwerp, Netherlands: Hart/Intersentia, 2000.
Dillon, M. *Religious Minorities and China*. London: Minority Rights Group International, 2001.
Dord, O. 'Entre laïcité et exigences européennes, une politique de lutte contre les dérives sectaires est-elle possible?' In *Laïcité, liberté de religion et Convention européenne des droits de l'homme*, edited by G. Gonzalez, 223–49. Brussels: Bruylant, 2006.
Dreifelds, J. 'Religion in Latvia: from Atrophy to Rebirth'. In *Religion and Political Change in Europe: Past and Present*, edited by A. Cimdina, 241–66. Pisa, Italy: Edizioni Plus – Università di Pisa, 2003.
Dupree, L. 'The Non-Arab Ethnic Groups of Libya'. *Middle East Journal* 12 (1958): 33–44.
Durham, W.C. 'Facilitating Freedom of Religion or Belief through Religious Association Law'. In *Facilitating Freedom of Religion or Belief: A Deskbook*, edited by T. Lindholm, W.C. Durham and B. Tahzib-Lie. Leiden, Netherlands: Martinus Nijhoff, 2004.
Durham, W.C. and L. Homer. 'Russia's 1997 Law on Freedom of Conscience and Religious Associations: Analytical Appraisal'. *Emory Law Review* 12 (1998): 101–246.
Durham, W. C. and B.G. Scharffs. *Law and Religion: National, International, and Comparative Perspectives*. Aspen Publishers, 2010.
Dvorkin, A. *Sekty Protiv Tserkvi*. Moscow: Moscow Patriarchate, 2000.
Eide, A. 'Minority Situations: In Search of Peaceful and Constructive Solutions'. *Notre Dame Law Review* 66 (1990–1991): 1311–46.
Eisgruber, C.L. and L.G. Sager. *Freedom of Religion and the Constitution*. Cambridge, MA: Harvard University Press, 2010.
Esau, A. *The Courts and the Colonies: The Litigation of Hutterite Church Disputes*. Vancouver, BC: University of British Columbia Press, 2005.
Esposito, J.L. and Voll, J.O. *Islam and Democracy*. Oxford: Oxford University Press, 1996.
Esquerre, A. *La manipulation mentale: Une sociologie des sectes en France*. Paris: Fayard, 2009.
European Consortium for Church–State Research, ed. *New Religious Movements and the Law in the European Union*. Milan: Giuffre Editore, 1999.
Evans, C. 'Chinese Law and the International Protection of Religious Freedom'. *Journal of Church and State* 44 (2002): 749–74.
Evans, M. *Religious Liberty and International Law in Europe*. Cambridge, UK: Cambridge University Press, 1997.

el Fadl, K.A., ed. *Islam and the Challenge of Democracy*. Princeton, NJ: Princeton University Press, 2004.

Filatov, S. and R. Lunkin. '"My Father's House Has Many Mansions": Ethnic Minorities in the Russian Orthodox Church'. *Religion, State, and Society* 38 (2010), 361–78.

Fournier, P. and E. See 'The "Naked Face" of Secular Exclusion: Bill–94 and the Privatization of Belief'. In *Religion in the Public Sphere: Interdisciplinary Perspectives across the Canadian Provinces*, edited by Solange Lefebvre and Lori Beaman. Toronto: University of Toronto Press. (2012): 63–76.

Geraci, R. and M. Khodarkovsky. *Of Religion and Empire: Missions, Conversion, and Tolerance in Tsarist Russia*. Ithaca, NY: Cornell University Press, 2000.

Ghanea, N. 'From UN Commission on Human Rights to UN Human Rights Council: One Step Forwards or Two Steps Sideways?' *International and Comparative Law Quarterly* 55 (2006): 695–705.

Ghanea, N. 'Phantom Minorities and Religions Denied'. *Shi'a Affairs Journal* 2 (2009). http://shiaaffairs.org/index.php/journal/article/viewArticle/4.

Ghanea, N. 'Religious or Minority?' *Religion, State and Society* 36 (2008): 303–25.

Glodenis, D. 'Legislation on Religion and the Challenge of Pluralism in Lithuania'. *Religion and New Religious Movements in Lithuania* (2005). http://en.religija.lt/content/legislation-religion-and-challenge-pluralism-lithuania.

Grim, B.J. and R. Finke, 'Religious Persecution in Cross-National Context: Clashing Civilizations or Regulated Religious Economies?' *American Sociological Review* 72 (2007): 633–58.

Grim, B.J. and R. Finke. 'International Religion Indexes: Government Regulation, Government Favoritism, and Social Regulations of Religion'. *Interdisciplinary Journal of Research on Religion* 2 (2006): 1–40.

Hallinan, D. 'Orthodox Pluralism: Contours of Freedom of Religion in the Russian Federation and Strasbourg Jurisprudence'. *Review of Central and Eastern European Law* 37 (2012): 293–346.

Harris, L. 2005. 'God and Caesar in China: Policy Implications of Church-State Tensions'. *Hong Kong Law Journal* 35 (2005): 532–5.

Hassall, G. 'Bahá'í Communities by Country: Research Notes', *Bahá'í Library Online* (2000). http://bahai-library.com/hassall_bahai_communities_country.

Hassall, G. 'Pacific Bahá'í Communities 1950–1964'. *Pacific History Papers from the 8th Pacific History Association Conference*, edited by Donald H. Rubinstein. Guram: University of Guam Press and Micronesian Area Research Center (1992): 73–95.

Henrard, K. 'Ever-Increasing Synergy towards a Stronger Level of Minority Protection between Minority-Specific and Non-Minority-Specific Instruments'. *European Yearbook of Minority Issues* 3 (2003–2004): 15–41.

Henrard, K. 'The Protection of Minorities'. *International Journal of Minority and Group Rights* 14 (2007): 141–80.

Hervieu-Léger, D. *Le pèlerin et le converti: la religion en mouvement*. Paris: Flammarion, 1999.
Hoppenbrouwers, F. 'Romancing Freedom: Church and Society in the Baltic States since the End of Communism'. *Religion, State and Society* 27 (1999): 161–73.
Isik, T. 'Sagci da Solcu da Misyonerlik Alarmi Veriyor'. *Radikal Gazetesi*, 20 April 2007. http://www.radikal.com.tr/haber.php?haberno=218964.
Jabareen, Y. 'Toward Participatory Equality: Protecting Minority Rights Under International Law'. *Israel Law Review* 41 (2008): 635–76.
Johnson, S.M. 'Junking The 'Junk Science' Law: Reforming The Information Quality Act'. 58 *Administrative Law Review* 37 (2006).
Johnson, S.M. 'Ruminations On Dissemination: Limits On Administrative And Judicial Review Under The Information Quality Act'. *Catholic University Law Review* 55 (2005–2006): 59–80.
Keane, D. 'Addressing the Aggravated Meeting Points of Race and Religion'. *Maryland Law Journal of Race, Religion, Gender and Class* 6 (2007): 353–91.
Keddie, N. R. *Modern Iran: Roots and Results of Revolution*. New Haven, CT: Yale University Press, 2006.
Khan, A.M. 'Misuse and Abuse of Legal Argument by Analogy in Transjudicial Communication: The Case of Zaheerudin v. State'. *Richmond Journal of Global Law & Business* 10 (2011): 497–523.
Khan, A.M. 'Persecution of the Ahmadiyya Community in Pakistan: An Analysis Under International Law and International Relations'. *Harvard Human Rights Journal* 16 (2003): 217–44.
Knox, Z. *Russian Society and the Orthodox Church: Religion in Russia After Communism*. London: Routledge, 2005.
Kolodner, E. 'Religious Rights in China: A Comparison of International Human Rights Law and Chinese Domestic Legislation'. *Human Rights Quarterly* 16 (1994): 455–90.
Kostovski, S. 'Church and State in Macedonia'. In *Law and Religion in Post-Communist Europe*, edited by S. Ferrari and W.C. Durham, Jr. Leuven, Belgium: Peeters, 2003.
Krumina-Konkova, S. 'New Religions in Latvia'. *Nova Religio* 3 (1999): 119–34.
Krumina-Konkova, S. 'New Religious Minorities in the Baltic States'. In *New Religious Movements in the 21st Century: Legal, Political, and Social Challenges in Global Perspective*, edited by Philip Charles Lucas and Thomas Robbins, 95–103. New York: Routledge, 2004.
Kuru, A. *Secularism and State Policies toward Religion: The United States, France and Turkey* Cambridge, UK: Cambridge University Press, 2009.
Kuznecoviene, J. 'Church and State in Lithuania'. In *Law and Religion in Post-Communist Europe*, edited by S. Ferrari and W. C. Durham, Jr, 77–196. Leuven, Belgium: Peeters, 2003.
Lacroix, B. *L'utopie communautaire: Histoire sociale d'une révolte*. Paris: PUF, 2006 [1981].

Lau, M. 'The Case of Zaheer-ud-din v. The State and Its Impact on the Fundamental Right to Freedom of Religion'. *Centre of Islamic and Middle Eastern Law.* www.soas.ac.uk/cimel/materials/intro.html.

Lefebvre, S. 'Between Law and Public Opinion: The Case of Québec'. In *Religion and Diversity in Canada*, edited by Lori G. Beaman and Peter Beyer, 175–98. Leiden, Netherlands: Brill Academic Press, 2008.

Leigh, I. 'Balancing Religious Autonomy and Other Human Rights under the European Convention'. *Oxford Journal of Law and Religion* 1 (2012): 109–25.

Leiken, R.S. and Brooke, S. 'The Moderate Muslim Brotherhood'. *The Fletcher Forum of World Affairs Journal* 86 (2007): 113–14.

Lewis, D. *After Atheism: Religion and Ethnicity in Russia and Central Asia.* London: Curzon Press, 2000.

Lieu, S.N.C. *Manichaeism in Central Asia and China.* Leiden: Brill Academic, 1998.

Luca, N. *Quelles régulations pour les nouveaux mouvements religieux et les dérives sectaires dans l'Union Européenne?* Aix-en-Provence: Presses Universitaires d'Aix-Marseille (PUAM), 2011.

Luca, N. 'Quelles politiques pour les sectes? La spécificité française face à l'Europe occidentale'. *Critique internationale* 17 (Octobre 2002): 105–25.

Lucas, P.C. and T. Robbins, eds. *New Religious Movements in the 21st Century: Legal, Political, and Social Challenges in Global Perspective.* New York: Routledge Press, 2004.

Macuka, J. 'Administrative and Financial Matters in the Area of Religious Freedom and Religious Communities in Latvia'. In *Legal Aspects of Religious Freedom*, edited by D. Cepar. Ljubljana, Slovenia: Office of the Government of the Republic of Slovenia for Religious Communities, 2008.

Mann, M. *The Dark Side of Democracy.* Cambridge, UK: Cambridge University Press, 2005.

Margiono, M. *No Middle Road: A Public Examination of the Decision of the Constitutional Court Concerning Review of Law No. 1/Pnps/1965 Regarding the Abuse and/or Defamation of Religion.* Jakarta: Indonesian Legal Resource Center, 2011.

Marshall, P. and N. Shea. *Silenced: How Apostasy and Blasphemy Codes Are Choking Freedom Worldwide.* New York: Oxford University Press, 2011.

Mednicoff, D. 'The Importance of Being Quasi-Democratic – The Domestication of International Human Rights in American and Arab Politics'. *Victoria University of Wellington Law Review* 38 (2007): 317–40.

Mendras, M. *Russian Politics: the Paradox of a Weak State.* London: Hurst, 2012.

Meral, Z. *No Place to Call Home.* London: CSW, 2008.

Meral, Z. *Prospects for Turkey.* London: Legatum Institute, 2009.

Miner, C.J. 'Losing my Religion: Austria's New Religion Law in Light of International and European Standards of Religious Freedom'. *Brigham Young University Law Review* 2 (1998): 607–47.

Minnerath, R. 'The Right to Autonomy in Religious Affairs'. In *Facilitating Freedom of Religion or Belief: A Deskbook*, edited by Tore Lindholm, W. Cole Durham, and Bahia G. Tahzib-Lie, 292–319. Leiden, Netherlands: Martinus Nijhoff, 2004.

Minzarari, D. 'The Interaction between Orthodox Church and State in Post-Soviet Russia'. In *Spaces and Borders: Current Research on Religion in Central and Eastern Europe*, edited by Andras Mate-Toth and Cosima Rughinis, 103–16. Berlin: De Gruyter, 2011.

Mitrokhin, N. *Russkaya Pravoslavnaja Tserkov'*. Moscow: Novoe Literaturnoe Obozrenie, 2004.

Moon, R. 'Liberty, Neutrality and Inclusion: Religious Freedom under the Canadian Charter of Rights and Freedoms'. *Brandeis Law Journal* 41 (2003): 563–73.

Moon, R. 'Religious Commitment and Identity: Syndicat Northcrest v. Amselem'. *Supreme Court Law Review* 29 (2005): 201–20.

Mulík, P. 'Church and State in Slovakia'. In *Law and Religion in Post-Communist Europe*, edited by S. Ferrari and W.C. Durham, Jr. Leuven, Belgium: Peeters, 2003.

Narochnitskaya, N. *Russkiy Mir*. Moscow: Aleteya, 2008.

Oktem, K. *Angry Nation: Turkey Since 1989*. London: Zed Books, 2011.

Ollion, E. 'La secte sécularisée. Contribution à l'étude des processus de requalification conceptuels'. *Genèses* 78 (2010): 25–47.

Ollion, E. 'Les sectes mises en causes. Sociologie politique de la 'lutte contre les sectes' en France (1970–2010)'. Thèse de doctorat EHESS, Paris, 2012.

Pastorelli, S. 'The European Union and the New Religious Movements'. *Religion, State & Society* 37 (2009): 193–206.

Peerenboom, R. 'Globalization, Path Dependency and the Limits of Law: Administrative Law Reform and Rule of Law in the People's Republic of China'. 19 *Berkeley Journal of International Law* 161 (2001).

Pelletier, D. *La crise catholique. Religion, société, politique en France (1965–1978)*. Paris: Petite bibliothèque Payot, 2005.

Pollack, D. and O. Müller. 'Religiousness in Central and Eastern Europe: Towards Individualization?' In *Religions, Churches and Religiosity in Post-Communist Europe*, edited by I. Borowik, 22–36. Krakow, Poland: Nomos, 2006.

Ramet, P.S. *Religion and Nationalism in Soviet and East European Politics*. Duke, NC: Duke University Press, 1988.

Richardson, J.R., ed. *Regulating Religion: Case Studies from Around the Globe*. New York: Kluwer Academic, 2004.

Richardson, J. and J. Shoemaker. 'The European Court of Human Rights, Minority Religions, and the Social Construction of Religious Freedom'. In *The Centrality of Religion in Social Life: Essays in Honour of James A. Beckford*, edited by Eileen Barker, 103–116. Aldershot, UK: Ashgate, 2010.

Richardson, J. and M. Shterin. 'Constitutional Courts in Post-Communist Russia and Hungary: How Do They Treat Religion?' *Religion, State, and Society* 36 (2008): 251–67.

Richardson, J. and M. Shterin. 'Minority Religions and Social Justice in Russian Courts'. *Social Justice Research* 12 (1999): 393–408.

Riis, O. and L. Woodhead. *A Sociology of Religious Emotion.* New York: Oxford University Press, 2010.

Riigi Teataja RT I 2002, 24, 135. Kirikute ja koguduste seadus [Latvian Churches and Congregations Act.]

Ringvee, R. *Riik ja religioon nõukogudejärgses Eestis 1991–2008* [State and Religion in Post-Soviet Estonia 1991–2008]. Tartu, Estonia: Tartu University Press, 2011.

Rolland, P. 'La loi du 12 janvier 2001 contre les mouvements sectaires portant atteinte aux droits de l'Homme: Anatomie d'un débat législatif'. *Archives de Sciences Sociales des Religions* 212 (2003): 149–66.

Rouiller, C. 'Le principe de la neutralité confessionnelle relative: Réflexion sur la liberté de religion'. *Pratique juridique actuelle* 8 (2003): 944–58.

Rowley, C.K. and N. Smith. 'Islam's Democracy Paradox: Muslims Claim to Like Democracy, So Why Do They Have So Little?' *Public Choice* 139 (2009): 273–99.

Sanasarian, E. *Religious Minorities in Iran.* Cambridge, UK: Cambridge University Press, 2006.

Saroglou, V. et al. *Mouvements religieux contestés: Psychologie, droit et politiques de précaution.* Brussels: Academia Press, 2005.

Sauzet, Jean-Paul. *Le Renouveau Charismatique. Les chrétiens du Nouvel-Age?* Lyon, France: Golias, 1994.

Schröder, I. W. 'The Elusive Religious Field in Lithuania'. In *Religious Diversity in Post-Soviet Society: Ethnographies of Catholic Hegemony*, edited by M. Ališauskiene and I. W. Schröder, 79–98. Aldershot, UK: Ashgate, 2012.

Shterin, M. *Cult Controversies in England and Russia: A Sociological Comparison.* PhD dissertation, London School of Economics and Political Science, 2002.

Shterin, M. 'Legislating on Religion in the Face of Uncertainty'. In *Law and Informal Practices: Post-Communist Society*, edited by John Gallighan and Marina Kurkchiyan, 113–33. Oxford: Oxford University Press, 2002.

Shterin, M. 'New Religious Movements in Changing Russia'. In *Cambridge Companion to New Religious Movements,* edited by Olav Hammer and Michael Rotstein, 286–302. Cambridge: Cambridge University Press, 2012.

Shterin, M. 'Religion after Atheism: Moving Away from the Communal Flat'. In *Challenging Religion*, edited by James Beckford and James Richardson, 56–69. London: Routledge, 2004.

Shterin, M. and J. Richardson. 'Effects of the Western Anti-Cult Movement on Development of Laws Concerning Religion in Post-Communist Russia'. *Journal of Church and State* 42 (2000): 247–72.

Shterin, M. and J. Richardson. 'Local Laws on Religion in Russia: Precursors of Russia's National Law'. *Journal of Church and State* 40 (1998): 319–42.

Shterin, M. and J. Richardson. 'The Yakunin vs. Dvorkin Trial and the Emerging Religious Pluralism in Russia'. *Religion in Eastern Europe* 22 (2002): 1–38.

Shterin, M. and A. Yarlykapov. 'Reconsidering Radicalisation and Terrorism: the New Muslims Movement in Kabardino-Balkaria and Its Path to Violence'. *Religion, State, and Society* 39 (2011): 89–113.

Sibireva, O. 'Freedom of Conscience in Russia: Restrictions and Challenges in 2011'. In *Xenophobia, Freedom of Conscience and Anti-Extremism in Russia in 2011*, edited by Alperovich Vera et al., 62–86. Moscow: Sova, 2012.

Siddiq, N.A. 'Enforced Apostasy: Zaheerudin v. State and the Official Persecution of the Ahmadiyya Community in Pakistan'. *Law and Inequality* 14 (1995): 276–337.

Simkin, L. 'Church and State in Russia'. In *Law and Religion in Post-Communist Europe*, edited by S. Ferrari and W. C. Durham, Jr. Leuven, Belgium: Peeters, 2003.

Slezkine, Y. 'The USSR as a Communal Apartment, or How a Socialist State Promoted Ethnic Particularism'. *Slavic Review* 53 (1994): 414–52.

Smart, N. *The World's Religions*. Cambridge, UK: Cambridge University Press, 1992.

Smart, N. and R.D. Hecht, eds. *Sacred Texts of the World: A Universal Anthology*. 1984. Reprint, New York: Crossroad 2007.

Sorenson, D.S. 'Global Pressure Point: The Dynamics of Political Dissent in Egypt'. *The Fletcher Forum of World Affairs Journal* 27 (2003): 207–28.

Stahnke, T. and R. Blitt. 'The Religion–state Relationship and the Right to Freedom of Religion or Belief: A Comparative Textual Analysis of the Constitutions of Predominantly Muslim Countries'. *Georgetown Journal of International Law* 36 (2005): 947–1077.

Stašulane, A. New Religious Movements in Latvia. *Soter* 32 (2009): 107–23.

Streikus, A. 'The History of Religion in Lithuania since the Nineteenth Century'. In *Religious Diversity in Post-Soviet Society: Ethnographies of Catholic Hegemony*, edited by M. Ališauskiene and I.W. Schröder, 37–55. Aldershot, UK: Ashgate, 2012.

Strmiska, M.F. and V.R. Dundzila. 'Romuva: Lithuanian Paganism in Lithuania and America'. In *Modern Paganism in World Cultures: Comparative Perspectives*, edited by M.F. Strmiska, 241–98. Santa Barbara, CA: ABC-Clio, 2005.

Sullivan, W. *Prison Religion: Faith Reformers and the Constitution*. Princeton: Princeton University Press, 2009.

Sullivan, W. *The Impossibility of Religious Freedom*. Princeton: Princeton University Press, 2005.

Tadros, M. *The Muslim Brotherhood in Contemporary Egypt: Democracy Redefined or Confined?* Milton Park, Abingdon, UK: Routledge, 2012.

Taylor, P. *Freedom of Religion: UN and European Human Rights Law and Practice*. Cambridge, UK: Cambridge University Press, 2005.

Temperman, Jeroen. *State-Religion Relationships and Human Rights Law: Towards a Right to Religiously Neutral Governance.* Leiden, Netherlands: Martinus Nijhoff, 2010.

Tēraudkalns, V. 'Religion and Politics in Latvia in the Beginning of 21st Century'. *Religion in Eastern Europe* 31 (2011): 10–18.

Thomas, K.A. 'Falun Gong: An analysis of China's national security concerns'. *Pacific Rim Law & Policy Journal* 10 (2000): 471–96.

Thornberry, P. *International Law and the Rights of Minorities.* Oxford: Oxford University Press, 1991.

Tretera, J.R. 'Church and State in the Czech Republic'. In *Law and Religion in Post-Communist Europe*, edited by S. Ferrari and W.C. Durham, 81–98. Leuven, Belgium: Peeters, 2003.

Turner, B. *Religion and Modern Society: Citizenship, Secularisation and the State.* Cambridge, UK: Cambridge University Press, 2011.

Vaišvilaite, I. (2001) 'Tradicinių ir kitų religinių bendruomenių perskyra Lietuvoje' [Traditional and religious communities split Lithuania]. In *Religija ir teise pilietineje visuomeneje*: materials from an Internation Conference, 127–9. Vilnius, Lithuania: Juistitia, 2001.

Van der Vyver, J.D. 'Constitutional Protection of Children and Young Persons'. In *The Law of Children and Young Persons in South Africa*, edited by J.A. Robinson, 265–320. Durban, South Africa: Butterworths, 1997.

Van der Vyver, J.D. 'Limitations of Freedom of Religion or Belief: International Law Perspectives'. *Emory International Law Review* 19 (2005): 499–538.

Van Dyke, V. 'The Cultural Rights of Peoples'. *Universal Human Rights* 2 (1980): 1–21.

Van Dyke, V. 'Human Rights and the Rights of Groups'. *American Journal of Political Science* 18 (1974): 725–41.

Verkhovsky, A. 'Russian Approaches to Radicalism and Extremism as Applied to Nationalism and Religion'. In *Russia and Islam: State, Society and Radicalism*, edited by Roland Dannreuther and Luke March, 26–43. London: Routledge, 2010.

Vickers, L. 'Freedom of Religion and the Workplace: The Draft Employment Equality (Religion or Belief) Regulations 2003'. *Industrial Law Journal* 32 (2003): 27–8.

Walzer, M. *On Toleration.* New Haven, CT: Yale University Press, 1997.

Wanner, C. *Communities of the Converted, Ukrainians and Global Evangelicalism.* Ithaca, NY: Cornell University Press, 2007.

Wanner, C. and Steinberg, M. 'Reclaiming the Sacred'. In *Religion, Morality, and Community*, edited by Mark Steinberg, Catherine Wanner and Mark Wanner, 1–20. Bloomington, IN: Indiana University Press, 2009.

Waye, V. and P. Xiong. 'The Relationship between Mediation and Judicial Proceedings in China'. *Asian Journal of Comparative Law* 6 (2011): 29–60.

Weil, P., ed. *Politiques de la laïcité au XXe siècle.* Paris: Presses Universitaires de France, 2007.

Witte, J., Jr and M. Bourdeaux, eds. *Proselytism and Orthodoxy in Russia: The New War for Souls*. New York: Maryknoll, 1999.

Woodhead, L. 'Accommodating Religion in the Public Sphere: looking beyond existing models'. Paper Presented at Religare International Seminar – Religious Communities and State Support, Sophia, Bulgaria, 2011.

Xin, X. 'Judaism in China'. *Studies in World's Religions* 2 (2000).

Xu, M. 'Qiang People's Worship of White-stone Godess [J]', *Journal Of Southwest Institute For Ethnic Groups* 3 (2009).

Zablocki, B.D. and T. Robbins. *Misunderstanding Cults: Searching for Objectivity in a Controversial Field*. Toronto: University of Toronto Press, 2001.

Žiliukaite, R. and D. Glodenis. 'State and Church in Lithuania'. In *State and Church in the Baltic States: 2001*, edited by R. Balodis, 67–94. Riga, Latvia: Religijas Brivibas Asociacija, 2001.

Index

About-Picard Law (France), 118, 124
abusive proselytism, notion of, 103
Ahl al-kitab (people of the book), 49
Ahmadis in Pakistan, 84–6
    judicial treatment of, 86–92
Ahmadiyya Muslim Community, 81–2, 85
Ahmad, Mirza Ghulam, 81, 84
Amnesty International (AI), 59
Anderson, John, 188
anti-cult organizations, 124–5, 128–9
    ADFI volunteers, 126
    Centre Against Mind Control
        (CCMM), 125
    UNADFI, 125, 127
anti-extremism legislation, 11
anti-religious ideology, 8
Arab Spring movement, 45
    Egypt, 53–9
    Libya, 59–63
    Tunisia, 51–3
Armenia Secret Army for the Liberation of
    Armenia (ASALA), 41

Badan Kongres Kebatinan Indonesia
    (BKKI), 73
Bahá'í Faith, 49
Baltic states
    anti-cult movement, 179
    cultural identities and traditions, 167
    Estonia. *See* Estonia
    European Court of Human Rights
        (ECtHR) and, 180–81
    Herrnhut movement, 168
    Latvia. *See* Latvia
    legislation on religion, 170–71
    Lithuania. *See* Lithuania
    New Religious Movements (NRMs)
        and, 178–80
    religious communities, 171
    similarities and differences, 167–70
Beckford, James, 224

Ben Ali, Zine Abidine, 48, 49, 51
Berger, Benjamin L., 227
Bhagwan movement, 112
blasphemy laws
    Egypt, 57
    Indonesia, 73, 75
    Pakistan, 82, 84
blood money, 35
Boko Haram (radical Muslim group), 249
Bolshevik Revolution (1917), 186
Bouchard Taylor commission (Canada),
    224
Buddhism
    in China, 199
    in Laos, 244
    in Sri Lanka, 244
Buddhist Association of China, 200
Bureau of Democracy, Human Rights and
    Labor (USA), 5

Campbell, Angela, 221
Canada
    Bouchard Taylor commission, 224
    Charter of Rights and Freedoms, 218,
        226, 231, 233–4
        infringement of, 236–7
    civil disobedience, 240
    corporal punishment, 239
    equality and anti-discrimination case
        law, 240
    freedom of religion in, 217
        decisions on, 226
        interpretation of, 226
        protection and enforcement of, 225
        realms of, 218–25
        scope of, 234
        state and civil responses to, 220
    Fundamentalist Latter-day Saints
        (FLDS), 221
    Hutterian Brethren case, 226–8
    polygamy, provisions against, 221–2

religious belief systems, 232, 235
religious minorities
  non-state actors, role of, 224
  power relations, 225
  regulation of, 224, 226–8
religious practices
  conflict with law, 238
  courts' accommodation of, 233–7
  insulation from state restriction, 232–3
  non-trivial interference with, 235
  public decision-making and, 242
  reasonable accommodation and balancing of, 237–41
state neutrality towards religion, 232
Wilson Colony case, 237–8
Capotorti, Francesco, 18, 65–7
Catholic-Protestant conflicts, 138, 140
Central Intelligence Agency (CIA), USA, 43
children, rights of, 251
China
  Administrative Procedure Law (1990), 203
  Administrative Review Law (1999), 203
  adoption of the open door policy (1978), 200
  Article 36 of Constitution of the PRC, 201
  Criminal Law, 211
  evil cults in
    declaration against, 207
    laws relating to, 208–13
    punishment, 212
  Falun Gong movement, 206–8
  freedom of religion, protection of, 201–2
  laws relating to, 202
  'house church' movement, 200
  major religions practiced in, 199
  minority religions in
    administration in the future, 213–14
    historical background, 199
    present situation of, 200–201
  persecution of religious minorities
    Falun Gong practitioners, 246
    Tibetan Buddhists, 246

Regulations on Religious Affairs, 203
religion administration in
  activities of foreigners and, 204–6
  religion administration and religious bodies, 201–4
religion extremes, responses to
  Falun Gong, case study, 206–8
  laws relating to evil cults, 208–13
sites for the conduct of religious activities, 204
State Administration for Religious Affairs (SARA), 205–6, 213
White Paper on Freedom of Religious Belief, 202
Chinese Patriotic Catholic Association, 200
Chinese People's Political Consultative Conference (CPPCC), 203
Chinese Taoist Association, 200
Chirac, Jacques, 248
Christian Charismatic movements, 178
Christianity, 3–4, 15, 34–5, 41, 49–50, 79, 88, 178, 184, 199, 244
Christian missionaries, 41, 42
Church of England, 244
The Church of Jesus Christ of Latter-day Saints, 158, 178, 190n, 197, 199, 227n
'clash of civilizations', 46
Commission on Human Rights on the Defamation of Religions, 93
Committee on Economic, Social and Cultural Rights, 162
Committee on the Elimination of Discrimination against Women (CEDAW), 162
Coptic Christian, 49, 54–5, 57
Coptic Orthodox Church, 245
corporal punishment, 239
Council of Europe, 179
  Framework Convention for the Protection of National Minorities, 251, 252
  Parliamentary Assembly, 101, 113
cults, 147
  anti-cult movement, 194
  anti-cult organizations, 124–6
  children's involvement in, 126
  controversies in Russia, 189–91
  criminal offenses and penalties, 104

cultic behaviour, 128
dress, 21
French anti-cult policy, 121–2
   aspects of, 123
   intensity of, 123–30
   legislations, 124
   Parliamentary investigation, 126
   rapid establishment of, 125–7
   religion and, 128–30
   of surveillance, 123–5
illegal practices, 102–4
mass murder-suicide, 126
official status of, 112
Order of the Solar Temple (Switzerland), 126–7
Parliamentary Assembly of the Council of Europe, 101
policies relating to registration or recognition, 104–5
psychological definition of, 129
public funding, 104, 125
public information about, 110
regulation of, 101
versus religion, 128–30
'religious, esoteric or spiritual' groups, 101
'War on Cults', 122–3, 130, 133, 135

Dahlan, Muhammad, 69–70
Diyanet, 158
Doctrine of National Security of the Russian Federation (2000), 192
domains of public religion, notions of, 218–19
Dvorkin, Alexander, 190–91, 194, 196

Eastern Orthodox Church of Christ, 243
Egypt
   Arab Spring movement, 53–9
   ban on female genital mutilation, 58
   blasphemy laws, 57
   as a 'country of particular concern', 57
   freedom of religion and associated rights, 58
   human rights violations, 57, 58
   Islamic principles and rulings, 54
   Muslim Brotherhood, 47, 55–6
   Salafist movement, 55
   Supreme Command of the Armed Forces (SCAF), 53, 56
employment, in religious schools, 159
en-Nahda (Ennahda), Tunisia, 48, 51–2
Equality Act, Ireland, 161, 163
Estonia
   Church of Satan, 177
   Churches and Congregations Act (1993), 176
   Council of Churches, 177, 179
   House of Taara and Native Religions, 177
   Law of Civic Associations, 176
   legislation on religion in, 176–7
   Maausk and the Taara faith, 178
   registered religious associations, 177
   religious organizations in, 176
ethnic cleansing, policy of, 247, 253
ethnic minorities, 15, 17
   right of self-determination, 250–51
      limitations to, 251
      and violation of national laws, 251
   right to secession, 252–3
European Convention for the Protection of Human Rights and Fundamental Freedoms, 170, 243
European Court of Human Rights (ECtHR), 116, 158, 183, 198, 243, 245, 248
   appointment of religious leaders, 157
   common law jurisprudence, 108
   criminal intelligence services, 106
   fact-specific treatment of policies, 110
   favor minoritatis guide, 102
   gathering information, methods of, 107
   Grand Chamber of, 109
   illegal practices, repression of, 102–4
   informed consent, 106
   Jehovah's Witnesses v. Russia, 107
   non-discrimination and selection by policy incentives, 104–6
   nondiscrimination, principle of, 106
   Parliamentary Commission (1995), 112
   protection of socially contested movements, 103
   public information policies, 106–7
      dissemination of information by the state, 110–13

freedom of expression in the public debate, 108–10
sectarian public policies, 102
value judgment and judgment of fact, 108
European jurisprudence, 102, 109, 159
   on freedom of religion, 101
   principles of, 103
European Social Survey (ESS), 137
European Union (EU), 39
   Council Directive, 160
Evangelical Lutheran Church, 174, 177, 243

Falun Gong movement (China), 206–8
   persecution of, 246
fatwa (rulings on Islamic law), 34, 75, 78
female genital mutilation (FGM), 58, 251
France
   About-Picard Law, 118, 124
   anti-cult policy, 121–2
      aspects of, 123
      intensity of, 123–30
      legislations, 124
      Parliamentary investigation, 126
      rapid establishment of, 125–7
      religion and, 128–30
      of surveillance, 123–5
   Code of Education, 248
   Common Law, 118
   cults *versus* religions in, 128–30
   Grenoble Court of Appeal, 117
   human rights and fundamental freedoms, infringement of, 116
   Inter-ministerial Commission on Sects, 115
   Inter-ministerial Mission for Monitoring and Struggling Against Sectarian Deviations (MIVILUDES), 116, 119, 123–4
   Law on the Exploitation of a State of Weakness, 118
   Parliamentary investigation on cults in, 126
   principle of freedom of belief, 115
   principle of the separation of church and state, 248
   sectarian movements, 115, 117
   state intervention on minority groups, effect of, 130–31

Jehovah's Witnesses, case of, 131–3
state-led Second Inquisition, 122
'War on Cults', 122–3, 130, 133, 135
freedom of expression, 45, 52, 106–7, 159, 255–6
   in public debate, 108–10
freedom of religion. *See* religious freedom
freedom of speech, 110, 255–6
freedom of thought, 31, 45–6, 50, 71, 103, 109, 170
French Revolution, 115
Fundamentalist Latter-day Saints (FLDS), 221, 227n, 229

Gaair, Mohamed, 60
Gadhafi, Muhammar, 48–9, 51, 60, 62
gender-based discrimination, 251
genocide, 41, 248
Gerbi, David, 62
German Constitutional Court, 112
Gest-Guyard report (1995), 112
Gills, Nikandrs, 170
global terrorist networks, 194
Greek Orthodox Church, 34, 248
Guyana Massacre (1978), 126
Guyard-Brard report (1999), 112

Haleem, Muhammad, 91
Hare Krishna movement, 178, 195, 197
'heavenly revealed' religions, 58
'house church' movement, China, 200
Human Rights Committee, 18–21, 23–5, 95, 153, 159, 162–3
human rights violations, 15, 57, 95, 129
Hungary, 154, 244
   registration of churches
      benefits of, 246
      requirements for, 245–6
Hurd, Elizabeth, 224–5

Independent Expert on Minority Issues, 19
Indonesia
   Belief in the One and Only God, principle of, 67–8, 73, 77
   Bill of Religious Harmony (2003), 69
   'The Birth of Pancasila', 67, 70–71
   blasphemy laws, 73

discrimination, against religious
minorities
  Bakor Pakem, 77–8
  blasphemy law, 75
  conflict, 76
  post-conflict, state prosecution of
    the minority, 76–7
  pre-conflict, provocation, 75
  problems surrounding minority
    houses of worship, 79–80
ethnic groups, 65
Forum Kerukunan Umat Beragama
  (FKUB), 70, 79
Human Rights Law (1999), 70
inter-religious dialogue, 70
Ministry of Religious Affairs, 69, 73
minorities' rights, 66
National Revolution, 67
persecution of religious minority
  groups, 72–3
aliran kepercayaan, 73–4
religious harmony *versus* religious
  freedom in, 69–72
religious minority in, 65–7
  discrimination against, 75–80
religious representatives, 70
Rule of Law and *rechtstaat*, 71
'Trilogy of Harmony', 69
Information Network Focus on Religious
  Movements (INFORM), 124
Injunctions of Islam, 83
institutionalized bias, against religious
  minorities, 5
Inter-ministerial Commission on Sects,
  France, 115
International Bible Students Association,
  175
International Convention on the
  Elimination of All Forms of Racial
  Discrimination (ICERD), 95
International Covenant on Civil and
  Political Rights (ICCPR), 18, 22,
  66, 90–92, 95
International Religious Freedom Report, 5
inter-religion marriage, 248
inter-religious competition, 10
Iran, Islamic Republic of
  Bahá'í community, 34–6
  discrimination against non-Muslims, 35

  Islamic Penal Code bill, 35
  Muslim-background Christians
    (MBCs), 35
  punishment for apostasy, 35
  reasons behind policies on religious
    minorities, 36–8
  religious freedom in, 34–6
  revolution of 1979, 33, 35
Islam, 3–4, 15, 22, 32, 34–7, 40–43,
  45–65, 78, 82–3, 86, 87, 93, 96,
  137, 142–3, 147, 193–4, 199, 223,
  243–4
Islamic Association of China, 200
Islamic Council, Pakistan, 83
Islamic headscarf or other headdress,
  wearing of, 21–4
  ban on, 243
  in Turkish law, 243
Islamic law court, Pakistan, 87
Islamic movement, in Tunisia, 48
Islamic Sharia law, 249
Israelite Religious Society, 245
Israel–Palestine conflict, 41

Jahangir, Asma, 121, 130
Jebali, Hamadi, 51–2
Jehovah's Witnesses, 49, 104–8, 112, 128,
  130, 131–3, 175, 178, 180, 184,
  186, 187, 197–8, 222, 226, 245
  degradations in places of worship, 134
  Kingdom Halls, 132
  Russian campaign against, 196
  variations in the membership of, 133
  Watchtower (book), 195
Jinnah, Muhammad Ali, 82–3, 96
Judaism, 34, 49, 67, 137, 142–3, 147, 199,
  235, 244, 247

Khan, Muhammad Zafarullah, 83
Khomeini, Ayatollah, 33, 37

Latvia
  Church of Scientology, 176
  Dievturiba movement, 178
  Free Orthodox Church, 176
  Law on Compulsory Military Service,
    180
  Law on Religious Organizations and
    Associations, 174, 175

legislation on religion in, 173–6
New Religions Consultative Council, 180
traditional religion in, 175
Law on Freedom of Conscience and Religious Associations (1997), Russia, 10, 195, 244
Law on Guarantees Regarding the Freedom of Conscience and Belief (1989), Poland, 244
League of Nations, 15, 16
Legal Status of Religious Belief Communities (1998), Austria, 244
Libya
   Arab Spring movement, 59–63
   Constitutional Declaration for the Transitional Stage, 59
   Gadhafi, Muhammar, 48–9
   Muslim Brotherhood, 60
   non-Arab ethnic groups, 50
   official interpretation of Islam, 48
   religious discrimination, 63
   sharia law, 60
   Sufi Sanusi order, 48
   women's rights, 63
linguistic minorities, 17, 26
   right of self-determination, 250–51
      limitations to, 251
      and violation of national laws, 251
   right to secession, 252–3
Lithuania
   Catholic Church, 168
   Law on Religious Communities and Associations, 172
   legislation on religion in, 172–3
   Osho Ojas Meditation Centre, 173
   Romuva movement, 178
   Working Group on Issues of Spiritual and Religious Groups, 179

Mandras, Marie, 193
maslahat, doctrine of, 37
mass murder-suicide, 126
Mayer, Jean-Francois, 141
membership, of religious organizations, 161–2
'mental manipulation' laws, 11, 103, 107, 122, 128, 130
Middle East/North Africa (MENA) region, 46
   intolerance towards 'non-traditional' faiths, 47
   restrictions on foreign missionaries, 47
Millet system, 16
minorities. *See also* religious minorities
   concept of, 15
   discrimination against, 18
   historical antecedents, 15–17
   rights of, 17
   separation of religious minorities from, 17–19
Morsi, Mohammed, 54–6, 58, 64
Mubarak, Hosni, 47–8, 51, 54, 57–8
Muslim-background Christians (MBCs), 35
Muslim Brotherhood, 47, 56, 60
   political agenda, 55

najess, idea of, 37
Nepal
   12-point peace agreement, 247
   civil war, 246–7
   Constitutional Assembly, 247–8
   as Hindu state, 246
   Maoist insurgency, 246
   polarization of ethnic and religious population, 247
   religious tension, 247
   rights of religious minorities, regulation of religious homogeneity, 248–9
   segregation, 247–8
New Testament, 247
Nigeria
   Boko Haram (radical Muslim group), 249
   inter-religion marriage, 248
   Islamic Sharia law, 249
   religious violence, 249
Non Governmental Organization (NGO), 63, 183, 197
North Atlantic Treaty Organization (NATO), 38

Order of the Solar Temple (OTS), Switzerland, 126–7, 138, 140

Organization of Islamic Cooperation
(OIC), 11, 93

Pakistan
  Ahmadis in, 84–6
    future aspects of persecution of,
      93–6
    judicial treatment of, 86–92
    protection of, 92
  Ahmadiyya Muslim Community, 81–2
  anti-Ahmadiyya sentiment, 82
  blasphemy laws, 82, 84, 93–4
  Constitution's Repugnancy Clause, 83
  Defamation of Religions Resolution,
    93
  discrimination against minorities, 94
  freedom of religion and belief, 96
  hate crimes against racial or religious
    minorities, 94
  intellectual property law, 86
  international obligations on religious
    minorities, 92–3
  Islamic Council, 83
  Islamic law court, 87
  Martial Law Ordinance XX, 85, 91, 94
  public order and morality, 83
  religious freedom in, 82–3
  religious violence in, 82
  Sunni Islamic theocracy, 83
  Zaheerudin court, 89–92
Pentecostal Church, 198, 248
Peter the Great (1682–1725), 186
Pew Forum on Religion and Public Life, 3
polygamy, provisions against, 221–2
Presbyterian Church, Scotland, 244
Protestant Three-Self Patriotic Movement,
  200

Quebec Charter of Human Rights and
  Freedoms, 234–6
Qur'an, 16, 36, 55, 83–4, 95

racial minorities, 16, 26
Raelian Movement, 109–10
*Regulating Religion: Case Studies from
  Around the Globe* (James T.
  Richardson), 224
religion legislation
  defamation of, 11–12
  and harassment of religious minorities,
    12
religion–state relationships, 7
  and chances of reconciliation, 27
  obstacles to, 25–7
  structural features of, 8
religion–state structures, for minority
    religions
  creation of, 12
  implications of, 7–12
  inter-religious competition, 10
religious adherence
  enforcement of, 32
  individual, 235
religious affiliation, 3, 32, 49, 85, 137, 140,
  160, 248, 252, 255
religious communities, 9, 80, 111, 137–40,
  146, 153–6, 239–40, 245–6, 253.
  See also religious groups
  anti-conversion legislation against, 12
  autonomy of, 181
  draft legislation on, 172
  identified as a minority, 66
  legally-recognized, 244
  registration of, 21, 24–5, 171, 173–4
  repression of, 5
  right to self-determination for, 251
  state-recognized, 244
religious conversion, 43, 47
'religious, esoteric or spiritual' groups,
  101
religious freedom, 7, 19
  in Egypt, 58
  in Iran, 34–6
  national security and, 105
  protections, 6
  religious harmony *versus*, 69–72
  religiously-based rivalries and, 249
  in Turkey, 39–42
religious groups. *See also* religious
    communities
  basic rights and protections, 152
  Employment Framework Directive,
    160–61
  forms of state discrimination against,
    152
  freedom of association, issue of, 151
  law of equality, 157
  multi-dimensional discrimination, 162

political rights, 162
registration of, 151–3
   duration requirements, 155–6
   numerical requirements, 153–5
   sui generis illegitimate registration requirements, 156–7
religious autonomy
   membership, 161–2
   other employment settings, 158–61
   religious officials, appointment of, 157–8
   services, 162–4
residual right, 162
special status, requirements for, 155
religious homogeneity, 9, 50, 248–9, 252
religious independence, 16
religious leadership, 25–6, 48
religious life, 48, 50, 69, 183
   State control over, 5
religiously-based rivalries, 249
religious migration, pattern of, 15
religious minorities, 16, 26. *See also* ethnic minorities; linguistic minorities; racial minorities
   characteristics of, 66
   discrimination in
      Austria, 245
      Canada, 224–8
      China, 246
      Indonesia, 65–7, 75–80
      Pakistan, 93–6
      Russia, 194–8
      Turkey, 40
      South Africa, 255
   persecution of, 246
   protection for, 16
      failure of national systems in, 246
   public's understanding of, 147
   regulation of rights of, 247–9
      religious homogeneity, 248–9
      segregation, 247–8
   right of self-determination, 250–51
      limitations to, 251
      and a right to secession, 252–3
      South African model for, 253–4
      violation of national laws and, 251
   right to secession, 252–3
   separation from minorities, 17–19

religious movements, 10, 67, 74, 80, 101, 109, 112–13, 124, 128, 135, 137, 139, 144–7, 200–201, 212, 224–5
religious officials, appointment of, 157–8
religious schools, 40
   destruction of, 63
   employment in, 159
   state funding for, 26
religious violence, 82, 249
right of self-determination, 250–51
   limitations to, 251
   and a right to secession, 252–3
   South African model for, 253–4
   violation of national laws and, 251
ritual murders, 251
Roman Catholic Church, 9, 128, 130, 167, 171, 173, 179, 244
rule-of-law principles, 9
Russia
   anti-extremist legislation, 197
   Bolshevik Revolution (1917), 186
   Byzantine tradition, 185
   cult controversies, 189–91
   democratic institutions and civil society, 198
   Doctrine of National Security of the Russian Federation (2000), 192
   ethnic minority religions, 189
   Federal List of Extremist Literature, 195
   Great White Brotherhood, 190
   Jehovah Witnesses. *See* Jehovah's Witnesses
   Krishna Movement, 195, 197
   Law on Combating Extremist Activity (2002), 195
   Law on Freedom of Conscience and Religious Associations, 195
   'the Moonies', 191
   Moscow Patriarchate (MP), 187, 189, 196–7
   new 'religious market' and competition for souls, 187–9
   New Religious Movements (NRMs), 184, 189–90, 192
   Orthodox Church, 183, 187, 189, 193, 194, 197
   Peter the Great (1682–1725), 186
   post-Soviet period, 191–3

religious minorities in
   Law on the Freedom of Worship (1990), 187
   legacy of state treatment of, 185–7
   management of, 186
   mechanics of discrimination of, 194–8
   post-Soviet state, 191–3
   'securitization of Islam' and, 193–4
   St Ireneus of Lyons Information and Consultation Center (SILICC), 190
   Western Evangelical missionaries, 190
Russian Academy of Civil Service, 191

St Ireneus of Lyons Information and Consultation Center (SILICC), Russia, 190
Salafist movement, 55
Satanism, 177
Sathya Sai Baba, 178
secularism and equality, policy of, 243, 248
self-worth and human dignity, concept of, 254
Sharia court, 249
Shari'a laws, 35
social hostilities, toward religion, 4–5, 12, 82
societal intolerance, 5
Society of Swiss Veterinarians, 138
Soka Gakkaï, 128, 130
South Africa
   Bill of Rights, 253
   freedom of expression, 255
   importance of religion, 253
   model for religion and religious diversity, 253–4
   Pan South African Language Board, 253
   Promotion of Equality and Prevention of Unfair Discrimination Act, 255
Soviet bloc, 26, 168
spread of religion, 15
state reactions, to minority religions, 4–7
Sufi Sanusi order, 48
Sunnah, 83
Swiss Animal Protection (SAP), 138
Switzerland
   Catholic Church, 137
   Control Committee of the National Council, 141
   educational measures, for religious communities
      creating an internet portal, 143
      Information Centre on Beliefs (CIC), 144–6
      teaching in public schools, 143–4
   Evangelical Reformed Church, 137
   Federal Commission against Racism, 142
   Federal Commission on Migration (FCM), 142
   Information Centre on Beliefs (CIC)
      features, 144
      scope of activity, 144
      utilization of, 146
      working methods, 145–6
   legal measures, for religious communities
      charitable status, 139
      freedom of belief and worship, 138
      jurisprudence, 139
      laws against religious discrimination, 138–9
   Order of the Solar Temple (OTS), 126–7, 138, 140
   political measures, for religious communities
      expert reports, 140–42
      national research programme, 143
      responsibility of local authorities, 140
   'Religion in Switzerland' programme, 143
   sectarian deviation, 141

Taoism, 3, 199–200
Tasser, Salman, 97
terrorism, Islamist, 194
Thirty Years War, 16
Transcendental Meditation practitioners, 178
Tunisia
   Arab Spring movement, 51–3
   Ben Ali, Zine Abidine, 48, 49
   crackdown on Islamic groups, 48
   en-Nahda (Ennahda), 48, 51–2
   Islamic movement, 48

Turkey, Republic of
  Directorate of Religious Affairs, 40
  ethnic and religious differences, 39
  integration with European Union, 39
  Justice and Development Party (AKP), 38–9, 42
  Lausanne Treaty (1923), 40
  National Security Secretariat, 41
  Ottoman Empire, 38, 40, 42, 43
  policy of exclusion and marginalization of non-Muslims, 40
  reasons behind policies on religious minorities, 42–3
  religious freedom in, 39–42
  reforms on, 42
Turner, Bryan, 185

Unification Church, 126, 191, 197
United Nations
  Declaration on the
    Elimination of Violence against Women, 251
    Religious Tolerance, 157
    Rights of Indigenous Peoples, 252
    Rights of Persons Belonging to National or Ethnic, Religious and Linguistic Minorities (1992), 19, 250–52
  Human Rights Committee
    jurisprudence, 18
    Article 17 of, 23
    Article 18 of, 21, 22, 25
    Article 27 of, 21–5
    headscarf or other headdress, wearing of, 21–4
    religious communities, registration of, 24–5
  Special Rapporteur on Freedom of Religion or Belief, 121
  Sub-Commission on Prevention of Discrimination and Protection of Minorities, 92
United States of America
  Central Intelligence Agency (CIA), 43
  Commission on International Religious Freedom (USCIRF), 56
  Office of International Religious Freedom, 223
  religious freedom jurisprudence, 88, 91
  'War on Terror', 194
Universal Declaration of Human Rights (UDHR), 31

Van Dyke, Vernon, 18
Versailles, Treaty of, 16
violence against women, 251. *See also* female genital mutilation (FGM)
Vivien Report (1983), 126

Wahid, Abdurrahman, 74
Wahid Institute Report on Religious Freedom and Tolerance (2011), 72, 76
Walzer, Michael, 186
'War on Terror', 194
Western Evangelical missionaries, 190
witchcraft, 251
Woodhead, Linda, 218–19
  'domains of public religion' model, 219
  limitations of, 220
World Jewish Congress, 142

zero tolerance policy, towards Islamic groups, 48
Zia-ul-Haq, General, 82, 84, 93
Zoroastrianism, 3, 34, 67, 199